VOICES
FROM THE
UNDERGROUND

VOICES
FROM THE
UNDERGROUND

Eighteen life stories from Umkhonto
we Sizwe's Ashley Kriel Detachment

Edited by Shirley Gunn and Shanil Haricharan

PENGUIN BOOKS

Published by Penguin Books
an imprint of Penguin Random House South Africa (Pty) Ltd
Reg. No. 1953/000441/07
The Estuaries No. 4, Oxbow Crescent, Century Avenue, Century City, 7441
PO Box 1144, Cape Town, 8000, South Africa
www.penguinrandomhouse.co.za

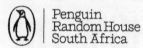

Penguin
Random House
South Africa

First published 2019

1 3 5 7 9 10 8 6 4 2

PUBLISHER: Marlene Fryer
MANAGING EDITOR: Robert Plummer
EDITOR: Alice Inggs
PROOFREADER: Lauren Smith
COVER DESIGNER: Ryan Africa
TYPESETTER: Monique van den Berg
INDEXER: Sanet le Roux

Set in 10.5 pt on 14 pt Minion

Printed by **novus print**, a division of Novus Holdings

MIX
Paper from
responsible sources
FSC
www.fsc.org   FSC® C022948

ISBN 978 1 77609 385 4 (print)
ISBN 978 1 77609 386 1 (ePub)

This book is dedicated to Ashley Kriel, Coline Williams, Robbie Waterwitch, Anton Fransch and Chris Hani, who gave their lives for our freedom

Contents

Foreword

I AM DELIGHTED TO write this foreword, given the fact that I was associated with this unit for many years as its front commander based in Botswana and came to appreciate the dedication, discipline and commitment of its members.

The testimony in this book is from a number of great patriots who joined the African National Congress (ANC) and Umkhonto we Sizwe (MK) and operated in the crucible of our struggle. All of them tell of great sacrifice and dedication; women and men, young and old, united in a single mission to attain freedom. Its members primarily come from the Western Cape, but over time comrades from Johannesburg and Durban joined them.

This unit takes its name from one of the young sons of the Western Cape and a darling of Bonteheuwel, Ashley Kriel. Ashley left the country having been active in the mass democratic movement's activities in the Western Cape and what was ambitiously called the BMW (Bonteheuwel Military Wing), a group of young activists influenced by Guevarean sacrifice and dedication. Ashley later joined the ranks of MK, trained in Angola and was deployed by Military HQ (MHQ) as part of a unit to Cape Town. Tragically, once back in South Africa, he was killed by one of the agents of death of the apartheid regime in circumstances that remain unclear. He never compromised any of his comrades and died valiantly in the true spirit of the great king Hintsa. Perhaps, as he wrestled with security policeman Jeffrey Benzien, who later applied for amnesty at the Truth and Reconciliation Commission (TRC), Ashley thought of the last words of Che Guevara to Sergeant Jaime Terán: 'I know you are here to kill me. Shoot, coward, you are only going to kill a man.'

By the time Ashley died, a number of comrades trained outside the country were already forming a nucleus of MK operatives in Cape Town. This unit was under the command of Aneez Salie and Shirley Gunn. In recognition of Ashley's heroism, we named it after him, with the support of MHQ.

Thanks to the iron discipline in this unit, it managed to operate for some time under the nose of the beast, evading arrest and detection. They carried orders from their commanders without any hesitation, and they fully understood the Oath of MK – to maintain and protect secrets and property of the

ANC and its military wing. Of great significance is that few of the members of this unit received formal military training in MK camps in Angola. Most were trained inside South Africa, and some in the frontline states, specifically Botswana, Zambia and Tanzania, as well as further afield in Cuba. The spirit of commitment in this unit is exhibited by one of its members, Kim Dearham, who says:

> There were thousands of people who were part of the wheels of resistance that finally broke the apartheid regime. If I am deemed a small bolt in this machinery, I am humbled. Through the AKD I met human beings who made invaluable contributions towards my view of the world. My children were affected by Mike's and my absence, but they have not grown into resentful adults. They respect the choices of the youth of the 1970s and the 1980s. Perhaps we were idealistic, but this is what pushed us to grow.

There were many casualties in the struggle for freedom, and this book is dedicated to preserving the memory of Ashley Kriel, Anton Fransch, Coline Williams and Robbie Waterwitch, young freedom fighters who made the ultimate sacrifice and must be celebrated. Also never to be forgotten are those who were an integral part of this great unit and have since passed away – Johnny Issel, Richard Ishmail, Paul Endley, Andrew Adams and Patrick Presence. As Charles Martin says in his story, 'Till the Sun Sets':

> Scared as we may have been at times, we were prepared to lay down our lives for freedom, right until the end.

This book will reveal how a group of people, joined by the umbilical cord of commitment to the values of the ANC, fought for a non-racial and non-sexist South Africa. It tells the story of their survival under intense conditions of repression in the Western Cape, and the bravery of Ashley Kriel and Anton Fransch who valiantly fought the security forces until their last breath. It also tells the story of the fateful mission undertaken by Coline Williams and Robbie Waterwitch, the wrenching pain their fellow unit members felt on hearing the news of their deaths and the efforts made to inform their parents and loved ones and salvage materials to protect the organisation from discovery by the apartheid security forces.

Anyone wanting to understand supreme commitment and discipline need look no further than the pages of this book. For me, the power of these stories is their uniqueness. Readers will make up their own minds about which stories resonate with them most, but I am certain that they will appreciate each one and what it took for them to be published.

JAMES NGCULU
MARCH 2019

Introduction

IN OCTOBER 1987, South Africa's minister for law and order, Adriaan Vlok, boasted that the apartheid security forces had broken the back of Umkhonto we Sizwe, the armed wing of the ANC, in the Western Cape. This claim followed the arrests of MK units commanded by Tony Yengeni and Ashley Forbes, and the killing of Ashley Kriel, who had recently returned from training in Angola. But Vlok's declaration of victory was premature. MK's Ashley Kriel Detachment (AKD), named after their slain comrade, conducted over thirty operations across the Cape between late 1987 and the day MK's founding commander-in-chief, Nelson Mandela, was released from prison on 11 February 1990.

Voices from the Underground tells the story of the AKD through the narratives of eighteen of its members, chronicling their political awakening and activism, their paths to taking up arms against apartheid at the height of its oppression in the late 1980s, their training outside South Africa and within the country, and the operations they executed.

The detachment targeted apartheid structures, including police stations, magistrate's courts, municipal buildings and civic centres. Perhaps the most audacious operation was the planting of a bomb inside the Castle of Good Hope – provincial headquarters of the South African Defence Force. The Castle was the official emblem of the army – supposedly the strongest in Africa – making this operation particularly symbolic. Other operations involved blowing up railway lines to support striking workers, targeting a rent office during a rent boycott, and bombing the turnstile at Newlands Cricket Ground before a rebel tour during the sports boycott.

The AKD pioneered a drastic shift in tactics, from the 'big bang' approach of a single, large-scale operation to several synchronised attacks in multiple locations. While no doubt impactful, a 'big bang' followed by months of little activity allowed the enemy time to mount a counter-offensive, usually smashing whatever MK structures were in place, whereas the AKD's approach successfully stretched and demoralised the enemy, and showed that MK could not be dislodged so easily. With these operations, a state of ungovernability through mass struggle, and international support, the stage was set for negotiations between the apartheid government and the ANC to commence.

Despite its impact in advancing the struggle, little is known about the AKD. More is known about other MK structures that were publicised through high-profile arrests, torture in detention and notable trials, such as those of Tony Yengeni and Ashley Forbes. The accused were sentenced to lengthy jail terms on Robben Island on charges of membership of the banned ANC and for acts of sabotage and terrorism, a fate that could befall any member of the AKD.

Aneez Salie and Shirley Gunn were joint commanders of the detachment, Shanil Haricharan commanded the Johannesburg logistics and communication unit and Melvin Bruintjies was the commander of operations. The AKD's mandate was to recruit and train members in area-based units in coloured, Indian and white communities in the Western Cape, as instructed by MHQ, as detachment members would be too conspicuous in black African areas. There were seven operational AKD units: Johannesburg, Bonteheuwel, Athlone, Hout Bay/Southern Suburbs, Mitchells Plain, Macassar/Hottentots Holland and Paarl. The Regional Politico-Military Committee (RPMC) included Aneez, Shirley, Melvin and Johnny Issel. James Ngculu was the AKD's front commander in Botswana, reporting to Chris Hani and MK commander-in-chief O.R. Tambo at the ANC headquarters in Zambia.

Shanil worked with Mike Dearham, Richard Ishmail and Joseph Nxusani in Johannesburg, and the unit couriered weapons and communications from Botswana into South Africa and all the way to Cape Town with the help of Ismail and Julie Vallie. Later, the Johannesburg unit's mandate changed as weapons were available in caches in the country, and Shanil, Richard, Mike and Kim Dearham moved to Cape Town to support the AKD command. Mogamat and Seiraaj Salie assisted by finding safe houses for their brother Aneez, removing weapons cached in hired cars, doing reconnaissance, assisting with vehicle maintenance and providing general support to the command structure. Anton Fisher also played an important role in supplies, logistics and politics for a time.

In the Western Cape, the Bonteheuwel unit included Coline Williams, Sidney Hendricks and Vanessa November; the Athlone unit was commanded by Anton Fransch and included Coline Williams and Robbie Waterwitch; the Macassar/Hottentots Holland unit included Andrew Adams, Paul Endley, Heinrich Magerman and Desmond Stevens; the Paarl unit included Andrew Adams, Charles Chordham and Charlie Martin; and Dicki Meter commanded the Hout Bay/Southern Suburbs unit, which included Patrick Presence. Timothy Jacobs, also of Hout Bay, left the country for military training in

Tanzania but returned after the ANC was unbanned and was therefore not part of AKD operations, but his story is included in this collection. The unit in Mitchells Plain was purged when it was suspected it was compromised by agents of the apartheid state.

The AKD could not have survived without financial support. Most of the funding came from outside the country via Botswana in cash. A few members held regular jobs while in the underground, including Shanil, Kim and Richard, and in so doing they provided a cover for their involvement in the AKD and a veneer of ordinariness to AKD safe houses. Their wages helped tremendously. In addition, there was a period when Zubeida Jaffer collected funds for the AKD every month, and the AKD was supported by various doctors and medical professionals at no fee.

This book grew out of a decision to document the service and sacrifice of the detachment's members, and to account to the people of South Africa, in whose name they had acted. Shirley and the Human Rights Media Centre initiated an oral history project in 2013 with the support of the majority of the AKD's members and funding from the National Arts Council, the National Heritage Council and the Western Cape Department of Cultural Affairs and Sport. The recording of oral interviews began in early 2014. Shirley conducted the majority of interviews; Shanil interviewed Shirley; and Dicki interviewed Patrick in Shirley's presence using an interview guideline. At each of these interviews, the contributor was encouraged to have someone close to them to listen and witness. Some interviews took as many as three sessions. Not everyone found the interview process easy, and instead chose to write their stories, such as Seiraaj Salie. Kim Dearham wrote her story following the interview guideline.

There were challenges involved in reconstructing events from thirty years ago. Memory can be unreliable and fragile, and because the AKD operated underground, it was too risky to keep journals, photographs and other records at the time. Each narrative had to be verified with research and collective memory processes, which included group conversations that helped to jog memory.

After the interviews were recorded and transcribed, they were lightly edited and given to members to read. In this way, valuable feedback was provided about gaps and details pertaining to their stories and the collection as a whole. The project had positive outcomes. Realising the gaps in their family histories, some members initiated their own enquiries, held long-overdue conversations and gave thanks to many generous and kind people who had supported them during the struggle. In the process of telling their stories, many were relieved of unexpressed pain and trauma. The stories were then edited again and returned to the members, allowing for further input. This process was repeated three times.

Not all members' stories are included in *Voices from the Underground*. Three members lost their lives in the line of duty: Coline Williams and Robbie Waterwitch died in July 1989 when a limpet mine exploded during an operation, and Anton Fransch was killed in a shoot-out with the security forces in November that year. Richard Ismail was murdered in 2007, and Paul Endley and Andrew Adams of the Macassar Unit passed away before the interview process began. Patrick Presence narrated his story while suffering from memory loss due to Alzheimer's disease. He passed away in 2017, and his story is included here. The four members of the Mitchells Plain unit, with which the AKD cut ties, were not invited to be part of the project.

Most members of the AKD share backgrounds rooted in coloured or Indian working-class communities. The exception is Shirley who grew up in white middle-class suburbs in Cape Town. Many members experienced the devastation of forced removals under the Group Areas Act and the humiliation of being treated as second-class citizens in the country of their birth. The fact that most were condemned to poverty because of the colour of their skin makes this collection particularly affecting: these are stories that the majority of South Africans can relate to.

This book traces the varying journeys people took to MK. The majority of AKD members engaged in activism as students, sacrificing their youth for the struggle, while others joined the underground from Christian organisations, community movements and the United Democratic Front.

Some members were trained outside the country – in Cuba, Angola, Zambia and Tanzania. The rest were trained inside South Africa – initially by Aneez and Shirley, then by Melvin and Anton Fransch – to minimise their exposure outside the country. Members were well trained and followed orders with precision; everyone made personal sacrifices and took calculated personal risks.

Living underground was not easy. There was a constant threat of arrest and detention, and the detachment lived in a state of hypervigilence and fear in order to stay alive and evade capture. Some members straddled the worlds of aboveground political activity and underground work and had to live double lives. Others were completely underground, living in isolation. Strict rules of secrecy were observed and members only received information on a need-to-know basis. This allowed the AKD to remain intact and operational until the armed struggle was suspended.

Some AKD members were captured and detained under Section 29 of the Internal Security Act or under state of emergency regulations, and in all instances their experiences of interrogation and torture were traumatic, yet those who share their stories here did not cooperate with their captors or divulge with whom they worked. Shirley also shares her experience of testifying to a TRC gross human rights committee hearing.

The AKD's track record – with over thirty operations to its name – meant that it did not get by unscathed. There has since been time to gain a greater understanding of what went wrong with the compromised Mitchells Plain unit, as well as the fatal Athlone operation that resulted in the deaths of Coline Williams and Robbie Waterwitch. However, the circumstances of their deaths remain unresolved. AKD members have been deeply affected by allegations that the entire detachment was compromised, which is simply not true.

The AKD took great care to avoid civilian casualties, but there was one occasion when things went wrong and a civilian was injured. The Bonteheuwel unit concealed a limpet mine in a milk carton and a young man, Moegamat Nurudien Bartlett, handled the carton and the limpet exploded. Despite serious injuries, Bartlett survived. The members of the AKD deeply regret this incident. Aneez, Sidney and Vanessa testified to the TRC regarding this event and received amnesty.

The Western Cape, where the AKD operated, was the only major region in South Africa where Wimpy Bars were expressly not targeted. This was the detachment's policy. O.R. Tambo would later reiterate that MK was not to hit soft targets, and no more Wimpys were bombed. The AKD acted strictly in accordance with the Geneva Conventions at all times.

After democracy was achieved in 1994 and the ANC came to power, the process of integrating the armed forces began. Three AKD members joined the new South African National Defence Force – Melvin Bruitjies joined the air force, Charlie Martin became a Reserve Force navy chaplain and later an officer, and Charles Chordnum joined the SANDF temporarily. Only Melvin has remained in the SANDF, today holding the rank of lieutenant colonel.

The rest of the members, bar one, demobilised from 1996, accepting the R22 000 package offered to non-statutory force members. They did not see themselves as career soldiers; serving to liberate South Africa from the shackles of white supremacist rulers was all that they wanted, and this had been achieved.

The fate of one member, AKD commander Aneez Salie, remains in limbo. While he was initially on the Certified Personnel Register (CPR), someone fraudulently demobilised using his name, and he could not get his name back on the register. Through his lawyer Taswell Papier, he challenged this, but was ignored by the Defence Ministry, until Papier served papers to litigate in the then Cape Town Supreme Court, at which point the Defence Ministry agreed to restore Aneez to the CPR. But this was never done.

For the members of the AKD, adjusting to civilian life was not easy. Without much support from the ANC, members returned to previous careers or entered new ones. Some studied, some have risen up the ranks of their professions, while others struggle to make ends meet. With steadfast commitment and hard work, most members have found satisfaction in a life of continued activism, holding on to their vision of a democratic South Africa for which they were prepared to die.

It is fitting that our life stories are bound together in this book. We never regarded ourselves as individuals in MK; we were a closely-knit structure of units, accountable to each other, to our commanders and to the cause for which we strove: an end to apartheid. Every AKD member was important and instrumental to the achievements of the detachment. We share our stories in this book with honesty and integrity.

The stories were initially edited and reviewed by Shirley, Shanil and Melvin, and proofread by Vaun Cornell. In 2018 we were ready to approach a publisher. Soon after receiving the manuscript in April 2018, Robert Plummer from Penguin Random House replied that he was interested in publishing the book, but that he was concerned about its length: around a quarter of a million words. We forged ahead together. With careful editing by Alice Inggs and Robert, together with Shirley and Shanil, who liaised with the contributors to address questions, facts and gaps in the narratives, *Voices from the Underground* was realised.

We ask readers not to be daunted by what is still a substantial book. The stories are riveting and we hope you will take in every detail to the very last page.

'The time comes in the life of any nation when there remain only two choices – submit or fight. That time has now come to South Africa. We shall not submit and we have no choice but to hit back by all means in our power in defence of our people, our future, and our freedom.'

– Umkhonto we Sizwe manifesto, 16 December 1961,
quoted by Nelson Mandela in his speech from
the dock during the Rivonia Trial

1

Shirley Gunn

Truth Is Like a Cork

O NE UNSEASONALLY WARM Friday afternoon in August 1988, wearing a sunhat, sunglasses and a dress, I took a bus from a safe house in Clifton to central Cape Town. In my handbag I was carrying a limpet mine inside a custard box. My target was the Castle of Good Hope, the headquarters of the Western Cape Military Command. To make sure I wasn't being followed, I did a route check that took me past the flower sellers on Adderley Street, where I bought a bunch of everlasting flowers to look like a tourist and to hide my face. I walked past the soldiers at the entrance of the Castle and stepped into the lion's den. Building renovations were under way and the place was teeming with construction workers. I went straight to the tearoom and had a cup of tea, careful not to leave fingerprints on the cup. As it was a Friday and the workers were knocking off early, I took the gap. One of our operatives, Seiraaj Salie, had conducted solid reconnaissance of the precinct.

I primed the limpet in a tunnel off an archway – open due to the renovations but clear of foot traffic – placed it against a wall inside the tunnel and hurried out of the area. I ditched the flowers in a bin at the Grand Parade as I headed to the bus terminus, where I boarded a bus to Sea Point. From there, I caught a taxi to Clifton. Back at the flat, I joined Aneez Salie, the other commander of the Ashley Kriel Detachment, and we monitored the news. According to the reports, the explosion had been extremely loud and had caused structural damage to the tunnel. The operation was successful – it was a great embarrassment to the South African Defence Force (SADF) that the Western Cape Military Headquarters wasn't properly secured – but I feared I might have been seen going into the tunnel where the limpet detonated, and that the security forces would retaliate.

My life journey has followed a path of resistance, with truth, justice and equality as my guiding stars. This is my story.

*

My parents were both medical professionals: my father, Kenneth Gunn, was a radiologist; my mother, Audrey Sauerman, was a nursing sister. Dad was born in Alexandria in Egypt, where his father, Dr James Gunn, worked at the time. Dad's father came from Orkney in Scotland and his mother, Marion Lamb, was from England. When the family moved to Cape Town, my grandfather took up employment at the University of Cape Town (UCT) medical school. They lived in a terraced house in Oranjezicht on the slopes of Table Mountain and, because they were Catholics, Dad and his brother John attended Christian Brothers College, a school in Sea Point. Later, when my grandfather became dean of the medical school, the family lived on campus in Observatory.

Mom was born in what was then Rhodesia. Her father, Victor Sauerman, grew up in Wynberg in Cape Town, and her mother, Cornelia Maré, was from Bedford in the Eastern Cape, but they met in Shabane (renamed Zvishavane in 1983). Gran was teaching and Granddad worked for an asbestos mine. My mom and her elder sister, Renee, grew up in this small mining town. They attended St Peter's Primary School in Bulawayo and completed high school as boarders at St Cyprian's School in Cape Town. My grandparents came to Cape Town in their eighties, to live closer to my parents' care, and I have fond memories of them. Granddad lived to the age of 98 and Gran to 102.

I am the fifth and lastborn of my father's children. Three of my siblings were born in Cape Town: John in 1944, Vandra in 1947 and Shaun a year later. They are the children of Dad's first marriage. After he divorced, Dad moved to Johannesburg with his three children, where he met my mother, and they married in November 1952. Jenny was born the following year. The family, including Zebulon the 'houseboy', moved to Cape Town when Mom was pregnant with me. I was born on 9 May 1955 at St Joseph's Hospital in Pinelands.

My early childhood memories begin in Sandown Road, Rondebosch. Dad left home early for work at his radiology practices in Claremont and Cape Town, and he came home late. When my siblings left for school, Mom and I often went to Cape Town to buy patterns, fabrics, zips and buttons, and when we returned she'd sit behind her sewing machine making our clothes. I don't remember ever shopping for clothes.

Vandra and Shaun were the 'big girls' and were expected to lend a hand when it came to Jenny and me, the 'little ones'. There was a playroom next to the garage, where my big sisters played rock 'n' roll records on an old wind-up gramophone.

Our large family lived in a series of old double-storey houses that our parents fixed up and maintained. Dad made the furniture, while Mom made the curtains and painted and wallpapered the walls. Her watercolour and oil paintings adorned our homes. Our parents were always busy with creative projects. They encouraged us to pursue our interests and never be idle. Dad had many hobbies. He was an active member of the South African Military History Society, had a library of rare books and spent much of his free time reading and writing in his study and designing heraldry and coats of arms, which he painted. He had served as a medical officer in the air force in World War II, but I don't remember him ever speaking about the war. Dad also took a keen interest in photography, and his images were developed as slides that we viewed on a carousel and handheld projector. He had an Akai reel-to-reel tape recorder and corresponded with friends across the world. I remember him as a large man in a white hospital coat smelling of disinfectant, settling into his favourite red chair in his study upstairs, surrounded by books. After supper, he'd drink red wine, smoke a Cuban cigar and read into the night. In those days, my sisters and I had pastel-coloured autograph books in which we'd write messages for our friends. I gave Dad my autograph book to write a message in and he drew a wooden ship with sails and oars, surrounded by wild seas. Underneath it he wrote: 'I hope your ship comes in someday.'

I started school at age five. My sisters and I attended Springfield Convent even though Jenny and I were baptised in the Anglican Church. Because I was the fourth Gunn girl at the convent school, my fees were waived up until Standard 3, when Vandra matriculated. This was how Catholic schools that opposed contraception rewarded big families.

We travelled to school in a black-and-white-striped school bus driven by a man called Gladstone. In Sub A and B, I had to wait for my sisters to finish school before travelling home on the bus and I often sat with Vandra in the music department while she practised the piano. In my middle-class family, my sisters and I could each choose one extramural activity: drama, dance or music. I chose dance. From the age of seven, I attended ballet classes twice a week at UCT's racially mixed ballet school in Woolsack Road in Rondebosch. By then, we had moved to a big double-storey house on Rosmead Avenue, opposite Kenilworth Racecourse. I had a friend called Rose Baumann, who lived close by in Putney Road, and we played together, climbing the fruit trees in her yard. She also did ballet and Mom would drive us to classes together. Rose gave up ballet when her family was forced out of Kenilworth by the Group Areas Act. The day her family was evicted, she came to say goodbye and explained that we wouldn't see each other again.

Mom worked on and off, but was always busy doing something, such as calligraphy, basketry, flower arranging, cake decorating, gardening, crochet, embroidery or dressmaking. When I was in primary school she worked at

Groote Schuur Hospital, and on Fridays she visited cancer patients who had discontinued their treatment. I often bunked school to accompany her on these house visits. Her patients were shack-dwellers and lived in very poor areas, like Vrygrond and Nyanga, and we'd go door to door trying to track them down. Most patients we visited had discontinued their treatment because they couldn't afford the bus fare to get to the provincial hospital in Observatory. I soon came to realise how health and poverty are inextricably linked. Although many things in South Africa were camouflaged, newspapers were censored and apartheid kept people apart, it was impossible not to know about the injustices in the country.

I attended high school at Springfield too, on the same grounds, with the same uniform and the same friends. By Standard 8, I'd achieved full colours in every sport the school offered. But that year something happened that would change everything for me.

I was sick one Monday morning, so I stayed home. Mom was visiting her parents in Bulawayo, Dad was at work, my sister Jenny was in boarding school in the Eastern Cape and my other siblings had moved out, so I was alone in our thatched double-storey house in Kenilworth. I woke up to the smell of smoke and angry flames licking my bedroom doorframe. I jumped out of my bedroom window, which faced the back of the house, and ran to the neighbours to call the fire brigade. When I returned, I saw Dad trying to enter the burning house while people held him back. He'd come home from work to fetch something and, having assumed I was inside the furnace, he was risking his life to save mine.

Almost everything I possessed was destroyed, including my clothes, books and files. My parents salvaged a few items of furniture and moved to another house, and then another soon after that.

The fire was a turning point. I had no material possessions and I lost my competitive edge and my interest in school. A few high-school teachers were supportive, such as Mother Thetler, our brilliant mathematics and English teacher, who pulled me into the Christian Leadership Group despite my apparent disinterest in Christianity. The discourse was stimulating and provoked deep critical reflection that I later learnt was contextual theology. When I completed matric, Mother Leo, the school principal, wrote in my testimonial: 'Shirley shows empathy beyond her years.'

In my high-school years, I always worked during the school holidays. At the end of Standard 9, at the age of seventeen, I applied for a nursing job at Victoria Hospital, telling the superintendent that I'd completed matric and was waiting for my results. I spent the entire six-week holiday working in the white-male ward and living in the nurses' hostel behind the hospital.

After school, I chose a medical career path. I began nursing training at Rondebosch Cottage Hospital, a surgical hospital, and did paediatrics at Red Cross Children's Hospital and medicine at Groote Schuur Hospital. I earned a monthly wage, which gave me independence. During apartheid, white student nurses could only work in white wards, which were adequately staffed and where patients were well cared for; black wards were understaffed and overcrowded. It was absurd. My medical-student friends with Marxist leanings and I discussed alternative health-care systems, but after graduating most of them ended up as cogs in the machinery of state hospitals, or opted to specialise abroad to avoid military conscription, like my brother John.

I left nursing in June 1976. That year, I got caught up in street battles in Adderley Street in Cape Town. I tasted teargas for the first time and was chased by the police. I worked in Johannesburg for three months and saved enough to travel around Europe, where I visited art galleries, hitched a ride from Athens to Turkey in a pantechnicon, and went to a Pink Floyd concert in Frankfurt.

Back home, I enrolled at UCT, majoring in social work and psychology. I enjoyed the practical component of these subjects. In my first year, 1977, my practical placement was at the Students' Health and Welfare Centres Organisation (SHAWCO) in the poverty-stricken, racially mixed communities of Factreton and Windermere. My second-year placement was in Bonteheuwel, and my third year in Retreat.

At the time, social work was one of UCT's few degree courses that admitted black students. In our fourth year, we had to specialise in counselling, group work or community work. Two black students and I chose community work; the majority chose counselling. My practical placement was with the National Institute for Crime Prevention and Rehabilitation of the Offender (NICRO) in the Hout Bay community of Hangberg. Through these placements I saw how apartheid and capitalism relied on the working class, and how inadequate the government's social-service provision for poor people was.

I went from door to door in overcrowded flats, listening to the residents' issues and needs, which pointed to the Cape Town Divisional Council's poor housing provision. Seasonal factory workers and fishermen were unable to pay the high monthly rentals. It was during this time that I encountered the powerful presence of the Food and Allied Workers Union (FAWU), which represented the workers on factory-floor issues. However, no civic organisation existed to fight the battles of inadequate housing and the lack of development plans for future generations. This was possibly because the FAWU leadership feared that if union members got involved in community struggles, FAWU would be at the receiving end of state brutality. Ultimately, workers defiantly downed tools and marched out of the fish factories at the harbour in their turbans and gumboots, bills in hand, to join residents protesting outside the rent office. These protests marked a significant shift in the workers' struggle.

I began reading the monthly *Grassroots* newspaper, which covered stories about civic and youth organisations in the Cape Flats and provided ideas for mobilisation. The Hangberg community would have better success in fighting for their rights if the people were united and organised, so every month batches of *Grassroots* newspapers were dropped at the NICRO office for us to sell in Hangberg, and every month we requested more copies because of the demand. I became increasingly militant, and set about organising the youth, workers and residents, while my rage grew at the injustices around us.

The problems within the social welfare system in South Africa under apartheid prompted me to look at radical alternatives. After I graduated in 1981, I continued working for NICRO in the Hout Bay Harbour community.

Working with the residents in the flats, maisonettes and cottages was extremely rewarding. We worked tirelessly, organising protests against the Divisional Council. We started the Hout Bay Action Committee (HBAC) that affiliated to the Cape Areas Housing Action Committee (CAHAC). Hout Bay was small compared to other City and Divisional Council communities and it was also isolated geographically from the Cape Flats, yet in a CAHAC signature campaign we gathered the most signatures. CAHAC meetings took delegates to different communities across the breadth of the Cape Flats. This had a positive spinoff as residents felt less isolated.

Slowly, the Hout Bay community 'agter die bult' (behind the hill) was incorporated into the struggles of the wider Western Cape. I served on the CAHAC organising committee with Nazeegh Jaffer from the Bo-Kaap, May Princ from Elsies River and Norma Gabriel from Grassy Park, and also on a housing research group with Trevor Manuel and Nicky Rousseau.

We fought tooth and nail in the struggle for land in Hout Bay, which had white ratepayers up in arms; they proclaimed that having a black squatter community in their midst would devalue their properties. I vividly remember the raids by Bantu Affairs Administration Board (BAAB) officials on the Disa River community, who had been living in shacks on that land for generations. BAAB officials usually raided at night, arresting any 'illegal squatters'. They were brutal. However, the unity of people in the quest for land and housing eventually resulted in the development of the Imizamo Yethu ('Our

Efforts') informal settlement, which Dicki Meter and many other comrades fought hard for.

One day, in the midst of the land struggle in 1982, Johnny Issel of the Churches Urban Planning Commission (CUPC) sent Bonteheuwel activist Leon Scott to tell me it was time I took on more responsibility. I'd been head-hunted to set up the Advice Office Forum, an advice office network across the Cape Flats, Paarl and Worcester. I had met Johnny, who was banned, during training workshops organised by the CUPC at the Dora Falcke Centre in Muizenberg, where we'd met with former Robben Island prisoners and held political discussions. Johnny knew the people of Hout Bay were mobilising around a radical agenda and engaging in significant land struggles in which I was deeply involved.

My meeting with Leon Scott took place in a tent – temporary housing for those whose shacks had been demolished by BAAB officials. I told him I was too busy to take on the task of coordinating the advice offices. Leon returned later to convey that CUPC accepted my concerns and that I could slowly phase out some of my responsibilities in Hout Bay, which I agreed to do.

The starting point in establishing the Advice Office Forum was finding common issues faced by poor people seeking advice. One common issue was hire purchase. We created a cartoon-type poster that explained people's rights, which the offices found very helpful. At the same time, a wage strike by the Clothing Workers Union (CLOWU) had begun at Cape Underwear, and I helped coordinate the relief effort for the striking workers and the educational programme. The advice offices took turns providing pots of food for the striking workers – mostly women – whose wages were insufficient to support their families. Again, solidarity among the workers and the community was demonstrated.

Coordinating the advice offices was a departure from the grassroots work I loved, but with the Cape Underwear strike, I used my experience to assemble a group of striking workers and we went from shop to shop in Athlone and along Klipfontein Road asking for donations. The shopkeepers and butchers were members of the Western Cape Traders Association (WCTA), which later affiliated to the United Democratic Front (UDF), and the support they offered was amazing; at the end of the day my car would be packed full of donations.

During this time, there was a daily educational programme of discussions and films at the Bonteheuwel Church hall, where the strikers assembled every morning. At the end of each week, the workers received food parcels. Their morale was high and the strike was sustained for six weeks. Then, victory!

There was an agreement to a national wage increase for all workers across the industry.

In 1982 I travelled to Zimbabwe with Shirley Chaplog, a close friend, to meet the ANC. Shirley and I had met through CAHAC; she came from Kimberley but worked and organised residents in Belhar after graduating from the University of the Western Cape (UWC), a designated coloured university. We hitchhiked from Johannesburg to Harare, where we met Mish Middlemann, a close friend who had left the country to avoid conscription. Mish put us in contact with the ANC leadership in the Zimbabwean capital.

The ANC decided that we would both work in the political underground while continuing our aboveground political work. I was prepared and willing to join Umkhonto we Sizwe and be part of the military underground, but I was told that I was better positioned to do political underground work and that I should continue until I couldn't operate aboveground any longer. A decision would then be made regarding my joining MK.

Shirley and I received training in coding communication, and we discussed Marxist–Leninist texts and the political situation in South Africa. We were instructed to set up a dead letter box (DLB) in Cape Town where we could receive communication from the ANC. When we returned to South Africa, I spoke to my cousin Beverley. She had good reason to receive post from Zimbabwe, her former home, and seeing as she was my cousin, I had good reason to visit her. I instructed her to never remove post from her letter box that wasn't addressed to her.

Political assignments, conveyed through coded messages, were disappointingly slow to arrive at the DLB. To make matters worse, the security police observed me going to Beverley's flat and opening her letter box. The DLB was compromised and Beverley's flat was surveilled.

In mid-1984, after the launch of the Western Cape Advice Offices Forum, I left CUPC and continued working for CLOWU as an organiser at Cape Underwear. In the wake of the strike and wage increase victory, I continued organising the workers, as some of the workforce hadn't gone on strike and needed to be signed up. I spoke to them at the factory gates at lunchtime and did house visits at night, during which workers could ask questions and join CLOWU. Levona Liberty from Elsies River, Gawa Hartley from Belhar and Evelyn Holtzman from Bonteheuwel served on the committee, and together we'd attend house meetings across the Cape Flats. We spent most nights and weekends visiting workers, explaining the difference between CLOWU and the pro-government Garment Workers Union, and discussing political issues. Eventually, the majority of workers at Cape Underwear signed up with CLOWU. The union was finally ready to enter formal wage negotiations with management and the powerful Aaron Searle, the company owner.

It took time and patience recruiting workers to CLOWU, and in the process I drove my car, Mom's old Alfa Romeo, into the ground. Late one night in early 1985 when it was parked outside my place in Athlone, the security branch placed a Molotov cocktail under the petrol tank, hoping the car would go up in flames. The same night, two security policemen pitched up at Mom's Kenilworth home, asking her if she owned the Alfa that had been found burnt out. But it hadn't burnt out; my petrol tank was flat empty! Wembley Roadhouse workers had spotted men running away, seen the smoke, and rushed to douse the flames with fire extinguishers. Nevertheless, the car was scorched – a baptism by fire!

By then, Aneez Salie and I had been recruited to the military underground by Leon Meyer, an MK soldier based in Lesotho but originally from Kensington in Cape Town. I'd met Aneez in 1981 at protest action at the Hout Bay Rent Office when he was working as a reporter for the *Cape Herald*. We had occupied the building, demanding that the officials respond to tenants' demands. Aneez and I got to know each other better over time; he stayed in a granny flat in Crawford and I stayed within walking distance in Belgravia, in a house on Denchworth Road shared with a number of comrades, including Johnny Issel, who was banned, and his partner and the secretary of CLOWU, Zubeida Jaffer. We hadn't been a couple for very long when Johnny informed us that Aneez was going to live in our house for a short while. Neither of us had a problem sharing a room. Meanwhile, Leon Meyer lived in Aneez's flat during his brief stay in the country.

We were trained in firearms, homemade explosives and reconnaissance. During the day, I worked as a trade unionist at CLOWU's office in Corporation Street in Cape Town, rushing to factory gates at lunchtime, attending meetings or writing and printing *Unity* pamphlets – CLOWU newsletters. At night, I visited workers at their homes before undergoing military training until 2 a.m., sleeping until 5 a.m., then distributing *Unity* pamphlets in Epping. It was a crazy existence. Bonteheuwel students assisted with our early-morning pamphleteering, which radicalised them. Ashley Kriel, a student at Arcadia High at the time, mobilised the student pamphleteering taskforce.

I was involved with the Release Mandela Campaign (RMC), which was planning a massive march on Wednesday 28 August 1985 to Pollsmoor Prison in Tokai, where Mandela had been moved from Robben Island three years earlier. Five days before the march, there was a crackdown and seventeen of us in the Western Cape, and many others nationally, were arrested. It was cold that evening and after work I had dashed home to Denchworth Road to fetch a coat. I entered the house through the front door, grabbed my coat and exited around the back. We'd received a tip-off during the day that comrades were being detained and I went to alert our neighbours to the crackdown. While I was doing this, three white security policemen crossed the veranda and began knocking on the front door. Then one came around the side of the house and spotted me. 'Are you Shirley Gunn?' he shouted. 'Come with us!'

The three men escorted me back into the house and searched my bedroom, where they found two copies of the South African Communist Party (SACP) periodical, *African Communist,* in the cupboard. They then took me to a car waiting outside. I was driven to Caledon Square Police Station in central Cape Town, flanked by two large men on the backseat. That same night, having been told I was being held under Section 29 of the Internal Security Act, I was driven to Pollsmoor and held in the women's F-section. Although I didn't hold an elected position as many of the other Western Cape detainees did – including Dullah Omar, Mildred Lesia, Wilson Sedina and Christmas Tinto – I ended up being held in detention the longest, probably because I was suspected of being a member of the SACP and MK.

Most days, the security police took me to Caledon Square for questioning, but I was sometimes interrogated in the major's office of the women's section of the prison. Among the many lines of questioning, they wanted to know about my connection to Johnny and Aneez, about Beverley and her postbox, and about my ANC and SACP membership.

I refused to cooperate and I refused to write a statement. After some time, I discovered that a young man from Oudtshoorn who'd served in the SADF and who had briefly lived with us in Denchworth Road had been detained and had 'sung like a canary'. I was concerned about everyone, but especially Aneez.

As required by law, the district surgeon visited me fortnightly, as did the inspector of detainees, Mr Gerber, a retired magistrate, to establish if I'd been tortured or maltreated. These provisions were in place because of atrocities committed over the years by the security police that had resulted in the deaths of detainees such as Steve Biko, Ahmed Timol, Dr Neil Aggett and Imam Abdullah Haron. Apart from these visits, the only other people I had contact with were the security police, my interrogators and a few female prison warders.

Mildred Lesia was also held at Pollsmoor. I'd seen her at Caledon Square on the night of our detention, but we were kept in solitary confinement at opposite ends of the women's F-section. My only comfort was seeing her underwear hanging on the washing line in the yard where we both exercised at different times. I tried to keep fit by running in the yard for the allocated half hour, steadily increasing my laps, until one day the security police asked me: 'Where were you trained?' So I stopped running in the yard.

The F-section had many single cells leading off two parallel corridors. It was empty except for the cells Mildred and I occupied. Initially, a warder was positioned behind a desk at the end of the passage, guarding me day and night, but after a while I was left locked up and unguarded and the warder on duty would check up on me every few hours. After some months, Mildred's underwear no longer appeared on the line. I assumed she'd been released and that I was in F-section on my own.

The security police continually asked me about the whereabouts of the comrades living in our Denchworth Road house, so I assumed they had managed to evade arrest. This was reassuring.

There was a period of about ten days when I wasn't interrogated, following a crackdown and mass arrests during the 1985 state of emergency, as I would discover later. When the security police returned to interrogate me, they appeared exhausted. Often, after I was interrogated in the major's office, they'd yell: 'You fucking liar, if you are working for the ANC you should be proud to say so. Go back and rot in your cell, you coward!' When they shouted, my morale was briefly elevated: I'd survived another interrogation session without breaking, although the terror would return when I got back to my cell.

During this time, Father Robin van der Spuy, the Catholic priest serving prisoners, requested to see me. 'Father Robin van der Spuy,' I thought. 'What kind of name is that for a Catholic priest?' Those I'd known at school were Irish and named after saints. I refused to see him. He persisted and I figured a meeting would at least break the monotony of solitary confinement. Still, I was suspicious of him and since I'd read the Bible – the only thing I was allowed in my cell besides two sets of clothing – I thought I'd test his biblical knowledge to see if he was genuine.

I gave Father van der Spuy a hard time, grilling him like the security police grilled me, but he continued to return. Eventually, I looked forward to his visits. I discovered later that this kind South African priest visited and comforted Mom too. On one occasion, out of the warder's hearing, he told me that Andrew Mlangeni sent me his regards. What a reassurance it was that a Rivonia trialist locked up in the maximum-security section in Pollsmoor was aware that I was being held in solitary confinement, and that Father van der Spuy was a trusted messenger.

After some time, I accepted the exercise book and pen the security police pressured me to take to write a statement. Back in my cell, I asked a warder for a pencil and eraser. I drew. The first drawing was of my cell, in perfect proportion: the small wooden shelf attached to the wall at the foot of my single metal-framed bed, the toilet pot and the window above it with its narrow windowpanes and vertical bars. The next drawing was of my worn-out takkies, and another was the repetitive blue-and-white design of the bedspread that reeked of rolled tobacco. The security police returned a few days later, demanding to see my statement. They fumed when they saw that I'd drawn in the exercise book. The few days with paper and pencil were worth their anger and verbal abuse, though, and the drawings are etched in my memory.

About a week later, the warders told me to pack up but refused to say more. It was an intense period at a time when the security police seemed to be making a breakthrough in their investigation. Earlier, they had brought the young man from Oudtshoorn who knew me from Denchworth Road into the interrogation room at Caledon Square. I knew that he'd been recruited into the SADF but had deserted. 'Shirley, you must speak,' he'd said to me. 'There are many of us behind bars because of you and Aneez. You must speak so we can be released.'

'Take him away,' I'd said dismissively. 'I don't know what he's talking about. He's telling you a pack of lies. How can you trust an SADF deserter?'

As ordered, I put my clothes in a carrier bag. I was taken deep into the prison to a cell next to the hospital section. It had a high window covered by dirty mesh. I could not see the sky or feel direct sunlight, as I had in my previous cell, but if I pushed the heavy metal locker below the window and climbed onto it, I could see out over the tunnel-like prison corridor. Opposite was another row of cells with windows similar to mine. I could hear the prisoners talking indistinctly. I didn't know why I'd been moved, but I presumed the reasons were sinister.

I'd warmed up to Dr Edelstein, the district surgeon who visited me every fortnight. I gathered he'd known my granddad, and Dad too, who'd passed away the year before. This connection was reassuring. When I complained about the food, which glistened with uncooked fat, he put me on a fat-free diet and prescribed a mild sleeping pill that I took at night. On one of his visits, he told me something that has stayed with me: 'Truth is like a cork; it always comes to the surface.' This scared me because I was withholding information, but I would later come to appreciate the wisdom of his words.

When I was shifted to the hospital section, an Afrikaans-speaking district surgeon took over his duties and I was told Dr Edelstein had left after suffering a nervous breakdown. Meanwhile, the security police told me I'd be lucky if I got ten years. Helpless and depressed, I prepared myself for a long stay behind bars.

I was allowed to see my mother on a few occasions. We couldn't say much, but at least she saw I was clear-headed and strong and she let others know that, including Essa Moosa, my lawyer. I'd been arrested in winter and I lived in the blue coat in which I'd been detained. Mom had given it to me for my birthday three months earlier. Summer came and I cut the sleeves off my T-shirt and the legs off my jeans using scissors provided by the warders. Mom kindly brought me an outfit: a pale-blue pleated skirt and matching top made of Zimbabwean cotton – ideal, I thought, for the day I'd be released or charged. The beautiful outfit was neatly folded in my locker, awaiting that big day.

Eventually, the security police told me that the docket had been prepared and handed over to the Attorney General (AG). There was a period of waiting for the AG to decide on the charges to be brought against me. On one of his visits, Father van der Spuy conveyed that I'd be out soon and I got the distinct sense that people were mobilising for my release. Mom had campaigned tirelessly for my release.

During this time, I was allowed to get one book at a time from the small library in the women's section. The only South African writer on the shelves was Wilbur Smith. I read all his books that were in the library and became completely absorbed in fiction that took me into the African bush. Later, the security police said I could choose a magazine. I didn't read magazines and wondered why they were offering me one, but I asked for a *Cosmopolitan* – it was the only name that came to mind. I duly received a *Cosmopolitan* and in Jane Raphaely's editorial I read about the large number of children arrested under the state of emergency regulations declared on 26 October 1985. From this editorial I deduced why I'd been shifted from F-section to a hospital cell; Pollsmoor needed space for female detainees.

In November 1985, Essa and Mom applied to the Cape Town Supreme Court for my urgent release, but the application was withdrawn when they read the state's replying affidavit that I was to be charged with terrorism and attempting to overthrow the state. That scared them off and I was stuck in Pollsmoor while the AG assessed the docket and came to a decision.

In the early morning of 13 December, the warders told me to pack up as the security police had come to fetch me. With no idea what to expect, I threw everything in a Checkers packet, including my light-blue outfit, and waited for my cell to be unlocked. The security police were waiting in the major's office with a charge sheet that read: Possession of Communist Party literature. I was about to sign the document when I said to myself: 'This is not the time to show an ounce of relief. Go for them.' I put down the pen and looked up from the charge sheet. 'Are you crazy?' I said. 'I have been here for 112 days and you're charging me with what you had on day one?' They had nothing to say to this. I signed the paper and another for the return of my wristwatch. The four security policemen were silent as they drove to Wynberg Magistrate's Court, where I met Essa in the court's underground holding cells. It was a great relief to see him again.

I finally appeared in court and the magistrate read out the charges. He didn't want to release me and stated that it was likely I'd skip the country, so there were conditions to my release: bail of R750 and I had to hand over my passport and report to Claremont Police Station on Fridays between 4 and 6 p.m. I also had to stay with Mom in Kenilworth, as they required my physical address. Finally, I was released. I remember feeling completely disorientated and overwhelmed by the noises and sounds of the outside world. A press conference was held in Mom's back garden. Many people gathered, including members of the Detainees' Parents Support Committee (DPSC) and journalists I knew, such as Rashid Lombard. The first thing I said to the media was: 'Now I have steel in my bones.'

Detention had different effects on detainees. Some became subdued, fearful they'd end up in the hands of the police again. Others, like me, became more militant. The experience in solitary confinement and my refusal to give in to the security police's questioning had indeed put steel in my bones.

Just before Christmas, Mom and I attended the Wednesday-night candlelit vigil at the Buitenkant Street Methodist Church opposite Caledon Square where I'd been regularly interrogated. Besides the consumer boycott and call for a 'Black Christmas', a passive resistance response to the state of emergency, people across the country were mobilised to turn off their lights and burn candles for an hour on Wednesday nights in solidarity with detainees, and churches were challenged to take sides. I received a standing ovation when I urged people to continue protesting the draconian Section 29 detention laws that flagrantly disregarded human rights. The United Nations General Assembly had adopted the Universal Declaration of Human Rights on 10 December 1948, and South Africa was among the few countries in the world that refused to sign it.

There was so much catching up to do but Aneez was my biggest concern as I feared the security police would be ruthless if they captured him. I desperately needed to see him to communicate the angle of my interrogation and the accusations by the young SADF deserter. While I was in detention, however, images of Johnny and Aneez had appeared on national TV as wanted and dangerous persons and their photographs were pasted up at police stations. They'd gone underground and I didn't know where or how Aneez was. I stayed with Mom for a while and I couldn't sleep for weeks, another effect of solitary confinement.

Soon after my release, I was taken to a secret location to meet Johnny, Zubeida and some CLOWU workers. The workers thought that I had been detained because of my union work and were wonderfully supportive. We had a good laugh about the security police's raid on an Athlone factory where CLOWU workers were caught sewing ANC flags. A number of workers were arrested and detained briefly at Pollsmoor, but they were released after a court appearance when they denied knowing anything about flags; they said they were sewing colourful tablemats. The state's tactics were utterly counter-productive: instead of making the workers fearful, they politicised them.

Shortly thereafter, I received a message that Aneez was in Johannesburg waiting to see me before he left the country. I approached Sandra Nagfaal, an executive committee member of the Media Workers' Association of South Africa (MWASA), to go with me. I hired a car with money I'd received from the Western Province Council of Churches (WPCC) and Amnesty International. Sandra took a week's leave from work and we drove to Johannesburg in the window period before my signing in at the Claremont Police Station on Fridays. I met Aneez in a Hillbrow flat; we had the place to ourselves. Still traumatised, I hardly ventured out. It was wonderful seeing Aneez and we affirmed that leaving the country was his only option. I memorised the contact details he gave me of people who could take me out of the country should the security police continue to make my life a living hell.

On my return to Cape Town, I left Mom's house and stayed with Avril Seria in Vanguard Estate in Athlone, remaining indoors and out of harm's way. One Sunday, Avril organised a picnic at Voelklip in Strand, where I met Johnny again. While we swam in the ocean, I gave him the details of the security police's questioning so that if he was detained he'd know how to handle interrogation. I warned him that whatever the SADF deserter knew, the police would know too.

Johnny was arrested soon afterwards and so was Zubeida, at an advanced stage of pregnancy. After their arrest, I shared a room in Observatory with June Esau, a CLOWU organiser. June had also been detained for a month and had a horrible experience at the hands of the security police. Johnny and Zubeida were released without charges a few months later.

Aneez left the country via Botswana. We had elaborate communication arrangements via public phone boxes and I was concerned that he was struggling to connect with the ANC, which stalled his passage further north. I carried on organising at Cape Underwear and reported to the Claremont Police Station weekly, often accompanied by Mom.

The trial connected to my possession of two issues of *African Communist* commenced in the Wynberg Magistrate's Court in January 1986. Dullah Omar represented me and Mom was a witness. When I was first detained and others in the Denchworth Road house went into hiding, she and Ragmat Jaffer had packed up our belongings there. In court, Mom testified that among the items she had found in the cupboard in my room was men's underpants. She asserted that my room and the cupboard were shared, and their contents – including the banned literature – could not be assumed to be mine. Eventually, in May 1986, after four court hearings, charges against me were dropped.

On Friday 7 March 1986, soon after my release from solitary confinement, I was detained again, along with forty others at Cape Town's D.F. Malan Airport, where we were protesting against the deportation of German anti-apartheid activist and Lutheran church leader Pastor Gottfried Kraatz. We were charged with disorderly behaviour. Most were released that same day, but Johnny and I were held in custody over the weekend. Christina Kunz, a German volunteer who was arrested with us, refused to leave me behind and insisted on remaining in custody. Christina was able to communicate with the German consulate in Cape Town and we received food and board games to occupy us.

On the following Monday, the entire group of protestors appeared at the Bellville Magistrate's Court. The first hearing was chaotic. I was detained again by riot policemen outside the court for shouting 'Amandla!' to my co-accused, and everyone refused to leave the courtroom until I was released. Eventually, on 21 May, with Ebi Mohammed from Essa's firm as our defence lawyer, charges against all of us were dropped.

By mid-1986, I could no longer operate aboveground. The security police followed me wherever I went, so I prepared to exit the country, banking on the route Aneez had taken, which I'd memorised. I helped Anton Fransch, a student activist from Bonteheuwel, leave at the same time. He travelled in a pantechnicon with Ebrahim Vallie, who regularly transported Cape fruit to Johannesburg, and I travelled by air, heavily disguised. We linked up in Boksburg and stayed in Johannesburg briefly while I established communication with a contact I'd been referred to to take us out of the country.

Anton and I got over the border safely, buried under vegetables on the back of a truck. The driver arranged our accommodation in Gaborone, where we stayed for a couple of days until I managed to connect with the ANC.

The first thing the ANC comrade asked me was who I was following. I thought this question strange, until he added, 'Who's your boyfriend?' Then it hit me: the perception was that MK women were part of the movement because of their partners. I was offended. 'I'm on my own,' I replied. From that moment on, I kept that mentality.

Anton had a separate briefing and I don't know where he was taken, but I was placed with a Dutch international NGO worker, his Batswana wife and their two children. After roughly ten days there, I was told to get ready to leave. Anton was in the car with three other comrades when I was picked up. We were driven to a game farm close to the Zimbabwean border, where we waited until nightfall. Under cover of darkness, the five of us got back in the car and drove quite a long distance. Then the car slowed, the headlights were turned off, and we came to a halt. We waited and waited in the stationary car and the three comrades became agitated. All of a sudden, there was a tap on the window and MK soldiers with AKs appeared out of the dark. Anton and I were instructed to go with them. The soldiers took our bags, we were handed AKs and we marched through the bush into a swamp. We walked through the swamp for several kilometres until we came to the Zambezi River, where inflated dinghies were waiting in the shallow waters to take us across. Two MK soldiers quietly rowed the dinghy over the river, which was notorious for crocodiles and hippos and patrolled by armed border guards. On the other side, a 4 x 4 was waiting for us in the bush on Zambian soil. We were taken to an ANC house in Livingstone. There, the comrades wanted to hear news from home. They had an insatiable thirst to hear how the mass democratic struggle was advancing and seemed desperately homesick.

The next day, we continued our journey to Lusaka. I was taken to Andrew's Motel, a place outside town, where I had briefings with Chris Hani, Charles Nqakula, James Ngculu and others. The ANC leadership wanted to hear my insights on the conditions at home and were excited to hear how the revolution was maturing. Finally, I got my briefing. Chris Hani advised that I would receive specialised training in military intelligence in Cuba before undergoing basic military training in Angola. Since I'd experienced detention, they felt it appropriate that I focus on military intelligence. I didn't know where Anton was but I was confident he was in good hands.

Some weeks later, I flew to Angola on a Zambian aircraft with a number of other comrades. From Viana Transit Centre outside Luanda, I was taken to an ANC safe house in the capital, a fourth-storey flat in an area called São Paulo.

The infrastructure was such that water had to be collected in buckets at the tap in the courtyard, carried upstairs and stored in our bathtub for washing and cooking. To stay busy, I catalogued the library of books and magazines in the flat and embroidered a small piece of linen I'd brought with me. We were all on a roster to prepare meals using provisions delivered by the ANC.

As the trip to Cuba approached, we underwent medical examinations and had to work on our legends, or cover stories, in case the CIA or another intelligence agency apprehended us.

Finally we set off in a Russian aircraft, and on landing in Havana we were taken to a tropical hospital where our group of about twenty-five men and women underwent further tests for tropical diseases. After being given a clean bill of health, we were taken to a large house in Havana with small dorms, women in one and men in the other two, where training was conducted. There were four of us in my group being trained in military intelligence and security – myself and three men. In another part of the house was a group learning to make dead letter boxes to cache materials and communication. They were forever banging and hammering. I learnt later that the comrades in the third group, including Ivan Pillay and Janet Love, were part of the ANC's Operation Vula, an underground operation aimed at smuggling freedom fighters into the country.

Two of us were made responsible for logistics in the underground house. Provisions such as food, toiletries and cigarettes were delivered on a weekly basis. Provisions had to be requested and shared. The comrades loved the Cuban staple diet – pork and beans, delivered in enormous pots. We received Cuban army non-filter cigarettes made with sugar paper that burnt to nothing, but we had to be careful when smoking in public as they were not sold in shops and would draw attention to the smoker. If there were a few packets over after distributing them evenly among the smokers, I divided loose cigarettes equally too. A few comrades remarked that they'd never had such a fair deal. That seemed strange, but opened my eyes to potential corruption within logistics.

The intensive course was translated from Spanish to English; the Cuban instructors were men; the translators, women. One of our instructors, a master at espionage, had been a double agent working inside the CIA for twelve years. I knew first-hand how our security police operated, so I shared their tactics. Intent on going back home after training, I needed to learn methods of outwitting the security forces. I learnt many different conspiracy and counter-conspiracy tactics that I would need at home.

The course was very interesting and useful, especially as I felt that I was not in exile but in transit, upgrading my skills before going home. I thoroughly enjoyed the underground photography course. We monitored buildings with telescopes and were taught clandestine photographic techniques, developing the film in the communal toilet that doubled as a darkroom. I presented my portfolio of photographs related to the course, but also images of everyday life that I'd taken conspiratorially in Marianao, a suburb about ten kilometres south-west of Havana. Our instructor showed great appreciation for my second portfolio. On the last day of the course he gave me a red rose – most unmilitary – but I appreciated his encouragement.

The other comrades doing the course with me had been in exile for a long time and didn't exert themselves, especially when it came to the practical assignment we performed in Marianao. We received weekly stipends to travel there by bus. The first part of one of the assignments was to map out the entire infrastructure of Marianao – shops, factories, clinics, hospitals, parks, schools, houses, small traders, roads and footpaths – on a massive piece of hardboard. The other three comrades relied on me to do this work; little did they know this was my expertise as a community social worker.

I was grateful for the time in Marianao, as we were otherwise confined to the underground house. I witnessed Cubans queuing to exchange coupons for food rations at the small warehouse, which ensured every household had enough food. Local doctors lived in small apartments above their clinics, so the community always had access to medical help. Each street had its own noticeboard displaying past and upcoming events. There were small factories where women workers sewed school uniforms: white shirts, short grey pants and variously coloured bowties that attached to the collar to distinguish different schools. People built extensions to their houses that were painted in bright colours – a stark contrast to the monotonous council housing in South Africa. I was inspired and there were many moments when I wished South African workers could experience Cuba too. I mapped the ground plan of the community of Marianao on the large board with careful precision.

The second part of our practical was a clandestine handover after doing a route check. My route check started in old Havana. I had identified a narrow L-shaped footpath where I could see who was behind and in front of me as I turned the corner to do the handover. Plan B was an ice-cream parlour with umbrellas and outdoor tables where it would be easy to speak to a stranger and exchange a message without it seeming suspicious. We presented our practical assignment individually to eight military generals. They listened and smiled at one another. We'd been monitored and they were very happy with my presentation.

I left Cuba after three months, in February 1987. Back in Luanda, I met

Aneez and Ashley Kriel, who had returned from the camps. I had known Ashley as a student leader in 1984 and 1985, shortly before he left for exile. Aneez had got to know him well in Lusaka; they lived together in the same house and were planning their return to Cape Town where they would work together.

I remember conversations with Ashley in Luanda. He felt conflicted, as the MK leadership wanted him to undergo officer's training abroad to equip him to take greater responsibility in the military after we'd achieved liberation. My response was to tell him that it was an honour that the leadership saw advanced officer training as fitting, but that he had to make up his own mind. I had done so and was going back to fight the battles on the home front. But first I had to continue my training.

I was driven in a jeep from Luanda to Pango, also known as the David Rabkin Centre, to do the basic military training course. The ANC fast-tracked my training so I could be sent back to South Africa quickly. They also tried to minimise my exposure to MK soldiers there – the more well known you were, the more compromised you became as an operative – so I received classes on my own. I had absolute confidence in my instructors, who taught politics, military combat work (MCW) and military engineering and conducted fire-arms training. I did plenty of firearms training, practising with different types of weapons, even R4s, in the event that we ambushed SADF armouries. I also practised with the Israeli Uzi, which is deadly accurate and has little recoil, and the AK-47, which I was comfortable with at short and long range. I practised in prone, kneeling and standing positions, and also while running. I think I would have made an excellent sniper, as I'd usually get eight or nine out of ten shots dead on target. In a short time, I was confident with firearms and explosives and felt equipped to return home. The only thing I found lacking in the course was how to handle detention and interrogation. When I returned to Lusaka, I wrote notes for the instructors to teach comrades in the camps, as many MK cadres were captured after infiltration into South Africa. At the time, the average lifespan of a trained freedom fighter inside the country was only three months.

I eventually left the camp on Sharpeville Day, 21 March 1987, before the commemoration, which involved the entire camp. I was driven in a truck to Luanda and stayed at an underground flat for a few days before flying to Zambia. On my arrival in Lusaka, I was taken to an underground house on a large property enclosed by a high wall with a solid metal access gate. Charles Nqakula and his partner, Nosiviwe Mapisa-Nqakula, lived in the house oppo-site. Sometimes, the ANC leadership held meetings in the house in which I was staying and it was where I received my briefings.

During one of my briefings, Chris Hani asked me about my experience as a woman in the army. I told him I'd had fantastic treatment from the instructors and everyone else, but was aware we were regarded as subordinate to our male counterparts, and I described certain situations that had shaped that awareness. Chris listened intently. 'That is why we need women like you in the post-apartheid defence force,' he said. 'You must keep this option open.'

In June 1987, I was sent back to South Africa on a high-security mission. I was given additional training in Lusaka and money in order for me to operate on my own. But just before I was to return home, I picked up malaria, with symptoms of acute stomach pain, diarrhoea and excruciating headaches. I became extremely weak and dehydrated. I was finally treated by one of our doctors at a Zambian hospital, but it would take weeks to regain a reasonable level of strength. When disembarking the plane in Botswana, I was too weak to carry my bag. The malaria gave me a great disguise, though – I was so thin that not even Mom would have recognised me.

My contact in Botswana was Thengiwe Mtintso, known as Molly. She took me to a leather shop outside Gaborone and said, 'Choose a bag that you wouldn't be seen dead with.' I chose an old-fashioned black leather bag, big enough to carry a Makarov pistol. I was to communicate with Molly regarding my special mission when I got back home. As I was about to board the train in Gaborone for Johannesburg, she asked if I was sure I could carry out the mission. I told her I was. 'You're very brave,' she said. This particular mission was ultimately aborted. If it had gone ahead, I probably wouldn't be here to tell my story.

I returned to Cape Town and, once there, moved into a one-bedroom mountainside cottage in Clifton, sharing with a woman doing a master's degree in psychology at UCT. While I was there, in July 1987, I learnt that Ashley Kriel had been shot and killed by the security police soon after returning to South Africa. He was only twenty years old. I was absolutely devastated, unable to talk to anyone about the tragedy.

When Aneez returned the country, I linked up with him, and we had a couple of meetings in the Clifton cottage during the day when we had the place to ourselves. I told him I was struggling to reach my contact in Botswana, but I didn't disclose what my deployment was.

As time passed, there was mounting pressure from the student to move out – she had gone through my bags and become fearful of harbouring me – so I settled for a tiny rented space behind a block of flats in Skye Way above

High Level Road in Green Point. The room had a kitchen on one end, a toilet on the other and the connecting passage was the bedroom. It appeared to once have been servants' quarters. My cover to the owner was that I was a writer and wouldn't stay long as I was looking for somewhere more suitable, and that the little room was perfect in the interim. I paid the monthly rental in cash, which I'd received when I returned and which I kept with me, not in a bank.

Around the end of 1987, Aneez and I got a bigger one-room bachelor flat in Clifton, which we kept until 1990. The flat was on the second floor, above the entrance, and had a side window that could function as an escape route. We'd agreed that if one of us was captured, we'd remove the weapons stored there, and anything else that could incriminate us, and evacuate the flat. Aneez was having difficulty linking up with comrades he was assigned to work with to build an underground detachment in Cape Town, and he had no money. Communication problems with Molly continued; the SADF was attacking ANC bases in the frontline states, so my special mission was on hold, but I didn't know for certain what had caused the delay.

We communicated our difficulties to the ANC leadership in Lusaka and proposed that Aneez and I work together to set up an underground detachment, since neither of our missions were going according to plan. We received the green light, and in September 1987, Aneez and I joined forces to start building what would become the Ashley Kriel Detachment, named after our comrade who had made the ultimate sacrifice for our freedom.

Our mission was to set up the AKD within the coloured, Indian and white areas. It was great working with Aneez; we shared a common understanding of the political conditions, and our approach to building a secure underground detachment was the same. We knew many community activists because of our work: he was a journalist, I was a civic and youth activist, and both of us were unionists.

We'd learnt from the mistakes of the MK detachments preceding us and didn't communicate directly from Cape Town with our MK commander in Botswana, James Ngculu, known as Faiz. Instead, our communication went via Johannesburg; the movement of people and communication between Johannesburg and Botswana was constant and hence more difficult to trace and less likely to raise suspicion. Aneez was instrumental in setting up the Johannesburg unit in early 1987, commanded by Shanil Haricharan, whom Aneez introduced to Faiz in Botswana. We communicated with Shanil from difficult-to-trace public phone boxes that changed constantly for security reasons, and he'd communicate with Faiz, also from public phone boxes. Over time, the Johannesburg unit expanded and it worked effectively as the conduit for weapons and communications between Gaborone and Cape Town.

In 1988, I recruited Ismail and Julie Vallie from Cape Town to assist with the conduit for weapons and communication from Gaborone. They had started a plastic packaging company and therefore had a good cover: a respectable Muslim couple doing business. They entered Botswana via Johannesburg with plastic-bag samples on the car's back seat as proof of their purpose. Shanil accompanied Ismail and Julie on their first trip to introduce them to Faiz. On their arrival back in Cape Town, they handed the car over to the AKD – mission accomplished. Ismail and Julie undertook three such missions successfully.

Aneez and I set up the Regional Political Military Committee (RPMC) with Johnny Issel to discuss the political situation on the ground and advise military responses. At our first meeting, which took place in a caravan on a farm, we decided to recruit Melvin Bruintjies, who worked for CUPC, mobilising the church youth. As his boss, Johnny gave assurance that Melvin would receive the support and protection he needed. I knew Melvin – he'd assisted us with CLOWU pamphleteering in Bonteheuwel – so I made the initial contact to recruit him. My first meeting with him was in Muizenberg and the next soon afterwards at Queens Beach car park on Beach Road in Sea Point. Besides Shanil, who was deployed to command the Johannesburg–Botswana–Cape Town logistics and communication pipeline, and Mogamat and Seiraaj Salie, Aneez's older brothers whom he'd recruited to assist on a number of fronts, Melvin was our first recruit in our formation of AKD units in the Western Cape.

Before we expanded the detachment, we performed a number of sensitive operations. One of these was in response to the assassination of anti-apartheid activist Dulcie September in Paris on 29 March 1988. Aneez and I felt that by targeting a French bank overlooking the historic Church Square in central Cape Town, we would be sending a clear message to the complicit French government that such actions against our people would not be tolerated. Aneez and I did reconnaissance of the building, as did Shanil during one of his trips to Cape Town.

There would be casualties if the limpet mine went off in the bank during working hours, so we decided to place it in the Parliament Towers building adjacent to the bank. The objective was to damage the building without injuring anyone. I did reconnaissance from the coffee shop nearby, monitoring the movement of people entering and exiting the building, which had offices near the ground floor and apartments above, and carried out a dummy run.

On the day before Parliament opened in April 1988, I travelled on public transport from our flat in Clifton to Church Square. I placed the charge inside the entrance of the Parliament Towers building, facing the bank's side wall. I wore socks on my hands, as gloves were a giveaway if you were caught. I then fled town in a meter taxi from Adderley Street and told the taxi driver to drop me off on Sea Point Main Road near the police station – who would think that the bomber would want to be anywhere near a police station?

Back at our Clifton flat, Aneez and I watched footage of the limpet explosion aftermath on the news. The outcome was unexpected: Amichand Rajbansi of the House of Delegates and Allan Hendrickse of the House of Representatives – both considered to be puppets of the regime – as well as senior white government cronies, all came running out of the building in front of the SABC newsmen saying: 'We've been attacked!' By sheer coincidence, they'd been holding a special caucus in the building next to Parliament Towers, as Parliament was opening the next day. They were certainly not the target.

Another operation was in response to the planned launch of a Conservative Party (CP) branch in Sea Point on 16 June 1988, the anniversary of the student uprisings. Their public launch was held in the main hall of the Sea Point Civic Centre on Main Road. Diagonally opposite the civic centre was a restaurant on Glengariff Road, where Aneez and I drank coffee and observed activity around the civic centre. The lights were on inside and there was no foot traffic; the meeting was in progress. I was to execute the operation. Aneez went back to Clifton to monitor the news.

My plan was to approach the civic centre from the flats behind the chemist on Glengariff Road, where I would prime the limpet mine. I would place the limpet against the glass façade of the civic centre, then leave the same way, exiting via the back entrance of the flats in order to catch a taxi on Main Road back to our base in Clifton.

It was not that straightforward. It was a misty winter night and I was wearing a hand-knitted jersey to which I'd added an extended polo neck that I could pull over my head like a hood. Everything seemed to be going according to plan, but then, as I was approaching the civic centre with the charge ready, a white woman – Gaye Derby-Lewis, I later discovered on the news – left the main building and entered the minor hall. I turned my back to her and waited to see what she was up to. She walked out of the minor hall and back into the main building, and then came out again with two men, entered the minor hall again and exited, carrying chairs to the main building. I waited a while longer, hoping they were not coming to fetch more chairs and, when it was clear, I dashed through the flowerbed and placed the charge facing the glass façade. I disappeared back into the flats, whipped off the jersey, exited through the back entrance and jumped into a taxi. According to news reports, the explosion shattered the glass while the CP members were singing *Die Stem*, apartheid South Africa's national anthem. This must have been a shock to them, and the expansion of the CP was abruptly stopped right there.

All our operations thus far were in close radius of the city centre, and Sea Point was often sealed off in search-and-seize operations. These joint operations by the South African Police (SAP) and SADF entailed cordoning off an entire area and searching every car and person within it. I missed one by a few minutes and it became very dangerous to move around.

After the explosion at the Castle of Good Hope in August 1988, I was concerned that I had been seen planting the limpet mine. I was aware that the profile of a white woman in a mixed-race couple was doing the rounds. To throw the security forces off our track, the detachment needed to expand and continue with operations away from the city. We already had the means to do so: weapons, materials and money that came into South Africa cached in cars from Botswana, and we'd dug ourselves in deep.

We obeyed the rules of conspiracy rigidly. Every Friday evening we'd pack our bags and line them up at the door of the flat, ready to flee if we were profiled on the SABC's *Police File*. To our relief that never happened, but we went through the same weekly drill for months. We monitored the print media, radio and TV around the clock. On Sundays, Julie and Ismail brought us the weekly newspapers. We were holed up indoors at this point and I looked forward to the brief contact with the couple, who were nearing the end of their roles as operatives – roles they'd played courageously. I'd sit on a bench on High Level Road in a sunhat, admiring the sea view, waiting for them to arrive with newspapers, *koeksisters* and other treats.

Aneez and I conceived our first child in the Clifton flat round May 1988. When I missed my period, I took a bus to Victoria Hospital in Wynberg, where I posed as 'Sharon Hendricks' for an examination. The pregnancy was confirmed. A conversation I'd had with Chris Hani in Lusaka a year before flashed through my mind. 'Don't fall pregnant. Don't have children,' he'd said. My reply to our MK commissar and Communist Party leader was: 'You're a fine one to say "don't have children" – you've got three beautiful daughters. Have they held you back in any way? Why would it be different for me, a woman?' He didn't defend himself or contradict me; he seemed to accept this feminist argument. I spent many hours reflecting on my conversation with Chris, asking myself how being a mother and rearing a child in the underground would change things.

Aneez and I decided to get married and Zubeida and Johnny organised our wedding, which took place on 12 September 1988 in a British admiral's beach house alongside the naval dockyard in Simon's Town. We looked very smart on our wedding day, in new clothes, our hair neatly cut. Our families knew I was four months pregnant. The invited guests were: Aneez's parents, Amina and Salie Salie; my mom; Aneez's brothers Mogamat and Seiraaj; Johnny and Zubeida; and Imam Gassan Solomon, who performed the *nikah* (Muslim matrimonial vows). This wasn't the usual *nikah* with men and women apart; we were together in one room, which Mama said made it very special. After a lovely meal of biryani, tea and cake, the guests left the way they had come, some lying low in their cars to avoid being seen. Zubeida, Johnny, Aneez and I stayed in that Simon's Town house for two nights. It was wonderful being with family and socialising like normal people, if only for forty-eight hours. Zubeida was a great support, as was Johnny.

After Melvin was recruited, the AKD expanded. The units operated well, and many successful operations were executed. Towards the end of 1988, we needed to establish another secure, discreet base where I could give birth. We kept a close watch on rental properties advertised in newspapers and spotted a garden cottage in Pear Lane in a beautiful area of Constantia called Witteboomen that seemed ideal. The property owner was Richard Rosenthal, a well-known lawyer. His father, the brilliant Eric Rosenthal, was an author of encyclopaedias and a general knowledge expert on a Springbok Radio quiz show that my sisters and I had listened to as children. In the last trimester of my pregnancy, in late November 1988, I made an appointment to meet Richard and his wife, Hillary, to see the cottage.

My legend was that I was Wendy Adams, a preschool teacher from Johannesburg. I was relocating to Cape Town and would soon be joined by my husband. I needed a quiet place to have the baby and settle down before resuming work. The cottage was a renovated stable, completely secluded and surrounded by old oak trees. The peaceful environment was perfect. Richard and Hillary wanted quiet tenants and they took an instant liking to me, perhaps taking pity on me, and I signed the lease, assuring them I'd hand over a copy of my ID when I'd found it among my packed possessions.

Zubeida and Johnny had given Aneez and me two comfortable second-hand chairs as a wedding present, and Mom had given us a duvet and covers, so the two-bedroom cottage with its lounge and fireplace separating the two rooms looked sparse but decent. I settled in first and Aneez joined me some days later. Richard and Hillary were curious. Hillary often arrived at the front door around suppertime with an enormous bunch of hydrangeas from their beautifully cultivated garden. When we saw her approaching, Aneez would grab his plate and hide in the toilet, but the strong smell of curry permeated the air. I always accepted Hillary's kind offering graciously, but never invited her in. Later, I established that the Rosenthals suspected we were a mixed-race couple and that I didn't trust them enough to tell them.

The Pear Lane cottage was safe. I didn't have to helter-skelter inside when helicopters flew overhead as the canopy of trees and greenery provided camouflage. There were numerous political trials going on at the Cape Town Supreme Court, including that of Ashley Forbes and his fourteen co-accused, who were part of an MK detachment that had been uncovered. Fearing that the convoys of trucks taking the comrades between Pollsmoor and the court would be ambushed, the security forces deployed helicopter surveillance. Even with police sirens screeching down Constantia Road and helicopters clamouring overhead, I didn't have to move. I could sit on the garden bench in my sunhat with my big belly, reading the daily newspapers under the oak trees in absolute peace. We monitored the news, and from time to time I went out to connect with comrades – mostly Melvin and Shanil via prearranged calls at different public phone boxes – or to buy provisions at Pick 'n Pay in Constantia Village.

In 1988, our units executed a number of successful operations after Melvin set up units in Bonteheuwel and Mitchells Plain, and later in Macassar, Athlone and Boland. It was a slow process training operatives and cautiously expanding to intensify operations. Melvin was fantastic: a reliable, dedicated, committed commander. We'd discuss who would be recruited into our units and he carried out the instructions. By then, my work was primarily communicating with him on public phone boxes. Aneez and I, and sometimes Aneez on his own, were involved in training our operatives until Melvin was proficient enough to take over. The people on the ground were not permitted to meet those of us in the command structure; we were to be fully protected by a buffer of competent unit commanders.

Up until that point, all of our operations were responses to the political situation, such as rent boycotts and labour strikes, and were defensive rather than offensive. We targeted civic centres and rent offices, as they housed rental records, as well as courts, railway lines, police stations and police barracks, but we were always careful that no one would be injured. We often pulled off simultaneous operations that had the security forces scurrying all over the peninsula. They did not know which way to turn, or where to begin to find us.

We wrote reports on the intensifying political conditions and the motivation behind each of our operations. The Johannesburg unit delivered these to James in Botswana and he would communicate with Chris Hani in Zambia. Shanil recruited Joe Nxusani, Mike Dearham and Richard Ishmail in Johannesburg, so that when he was deployed to Cape Town in December 1988, that unit remained operational. Our commanders appraised our work. We received their instructions clandestinely cached in vehicles or in fruit-juice boxes, and once in a chocolate box. With our forward-thinking strategies approved, we gave orders to the unit commanders to carry out the instructions with operatives on the ground. Command structures were vertical, not horizontal, as was communication, and our unit operatives only knew their immediate commander.

On 10 January 1989, we suffered a major security threat and setback. Two days after the ANC's anniversary, while Aneez and I were playing darts in the spare room of our Pear Lane cottage, we heard on the radio that I was being accused of bombing Khotso House, headquarters of the South African Council of Churches (SACC) in Johannesburg, which had taken place on 31 August 1988. The first announcement reached the airwaves at 4 p.m. At a press conference held in Johannesburg, Major-General Jaap Joubert named me as the prime suspect. We were shocked and horrified, and our ears were glued to every radio bulletin thereafter, where the breaking news was repeated again and again.

At 6 p.m., SABC TV news released my image: the white woman responsible for the terrorist attack on the SACC. They also released identikits of two alleged accomplices seen going into Khotso House carrying military-type explosives in a heavy, round case, apparently weighing more than thirty kilograms, which the SAP alleged went off prematurely in the basement. Twenty-one people sustained injuries and a manhunt was launched to get the 'terrorist' responsible for the bombing, as well as those responsible for the October 1988 arson attack at Khanya House, the headquarters of the Congress of South African Trade Unions (COSATU) in Johannesburg. It was clear as day to us that right-wing elements were to blame. They were preparing the public to see me flushed out of hiding and taken out horizontally, feet first, dead not alive.

My mom, who was on holiday with Jenny in Namibia at the time, later told me that she'd received a call from a policeman who had forewarned her that I would appear on national television that day. They were monitoring her movements to see if she would try to alert me, but we had observed the rules of conspiracy and she had no way of contacting me.

The bombing accusation turned our lives upside down in a flash. There we were, safely tucked away on the Rosenthals' property, preparing for the new arrival in February, when we had to stop everything, analyse what this meant and figure out our response. Why had the police framed me for bombing Khotso House, which housed many anti-apartheid organisations? We concluded that they were trying to discredit me personally, as well as the ANC, deceiving the public in an attempt to show that they were on top of the investigation. It was a desperate measure. Perhaps they also wanted to intimidate the tenants of Khotso House and Khanya House and suppress their anti-apartheid activities. By airing my image on TV and in newspapers, the security forces hoped that someone would come forward to provide information about where I'd been seen, and I would be captured or killed. At the very least, our operations would be disrupted.

The photograph of me that appeared in the newspapers and on SABC TV had been taken by the SAP at Pollsmoor in 1985. Two men had come to my cell, told me to take off my spectacles and pose in front of the cell's metal door. We wondered if Richard and Hillary, on holiday in Knysna, would recognise their quiet tenant. A prominent advocate from Johannesburg, Arthur Chaskalson, was staying in their house while they were away. I had seen Arthur in the garden. He'd represented many comrades in treason and terrorism trials over the years so I knew I could trust him, but I didn't speak to him. Aneez and I concluded that it was doubtful any of our neighbours would recognise me from the police's outdated image of their 'wanted suspect' – we had been there only a month, I didn't move around much, and when I did I was disguised. The police were desperate to close their net around us though, so we decided to play it safe by moving and monitoring the situation for the time being, then returning to Pear Lane later if it seemed safe to do so.

I phoned Dr Roli Bloomberg, a pathologist at Groote Schuur Hospital and a member of our medical unit, or *médico*, and asked him to fetch me immediately. Aneez and I hurriedly packed an overnight bag, thinking we wouldn't be away for very long. Roli took me to his house in Mowbray and Aneez drove to the Clifton flat to warn Shanil of the security scare. He'd recently joined us in Cape Town and was staying in the flat, but needed to evacuate as I'd lived there for some time and the other residents might recognise my photograph on TV. We always considered the worst-case scenario when it came to our safety and security, and erred on the side of caution. Roli offered his bedroom to Aneez, Shanil and me, and we re-strategised. Both the Clifton flat and Pear Lane cottage were put on ice while we monitored what was going on.

*

When families went away for the summer holidays, daily newspaper deliveries built up in their letter boxes. This was a telltale sign to thieves that nobody was home. We'd taken out newspaper subscriptions at the Pear Lane cottage, so we got Roli to remove them every other day and monitor the security situation. Roli reported that everything was normal each time, so Aneez went to the cottage a week later, believing it was safe. He drove there in Shanil's silver Toyota Corolla and parked in the deserted lane close to the cottage's entrance. When he went to have a look around, he heard a story that contradicted Roli's report: the gardener, whose small flatlet was attached to our cottage, was extremely upset because there'd been a burglary and his portable TV had been stolen from his room. Our cottage was broken into as well, and the police had been notified.

Aneez sped off in the Toyota. The police must have watched him entering the property and placed a tracer under the Toyota, hoping he'd lead them to me and possibly others too. Suspecting he was being followed, Aneez did a route check in Cecilia Forest car park, which confirmed the worst. He sped off again, past Kirstenbosch Gardens and all the way to Athlone, where he dumped Shanil's Toyota near the house of a South African Council on Sport (SACOS) member he knew, and sought assistance.

When Aneez finally reached us in Mowbray, he was in a flat panic. We deduced that the police must have picked up my fingerprints in the cottage (they'd taken them when I was detained in 1985) and then returned to do a thorough investigation, hoping to find weapons and military hardware hidden in the cottage and on the property to build a case against us. Pear Lane was compromised; we couldn't go back. As a safety measure, we couldn't return to the Clifton flat either. We had to start afresh and quickly find another place to live. During this time, on 18 January 1989, Prime Minister P.W. Botha suffered a mild stroke and F.W. de Klerk became acting president.

For a short while we stayed in a flat close to Roli's with brothers Ahmed and Yusuf, friends of Saaliegah Zardad. We then found a single-storey, three-bedroom furnished rental house in Northpine near Brackenfell. Shanil brokered the lease agreement with the landlord and we moved in on 1 February 1989. The house didn't have a surrounding wall but it had a garage and concealed yard, so it offered a degree of security. Aneez and I remained hypervigilant, monitoring the news around the clock, waiting for the birth of our baby.

Over the years, we had recruited a *médico* unit of doctors and medical professionals to treat us in the underground. We went by other names and made special arrangements to be seen at night. Besides Roli, there was Dr Shreef and Dr Michael Michalowsky, our dentists; and Dr Peter Roos, a gynaecologist in private practice at Vincent Pallotti Hospital who also worked at Somerset Hospital. Later, when our son needed his inoculations, we recruited Dr Dubois, a paediatrician at Red Cross Children's Hospital, and Sue Kramer when Shanil needed physiotherapy after being injured in a car accident on the way back from Botswana. Our *médico* was unlike other units – we communicated with each person individually and they did not know each other. We trusted their loyalty and commitment to assisting us.

I first visited Dr Roos after hours at his Vincent Pallotti consulting rooms while staying at Roli's house in Mowbray, and I had two or three further consultations when we moved to Northpine. We were assured from scans that the baby was growing well and that I was healthy and strong for the delivery. We'd wanted a homebirth for security reasons, but Dr Roos was against this in case something went wrong. My legend was that I had been seeing a midwife and was preparing for a homebirth, but at the last minute she and Dr Roos advised that I should have the baby at Somerset Hospital. I would be admitted under a false name and my file would be destroyed after the birth. My cover was solid; I was in good hands.

The contractions woke me with a jolt in the early hours of 21 February 1989. Shanil drove me to Green Point, the contractions a few minutes apart, and we entered Somerset Hospital via the back entrance. I was admitted immediately in a general ward under the name Sharon McKenzie, while Shanil posed as the baby's father to complete the admission forms. The nursing sister who examined me said I was ten centimetres dilated and ready to give birth. I was made comfortable in a hospital bed in a whites-only ward and Dr Roos arrived soon thereafter.

Shanil, whose underground name was Ben, was told the birth would take a while, so he waited with me until I said 'Fetch Joe now!' Joe was Aneez's underground name at the time. Shanil left, and within an hour the birth was over. 'Baby McKenzie' was born at 8 a.m. The birth was easy, so much so that the nurse commented over my head to Dr Roos, 'I don't know why she had to come in; she could have had a homebirth.'

Shanil and Aneez were held up in the peak-hour traffic on the N1 and arrived late. The Immorality Act had been repealed back in 1985, but mixed marriages were still uncommon in South Africa and hospital wards were still racially segregated. Fortunately for us, 'Baby McKenzie' was fair in complexion, so he didn't raise eyebrows. 'Joe' and 'Ben' saw me in the ward and then went to the nursery to see the baby lying peacefully in his crib. Aneez and

I named him Haroon, after Imam Abdullah Haron who was killed in custody by the police in 1969.

It was hilarious receiving a florist's bouquet with a blue plastic skewer in the bunch with the words 'It's a boy' and a note saying 'With love, Ben and Joe'. Shanil often bought fresh flowers when purchasing our daily provisions, a memory I still cherish. Not only was it a lovely gesture but an excellent cover. Who would suspect he was buying fresh flowers and provisions for MK comrades in the underground?

When Haroon was a few weeks old, we organised a clandestine meeting of our families to see our baby boy, whose underground name was 'Timmy', after Ahmed Timol. Shanil fetched Aneez's parents and my mom, who were blindfolded and seated in the back of our VW Kombi. Shanil drove the vehicle into the garage and they entered the house, clueless about where we lived. They were understandably worried, what with my having been framed a month before, so this was an opportunity to discuss our security situation and reassure our parents that we were able to cope under the difficult circumstances.

As the primary nurturer, I remember feeling a sense of loss knowing that my MK role would change. Simple things like not always being available to participate in discussions if I was breastfeeding or putting Haroon to sleep reinforced the feeling. Most cadres in my position would have gone into exile, but we chose to stick it out, going even deeper underground.

Shanil had a part-time teaching post. He left the house in the early morning, and returned in the evening with our daily provisions. I continued the risky work of communicating with Melvin at night, cradling our newborn baby in my arms. The security of the AKD needed strengthening, and a month after Haroon's birth we received communication from Chris Hani that we were to get reinforcements. We also received a message from Oliver Tambo that we should retreat to Lusaka because our lives were in danger. But we resisted, saying that we believed we were still able to make a contribution and that we would retreat if things became completely impossible for us.

Aneez mostly stayed indoors. He ventured out for specific meetings, did reconnaissance initially, and was centrally involved in training and ordnance. Just after Easter, two trained cadres, Anton Fransch and Mark Henry, arrived in Cape Town to defend, consolidate and advance the work of the AKD.

The detachment suffered a massive setback when Mark Henry climbed out the window and disappeared, deserting the AKD. Soon afterwards, he went to stay at his parents' home – an unspeakable risk for him and us. Mark knew too much after living with us in the command structure, so once again we had to pack up everything and flee. We found a smallholding near Kuils River where we stayed for a short while.

We decided to find Mark Henry and insist that he leave the country. If he refused, we'd be forced to follow orders and take more drastic measures. Risking exposure, we asked a few comrades, including Leon Scott and Ashley Forbes's partner Yasmina Pandy, to help us track him down so that we could convince him to go into exile if he valued his life. Our efforts were in vain.

While we were living on the smallholding, Anton Fransch was set up in a separate entrance on 57 Church Street in Athlone, and was deployed as commander of the Athlone unit, assisting the Macassar unit as well. The rest of us – Aneez, Shanil, Haroon and I – moved to another house in Northpine with a small swimming pool in the yard. Mike Dearham joined us there when he returned from training in Tanzania and Lusaka. After a few months, his partner, Kim, joined us too.

One day, Anton bumped into Mark in Athlone and made the fatal error of taking him to his place in Church Street. He spent several hours talking to Mark, who eventually agreed to meet us at an arranged place and time. Believing he would honour the agreement, Anton let him go. Mark didn't meet us and, as we'd feared, he was arrested and detained not long afterwards, on 17 November 1989. I had a meeting with Leon Scott that night, and on hearing this news I cut the meeting short and hurried back to base so we could figure out how to alert Anton. We feared that when the security police interrogated Mark, he would lead them to Anton's place.

Shanil was instructed to communicate with Anton's landlady to let Anton know he needed to move immediately. The landlady answered his call and said Anton wasn't in as his lights were off. Shanil kept calling, but the landlady told him to stop bothering her and to phone again in the morning as it was late and she didn't want to be disturbed.

Early the next morning Shanil called the landlady again and was told that Anton had been killed by the police. On the news we learnt that a seven-hour standoff had ensued between Anton and a large contingent of SADF soldiers on foot and in armoured vehicles. Anton had heroically defended his base to the end and was killed before he could be captured. Mark, all the while, was handcuffed inside one of the police vehicles, having been forced to point out where Anton lived.

By this time, we had a number of operational units on the ground. Coline Williams, Sidney Hendricks and Vanessa November operated in Bonteheuwel. After Anton's death, Coline was made commander of the Athlone unit, working with Robbie Waterwitch. Raphael Martin, Desmond McKenzie, Andre Bruce and Gloria Veale were based in Mitchells Plain, and Andrew Adams, Heinrich Magerman, Desmond Stevens and Paul Endley were in Macassar.

In the Southern Suburbs there was Dicki Meter and Patrick Presence. Later, the detachment also included Timothy Jacobs, who returned in 1990. In the Boland there was Charles Chordnum and Charlie Martin. Working with ordnance from Johannesburg was Shanil, Richard Ishmail, Joe Nxusani and Mike Dearham. Julie and Ismail Vallie from Cape Town also worked with that unit. Kim Dearham joined us to support the command base, while Anton Fisher arrived after Mandela's release in 1990 to support the AKD.

As a security measure, none of the operatives had contact with Aneez and me, nor did they know the detachment's name. We had *noms de guerre* that changed regularly. If a unit operative was arrested, he or she would only know of a few people, not other units or the command structure. The AKD was responsible for over thirty operations between 1987 and 1990. With the avalanche of security threats, our Johannesburg cadres were brought to Cape Town to provide additional capacity and protection to the high command: first Shanil, then Richard, Mike and later Kim, but they had no contact with unit operatives on the ground. Only Joe, who had accompanied Shanil on a trip to Botswana, remained in Johannesburg. At this point, we no longer needed to cross the border to collect weapons because another MK unit had taken over this dangerous work and was caching the weapons inside the country, smuggling them in under the seats of unsuspecting tourists on safari. We received communications, money and route maps whenever we delivered reports to James, and once back in South Africa we would retrieve the weapons using the maps. Melvin commanded our units in Bonteheuwel, Macassar, Paarl and Athlone, and for a short while in 1989 Anton Fransch took over command of the Bonteheuwel and Athlone units.

The Mitchells Plain unit was more complicated. In a short time, for reasons we could not figure out, operations did not go according to plan. For security reasons, once again erring on the side of caution, we couldn't risk any further exposure to the unit, so we cut ties completely: the unit of four young comrades was purged. I was Melvin's contact in the command at the time. We had scary moments at phone boxes, and he narrowly escaped arrest at his house in Wynberg. Melvin was forced to go underground and live with us in the command base. His partner, Ruth, and their baby daughter, Coline, joined us soon afterwards.

Three months later, on 11 February 1990, in our underground house in Northpine, we watched Nelson Mandela's release from Victor Verster Prison on TV. What a joyous moment! We were aware that Mandela would not be calling for the disbanding of MK. In his speech at the Cape Town City Hall, he reaffirmed this, pronouncing: 'The armed struggle is not abandoned.' To demonstrate that we were combat ready and poised to follow through on the orders of our freed commander-in-chief, we pulled off three simultaneous operations that evening, at Newlands Cricket Ground, the Parow Civic Centre and the Paarl Magistrate's Court.

We understood that the unbanning of the ANC and the release of Mandela wasn't going to change our lives overnight, and that we'd remain in the underground for some time yet, but the South African political landscape had changed irreversibly and we felt elated and proud to have contributed to that change. We had survived in the underground for a number of years and I don't know if words can adequately describe the toll it took on us – we never talked about it and we didn't consider the personal cost. Some of us are only beginning to reflect on this now.

Despite the hardship of isolation and living in constant fear, we got up early every day, did our chores and performed our duties to the best of our abilities, without complaining, always united in our efforts. Living under these conditions for so long was very difficult, but we believed we were in it for the long haul and we kept going while everyone else was beginning to enjoy the fruits of the liberation struggle. ANC exiles were returning and being given platforms to address the applauding, appreciative masses who had borne the brunt of our mass democratic struggle. We remained underground awaiting fresh orders.

Haroon turned one ten days after Mandela's release. To mark this milestone, Shanil, Mike, Kim and I took him for a picnic at Antoniesvlei in Wellington in our blue Mini panel van. Haroon's birthday fell on a weekday so we had the enormous swimming pool and braai area to ourselves, and although we kept to the shade of the bluegum trees, the day outside did us the world of good. Aneez stayed behind in Northpine holding the fort. I have a few photographs of that day; they're the only photographs I have of us in the underground besides those taken on our wedding day and a few photographs Sue Kramer took of Haroon in September 1989 when we camped in Arniston while I was on a reconnaissance mission. He looked confused sitting in a swing with a camera pointed at him; he'd never seen either before.

By mid-1990 I was physically and emotionally depleted by the demands of breastfeeding and living in a state of constant hypervigilance. Mom and Jenny and her three boys, Kyle, Murray and Nick, were planning a holiday for the June–July school holidays, and we figured out a way for Haroon and me to connect with them and take a short break. Everything was arranged clandestinely. Mom and Jenny were instructed not to speak over the phone about our joining them. On 23 June 1990, Mom's good friend Norma Beattie and her husband Paul dropped Haroon and me in Stellenbosch, where we were picked up by the family; three adults, four children and our bags squashed in a small car.

When we arrived at Melton Wold Guest Farm outside Victoria West, I became worried when the receptionist said that there'd been a change to our reservation. 'You are no longer in the rooms inside the building,' she told us. 'You're together in the outhouse with its own bathroom and toilet, better suited to your family.' She added that the lounge to the right of the passage was out of bounds.

After having a look at our quarters, I went directly to the lounge that was out of bounds. I opened the door and took in the room: a large contingent of white men stood around the fireplace, talking and drinking beer. They immediately went silent when they saw me in the doorway. Who were these men? Were they policemen? What was I to do? Running on foot or leaving by car would be suicidal in this remote and conservative part of the world. I'd have been pursued and assassinated on the farm road – a 'dangerous terrorist killed while running away' – playing directly into their hands. All I could do was stay close to Mom, Jenny and the other guests, never allow Haroon out of my sight and observe what the men were up to. The winter of 1990 was unusually cold; the water froze in the pipes, we froze in the outhouse, and I was numb in every other respect.

I was certain that the men I'd seen were security policemen and that they'd observed our arrival from the lounge window that faced the front of the farm and were having a drink to celebrate. But within a few minutes of my arriving, I had exposed them and foiled their sinister plans. This was a counter-intelligence tactic I had learnt in Cuba in 1987 to expose and disarm the enemy. Now I had to build relationships and befriend the workers and residents while monitoring the security policemen's movements.

I didn't sleep a wink. Mom and Jenny didn't understand why I wouldn't allow Haroon out of my sight, not even to feed the animals with his cousins, a drawcard of the family-friendly guest farm. I didn't tell them I suspected the place was teeming with security police. At mealtimes, I watched the men eating at the table at the far end of the dining room and observed a man sitting alone at a table near the door. My family probably thought that living in the underground had made me paranoid. I was on my guard every second of every minute, panic-stricken. I felt like I was in a cul-de-sac, with no way out.

Two days later, on 25 June, the day before we planned to leave this god-forsaken place, I used the same counter-intelligence strategy, and it may have saved our lives. Jenny coerced me into going for a short walk with the children, even though I knew the other residents at the farm were my protection. We walked a little way and I sensed we were being followed. Spotting a bloated sheep grazing in the lands, I slowed down and said to Jenny, while glancing over my shoulder, 'That animal looks sick.' We were definitely being followed. I turned around with Haroon in my arms, walked straight through the row of five large men behind us and hurried back to the farmhouse. Five minutes later, Major Johan Kleyn and other security policemen apprehended me in the passage. 'Don't scream or shout or do anything,' Kleyn said. 'You're under arrest. We're taking you to your room to pack up and you're coming with us.'

We were escorted to our room and I began packing as slowly as possible. While putting things in a bag, I told the policemen that we hadn't eaten and it was almost supper time. 'What are you going to do about that?' I asked. Kleyn said provision would be made for us. Jenny generously packed a small brown children's suitcase with her boys' dinky cars for Haroon, and I told her softly to go inside the farmhouse and tell as many guests as possible that her sister was being detained by the security police and that they must come outside. She dilly-dallied. 'Jenny,' I snapped, 'go *now*!' I will never forget her expression of complete surprise and affront as she obliged.

When I was finally escorted out of our family quarters with Haroon and our bags, a crew of unsuspecting guests that Jenny had gathered was standing at the back entrance of the guest farm. 'Do you see these men?' I shouted, 'They are security policemen. Do you see their cars? I'm being detained, probably under Section 29 of the Internal Security Act. I don't know where my baby and I are being taken, but you are witnesses to this.' The policemen tried in vain to stop me, leading me to the waiting cars in the parking lot. There was no space for our bags in any of their car boots as they were all filled with metal trunks, presumably full of firearms and ammunition. Our bags were taken from one car to the next and then squeezed into the car we were in. Then the convoy of cars drove off.

We were taken to the Victoria West Police Station. I was ordered to remain in the car with Haroon while under police guard and most of the other police-men went inside. It felt like ages before they eventually came out with orders to drive us back to Cape Town.

When we arrived at Milnerton Police Station, the commander seemed sur-prised to see me and Haroon; clearly he was not expecting us, and certainly not at 2 a.m. 'It's only for one night,' Kleyn told the commander. 'We are mak-

ing arrangements for them elsewhere. We'll fetch them early in the morning.'
I was forming a picture of what was going on: They'd received fresh orders
to bring me to Cape Town, but this had not been their plan. What *was* their
plan, though? Considering all the arms they had with them, they were most
likely prepared for a shoot-out or to take me out and dispose of my body on
the farm. However, their mission had failed and now they were humiliated.
I braced myself for the hell ride ahead.

The next morning we were taken to Culemborg, the railway police headquarters on the Foreshore, where I was interrogated. Late that afternoon,
Haroon and I were transferred to Wynberg Police Station and locked up in
the holding cells. The conditions were disgusting. The toilet was blocked and
every time I flushed it, excrement rose out of the bowl and flooded the floor.
It was mid-winter and freezing. The policewoman guarding me sat in the
passage on the other side of the yard and our hospital-style metal bed was
positioned in line with the open door so she could observe us. The shower
water in the uncovered yard was icy cold. I tried to maintain some sort of
routine with a toddler in this filthy concrete environment, washing nappies
and singing songs. Haroon had complete trust in me and in the few adults
he knew in the underground, but we were now at the mercy of the enemy.
I didn't know what had happened to Mom and Jenny after the security police
took us, but I hoped they'd gone straight to inform Essa Moosa. I was certain
he'd assist me somehow, and I was sure comrades aboveground and in the
underground would kick up a storm too.

I would learn later that during my detention, over 150 women, many
of whom were members of the Wynberg branch of the United Women's
Organisation (UWO), marched to the security police headquarters in Loop
Street, led by Mom, Ragmat Jaffer and Dorothy Boesak, demanding my release
and that of all Section 29 detainees.

Most days, we were taken to Culemborg and I was interrogated. Haroon was
always with me. To keep him busy during interrogation, the security police
brought him wax crayons and a colouring book. I didn't let him out of my sight.

On Wednesday 4 July 1990, two senior social workers from the Department
of Health and Welfare Services, Mrs Robertson and Mrs van den Heever, came
into the interrogation room at Culemborg. They spoke about the Children's
Act and said that the Wynberg Police Station cells were an unsuitable place
for a child, according to the Act.

'I know the Act, I'm a social worker,' I replied. 'I got my degree at UCT;
where did you get yours?'

'At Free State University in Bloemfontein,' Mrs Robertson said.

'I'm surprised,' I countered. 'You're not acting ethically. Shame on you!' I put Haroon on the table and I lifted up his top. 'Do you see any bruises? No bruises! No scratches!' I said. 'What does that say? It says he's well looked after, even in inhumane living conditions, as you correctly call them. There's no reason why he should be removed from me. He's breastfed and doesn't know anyone besides me.' Mom had only spent a few days with us in Melton Wold so she barely knew Haroon; neither did Jenny and her children. I certainly wasn't going to tell the social workers the only people Haroon knew were a handful of cadres, among them his dad, Aneez Salie.

But the social workers persisted: 'It's no good you talking. We've got an arrest warrant for Haroon and we are taking him away.' They slapped the warrant on the table, yanked Haroon out of my arms and took him, screaming at the top of his lungs, to their car outside. They drove off as I stood there, enraged and helpless, trapped behind the metal gates. I stormed back to the interrogation room and announced that I was going to stop eating until Haroon was returned to me. This snap decision went completely against my better judgment. The worst thing for a detainee to do is go on a hunger strike. Starvation makes you weak and detainees should do everything in their power to stay strong. That was my philosophy and it worked in my favour when I was in detention in 1985, but this was early July 1990 and it seemed as though it was my only option against the security police. Their response was to threaten that if I persisted with the hunger strike I'd be sent to the notorious Kroonstad Prison in the Free State.

When I was back at the Wynberg police cell that evening without Haroon, my breasts started to become painful and engorged and I realised I had made a terrible decision. If I didn't eat, my body's ability to produce milk would be affected. I decided I was going to eat and drink and I was going to express my milk and insist that they give it to Haroon, wherever he was. Breast milk would be my new weapon.

Over the next few days, when the interrogation was getting tough, I told the security policemen that my breasts were sore and I needed to express milk. I demanded a basin of hot water to make the task easier. The men exited the interrogation room and a security policewoman stayed behind with an empathetic cleaner who brought the basins of hot water. I expressed the milk into the basin, turning the water milky white. When it cooled down, I'd ask for more hot water. The cleaner would leave the room with what looked like basins of milk. The men outside the interrogation room must have thought they'd captured a Jersey cow.

When questioning resumed, they'd be disarmed, struggling to pick up where they had left off, so I'd express my breast milk strategically as a diversion tactic. I spoke about this later at a special women's Truth and Reconciliation (TRC) Human Rights Violations Committee hearing on 7 August 1996, illustrating how it was possible to use our gender to our advantage.

The days went by and because Haroon was no longer present, interrogations intensified. By then I knew he'd been taken to Tenterden in Wynberg, a place of safety for children, but the knowledge didn't make things easier. The security police then brought tape recordings of his crying voice calling for me. They told me I was a terrible mother, but that Haroon would be returned to me if I cooperated with them. I was traumatised, but I understood that this was their strategy to break me. I had to keep on withholding information, not break down, not let them see any sign of weakness. I relied on my training and my previous experience in solitary confinement. 'Their tactics must not work,' I told myself, while terrible conflict and guilt raged inside me.

Since Aneez and I had agreed we'd forfeit the Clifton flat if anything happened to either of us, I eventually took the security police there, convinced that Essa would know I'd been detained by then and that Aneez and the comrades with him would know too. The security police got me to open the door, pushing me in front of them as a human shield so that if we were shot at by whoever might be inside, I'd be the one to take the bullets. Our sparsely furnished flat was neat – and deserted.

A week later, the security police informed me that I would get Haroon back; no further details. On Thursday that week, they brought him to me at Culemborg. We were then taken back to the Wynberg police cells and told we'd be taken to another prison the next day. Haroon's beautiful, smiling eyes were sunken; he was dehydrated and had lost weight. He adjusted very quickly to the police cell, though, trotting around, happy to be reunited with me after eight days of separation, and he soon started suckling again.

We were fetched the next day. I was handcuffed and the two of us were ushered to the back seat of a police car and guarded by a black security policewoman. Two security policemen sat in front. They took a route that went via Sunset Beach, driving around Sunset Circle a number of times to check if we were being followed, then along Baden Powell Drive, past Monwabisi and Macassar, and over Sir Lowry's Pass. They were silent as they drove, and demoralised, I thought, as it was not their plan for Haroon and I to be reunited. That order had come from elsewhere.

They drove further and further away from Cape Town and eventually turned right at the Caledon off-ramp. A little further on, they parked at the

Caledon Medium-Term Prison. We were locked up in the hospital cells of the women's section. There were two toilets and a bathroom with a big bathtub as you entered the section via a small adjoining yard. Along the left-hand side of a passage to the right were three lock-up cells. We had the first cell, but I made sure another was kept open and used it to store our clothes. I put the mattress on the cold passage floor for us to sit on. We had the hospital section to ourselves – much bigger and cleaner than the Wynberg police cells – but for how long I did not know.

That Friday night, Haroon started vomiting and had acute diarrhoea. No one responded when I pressed the bell in the cell. By Saturday his condition had worsened, but the warders insisted we'd have to wait until Monday for the district surgeon to attend to him. By nightfall, Haroon had deteriorated. Rain was hammering down and the wind was howling. I rang the bell incessantly and shouted for help through the metal mesh and bars, but nobody came. By Sunday, my child was disappearing in front of my eyes. He was so ill that he flopped in his pushchair, too weak to hold up his head. Again I was told we'd have to wait until Monday. I tried to feed Haroon but nothing stayed down. I was hysterical and started fearing his gastroenteritis was engineered and he'd been deliberately infected.

At 10 a.m. on Monday, the district surgeon Dr du Plessis sauntered in and after examining Haroon said, 'There's nothing wrong with him. He has gastroenteritis that I can treat. There's something wrong with you.' It was obvious that in his mind I was a terrorist. The way he looked at me was just like how the security police did. I kept the medicines Dr du Plessis prescribed for Haroon with his name on the bottles as an exhibit in case I ever had to go to court. The fact that nobody came to my aid over the weekend was inexcusable; a child of Haroon's age could have died without prompt treatment. I slowly nursed him back to health and eventually he was his old self again, toddling about. The passage was perfect for the dinky cars Jenny had packed for him: they sped down the shiny, polished surface at tremendous speed. We'd play for hours. Once, Haroon attempted to unlock the grid-door lock to the yard with wax crayons and ended up jamming it instead.

Two female warders saw to us, bringing us our three daily meals on trays, letting us out when the security police came to interrogate me and supervising our exercise time in the yard. We were let out to exercise for an hour each day – half an hour in the morning and half an hour in the afternoon. To prevent Haroon from falling and scraping his knees, I put him on my shoulders and we walked around the yard together. I drew a large happy sun on the wall with the multicoloured crayons. The warders didn't stop me, but they didn't like the sketch of a female warder with a large bunch of keys that I drew on the ground in the yard. The winter rains washed it away, but the bright, smiling sun remained visible until we were released.

Perched on my shoulders, Haroon had a bird's-eye view of a mother kiewiet sitting on her eggs in a vent in the yard and a father bird observing her from the top of the surrounding high wall, bringing her things to eat. As time went by, the eggs hatched and the father bird worked harder, bringing more worms for the mother and chicks. We were there long enough to witness the lifecycle from eggs to chicks, but not long enough to see them flying to freedom. There was so much symbolism about these birds in our lives – the father outside, free but not free, while inside the prison were the mother and child who would someday fly off and reunite with him.

Pear Lane hadn't come up much in interrogation, but the question of where we stored arms had. We'd left an incriminating item at Pear Lane – a Makarov pistol in a white leather handbag with a small, laminated Islamic prayer in the inside pocket. I was confident that my fingerprints weren't on the pistol as we were meticulous about security and cleaned our weapons. During interrogation, I refused to admit that the pistol was mine.

One Thursday at midday there was an incident that scared me to death. An important rule of the underground was never to get into a pattern or routine because, by doing so, you could set your own trap. I broke this golden rule. After lunch at noon, I usually took a nap with Haroon on the single bed in our cell. I remember it was a Thursday because the major in charge of the prison was routinely off on Thursdays. As on other days, I lay down with Haroon after lunch and fell asleep.

I woke suddenly when I felt the presence of someone in the cell. A white man was standing there alone, without a female warder, which was against the law. He was elderly, with white hair and very pale skin. 'What the hell are you doing here?' I shouted. For a moment he look shocked, like a rabbit blinded by headlights, and he quickly put his hands behind his back and took a step back, away from the locker next to our bed. Then he left without a word, scurrying down the passage, out of the door to the yard, which he locked behind him, and across to the passage that led to reception.

I wondered what he might have had in his hands. On top of the locker was a jug of rooibos tea, brought in warm in the morning but equally delicious when cool later in the day. Also on the locker was fresh cow's milk. Initially, when we were booked in, I was given an enamel cup of powdered milk, but I demanded cow's milk because I was breastfeeding. After that, we were given a jug of creamy, fresh milk every day. I was told it was from a nearby prison farm. Fresh produce from the farm was delivered to Caledon Prison daily, so my request was not a tall order and the major in charge obliged. The white man in my cell had had his hands close to the jugs. Was he about to poison the liquids on the locker? That was another wake-up call to stay vigilant at all times. I didn't fall asleep in the daytime again.

The next day, when the major came to me on his routine morning rounds to check on the inmates, I asked who the man in my cell was. I described him and told the major that he'd exited very quickly when I woke up – with the keys. The major looked surprised and said he'd look into it, but he did not come back with an explanation.

In 2001, I got to examine the prison register and found that the man's visit to the prison and my cell was not recorded in the logbook. I concluded that he was a death squad operative and had taken the gap when the major was off, intending to poison Haroon and me. This wasn't my imagination running wild. I had been framed eighteen months prior to this incident and it clearly wasn't the security police's plan for me to be alive. I believe that it was a foiled attempt on my life; on our lives.

Towards the end of my stint in detention, the security police finally managed to hold one of the many identity parades they had threatened all along. I was told Gaye Derby-Lewis would be flown from the Free State to point out the person she had seen on the night of the explosion at the Sea Point Civic Centre. I challenged them, saying that my image had been in the newspapers. Besides, if I was lined up with other women in my old jeans I'd be easily identified. I also demanded to know what would happen to Haroon while they held the parade and suggested that he be handed over to Mom for the morning. They conceded to my demands and I continued to monitor the flaws of their ID parade with the view to challenge its fairness in court, if necessary.

On the day of the parade we were taken to Culemborg, where the security police gave me an awful black and red Saucy Cats dress to wear, the price tag still attached, and a pair of black pumps, loaned from OK Bazaars. Haroon was handed over to Mom and I was taken to Bishop Lavis Police Training College, where the parade would take place. I was led into an auditorium full of policewomen and, bizarrely, I was asked to select ten women to be part of the ID parade. I tried to imagine how I'd looked that night in June 1988, and picked five white women with light hair like mine. The remaining five I selected randomly. The eleven of us were led into the ID parade room and we were told to stand in a line against the wall. Leonard Knipe, who I recognised from media coverage as someone who worked in the SAP's Murder and Robbery division, was in the room, overseeing the line-up.

Gaye Derby-Lewis entered the room and walked up and down the row of women, staring into our eyes. She told Knipe that she was unable to recognise any of us, as the woman had turned her back to her that night, so Knipe asked us all to turn around. In that moment I knew it was over. She walked up and down again trying to identify the woman she'd seen from behind two years back. 'No,' she said eventually. 'I can't positively identify anyone.'

Haroon, wearing a pair of new lace-up leather shoes, was all smiles when we were reunited back at Culemborg. He'd been sad and weepy without me, Mom said. We were then driven back to Caledon Prison.

A few days later, the security police arrived with albums of outdated photographs of suspected ANC members. I was expected to identify them. I knew then that we'd be released soon.

We were released on 26 August 1990 after sixty-two days in captivity. The single charge against me was possession of a Makarov pistol and ammunition, for which I had to appear in the Wynberg Magistrate's Court on 24 October 1990.

On the day of my release, I was taken to the prison reception to sign out and was handed some items of clothing – presumably stolen from our Pear Lane cottage – which I had to sign for, as well as a small parcel of hand-knitted newborn baby clothes from Aneez's mom. As I signed the document, I considered two possible scenarios: either the security police had broken into our cottage and created the impression it was burgled, or they had apprehended thieves with stolen goods and the Makarov who led them to Pear Lane. I would only find out the truth ten years later, in 2000, when, at my request, Western Cape Crime Intelligence Chief Jeremy Veary led an investigation into a range of matters relating to my arrest. I learnt that the National Intelligence Service (NIS) had arranged 'static surveillance' at Pear Lane and had staged the break-in by removing a windowpane. When we met after my release, Richard Rosenthal told me that hordes of policemen with metal detectors had scoured every square inch of his property. It was an old farm, so pieces of metal were buried everywhere and they dug whenever the detectors screeched, only to find horseshoes and other useless pieces of scrap metal. They caused havoc on the property and even ripped open the roof of the cottage.

After the signing-out procedure, the security police asked me where I wanted to be dropped off. Rather than having to endure their company all the way to Cape Town, I told them to drop us off at Mom's place at Helderberg Village in Somerset West. At the entrance to the complex the security booms were lifted, no questions asked, and they drove directly to Mom's small cottage. They knew exactly where she lived and the security personnel at the gate were clearly accustomed to their comings and goings. Mom wasn't at home, so I asked to be taken to Essa's house in Surrey Estate.

Over tea in Essa's small, familiar kitchen, he told me about the Shirley Gunn Support Group, set up after my arrest with Haroon. The group had held protest marches to the security police headquarters in Loop Street in Cape Town, led by Imam Solomon and Mom, demanding our release and that of all political detainees. He also told me about his legal firm's urgent application to the Cape Town Supreme Court on 4 July 1990, with Advocate Siraj Desai as senior counsel, Mom as applicant and Ralph Diedricks, a paediatrician, as an expert witness. The application challenged that my detention was not in the spirit of the Groote Schuur Minute, a commitment negotiated between the government and the ANC to resolve the climate of violence and intimidation in the country, and demanded that Haroon be reunited with me. The respondents were the director general and regional head of the Department of Health Services, the commissioner and regional head of the SAP, and the superintendent at Tenderton Place of Safety. The application had been successful and the court had ultimately ruled that Haroon be placed with me in more suitable detention facilities. A press conference was held at Essa's offices in Athlone on 27 August, a few days after our release, with Cheryl Carolus as the only official ANC representative present.

I have little recollection of appearing in court on charges of unlawful possession of an unlicensed firearm and ammunition of Russian origin, although in my archive of newspaper clippings there are articles from *Die Burger* on 25 October 1990 when I was asked to plead, but the case was postponed to 16 November. There is another article, dated 17 November 1990, with the headline '*Shirley Gunn versuim om te verskyn*' (Shirley Gunn fails to appear). The case was eventually dropped.

After our release, Haroon and I stayed with my in-laws, Amina and Salie Salie, whom we called Mama and Boeya, in Second Avenue, Crawford, for over a year. Aneez's parents were wonderful. Boeya was so patient with Haroon. When praying on his knees with his head on the floor, he tolerated Haroon jumping on his back and riding him like a pony. He tried to coax Haroon into going to the shops with him, but despite all his gentle persuasion Haroon wouldn't allow me out of his sight. I grew to love my in-laws, who gave us the protection of a loving family. I had few responsibilities and I was under no pressure to rush off and find work, but I resumed some responsibility for AKD members still in the underground. I kept a low profile, sometimes staying in the underground house with the comrades for a few days at a time.

I had been detained in June 1990, four months after the ANC was unbanned, and my experience in detention was that the security forces didn't know what to do about MK, and our detachment specifically. I was extremely anxious after my release, vulnerable, and terrified that I might lead the security police to comrades in the underground. One of my responsibilities after my release was connecting with Mathews Phosa who, on Chris Hani's instruction, made a special trip to Cape Town to meet me to discuss indemnity for our members. 'Your detachment's indemnity is a simple matter,' Mathews told me. 'Unlike others I'm dealing with.'

A year later, in 1991, the Salie family needed space in the house for Ibrahim and Miriam, Aneez's eldest brother and his fiancée, who were getting married. I found a rental house in Crawford and Haroon and I moved there. Shanil and Richard, who were still in the underground, stayed over for a few days and helped clean the house and garden. Aneez joined us when he surfaced in January 1992.

To mark Aneez's homecoming, we went on a one-month road trip across the country in our old gold Alfa Romeo. We were in Port Elizabeth at the time of the referendum on 17 March 1992, when white South Africans voted on President F.W. de Klerk's reform initiatives, announced two years earlier, in which he proposed an end to apartheid. He received a 68.73 per cent yes-vote outcome, opening the way to general elections for all South Africans. We stayed with Vandra and Chris in Dordrecht, spent ten days in Coffee Bay where Haroon turned three, drove to Tongaat and stayed with Shanil and his parents, spent a few nights with my cousin Penny in Pietermaritzburg, and finally drove back to Cape Town to start a new life together.

It was an adjustment living together normally as a married couple. Our strategy was that Aneez would demand his job back at Independent Newspapers and I would look for work. In mid-1992, the New York chapter of the Social Service Workers' Association invited me to the United States to speak at their conference. Haroon and I stayed with Marilyn Moch, a social worker and one of the organisers of the conference, in Manhattan and on Long Island. Besides speaking at the conference at Columbia University, where I made lifelong friends, I had other speaking engagements in New York and Washington. When I was detained, the association had launched a petition for my release that was sent to F.W. de Klerk. Their role and that of the Bertha Reynolds Society was to defend the rights of radical social workers around the world who were persecuted by oppressive regimes. They had celebrated our release in August 1990 as their victory too. It was a relief not having to look over my shoulder, and being abroad gave me a break from the struggle to reintegrate and adjust to civilian life together with Aneez.

On my return to South Africa, I found a suitable preschool for Haroon – Vuyani Educare Centre in Lansdowne – which was close by and where Zubeida's daughter Ruschka went. At first, Haroon was very anxious without me close by, and so was I. In psychological terms it's called separation anxiety; others may go as far as labelling it post-traumatic stress disorder (PTSD).

In September 1991, I attended the ANC's National Conference in Durban as a regional MK delegate. I also attended the MK Conference held at the University of Venda in Thohoyandou, where I met many MK cadres for the first time. By force of habit, everyone was cagey in conversation, but there was nevertheless a wonderful feeling of solidarity and connection. After a number of speeches by the leadership, delegates moved into different commissions and I participated in the commission on the social welfare needs of MK cadres. Winnie Mandela, a social worker like me, had developed the position paper and Chris Hani asked me to report back on the commission's deliberations to the plenary the following day. I stayed up most of the night writing the report and wish I had a copy because it was comprehensive and well received.

I was fortunate with finding work. In 1992, I was offered a job as programme assistant to Vivienne Taylor at the Southern African Education Development Programme (SADEP). Based at the University of the Western Cape, SADEP trained development workers across southern Africa. The work aided my integration into society, as my responsibilities included coordinating the practical component of the course and put me in touch with the development needs and challenges facing communities across the country. I ended up writing a book on community needs assessment, which was published by the university.

Aneez and I wanted a second child and I conceived in March 1993. A month later, on 10 April, our revolution suffered a severe setback with the assassination of our commander, Chris Hani. Vivienne gave me time off work, Mom took care of Haroon, and I flew to Johannesburg and stayed with Richard Ishmail in his Hillbrow flat. We walked in a procession to Chris's funeral in Soweto on an extremely hot day and I remember feeling emotionally numb, coupled with the strain of that long walk in the first trimester of my pregnancy. In that year, Andy Dawes, a psychologist at UCT, counselled Aneez and me. I was angry and depressed and I was prescribed antidepressants.

Haanee, named after Chris Hani, was born on 2 November 1993.

On 27 April 1994, Aneez, Haroon and I, with Haanee in a pushchair, waited in the long queue at St Mary's Parish in Athlone to cast our votes in our country's first democratic election. The official results, which were announced by the Independent Electoral Commission (IEC) after seven days of count-ing, and confusion over allegations of fraud, gave the ANC 62.65 per cent of the national vote. In the 400-member National Assembly, the ANC secured 252 seats and won control of six of the nine provincial parliaments. Mandela, a true democrat, told journalists that he was relieved the ANC did not secure a two-thirds majority because of tensions and fears that the ANC would write its own constitution and that the Government of National Unity would be an empty shell for opposition parties.

Later that year, all of us who served in non-statutory armies had to decide whether we wanted to demobilise or integrate into the new South African National Defence Force (SANDF). An elite unit from the United Kingdom oversaw the demobilisation process. I had substantial conversations with Richard Cook, a UK officer who told me that with my qualifications and experience I'd probably walk in as a brigadier. I remembered the conversation I'd had with Chris Hani in Lusaka about women like me being needed in the post-apartheid defence force and I decided I'd find out where I could fit in. Bongani Jonas from the ANC regional office set everything up: I'd go by bus up to Wallmansthal outside Pretoria with five-month-old Haanee to establish my rank and potential role in the SANDF. The morning I was about to leave for Pretoria, Haroon was extremely upset I was leaving him behind, so I packed some clothes for him too and Melvin took the three of us to Youngsfield Military Base in Wynberg to catch the bus.

As I was sitting in the bus with my two children, a white soldier approached me and asked what I was doing there. 'I've been told to tell you to get off the bus,' he said.

'Speak to Bongani Jonas,' I replied. 'He's in the kombi with the tinted win-dows over there. He's the ANC person responsible for my arrangements.'

The soldier left, but returned a few minutes later. 'Look, I have been told that you *must* get off the bus,' he said.

I told him firmly that I was not getting off the bus, thank you very much, and that he could repeat that to his superiors. Once again he left. He then returned a third time.

'If you don't get off the bus we're going to arrest you,' he said.

On hearing the word 'arrest' spoken by a white policeman, Haroon got very upset and began screaming 'No, no!' The only way I could pacify him was to get off the bus as per the order. Bongani Jonas was nowhere to be found to sort out this misunderstanding, so I went home and phoned the ANC regional office and the headquarters in Johannesburg to get assistance. No one explained or apologised. Something snapped inside me and I came to the realisation that I was on my own. A feeling of absolute abandonment hit me. I demobilised, took the R22 000 package, and moved on.

The 1990s were the most difficult years of my life. In November 1994, former police operatives Dawid Brit and Willem Nortje publicly confessed in affidavits that Adriaan Vlok, former minister of law and order, had personally congratulated them at a braai at Vlakplaas after the bombing of Khotso House and Khanya House in 1988. The two men went into a witness protection programme arranged by the Goldstone Commission. A month later, with Essa Moosa's counsel, I charged Vlok with *crimen injuria*, defamation and defeating the ends of justice, suing him for R1 million. Dr Rina Venter, former minister of health services and welfare, and Kobie Coetsee, former minister of justice, were included in the civil action. The case dragged on and three years later, after the establishment of the TRC, I reached an out-of-court settlement of R70 000. I was satisfied with this settlement as I knew Vlok and others would have to apply to the TRC's Amnesty Committee for their role in the attacks.

When the TRC began its work in 1996, I was working part-time at UWC. In June that year, the apartheid generals seeking indemnity approached the TRC claiming collective responsibility for a number of apartheid-era crimes, including the Khotso House and Khanya House bombings. Two days before Women's Day in August 1996, I presented my testimony to a special women's hearing of the TRC. Prior to testifying, I was called to an ANC women's caucus at the regional offices. In the room with me were Mildred Lesia and Zou Kota, both members of Parliament, and other prominent women from the ANC. They were talking about women's roles in the struggle: 'If you look at women's testimonies to the TRC, they're partners, cousins, witnesses, parents or innocent bystanders. None have been active agents of change and this needs correcting.' I went away from the meeting, contemplated deeply, and arrived at the conclusion that I'd testify and contribute to addressing this imbalance. I wept like I'd never wept before as I typed up my statement, and after giving it to Aneez and attorney Taswell Papier to read and approve, I handed it to Advocate Denzil Potgieter, a TRC commissioner.

I was called to testify in the Great Hall at UWC on 7 August 1996. Besides Mom sitting in the front with Ragmat and Zubeida Jaffer and a few comrades,

I testified to a hall of strangers. The experience was impersonal and the camera lights were blinding, but I'd agreed to participate.

Testifying to the TRC made me extremely vulnerable and had consequences I did not anticipate. I was inundated with interview requests, which I accepted as I felt I had a duty to do so in order to raise awareness about human rights abuses in the country. Everyone was interested in my story and I gave interview after interview to local and international media and to academics from many different fields. The result was having to relive the trauma over and over for other people, none of whom were equipped to deal with or respond to it. The toll was extreme.

Aneez and I divorced in 1998. According to our divorce agreement, Haroon and Haanee would spend every second weekend with their dad. Both Haroon and Haanee attended Westerford High School and attained decent matric passes. They both went on graduate with degrees at UCT: Haroon in fine art, majoring in sculpture, and Haanee in social science, majoring in history and international relations. Haroon is an internationally acclaimed artist; his collaborative practice translates community histories into artistic interventions and installations based on dialogue and exchange. He carries the world on his shoulders and his heart on his sleeve. Haanee, who has always demonstrated an independent spirit and responsible work ethic, went on to teach English as a second language. She worked in Vietnam for fourteen months and now teaches English online to students in different parts of the world.

The year Aneez and I divorced, I got a call from Eric Harper, a London-trained psychoanalyst working at the Trauma Centre in Woodstock. He had been tasked with following up with those who testified at the TRC, as many were not taking advantage of the Trauma Centre's services. I took Eric's advice and saw him at the Trauma Centre every week for more than a year, and he offered eight sessions to Haroon as well. It was helpful, but towards the end my sessions focused more on the group of community people who needed counselling, as the Trauma Centre's one-to-one therapeutic model was neither effective nor culturally appropriate for those affected by apartheid violence and torture. They were thinking of starting group counselling, as psychosocial group-work techniques are effective when people have common histories and members can support each other rather than being closed in a client–therapist relationship where power resides with the therapist. The group interested me, and I advised Eric on how to get it going. One day, I announced to him that I wasn't going to attend sessions with him any more: 'I want to belong to the group,' I said.

I joined the Ex-Political Prisoners and Torture Survivors group and quickly became centrally involved. The executive committee on which I served met weekly, and we held monthly meetings at St John's Church Hall next to the Trauma Centre in Chapel Street. Membership soon quadrupled, so we moved our meetings to the Ashley Kriel Hall at Community House in Salt River, and set up offices there too. Many members had not made statements to the TRC, so our advocacy work involved appealing to the TRC to remain open to those victims who were excluded, rather than close down as the Act prescribed.

Throughout 1998, I also worked for a UWC-based project called Fair Share. I enjoyed the work, which had enormous scope and impact, but I found the academic environment to be uncreative and I resigned at the end of 1999. In August that year, Adriaan Vlok and eighteen others, including Eugene de Kock, received amnesty for bombing Khotso House and Khanya House. Their amnesty hearing was held in Pretoria and I attended the first two days, my arms filled with files of their statements to the Amnesty Committee. The hearing on the first day was postponed, so I flew home and back the next day at the expense of the TRC. I sat next to the Khotso House caretaker, who wore a neck brace as a result of injuries he sustained in the explosion. Many others who had been injured were present too. I didn't have legal representation, so my presence was symbolic. At one point, Vlok addressed the commissioners: 'I'm sorry for what Shirley and her baby went through,' he said.

At the end of the day, the media asked how I felt hearing Vlok say he was sorry. 'He didn't say sorry to *me*,' I replied. 'His apology means nothing to me.' An apology wouldn't give him amnesty, I explained. The requirements for amnesty were that he and his cohorts made full disclosures and that they proved that their crimes were politically motivated.

After this, and drawing on my own experience of the TRC and the Ex-Political Prisoners and Torture Survivors group and how people's life stories helped in shaping consciousness and our understanding of human rights abuses, I saw the need for a media organisation whose work would focus on people's narrative histories, going further and deeper to challenge and build our fragile democracy. As a social worker, I had interviewing experience and felt equipped to work with traumatic memories. I envisioned how media practitioners could work ethically, and how participants could retain active agency over their stories. I took the risk and in 2000 I set up the Human Rights Media Centre (HRMC), an NGO that works with people's individual narratives and history for human-rights awareness and education. To date, we have published 132 life stories, made a number of documentary films, and done amazing work on many human-rights-related fronts, much of which relates to matters of transitional justice.

In 2000, the Ex-Political Prisoners and Torture Survivors amalgamated with the Khulumani Support Group. The headquarters were in Gauteng, but there were members in all the provinces. We launched the reparations campaign, as survivors who had testified at the TRC were in limbo, not knowing when they'd receive the monetary reparations promised. Just before Christmas in 2003, after endless protest action, the Department of Justice paid out R30 000 to each TRC-identified victim, far less than the TRC had recommended, but a small victory nonetheless. We continue to fight for truth and accountability, including prosecutions relating to apartheid-era crimes, as well as community reparations.

During this time, I went back to Caledon Prison and spoke to one of the two female warders who had guarded Haroon and me. She said that the security police had placed listening devices in the hospital section and inter-rogation room at the prison before we arrived. She also told me that she had thought it very cruel that Haroon and I were kept there for nothing, and getting to know me had been a turning point in her life. Although previously apolitical, she was later elected as chairperson of the ANC Women's League in her community in Caledon.

I didn't get to see the major in charge of the prison, whom I'd grown to trust. He was a bird-lover and showed interest in Haroon and my fascination with the kiewiets breeding in the yard.

Mom and I also tried to make sense of what could have led to my arrest on the farm at Melton Wold. We suspected her neighbour at Helderberg Village may have cooperated with the security police, as she was in a perfect position to monitor Mom's movements. On the morning Mom, Jenny and the boys left to fetch us in Stellenbosch, she'd phoned Mom to ask what time she was leaving.

A few years later, in 2003, I was in Victoria West for the Apollo Film Festival and decided to do some research at Melton Wold. I discovered that the guest farm owner was an active SADF civilian force member, so I can only assume he allowed the security police to be stationed on his farm and cooperated with them. I spoke to some of the workers, who still didn't feel free to talk about the incident. Even so, I managed to find out that the chef had been upset because the police dug up his vegetable garden, located behind the outhouse near the kitchen. Another worker said that every day men drove off in a bakkie past their houses far into the lands, where they also dug. Given such infor-mation, my imagination ran wild. Had the security police been planting arms in the garden to frame me again and claim I was armed and dangerous so that they would have licence to shoot and kill me? Or were they planning my assassination and preparing my grave?

It was only in 2006 that I received more substantial information about my arrest. Out of the blue, Donald Alanby, a security policeman, phoned to say he was writing his autobiography and had something he wanted to tell me before it was published. I agreed to meet him on condition that our meeting was recorded. He accepted my terms and we met at a coffee shop in Gardens. He began by apologising to me, and admitting that he was instrumental in my arrest. He confessed that when he was based in Walvis Bay in 1990, he'd illegally tapped Jenny's Swakopmund landline, which was against sovereignty protocol. Mom and Jenny's conversations, however cryptic, had provided the security police with the details of our holiday. He gave me the transcript of their conversations and the section in his book dealing with the events that led to the arrest of 'South Africa's most wanted woman'. From the transcripts I could see that Jenny and Mom were careful about what they said on the phone and Mom diligently phoned her from public phone boxes, but it was in vain – the tapped line gave the police enough details to be able to arrive at the guest farm before us.

Thanks to Jeremy Veary's investigation, I also discovered that the security police had rolled three cars on the way to Victoria West, where I was arrested. Three death squads had apparently been chasing each other for the reward offered for my assassination. If the security police had succeeded in their mission to take us out, Adriaan Vlok and his henchmen's role in the bombing of Khotso House and Khanya House may never have been challenged and the truth may never have surfaced.

Twenty-seven years after I was framed for the 1988 bombing of Khotso house, I received a request from the Vlakplaas commander and apartheid assassin Eugene de Kock to meet him at Pretoria's B-Max prison. In 1996, De Kock had been sentenced to 212 years behind bars. At some point during the hour I sat across from him, he told me that in 1989, when he heard that I was to be framed for the bombing, he'd told his superiors that it was unfair, but they had gone ahead anyway. I stared at him. I didn't have to listen to this; I didn't want to listen to this. I hadn't got the truth about the security police's plans for me from Adriaan Vlok during the TRC amnesty hearings, so why should I listen to De Kock? I had told Vlok to his face that he was a liar, and was considering telling De Kock the same, but his time was up. As he was walking towards the entrance to the cells, he turned around and said: 'Your baby saved you.' I felt the blood drain from my face and was on the verge of fainting. Hearing this gave new meaning to the concept of a human shield. I realised that this was the closest I'd come to hearing the truth that they had planned to kill me.

2

Aneez Salie

The Last Order

BY 1985, I was on the run from the security police. The *boere* and my bosses at Independent Newspapers were colluding, trying to lure me into the office so that I could be arrested. I took three boxes of my most precious belongings and LP records to Moegsien Williams's house in Fairways in Cape Town for safekeeping. He was a good friend and comrade, and we had been through quite a few scrapes before. Shortly afterwards, he was detained under Section 29 of the Internal Security Act because of our association, but he did not cooperate with his interrogators or reveal where I was. While he was detained, his wife, Gadija, became nervous about my boxes and got word to my brothers, Mogamat and Seiraaj. They retrieved the boxes from her home and burnt everything – all of my photographic negatives, copies of my news-paper articles, and my books. As a consequence, there are no records of my life before 1985, and not much of a record from 1985 to 1992, when I was in the underground.

In 1987, I was deployed to be part of the Western Cape machinery of MK, with Ashley Kriel, Ashley Forbes and Peter Jacobs, all of whom had also received military training in Angola. Soon after they returned to the country in 1987, the apartheid security forces captured Ashley Forbes and Peter, and on 9 July 1987 they killed Ashley Kriel. I was subsequently instructed to work with Tony Yengeni, but he was also captured that same year. I was then given command of the MK in the Western Cape and started implementing the ANC-led alliance's struggle strategy. I did so mindful that no matter how well trained we were, it was only the people in the mass democratic struggle, supported by the military wing, the political underground and international support, that could liberate the country.

My name is Moegamat Aneez Salie. The previous generation gave each boy the name Moegamat (spelt in a number of different ways) as a prefix to honour the

Prophet, so I am actually Aneez Salie. Aneez means 'friend for life' in Arabic. Historically, Aneez was a scribe who accompanied the Prophet Muhammad. The very first word that Allah said, through his angels, to Prophet Muhammad was *iqra*, which means 'read'. The Prophet's reply was: 'But my Lord, I cannot read.' So Angel Gabriel said: 'Read in the name of thy Lord', and Muhammad began to read. But one cannot read unless somebody writes. This story would eventually become a powerful influence in my life and career as a journalist, although I started off as a photographer and only made the connection between my name and the scripture much later.

I was born on 5 August 1956 in Mark Road, Claremont, four days before the historic women's anti-pass march to the Union Buildings, led by Lilian Ngoyi, Helen Joseph, Rahima Moosa and Sophia Williams de Bruyn. I am the sixth of seven children; I have four brothers and two sisters: Mogamat, Ibrahim, Seiraaj, Adenaan, Tourhiera and Ayesha.

My grandfather owned houses in Wynberg and Newlands, and four houses in Mark Road, Claremont, occupied by his four offspring. Our home was a typical suburban, Victorian-style semi-detached house. Our maternal uncle Achmat and his family lived next door, and our maternal aunts, Auntie Gabiba (known as Auntie B) and Auntie Hajeera, both businesswomen, lived across the road in adjoining semi-detached houses. Auntie B was quite progressive and loved music. She had a collection of LPs, including Nat King Cole and Ray Charles.

My maternal grandfather, who came from India as a young man, started off as a humble vendor, selling fruit and vegetables from a large barrow he pushed from Claremont to Simon's Town. Through sheer hard work and sacrifice, he worked himself up and later owned two shops on Main Road in the Claremont central business district, one on the corner of Station Road and the other on the corner of Ralph Street.

I had a happy childhood, but my earliest memory is traumatic. I was four years old and it was Eid al-Adha, the Festival of Sacrifice, when Muslims slaughter a sheep or other animal. My mother had started teaching me to read before I went to school and my association with sheep came from the nursery rhyme 'Mary had a little lamb'. On Eid al-Adha, I witnessed the slaughter of a sheep, which to me looked like Mary's little lamb, and I cried so much that my father was told to do something about *that* boy.

The banks of the Liesbeek River were my playground, and my siblings and I often walked to Kirstenbosch Botanical Gardens from our home. Auntie B would take us. It was quite a stretch for me as a little boy and on one extremely hot summer's day, when I was about four or five, I arrived at Kirstenbosch very sweaty. Not far from the entrance was a cool, flowing stream, and like any child would do, I stripped naked and jumped in. Auntie B was very upset. '*Nee, wat sal die wit mense sê?*' she cried (No, what will the white people say?), and ordered me to get out of the water and put my clothes back on.

White people did live in Claremont, but not next door or on the same street as us. I used to see white children riding their bicycles and I prayed to Allah to give me a bicycle too. When the children went to buy sweets at Mr Dawood's corner shop on Mark Road and left their bicycles outside, my friends and I would take them for a quick ride and the children would have to wait outside the shop until we returned.

I was aware of interracial marriages; some white people married coloured people and chose to be coloured, and there were coloured people who pretended to be white so that they could have a better life. I did not have white friends, unless my best friend, Clive Bath, counts. His family was coloured, but they were fair-skinned and aspired to be white. Clive and I once caught a trout in the Liesbeek, and we removed empty Oom Tas wine bottles from the river. We dragged the bottles we collected in a little handmade wagon on wheels, all the way to a recycling depot near Maynard Mall in Wynberg, to get the deposit on the empties. Clive and his family eventually emigrated to Australia in 1970.

I went to Stephen Reagan Primary, on the corner of Protea Road and Main Road where the Deaf Federation of South Africa is today. It was here, in Sub A, that I had my first political lesson. The apartheid government ordered that on 31 May 1964, Republic Day, all coloured and black schools must sing their anthem, 'Die Stem', at assembly, and raise the apartheid flag, as was done at white schools. I picked up a lot of uneasy chatter among the older pupils on the playground and I asked my sister Tourhiera, who was in Standard 5, what the fuss was all about. 'Don't you worry,' she said. 'All you need to remember is that at assembly you must not stand and you must not sing.' When the music for the anthem played, the teachers rose and the flag was raised, but none of the children stood up and nobody sang. This was my first act of defiance against apartheid.

My next definitive political lesson was in September 1969, when Imam Abdullah Haron was brutally killed in detention. I was thirteen. Imam Haron was closely connected to my family. He was a progressive leader in our Claremont mosque and the editor of the *Muslim News*, and I often attended his talks. He would arrive at the mosque on Fridays, neatly dressed with a shining *chiskop* (clean-shaven head), and a bundle of newspapers under his arm. I remember saying to myself: 'I want to be like him one day.'

Imam Haron had many intelligent ideas and came up with new and innovative ways of doing things. He was classified coloured, but he often visited black townships, and by listening to conversations between adults at the mosque I learnt that he was involved in the armed struggle through the Pan Africanist Congress (PAC). Apparently, he arranged for people to go to Mecca and they would stop over in Egypt to receive military training before returning home, or so it was said.

I attended his funeral at City Park in Athlone in September 1969. It drew 40 000 people, and I walked right in the front of the procession all the way to the Mowbray Cemetery, over ten kilometres away. At his gravesite I told Imam Haron that I would avenge his death one day. Saying this carried an enormous responsibility, which would influence me throughout my life. This was my second political lesson.

My father had to leave school in Standard 2 to support his family. His branch of the family came from Bo-Kaap and can be traced back seven generations to Saartjie van die Kaap, who was married to Achmat, both of whom came to the Cape as slaves from Indonesia. Under Dutch colonial rule, it was illegal for slaves to practise their religion, so they worshipped in secret. Saartjie was the leader of this underground practice, which made no distinction between black or white people. When they were finally allowed to practise their religion openly in 1798, during the first British occupation, the house in Dorp Street where they had previously worshipped in secret became the Auwal Mosque, the first mosque in South Africa.

My father worked as a builder all his working life and made his way up to senior general foreman at the Cape Town City Council. He also served as secretary at the Longmarket Street Mosque for twenty-three years, and was president of the Building Workers Union and chairman of the Cemetery Board in Mowbray, as well as serving on school boards.

My mom loved reading and learning but she was taken out of school in Standard 4 to assist with the family business. Like my father, she was socially conscious. We grew up in a tight-knit, working-class, community-orientated environment. This was best illustrated when my father was unemployed for a few years because the cement he worked with on construction sites had damaged his hands. Our neighbours in Mark Road came to our house with provisions: one with potatoes, another with meat and someone else with OMO soap. Because of this caring *ubuntu* culture, we got by during this cash-strapped period. This was our defining philosophy: you are a community first. Everybody has a responsibility towards you and you have responsibility towards everybody. When we were children, aunties from the neighbourhood would scold us when we did not conform because every child was everyone's responsibility. A *kanala* (favour) culture operated. For example, community members with carpentry skills were expected to fix roofs. People helped each other.

Our community was socially and culturally integrated: Muslims, Christians and Hindus living side by side. Our parents were quite open-minded in how we were raised and I remember having a Christmas tree and Christmas stockings at home. On New Year's Eve, Patrick from next door fetched soot from our coal stove to use as face paint for the *Klopse* (minstrels).

I went to madressa at Stegman Road Mosque. Sometimes I bunked and went to read in the Claremont Library. I read a lot: every single Enid Blyton book and all of Sherlock Holmes, among many others.

Being forced out of our Claremont home by the Group Areas Act in 1966 was a shock. It was the same year Imam Haron was killed and the memories I have are of defiance and anger. People had refused to move when the forced removals had begun a couple of years earlier, but the officials threatened us with expropriation: houses would be sold on auction for half of what was offered on the open market. Our community lacked bargaining power, so we were, in any case, forced to sell to white people, who paid peanuts.

We had to move to Crawford, where the community spirit we'd enjoyed in Claremont was absent. The railway line divided Crawford from Rondebosch East, which was white, and Athlone. The area we moved to was in a kind of no man's land between two white communities. We spent most of our time in Athlone, the heart of the Cape Flats.

I was also forced to change schools and I spent the last years of primary school at Garlandale, which was within walking distance of our new home. After primary school, I went to Alexander Sinton High. The teachers kept the struggle alive and gave us a lot more than the gutter-education curriculum.

One of my teachers, Randy Hartzenberg, was our neighbour. I was the class clown, hyperactive and disrespectful of authority. One day, Randy pulled me aside after class. 'You know,' he said, taking my hand, 'you're not going to go far in life with that attitude.' He was a very progressive teacher, who encouraged free expression. Our relationship developed over time. I would pop over to his house to chat, and he introduced me to Bob Dylan. To my ears, Dylan's music was revolutionary and mind-blowing.

Randy was an artist and dramatist and I often went with him when he performed at The Space Theatre in Bloem Street in Cape Town, where progressive anti-apartheid plays were performed. I remember a 1977 play about

Dimitri Tsafendas, who killed Prime Minister Hendrik Verwoerd. The play gave Tsafendas all the respect, dignity and praise he deserved.

Education was a site of resistance against the bleak future that the apartheid government had designed for us. In Standard 7 we had a new young Afrikaans teacher, Mevrou van der Merwe, who taught us the Afrikaans proverb '*Eers baas, dan Klaas*' (First the superior, then the lesser) – the former referring to a white boss and the latter referring to a black worker. I rejected this in front of the whole class, and landed up in the the principal's office. 'It's wrong,' I told him. 'That proverb is racist.' He told me not to worry, and seemed to dismiss the matter. It later came to light that Mevrou van der Merwe was advised to remove that proverb from our curriculum.

My militancy started with our 1975 protest, the year I matriculated. We closed down the school because the apartheid government wanted to use it as a polling station for the Coloured Representative Council's (CRC) elections. Our teachers organised us, ignited the spark, and we demonstrated. The police unleashed their batons and threw teargas at us, but we succeeded in closing down the school. Our actions stopped Coloured Affairs from ever using our school for elections. It was our first victory.

After the 1975 protest, I joined the South African Black Students Organisation, led by Ashiq Mannie and Stephen Smith, and I was nurtured by activists who took me under their wing. In 1976, when the student uprisings started in Soweto and spread throughout the country, Alexander Sinton High became the centre of the student uprisings in Cape Town – a result of our activism the previous year.

Once I'd completed matric, I volunteered at my eldest brother Mogamat's newspaper business. Sometimes he'd wake me at 2 a.m. because the *Cape Times* had missed the delivery truck again and the newspaper had to be taken to Swellendam via Riviersonderend. I helped out because it was for Mogamat, and therefore for the family.

I also had a job as a work-study officer at Florida Fashions, a women's clothing factory in Woodstock. I was taught the inner workings of capitalism, and its heart – exploitation. I started as a trainee, measuring how long it took to complete each task or function on the production lines. The workers earned very little, but they could earn production and attendance bonuses at the end of each week.

The bosses wanted us work-study officers to set high targets to push production and increase profits, but I lowered them so that the workers could earn decent production bonuses. The bosses could see what I was doing and resented me for it.

Florida Fashions was my first formal job, working for a boss with a clock-card and paying income tax and unemployment insurance. I travelled to work by train from Athlone to Woodstock and walked to the factory with the workers. I was with my people, but my position required me to wear a tie. I hated wearing a tie; I felt that it set me apart from the general workers, and I would only put it on when we reached the factory gates.

One month into working at Florida Fashions, student uprisings prompted a national two-day stay-away. Although I was part of the supervisory staff, I joined the workers on 15 and 16 June. Some workers stayed away on 17 June, which was optional, and I did too. The bosses were unimpressed, and since I also refused to raise the work targets, I was sacked after ten months.

While I was working at Florida Fashions, I started freelancing, submitting photographs to newspapers, mainly the *Cape Herald* and *Muslim News*. One of my best friends at school, Shabir Allie from Rylands, had converted a tiny built-in wardrobe at his home into a darkroom, and introduced me to developing and printing black-and-white photographs.

I also started writing articles, but it was my photography hobby that really grew as an art. During my time at the factory, I enrolled to do a photography course at Ruth Prowse School of Art. I didn't last more than half a semester, though. Most of the students were at the art centre for reasons that were completely different from mine. I saw my photography as both art and a weapon in the struggle, while many others just wanted to learn how to use their expensive Nikon cameras and take photographs that were commercially rewarding. Furthermore, I had already learnt how to print and I was very good at it.

For one of our assignments, we had to photograph shoes. One of my *Muslim News* assignments at the same time was to cover the work St Athens Mosque did delivering soup to poor communities in Crossroads and Browns Farm. The photograph I submitted for the shoes assignment was taken while I was covering the soup kitchen one late afternoon, when the sun was low and the shadows long. In the foreground were the legs and boots of a woman serving soup, the four legs of a table and the legs of a child wearing one shoe. They were standing on a stretch of sand and the footprints in it made the sand look like waves. It was not the high-fashion photograph of catwalk heels that the tutors at Ruth Prowse apparently wanted and I got the lowest mark. At that point I decided the course was not for me and I quit. The photograph I took was later exhibited at a Domestic Workers Union's conference in Gugulethu.

My sister Tourhiera paid the R50 deposit on my first camera, which I then paid off using my freelance earnings. The camera was stolen the week I finished paying it off, and I had to start all over again. I had befriended a photographer, Joe Myengeza, and we worked together in his small photographic studio in Langa. We used film supplied by *Muslim News* and took pictures of the bleak and overcrowded Langa Hostels, which stood in contrast to the warmth and humanity of hostel dwellers. We also photographed the evictions at Modderdam, Unibell and other informal settlements that were taking place at the time.

It cost *Muslim News* more to pay me as a freelancer than it would to employ me full-time, so they offered me a job in August 1977, soon after my twenty-first birthday. James Matthews was the editor at the time. I learnt a tremendous amount from him and practically lived at his house in Silvertown. We worked every day of the week, which was also part of the struggle for freedom.

I had a wonderful time at *Muslim News*. We got to do everything: take pictures, develop the film and strip the photos to size. *Muslim News* and Sayed & Sons Printers were far more advanced than mainstream printing companies because they were computerised. The Sayed family had started the newspaper in 1967, and an iconic photograph of the founding editors, Zubaire Sayed and my hero Imam Haron, was prominently displayed at the offices.

In 1977 we were paid weekly. My first pay cheque was R20. Even though we received very little remuneration, I was committed to the work. In June that year I married Zuraida (Raidy) Dawood. She was living in Cashel Avenue, up the road from *Muslim News*. When our daughter, Shihaam, was born, I was still earning R20 a week, so James spoke to the Sayed family and my salary was increased to R50 a week. They also bought soya milk wholesale for Shihaam, because she was lactose intolerant.

One perk of the job was that journalists were given free petrol at the Shell petrol station in Camberwell Road, which was owned by one of the Sayed brothers. I had my own car, an old green Mazda that I bought second-hand for R700. We serviced and fixed it ourselves, and the free petrol meant that there was no restriction on where James and I could go.

Sayed & Sons Printers and *Muslim News* were constantly under attack from the security police, and a number of editions were banned and confiscated. Sayed & Sons also did printing for the National Union of South African Students (NUSAS) and other anti-apartheid organisations. Often, the staff were not paid. They did this for many years but it eventually all became too much. I was told to look for another job because they could no longer afford to employ both James and me.

I responded to an advertisement for a reporter at the *Cape Herald*, a biweekly newspaper for the coloured market in Cape Town and Port Elizabeth. The paper had a big circulation and was initially a mouthpiece for the apartheid government, propagating the idea that the coloured community should comply with the apartheid regime. We transformed it into a serious anti-apartheid newspaper and sold more copies than the *Cape Times* at one stage.

The general rule at the *Cape Herald* was that new employees were put on probation for a three-month period, but after producing my first stories, deputy editor Jimmy Atkins asked whether I was prepared to start straight away. I signed up immediately and started on 21 October 1979. My salary tripled, not that it was a fortune; newspapers were generally paying black and coloured employees far less than their white counterparts.

I had been with the newspaper company for less than a year when the staff went on a strike against this salary injustice in August 1980. While at *Muslim News* in early 1977, James had taken me to a meeting of the Union of Black Journalists (UBJ), and I had joined up. The UBJ had been founded in 1972, in response to the registering of the all-white South African Journalist Society in 1969. The apartheid regime ordained that only whites were allowed to be members of registered unions, enjoying the protection of the law. Many white journalists rejected standing in solidarity with black journalists, and chose state-sanctioned unions open only to whites.

The UBJ was part of the Black Consciousness Movement, which had been banned in 1977 along with twenty other organisations and a couple of newspapers. The UBJ was banned in October 1979, but before that happened we formed the Writers' Association of South Africa, which we transformed into the Media and Allied Workers Union (MWASA) in 1980. The point of MWASA was to organise all media workers, from journalists to those on the shop floor, into one union.

MWASA was very successful. We were able to take everybody out on strike, including messengers, cleaners and printers, all the way to the upper echelon, except management. Eventually, however, the deputy editor joined the strike too. In our meetings with the bosses we always took the lowest paid workers, not just the leadership. The first time we brought them in, the workers came straight from the factory floor with printing ink on their boots, leaving black footprints on the plush carpets in the bosses' offices. My union duties involved a lot of hard work, consisting of weeks and weeks of organising to reach people who were neither politically aware nor unionised. It was all very new and very dangerous.

I led that strike at the age of twenty-four, my first experience of leadership. I flew up to Johannesburg every couple of days because our members at the

Sowetan had started to stir and this was the first major strike in the South African media industry. We insisted on coming to work every day, based on the idea that if we came to work, they could not lock us out. Plus, the office was a good place to meet, make calls and organise in order to ensure that everybody was on the same page and in agreement regarding the action plans.

Our editor started going to people's homes to entice them to return to work, and the situation changed. The morale among the striking workers was like a bicycle tyre that deflated every night and had to be pumped up in the morning. That was the challenge of leadership: constantly pumping people up, convincing them of the righteousness of our course of action and motivating them to stand firm.

The bosses decided to wear us out by seeing how long we would last without pay. We had hurt them by withdrawing our labour, so they brought in scab labour to produce the newspaper. In response, we organised the delivery drivers so they would not deliver the paper, and the company took on more scab labour for distribution. But we were a step ahead: we organised the Western Cape Traders Association so that when the company brought the papers to the market, the retailers would not stock them or, if they did, they would put them under the counter. Not only that, we sent our advertising representatives to clients to tell them not to buy advertising space. We gave them the facts regarding the wage discrepancy between white and black journalists and asked them how they could continue advertising while we were trying to fight this injustice. We squeezed them hard and none of them advertised.

Meanwhile, the president of MWASA, Zwelakhe Sisulu, son of Albertina and Walter Sisulu, sent one of our members across the border to Swaziland. He came back with an attaché case full of bank notes from the ANC so that we could provide strike pay to MWASA's members. Thanks to the ANC we were able to outlast the bosses. The strike went on for thirty-three days – the record for the longest strike at the time.

One of the most wonderful days of my life was when we sat across the table from the bosses at Newspaper House and they folded and agreed to settle. We got them to agree to most of our demands and we instituted pay scales for every category of worker in the company. Our salaries increased by 64 per cent on average, which remains the record in South Africa. That victory was sweet, but after that I was a marked man. Motivating everybody had also taken a heavy toll on me, and I later sought professional psychological help for the anger and resentment I felt at having had to carry such a huge responsibility.

From 1981 I was MWASA's national wage negotiator and I played that role for years. Between 1981 and 1983, we set up human relations processes and structures dealing with wages, grades for every job, protocol, and time off. We survived on foreign funding because subscriptions alone could not cover the cost of flying or bussing people up and down the country.

In mid-summer of 1983, I went to Stockholm to represent MWASA at the Swedish Union of Journalists national congress. I spoke at the congress on 16 June, dressed in a black and gold MWASA T-shirt and green corduroy jeans – the ANC colours.

I was meant to stay for three days, but ended up staying for a month having struck up a friendship with the union's secretary, Anita Vahlberg. She and her mother Ann-Marie and daughter Emily Hall subsequently visited me in Cape Town, and I have been back to their beautiful city a few times. They typify Sweden's international solidarity and love. While I was there, the ANC in Stockholm asked Anita if they could see me, and I agreed. I met with the ANC representatives, facilitated by Anita, and was formally recruited to the ANC. My first assignment was to prepare dead letter boxes and start recruiting people. We met about three times after that in Stockholm, always clandestinely, and on a few occasions the ANC comrades came through my bedroom window instead of through the front door. This was probably because the *boere* were everywhere in Stockholm, as Sweden was an important ally and supporter of the ANC. The Swedish Union of Journalists congress was held at the Trade Union Centre outside the city. Apartheid police spies were monitoring the proceedings. I knew they were also watching me because, on my way to Stockholm, they had seized and broke open my suitcase, which was only returned a couple of days later.

On 16 June I was interviewed on radio in Sweden. The interview was broadcast live across Scandinavia as well as at the Trade Union Centre. At the time, the apartheid regime had just carried out death sentences on the Moroka Three: Marcus Motaung, Jerry Mosololi and Simon Mogoerane. The radio interviewer asked me about the execution of our three comrades and I clearly remember what I said: 'We are shocked to the bone that the regime has gone so far. But we are not despairing and we call on the world not to despair. South Africa is not a strong regime; a strong regime does not kill its opponents like the apartheid regime is doing. It is a weak regime; they are on their last legs, so we must intensify sanctions against South Africa.' I must have been bloody mad to say this publicly, but I did.

Newspapers interviewed me as well. 'Many of you have been very concerned about my safety,' I announced during a speech I made at the Swedish

Union of Journalists' congress. 'You have asked me what the state will do to me when I return home. I am not afraid. As journalists, the answer should be clear. We have a responsibility to tell the truth, no matter where we are, and no matter the consequences.' They appreciated that. After my speech, the congress passed a few resolutions, one supporting MWASA materially and financially, and another resolving that it would no longer buy South African products. The members collected money for me, which supported me for the thirty days I spent in Sweden. The ANC comrades supplied me with copies of the highly sought-after *Sechaba*, the official publication of the ANC, to take home with me. *Sechaba* was banned in South Africa, though, and on my way home I left them in a toilet at Heathrow Airport just before boarding. If I was caught with them I would go to prison, and I had too much work to do to take that risk.

At home, I got back to my MWASA work straight away. I was essentially working three jobs simultaneously, as I also had my journalism and my work as an underground operative for the ANC. On top of this, there were some evenings when I went with Shirley Gunn to work with the Clothing Workers Union (CLOWU). On these occasions I would get to bed at 2 a.m. and then be up again at 5 a.m. to distribute pamphlets at Epping Station. From there, I would go to the *Cape Herald* in the Cape Town CBD to do my journalism job, then to my union job, and then do work for the ANC.

Around Easter that year, a number of MK guerrillas, including Leon Meyer, were deployed to Cape Town. Leon told me that Charles Nqakula had referred him to me. Charles was from the Eastern Cape. We had worked with each other for years when he was elected as president of MWASA and I was vice-president, but he had been forced into exile and was now serving with Chris Hani in MK. Another comrade, Johnny Issel, brought Leon to my granny flat in Crawford, off Belgravia Road, within walking distance from where Johnny, Zubeida Jaffer and Shirley were staying. I had more or less moved in with Shirley by then, so my place was available and Leon moved in and began training Shirley and me.

Leon trained others too, and they carried out a number of operations. He left in October 1985 because he had to get back to Lesotho, but he said he would return. We never saw him again. In December, Leon and his partner, Jacqueline Quin, were killed in an ambush led by death squad leader Eugene de Kock in Maseru, Lesotho.

Shirley was detained that year too, and while she was in detention I conducted a military operation. We wanted to demonstrate to the *boere* that if they detained our comrades there would be hell to pay. Our message to the state was to release detainees, and as long as our people were inside we would continue with our operations. I had to go into hiding soon after this operation as I had been betrayed by a young man from Oudtshoorn who had shared a house with us and the *boere* were hunting me down. I knew I had no option but to leave the country.

I managed to leave clandestinely with the help of a number of people. I initially stayed in a flat in Hillbrow, Johannesburg, before crossing the border illegally into Botswana on 6 February 1986. I then travelled to Angola, where I received military training at MK's Pango camp for four months, from 16 July until November 1986. It was not a big ANC military camp, but rather an underground one for those who were receiving training and were to be sent back to South Africa to fight.

Getting to Pango was an adventure. I was driven in a convoy of four military jeeps from Luanda. It was a two-hour drive north on narrow roads through jungle and bush, where UNITA bandits often carried out ambush operations. There I was, a lone civilian, flanked by MK soldiers in military gear with AK-47s and bazookas. I was the only one in the convoy going to training.

There was a large, hand-drawn banner of two female guerrillas at the entrance to the camp. The slogan read: *No Liberation Without Women*. I was taken to the chief recording officer's quarters, which were in a dugout. I had to write my biography for the ANC and, as a voluntary recruit being inducted into MK, I had to take the oath of allegiance to obey the constitution of the ANC. I stood in front of the chief recording officer, the second in command of the camp, raised my right hand and took the oath. On the wall behind him was a portrait of the assassinated comrade Ruth First. That moment stuck in my mind forever. It was my first contact with the structured, organised army outside South Africa.

When the camp commanders asked who could type, I was reluctant to step forward. I did not want to pick up a typewriter again; I wanted to pick up an AK-47. Nevertheless, I admitted that I could type and ended up monitoring international radio stations and typing up the daily news bulletins for the camp. Being a journalist made this task very easy, but initially I resented having to do this work. There was no electricity in the camp, but there was a battery that powered the shortwave radio, so we were able to get all of the major stations, including Radio Moscow, Voice of America, the BBC and others. It took skill to find the stations at the camp, but fortunately I had experience. As a teenager, my friends and I had become 'DXers' – shortwave listeners who connect to frequencies in foreign countries. We logged the stations and sent them to an organisation in the United States that monitored which stations could be heard in South Africa. DXing is like birding: when you spot a rare bird somewhere in the bush, you send in a report.

At the camp, I monitored the stations from midnight to 4 a.m., and the bulletin had to be ready at seven. Besides this duty, I also participated in regular training and other daytime duties like everybody else.

There were distinct advantages to being the news monitor. The radio tent always had a lamp burning, making it one of the only places that always had a flame. Some of the comrades smoked cigarettes, and because there were no matches, lighters or fires at that time of night, they would come to the radio tent and offer me a couple of puffs in exchange for a light. Cigarettes were in short supply, so we collected the *topatjies* (stubs) that the officers had discarded, took the scraps of tobacco from them and made hand-rolled cigarettes. Another advantage to being the radio monitor was that I was exempt from some of the other duties. For example, I often had to monitor the news while the rest of the soldiers went to drill. I was very unfit from the many months I'd spent cooped up in hiding back in South Africa, so physical training was sheer hell, although I was fit and thin by the time I left.

The general military training was incredible and I took to it. The main subjects were military combat work (MCW); military engineering, which involved explosives; and tactics, but most of the time was spent on politics. We had classes every morning from 7 a.m. until 1 p.m., and we took notes in exercise books. I took such precise notes on the MCW course that my instructor asked for my notebook when I finished the course, to use as a textbook.

On 9 August, Women's Day, the head of the ANC Women's League, Gertrude Shope, arrived. It was incredible to see Ma'Shope and our women leadership armed and in military uniform, marching to our camp's meeting place. There, Ma'Shope addressed us and invited questions. As a cocky thirty-year-old, I stood up and asked whether any progress had been made in uniting the women's organisations, as the ANC leadership had been making very serious efforts to do so. Her reply stuck in my mind: 'We women do not go around ringing our bells.'

Shortly after starting my training at Pango, Ashley Forbes and Peter Jacobs arrived. When I first saw them I was returning from guard duty, wearing my peak cap, fatigues and boots and carrying my AK-47, my spare magazines and my grenades. They were still in their civilian gear and they were very impressed to see me in my uniform, and happy too, because they knew me from home.

Our camp had regular mock attacks to prepare us for potential UNITA attacks. These were terrifying. The camp made it as real as possible, with explosives going off, so that we really felt as though we were under attack. Officers from other camps inspected and evaluated our responses to determine if we were prepared for such eventualities. Once, I looked up from my designated foxhole during one of these mock attacks and saw an officer in a beret standing over me. It was Ashley Kriel!

Ashley was not based in our camp. Pango was essentially a specialised underground camp for people who had gone into exile to be trained and who would ideally return home as guerrilla fighters. Ashley was not going back, as it would be too dangerous for him. He had served as an officer at Quatro, the notorious ANC detention camp in Angola where enemy agents, real or perceived, were held and brutally tortured or killed. Had Ashley returned to South Africa and been captured by the security police, *he* would have been tortured or killed, as they sought information on Quatro, especially which of their agents were being held there.

Ashley Forbes and Peter Jacobs left Pango a few days before me to be deployed at home. Although everybody hoped to go back home to South Africa, some never got the opportunity because it was the most dangerous assignment of all. Ashley Kriel knew that Ashley, Peter and I were to be deployed back home. This affected him deeply; he wanted to return to fight too, but he'd been selected for officer training and was due to leave for the German Democratic Republic (GDR, also known as East Germany). The ANC often earmarked cadres for specialised training in order to run a modern, regular army. This was different to the training we received in MK, where we were not trained for conventional warfare against the SADF. Ashley's officer training was to prepare for the day when the ANC took over. The day before he was to leave for the GDR, he made himself physically sick. The ANC appreciated his determination to return home and decided to deploy him back to South Africa as well.

In early November 1986, a group of us left the camp on the back of a Soviet-supplied truck and headed for Luanda. As we departed, one of the instructors asked me what I had learnt. I thought back on the explosives and firearms training, and how we'd been taught to organise military structures, how to operate and stay alive, and the history of the ANC and its politics. Military training had taught me several important things: commitment, focus, determination and the belief that our war efforts were just. But the most important lesson had been about myself. I told the instructor that I'd learnt that one tends to give up just before the finish line, but it's important to persevere and soldier on to the end.

Ashley Kriel and I flew together from Angola to Lusaka, Zambia. Both of us were to serve in the same detachment as Ashley Forbes and Peter Jacobs. I was to command the detachment.

The months that Ashley and I spent together in Zambia are some of the most memorable of my life. We spent about four months in Chilanga Township, a distance outside Lusaka, where the Chilanga Cement factory dominated the skyline. This was a colonial town that the British had exploited. We stayed in a small two-bedroom house with a South African nursing sister who had been involved with the PAC and was living in exile, and her niece. Over decades, Zambia's president Kenneth Kaunda provided shelter for exiles from every country and every group in southern Africa, and as a result Zambia paid a heavy price at the hands of the *boere*, the Portuguese and Rhodesia.

Ashley and I walked every day, and ran through the farmlands most days to stay fit. We frequented the Chilanga Club, which had a full-sized billiard table beside the bar, a swimming pool and tennis courts.

The locals knew who we were and that our house sheltered MK soldiers. Although we had no money, we were able to barter our clothing for food. At times, we did not get enough supplies and our neighbours, many of whom were poor, taught us how to cook pap with a relish of pumpkin leaves. The house we shared with the nurse and her niece was only slightly bigger than a typical South African township house. Ashley and I had two single beds in one of the bedrooms. Sometimes we talked all night, and before we knew it the sun would be rising.

Before Ashley Forbes and Peter left Lusaka, the four of us met and strategised about our work back home. We set up lines of communication so that when Ashley Kriel and I returned we could work together.

The day finally arrived when Ashley and I were to return home. We were driven to the Lusaka International Airport, where we met Chris Hani and Charles Nqakula before departure. Chris Hani's wife, Limpho, was also there, on her way to her family home in Lesotho. As Chris gave us last-minute instructions, I noticed Comrade Limpho giving us a look that I will never forget. Her eyes were pleading for a few precious moments with her husband.

Ashley and I boarded a flight to Gaborone. Botswana was not always very receptive to the ANC, because apartheid security forces often conducted cross-border raids that resulted in civilian casualties, and the Batswana authorities would sometimes arrest undocumented comrades in transit. MK had therefore organised forged passports for us with false names, which enabled us to pass through customs at Sir Seretse Khama International Airport without problems.

Our first night in Gaborone was surreal. After living in the camps in Angola, and in Chilanga Township alongside poor neighbours, we were put up in the Gaborone Sun, a luxurious five-star hotel. Our room had two enormous beds that could have fit four people each. We also had room service because we were not allowed to leave the room. We could not believe that we had ended up in the lap of luxury. I cried that night when I heard Chris de Burgh's hit song 'Lady in Red' on the radio, because it reminded me of Shirley.

Ashley returned to South Africa a few days before I did. Before I left to join him, Ashley Forbes and Peter in Cape Town, I had to set up a communications and supplies pipeline between Gaborone and Johannesburg. Other MK units from Cape Town had been caught when they communicated directly with the ANC in Botswana, so we formed a unit of our detachment in Johannesburg in order to protect ourselves and secure our communications from being tapped and traced.

Shanil Haricharan, whom I had met at a mutual friend's flat in Hillbrow in 1987 before I went into exile, was the first person I deployed to command the Johannesburg unit. Shanil had returned from the Transkei, where he was an MK operative in 1986. He recruited Richard Ishmail, and I put them in touch with our commander in Botswana, James Ngculu, to make the pipeline work effectively. When I had completed this task, I went to Cape Town, where I connected with my brothers Seiraaj and Mogamat, as well as Johnny, Zubeida, and Shirley's mother, Audrey. Audrey's house was on Bolus Avenue in Kenilworth, and it was my first stop after returning to Cape Town. At one point, Audrey feared the security police had pitched up outside her home. She panicked and tried to hide all trace of my presence there, grabbing the washing off the line and hurriedly stuffing it into her aged mother's overnight bag. Fortunately, it was a false alarm. Granny was surprised to find my underwear stuffed in her bag, which made us all laugh, and it's a story that Audrey still finds hilarious.

I struggled for some time to make contact with Ashley Kriel, Ashley Forbes and Peter Jacobs because the lines of communication we had set up in Lusaka had broken down. I was not prepared to wait endlessly, doing nothing while risking capture or death, so I made my way back to Gaborone, crossing the border using my fake passport. I made contact with Charles Nqakula. 'My God,' he said when he saw me, 'you must like exile!'

I explained my predicament: contact with the other three had been lost. He instructed me to link up with Tony Yengeni's detachment and I supplied the number of a public phone box in Cape Town where Tony could call me on a particular day and time.

On Monday 13 July 1987, the comrades in Gaborone escorted me to a Botswana border post to cross into South Africa again. Just before I crossed, one of them stopped me. 'By the way,' he said, 'your friend Ashley Kriel was killed four days ago.'

Anger and devastation raged through me. Why hadn't the ANC told me? 'They knew you would be extremely upset, seeing how close you'd been,' said the comrade. He explained that he was telling me because it was important that I knew what the prospects were if I returned to South Africa. Alternatively, I could abort my mission, turn around and stay in exile with no questions asked. But turning around was not an option; I had to persevere for Ashley. I crossed over the Ramatlabama border post into South Africa and made my way to Johannesburg to link up with Shanil.

The first thing I did was drive to a shopping centre in Roodepoort and buy the *Weekly Mail* to find out what had happened to Ashley. It was such a struggle to take in all the details that at one point while driving to Shanil, who was staying illegally with a Namibian friend in the nearby white suburb of Newlands, I completely lost track of where I was. It was frightening. This event marked the start of my time in the military underground in South Africa.

Back in Cape Town, on the day I'd arranged to receive Tony Yengeni's call, I waited at the designated phone box at the specified time, but the call never came. Usually, we did not wait more than five minutes for contact of this nature, but I waited for twenty. Mogamat was with me. We sat in his car, near enough to the phone box to be able to hear it ring. I was armed with my Makarov pistol in case something went wrong. After a while, we saw some white guys who looked like cops driving off very fast down a one-way street and figured they must have been watching the phone box. We decided to leave. Later, we found out that Tony had been caught using a phone box behind the Baxter Theatre in Rondebosch on the day I was supposed to hear from him. I suspected that he had been in direct telephonic contact with the comrades in Gaborone and the call had been traced. It was for this reason that our detachment had set up our own structures and did not communicate directly with Gaborone, but went via our unit in Johannesburg.

I was then put in command of a new detachment that the ANC and MK leadership had named in honour of Ashley Kriel. I linked up with Shirley, who had received military training with MK in Angola and Cuba. The last time I had seen her was in Luanda at an MK flat when she was one her way to Pango and I was returning from there. Shirley was meant to be with special operations, but with permission from our ANC commanders in exile, we started operating together. I asked Shirley to co-command the detachment, whose jurisdiction would include the coloured, white and Indian areas in the Western Cape. These communities made up the majority of the Western Cape population. We were instructed not to operate in the black townships because we would have stuck out.

First, we had to secure a safe underground base from which to live and operate. We rented a tiny, one-roomed flat without a kitchen, above Second Beach, Clifton. Then we started building the detachment by recruiting key youth, such as Melvin Bruintjies, who was identified by Johnny and Shirley as a suitable recruit. We set about establishing a Western Cape Regional Political Military Committee (RPMC), which was the overarching structure necessary to implement our 'people's war' strategy and tactics. We understood that no group of trained guerrillas would be able to liberate our country alone. The purpose of the RPMC was to link the military leadership to the political leadership. Our work would be informed by the political conditions on the ground. Shirley and I chaired the committee along with Johnny Issel, who provided political input, and Melvin, who was chief of operations. Shanil continued to head up the Johannesburg unit, linking us to Gaborone and Lusaka.

Over time, we set up AKD units in Bonteheuwel, Macassar, Mitchells Plain, Hout Bay, Paarl and Athlone. The RPMC met from time to time to assess the political and military situation and determine what our responses should be.

Johnny's approach initially differed from ours. He favoured 'big bang' tactics, such as an attack on a target like Sasol, which would have a major impact. We thought this would be counterproductive, as it would require us to get out of the country very quickly or go so deep underground that we would be unable to operate effectively. Instead, we advocated conducting several operations, some simultaneously, to stretch the enemy and show MK's presence across the city and Boland. Eventually, Johnny came to accept that our strategy was far more effective.

The RPMC's first meeting was in a caravan on a smallholding in Klapmuts, in the Northern Suburbs. Shirley and I travelled there by train from our Clifton base. We behaved as if we had no connection to each other, both of us armed with Makarov pistols and grenades.

Johnny had organised the meeting place through Moegsien Williams, and the caravan was parked on the property of one of Johnny's friends, an academic at UWC. We all spent a couple of days there, strategising, catching up and discussing our next move in expanding the detachment and what operations we would carry out. That session was very productive.

On our way home, we had a scare. There was a contingent of policemen with sniffer dogs at the Cape Town train station concourse. We slipped away undetected, hopped on a Golden Arrow bus and reached our base safely. From then on it was extremely dangerous for all of us to meet because Johnny was banned and on the security police's radar. Shirley and I were also wanted, so our meetings with Johnny became infrequent.

When Dulcie September was assassinated in Paris on 28 March 1988, we decided to take a stand. Comrade Dulcie, who was also from the Western Cape, was the ANC's representative in France at the time. We feared that this could lead to many other such assassinations. Our people were vulnerable, and we feared that governments abroad were colluding with the apartheid government to kill those who opposed the regime.

In response, we planned to bomb a French bank on the corner of Spin Street and Parliament Street, opposite the back of the Slave Lodge in Cape Town. The bombing would be a message to the French, and other apartheid allies around the world, that if there were more assassinations there would definitely be retribution from us.

I did the initial reconnaissance and we decided that Shirley would place the limpet. Shanil was visiting us, and we dispatched him to do additional recon of the area. It was common practice for us to have more than one person reconnoitring a target.

To minimise civilian casualties, we decided to place the limpet after hours in the adjoining building, on the wall shared with the bank building. Shirley did the dummy run and discovered that the Israeli consulate was located on the second floor of a building close to the bank. As a result there was a lot of security and surveillance in the area. This made the operation very tricky, but we pulled it off.

We heard on the radio that the bomb had successfully gone off, but we had to watch the news to see what had actually happened. Unbeknown to us, the former minister of law and order, Louis le Grange, was chairing a session of the Tricameral Parliament in the coloured House of Representatives chamber when the bomb detonated. We did not know this, but the French Bank building shared a back wall with the Marks Building in the parliamentary precinct where the session was being held.

We saw Le Grange on TV, shocked, sweating and angry, fuming about how 'terrorists' had come right into Parliament to attack them. We knew that this was not the real story, but the record showed that we hit Parliament, and we were not going to argue. Dulcie was the first and the last ANC operative killed in Europe.

*

Our work was to support the various struggles: community, students and, most importantly, the workers' struggle. In November 1989, we responded to the national railway strike. The apartheid government refused to recognise the South African Railway and Harbour Workers Union (SARHWU), which meant that they could not participate in the labour council to negotiate wages and working conditions. The government's refusal favoured the white minority unions affiliated to South African Transport Services (SATS), fracturing trade unions in the sector along racial lines. The railway workers were on strike because SATS management was *hardegat* (stubborn) and refused to negotiate with SARHWU. They had reached a stalemate. Many SARHWU workers were fired and some striking workers were injured and killed during the protracted strike.

At one of our RPMC meetings, we decided that the AKD had to intervene and support the strike by hitting the railway lines. We originally wanted to do this in the evening, until Johnny pointed out that it would mean that workers got home late. 'Make it the early morning so SATS won't have time to fix the lines and everyone will be late for work,' he said. 'It won't be the workers' fault and it'll piss the bosses off terribly and affect profits. The bosses will then put pressure on the government.' We took Johnny's advice and instructed units to strike the railway lines in Eerste River, Bishop Lavis, Kuils River, Heideveld, Diep River and Athlone.

We also pulled off an operation in support of the striking workers at the Vineyard Hotel in Newlands. The establishment dates back two hundred years, to when the Cape of Good Hope was under British colonial rule. It always represented white privilege, greed and colonial conquest. I had grown up close to the Vineyard Hotel and as children we had passed it on our way to the Liesbeek River, but the hotel's whites-only policy meant we could never go inside.

I took Seiraaj with me on this operation, and chose to place a mini limpet mine in a blue plastic rubbish bin attached to a pole close to the bus stop on Colinton Road in front of the hotel parking area, where lots of luxury cars were parked. We carried out the operation late at night, when there were no pedestrians and the buses had stopped operating. I did not even have to get out of Seiraaj's old bakkie: I just stretched my arm out of the window, placed the limpet carefully in the bin, and we drove off. The mine damaged quite a few vehicles, and the hotel management settled the dispute with the workers soon afterwards.

During the sports boycott, we planned to target the South African Tourism Office (SATOUR) at the Golden Acre Shopping Centre in central Cape Town because SATOUR had a hand in organising rebel sporting tours, defying the international sporting ban on South Africa. Based on my reconnaissance, I thought SATOUR would be easy to bomb because there were plenty of places to put a limpet mine. However, there was a restaurant with outdoor tables and chairs opposite the office, and an operation would put civilians at the restaurant at risk of being injured or killed. Seeing this made me physically sick and I could not go through with the bombing, despite the legitimacy of the target, so I returned to base with the limpet in my bag.

Until then, MK's policy was not to go after soft targets or endanger civilians, and the AKD agreed that hitting soft targets was unethical and counterproductive. The AKD never hit a restaurant or bar, even if the patrons were policemen, because there would have certainly been civilian casualties. But then we received a message from the ANC in Botswana to say that the lines had become blurred between hard and soft targets and that we should pursue soft targets. The AKD chose to defy this order, knowing full well that we might be disciplined and perhaps even severely punished. Before then, the AKD had never defied an order. Because of our adherence to our policy, no Wimpy Bars were blown up in the Western Cape, unlike in other parts of the country.

In June 1988 we bombed a Conservative Party meeting in Sea Point. With its high-density residential flats, similar to Hillbrow, Sea Point was a battle-ground because the *boere* did not have much luck in enforcing apartheid there – black people could live in the area under the pretence of being workers. Two worlds existed in Sea Point: the white world of luxury, and the black world of workers who, under the law, had no right to be there. With the advancement of the struggle, the police colluded with the Cape Town City Council and came up with a by-law that gave the police copies of the keys of all servants' quarters attached to blocks of flats and residences. If they wanted to raid workers' premises, they could. This by-law was resisted and the Domestic Workers Union was at the forefront of opposing it.

As a result, the CP tried to set up a branch in Sea Point to enforce these sorts of racist laws. We did reconnaissance of the Sea Point Civic Centre where they were to hold their public meeting, and decided to bomb the library close to the main hall. Shirley placed the limpet mine and it detonated while they were singing 'Die Stem'. The CP members and potential Sea Point members inside got a massive *skrik* and fled the civic centre in undignified panic. That was their first and last attempt at setting up a CP branch in Sea Point.

Another of our operations targeted the Castle, the headquarters of the SADF in the Western Cape. The Castle was being renovated at the time and the construction companies' workers, such as my younger brother Adenaan, had access to blueprints and plans of the building. Adenaan gave the plans to Seiraaj without knowing his connection to the AKD.

Shirley completed the operation disguised as a tourist. She took the bus from our bedsit in Clifton, entered the Castle with a limpet mine and placed it where no one would get hurt. It was a warning to the SADF that we were capable of getting right into the headquarters of the Western Province command. No doubt that explosion hurt them psychologically. The chief of the SADF, General Constand Viljoen, even commented on it.

That year was critical for the racist government, which was trying desperately to hold on to power. The regime was imposing municipal elections across the country. Some black and coloured people supported the new dispensation and were co-opted. The AKD felt we had to respond, and we did so in various ways.

Our Macassar unit set off a limpet mine inside a local polling station on the night before the elections, within hours of minister of law and order Adriaan Vlok telling the public not to worry as the polling stations were protected. The bombing was the crowning glory of that campaign.

We also targeted municipal buildings and courts that were to serve as registration points for the elections, one of which was in Athlone. The Kismet Bioscope and the Athlone Magistrate's Court shared a narrow lane that ran between the two buildings, which I knew well from my youth when we bunked school to watch movies on Friday afternoons. The plan was for two AKD members, Coline Williams and Robbie Waterwitch, to walk up the lane and place the mine over the fence into the court premises. Because of our simultaneous operations that night, the bomb squad was sent helter-skelter. First they rushed off to Goodwood Court. A few minutes later, there was another blast at Somerset West Municipal Offices, so they had to rush to Somerset West. A fourth blast, planned to target the Heideveld Rent Office, was aborted.

Two days later, we learnt that Coline and Robbie were dead. The limpet meant for the Athlone Magistrate's Court had exploded, killing them both. When further details eventually emerged, we discovered that they had died at the back of the public toilets across the road from the lane between Kismet Bioscope and the court – the opposite side of the road from the target.

Coline was a veteran of a few operations; Robbie was on his first mission, observing Coline. She knew how a limpet worked. An explosive cannot go off by itself; it must be detonated. The heart of a detonator is the striking pin. When released, it hits the primer on the limpet and explodes. It is held in place by a wind-up spring, and at the top of the spring there is a hard U-shaped wire. The timing device is a lead plate of varying thickness, colour-coded according to the length of the delay. The lead plate goes under the spring. The AKD always used lead plates in the middle range, giving comrades about thirty minutes to get away safely before the limpet mine exploded. Temperature can also affect how long it takes for the wire to cut through the lead plate, and in warm weather it cuts through the plate faster. The limpet mine and its detonator are always stored separately from each other.

All MK members learnt how limpets worked, but mishaps did happen – for instance, when comrades forgot to put in the lead plate or it fell out. By the time we were instructed in handling explosives, the training was extremely methodical, as the ANC had lost a few of comrades to limpet mines in the early days of the struggle and did not want this to happen again. A limpet is not like a grenade. A grenade has two safety devices: a pin that you pull out and a lever on the side that you hold with your hand. When you pull the first safety pin, you are arming the grenade. When you throw the grenade you release the second safety device and four seconds later the grenade goes off. The security police distributed doctored zero-timed grenades with malfunctioning levers to politically active young people; when the first safety pin was pulled the grenade went off immediately, which led to many fatalities. However, you cannot zero-time a limpet mine because they do not have that kind of mechanism.

The only way you can really make a fatal mistake with a limpet mine is if you put the detonator into the limpet without the lead plate and then, when you pull the pin, the striking pin detonates the limpet immediately. To prevent this from happening, detonators should be armed away from the limpet to ensure the lead plate is in place. By the time of Coline's final mission, she had already detonated limpets in previous operations and had been made commander of the Athlone unit. It seemed inconceivable that with all her experience she would first put the detonator in the limpet, then arm it and try to pull the pin. You never mess with a limpet once it is armed.

However, errors are possible even when they're unlikely. When you conduct an operation, you might start off calm, but there are psychological and physiological responses beyond your immediate control. Your palms sweat, your heart races, you hyperventilate and become hypervigilant. Nervousness can cause you to shake.

On the other hand, if Coline *had* made a fatal mistake, then the explosion should logically have happened in the lane, because that was where they were meant to arm the limpet. They would not have armed the limpet and then carried it across the road. Unless, perhaps, they changed their plan because of a risk to civilians.

In Coline's previous operation at the Bonteheuwel Rent Office, a civilian had inadvertently been injured when he picked up a milk carton in which the limpet had been placed and dropped it, causing it to detonate. Coline explained to us what happened and we accepted her explanation and allowed her to continue to operate as we had full confidence in her. But perhaps this incident had led to her being extra cautious about harming civilians.

When it was confirmed that Coline and Robbie had been killed in the blast, we were devastated. The AKD wrote a pamphlet for distribution at their joint funeral, stating that there were three possibilities which could have led to their deaths. Firstly, they were human and could have made a mistake, although this was unlikely as Coline was a veteran of several successful operations and their training and modus operandi precluded such a mistake. Secondly, given that multiple blasts planned at magistrates' courts had been compromised by a leak in Mitchells Plain, evidenced by the presence of the police at targets in Mitchells Plain and Goodwood, Coline and Robbie could have been intercepted and been blown up. The third – and, to our minds, the most likely – possibility, was that Coline and Robbie had moved the armed limpet across the road to the toilets, against our orders and training, perhaps because they saw civilians near the target. Those civilians could have been *boere* checking out the magistrate's court, but neither Robbie nor Coline would have been aware that other operations that evening had been compromised. Moving an armed limpet to avoid civilian casualties at great danger to themselves might ultimately have cost them their lives. It is for this reason that we regard Coline and Robbie as among our nation's greatest heroes, like their AKD commander, Anton Fransch, who months later single-handedly fought off the *boere* for seven hours before they killed him, a few hundred metres away from where Robbie and Coline had died.

We distributed the pamphlet at the funeral, despite the risks involved, because we felt that it was important that the *boere* did not capitalise on our comrades' deaths by turning our people against us. Using dirty tricks was a common tactic to turn the masses against the people's army. Shortly after Coline and Robbie fell, the *boere* blew up the Early Learning Centre in Athlone. In August 1988 they had blown up Khotso House in Braamfontein in Johannesburg, and the following January Minister Vlok framed Shirley for it.

In late 1989, Nelson Mandela requested a meeting with Johnny Issel at Victor Verster Prison. Mandela was holding meetings with leaders from across the political spectrum. His release had not yet been announced, but other comrades had been freed, including Govan Mbeki and Walter Sisulu. The struggle was at a critical stage and we needed marching orders from Mandela.

Johnny went, taking with him a copy of 'The Path to Power' – the South African Communist Party's 1989 programme. He came back from the meeting with a profound message for our detachment from Madiba. I remember the exact words very clearly: 'Look, the leaders of the apartheid regime have basically agreed to everything we demanded, but we must not make it look as though we have won.' We knew then that our hard-fought struggle was over.

We suspended our operational work in 1990 because we wanted to give Madiba and the negotiation process a chance. In any event, we in MK were not authorised to issue orders; we followed them. We had to take our cue from the political leadership and we were given clear instructions not to humiliate the apartheid government, or make it look like we had won.

On 11 February, we watched Mandela's release on TV from our headquarters in Northpine. We shed tears when we saw him walk out from Victor Verster Prison as a free man. This was our final victory and there would be no turning back. We then waited for his first public address from City Hall, which we knew would indicate to us what we were to do. 'The factors which necessitated the armed struggle still exist today,' he said. 'We have no option but to continue. We express the hope that a climate conducive to a negotiated settlement will be created soon, so that there may no longer be the need for the armed struggle.'

The AKD command realised that we had to respond strategically to this statement. South Africa had been banned from international cricket because of apartheid, yet controversial rebel tours were still taking place. We had already done a lot of reconnaissance of related targets, and Mandela's release coincided with the last of these rebel tours. The English side was playing South Africa and one of the tests would take place at Newlands Cricket Ground. We had done reconnaissance around the British-owned Barclays Bank, which sponsored the rebel tour, and had executed a number of operations against British Petroleum (BP) in October the previous year, because British prime minister Margaret Thatcher had wanted to crush our struggle and there was a call to lift the sanctions against South Africa. A critical Commonwealth meeting with heads of state took place in Kuala Lumpur, which Margaret Thatcher attended. The AKD responded by bombing BP's headquarters in Cape Town. Thatcher certainly got the message because she issued a statement calling for a report, and sanctions were not lifted. Our efforts contributed somewhat to that.

When Mandela's call to continue the armed struggle came, we had initially planned to target Barclays Bank, seeing as we had reconnoitred it. However, we were mindful of the fact that Mandela had told Johnny that we must not do anything to sabotage the negotiations between the ANC and the National Party (NP). A few weeks earlier, we had discovered that there was another MK unit operating in Cape Town as part of Operation Vula. While we were holding back because of what Mandela had said to Johnny, a Vula sub-unit blew up a Barclays ATM in Claremont in response to the planned cricket test in Newlands. We complained bitterly to Chris Hani, via James Ngculu in Botswana, who took our complaint right to Oliver Tambo in Lusaka. 'What is going on?' we asked. 'You gave us command of the Western Cape, but clearly there is another unit operating here. We could have killed each other in the field!'

Seeing as Barclays Bank had already been targeted, we focused our attention on Newlands Cricket Ground. The city council had just built modern turnstiles at the entrance, so we blew them up with a large limpet mine. The beauty of the operation was that Newlands Cricket Ground was only a few kilometres away from the archbishop's residence in Bishopscourt, where Madiba would spend his first night of freedom. The operation in Newlands was thus within earshot of our commander-in-chief. We also hit the Paarl municipal building and the Parow Civic Centre that night. These three operations were symbolic – a demonstration that MK was still operational in the Western Cape. It remained important not to be compromised or captured. We had to stay in hiding and remain combat-ready so that when Mandela and ANC leaders sat down at the negotiation table, the ANC would have MK behind it.

Those three operations turned out to be our last. A few months later, when the ANC was unbanned, most political prisoners were released and exiles began returning home. Shirley left discreetly with our son, Haroon, to meet up with her mother and sister for a holiday. Shirley and I had arranged for her to keep in contact with Melvin in order to reassure the AKD that she was safe. Her first call was supposed to be to a public phone box in Muizenberg. When she didn't call we knew something was up, and we later learnt that she and Haroon had been detained by the security police.

The AKD mobilised and engaged lawyers to get them released. We also got Imam Gassan Solomon, who had married us and who was regarded as the ANC's priest, to help mobilise public support for Shirley and Haroon's release. He was overwhelmed, so we got advocate Siraj Desai involved. Shirley's mother Audrey played a role too, by resisting pressure from the state to take custody of Haroon and insisting that he remain with Shirley in detention because she was breastfeeding him. Their absence was agonising and it was terrible thinking about them in jail at the mercy of the security police. It took about two months to secure their freedom.

When Shirley was detained, we had left the Zeekoevlei safe house that we'd moved into after Northpine, when Melvin was compromised by the Mitchells Plain unit and came to stay with us. As a precaution, we rented a house in Church Street in Athlone, which was paid for by Richard Ishmail, who gave us his pay cheque at the end of every month. The money helped to support our operations and cover our living expenses.

After their release, Shirley and Haroon went to stay with my parents in Crawford, and we made plans to see each other clandestinely at the Athlone base from time to time. We would make food and spend time together, and we got a small inflatable pool that we put in the secluded backyard for Haroon to play in. We remained underground throughout the early 1990s. It was very tough – we had to be obsessive about rules and careful about the way we did things in order to keep everybody alive. If we relaxed, mistakes could happen.

Around this time, Anton Fisher returned from exile and was deployed to the AKD. He stayed with us in the underground, even though he desperately wanted to return home to be with his family. Anton played a supportive role: because he was not wanted by the security police, he could go out in public and shop for supplies.

Slowly, the negotiations between the ANC and the National Party advanced. In order to participate in the talks, people in leadership positions in the ANC and MK received indemnity. Attorneys Mathews Phosa and Taswell Papier handled indemnity for the ANC and AKD respectively. I received indemnity from prosecution in December 1991.

At the beginning of January 1992, I went to COSATU House in Johannesburg to meet with Chris Hani, our commander. It was an incredible thrill to meet openly with Chris. The last time I had seen him was at the airport in Lusaka, when he had given Ashley Kriel and me our orders. Because I was an operational regional MK commander, Chris had a number of career options in mind for me – an army general, a political role in Parliament, a business leader, or a fundraiser for the ANC – but I wanted to go back into the media. There were two camps in the media then: PAC black nationalists and the non-racial ANC. The ANC struggled to get its message out because the PAC journalists were at the helm of most of the papers. At the time, Paul Simon was in South Africa on his Graceland tour, performing with local artists. They made amazing music, but the PAC journalists questioned Simon's motives and claimed he was exploiting South African musicians. This kind of treatment was completely contrary to South Africa's revolution, and I told Chris that I needed to go back in and counter these tendencies. I was pretty persuasive. Chris discussed this decision with Charles Nqakula and eventually agreed that I should return to work in the media, revive its unions and contribute to its transformation, after which I would be redeployed. This turned out to be my last order from Chris.

Before I went back to Independent Newspapers, Shirley, Haroon and I went on a month-long vacation. Chris had given us permission because we hadn't had a holiday in eight years. We travelled across the country and visited Shirley's sister and brother-in-law in Dordrecht. We spent time in Coffee Bay, where Haroon turned three, and we had a party for him. We hiked along the beautiful Wild Coast and ate crayfish and other seafood brought to our door by the locals. We also visited Shanil and his family in Tongaat, KwaZulu-Natal. Being able to move around freely and be together as a family was wonderful. For the first time in many years, I was not constantly monitoring the news. I could have normal conversations with people. It humanised me. I was energised and prepared to face the next phase of my life: helping to transform the media.

Independent Newspapers was shocked when I turned up – they had not expected to ever see me again, and I had to fight to get my job back. Management claimed that I had accepted my dismissal in January 1986, which I had not. I had been forced to leave the country in September 1985 when Shirley was in detention and the security police were looking for me. I had arranged unlimited unpaid leave with my editor, Ted Doman, and told him that any money due to me must be paid to my lawyer, Essa Moosa, who would use the money to pay child maintenance for my daughter, Shihaam, while I was underground. My agreement with Doman was documented, but in January 1986, the company dismissed me, claiming that I had absconded.

I had the records to prove my story, thanks to MWASA's good record-keeping. Once I produced proof, Independent Newspapers was compelled to reinstate me, but they could not give me back my job at *Cape Herald* because the paper had since been closed down. I hoped to get work as a journalist at the *Cape Argus*, which was owned by the company, but Fred Collins, the company's regional manager, said the white journalists at *Cape Argus* would make my life hell because I had served with MK. Fred offered me work in the accounts department instead. I refused the position, but I agreed to work in the community newspaper division. I started at the lowest rank for the least pay, and soon discovered that the work consisted of filling spaces between paid advertisements. Working at the community paper was hard because I had a family to support. We were reintegrating into society with no money or state support, and the company paid me the least they possibly could.

It was my understanding that I could receive new orders from Chris Hani at any time, but the following year, in April 1993, Chris was assassinated. He had said to me that our biggest threat was the right wing, particularly the CP (to which Clive Derby-Lewis, who was involved in his assassination, belonged) and the Afrikaner Weerstandsbeweging (AWB), and that we must keep an eye on them. Maybe if we had taken him a bit more seriously he would not have been killed. I expected my assignment with the media to take about three years, but Chris never got the chance to give me my next order. I might have been deployed as a politician, business person or military general, but the order to leave the media never came.

For a little over two years I was stuck working for the community newspapers as a reporter. Then in 1995, the *Cape Times* became part of Independent Newspapers. My friend Moegsien Williams was appointed editor, and arranged an interview for me with the deputy editor. In August 1995, I got a job there as a journalist.

I became a specialist health writer. In 1996, I investigated and exposed corruption in the Department of Health, where millions of rands in donor money was misappropriated under the guise of organising an AIDS awareness play called *Sarafina II*. The health minister at the time, Nkosazana Dlamini-Zuma, who was married to Jacob Zuma, denounced me as a traitor in Parliament. Her spokesperson, Vincent Hlongwane, had been one of the instructors at Pango. When I saw him for the first time in Parliament at a press conference, he was giving a presentation attempting to cover up the corruption in the department. I confronted him. Afterwards, I saw him outside Parliament and asked if he remembered me from Pango. 'Yes,' he replied, and asked why I was giving them such a hard time. I didn't relent and went on to break the *Sarafina II* scandal, winning the Henry J. Kaiser Award for journalism in 1997.

On 28 October 1999, during the TRC, I appeared before the Amnesty Committee with AKD members Sidney Hendricks and Vanessa November. This was for the incident on 28 October 1988 when twenty-year-old Moegamat Nurudien Bartlett was injured outside the Bonteheuwel Municipal Rent Office when he picked up a milk carton and triggered the explosion of the limpet mine hidden inside it. As with our other operations, it was never our intention to injure civilians, and the chance that anyone would be out at night when the explosive was timed to go off had been negligible. We had packed thermite into the mine, hoping to burn down the rent office, and Bartlett was badly burnt. The incident troubled us and so we visited the Bartlett family to explain what had happened. His mother told me that Moegamat was in the habit of bringing her boxes, like milk cartons. She and her family accepted our apology. This was the only civilian casualty attributable to the AKD in over thirty operations in the Western Cape.

For this incident, the state accused us of attempted murder, which was clearly ludicrous. The Amnesty Committee at the TRC agreed with us that it was an accident, and unreservedly granted the three of us amnesty.

We also cooperated fully with the TRC investigators with regard to the deaths of Coline and Robbie. It was clear in the minds and consciences of AKD members that we did not do, or fail to do, anything that had caused their deaths. However, we were extremely dissatisfied with the way the TRC conducted their investigation into the deaths of our two comrades. Their incorrect conclusion that the AKD was infiltrated by enemy agents has led to rumours that the limpet mine was zero-timed, and this raised questions about the AKD's complicity in their deaths. Nothing could be further from the truth. This matter is unresolved and we have met with the families, who agreed with our proposal that we request the police reopen the investigation into their deaths, but Coline's sister, Selina, subsequently refused us permission to approach the police, yet she persists to this day to claim her sister was murdered. This has been a terrible strain on us for three decades. Therefore we have repeatedly called for their inquest to be reopened.

In 2001, the position of deputy editor opened up at the *Cape Times*. I applied, was interviewed and had to do a written test, which took place four days after my mother had died. Although the office offered to postpone the test, I told them I would take it. I was doing it for my mother, who had taught me to read before I went to school, and for my father who brought the *Cape Times* into our house every day for half a century.

The test involved writing an editorial on the Myburgh Commission's inquiry into the collapse of the rand. Afterwards, editor Chris Whitfield told me that I was the best candidate, but I lacked business acumen. Chris told me not to worry, though: they would organise business courses for me, after which I could take over the position. I soon discovered that they had no intention of offering me those courses, and instead of getting the deputy editor position, I had to go on working as a journalist. I stuck it out for twelve years. During that time Chris appointed Alide Dasnois as *Cape Times* deputy editor.

In 2013, the ownership of the Independent Media company changed, with Dr Iqbal Survé becoming chairman. I felt that he had liberated us in the media and that we were finally free to write what we liked. Gasant Abarder was appointed as *Cape Times* editor, and he asked me to become deputy editor in December 2013. I finally got the position I had applied for all those years ago.

In 2015 Dr Survé appointed me as editor of the *Cape Times*. It has been a long road, but I fulfilled my mission, carrying out my commander Chris Hani's last order.

3

Shanil Haricharan

The Fighting Spirit

MY FIRST TRIP to Cape Town was in 1975 with my family in a blue Peugeot 404 when I was fourteen. The second was in late 1987 with Shirley Gunn in a dented white Nissan Skyline packed with enough cached military hardware to wage a small battle against the apartheid state and its security forces.

Joe Nxusani and I had collected the weapons from Gaborone, but it was just Shirley and me in the Nissan heading back to Cape Town from Johannesburg. During the night, just after Kimberley, we entered a fog, making visibility very poor. I was in the middle of telling Shirley why the side of the car was dented and the back door was jammed (Joe's handiwork, swiping a bakkie outside Krugersdorp en route to Gaborone) when there was a loud *bang!* and the car jerked. Shirley pulled over and I got out. It was pitch dark and bitterly cold. Then I saw it: a dead sheep on the road. It looked pure white, except for a spot of red on its head. I was shaken by the sight of it, but I dragged it away from the road and went to inspect the car. Fortunately, the accident had not affected the hand grenades cached in the fender centimetres away. We drove on in sombre silence.

Sometime later, Shirley's eyes became sore and inflamed. She removed her contact lenses, but soon she could barely open her eyes. We swopped places and I drove through the night. My fatigued mind conjured up terrifying omens from the images in my mind: the bewildered eyes of the elderly farmer in the bakkie Joe had swiped, the dull darkness of the still-warm sheep's eyes, and now Shirley going blind.

When we approached Cape Town the following afternoon I was overcome by the sight of Table Mountain looming ahead. It was a hot summer day. I didn't know the city, so I read out the signboards and Shirley gave me directions to a location on High Level Road in Green Point. As soon as we arrived, Shirley stumbled out of the car and disappeared down the road. The bright afternoon sun stung my weary eyes. I longed for a hot shower and sleep, and most of all to deliver the car and its contents to fresh-eyed comrades. I waited, unaware of where Shirley had gone or what the next steps were.

I gazed across Table Bay and spotted Robben Island. I was ten months old on 16 December 1961 when Nelson Mandela, the MK commander-in-chief, had given orders for the first military attacks against the apartheid state. Now, twenty-six years later, here I was in a car laden with weapons, continuing the armed struggle.

Suddenly, a police van pulled up next to me and two policemen jumped out. 'What are you doing here? Where is your driver's licence? Whose car is this?' one asked bluntly. I showed them my ID. They looked at the car's Transvaal registration number and radioed it in. While this was going on, Aneez Salie appeared unexpectedly, walking straight towards the car. He'd obviously seen the police van, but it was too late for him to change direction, so he nonchalantly slid into the front passenger seat of the Nissan while the policemen were checking the boot. 'Call me at 7 p.m.,' he whispered, then casually got out of the car again, his Makarov pistol knocking against the door, and walked off down the road. I felt stranded.

Aneez's sudden appearance and disappearance upset the cops. My adrenaline was on overdrive, my heart palpitating wildly, but I had to keep cool and clear-headed. I knew that there were South African security agents in Gaborone who could have tipped off the Cape Town police, but the men searching the Nissan were in uniform, which meant that they weren't security police. Plus, I told myself, if they were aware of the weapons, the anti-terrorist unit would have been deployed. Hoping I was right, I boldly complained that they were harassing me. Just then, one of them noticed the dents in the Nissan. 'Did you knock an animal?' he asked, pointing to a scrap of wool stuck to the front bumper very close to where the hand grenades were stashed. I started telling him about the sheep and the fog near Kimberley, but he interrupted, asking whether I'd reported the accident to the police. I told him I hadn't, but that I planned to report it in Cape Town that day. Then, to my astonishment, the policemen apologised for the inconvenience: they were responding to a call from an elderly white resident about a suspicious-looking car and occupant.

I drove on, parked at the Sea Point Promenade and waited in the car for a few hours, anxious and exhausted. At 7 p.m., I called Aneez from a phone box and we arranged to meet. It was a relief to see him again. Sensing my anxiety, he teasingly reassured me: 'You can stop giving the *boere* a hard time now,' he said, smiling. 'You can relax.' For what felt like the first time in several days, I exhaled.

*

Close to a century earlier, my ancestors Ramesar Nimar and Sanjarie Panchoo, both in their twenties, journeyed thousands of miles across the vast Indian Ocean, disembarking from the *Umzinto XIV* at Port Natal on 1 April 1897. This married couple from Jaunpur in the North Indian state of Uttar Pradesh had travelled from Calcutta under horrid conditions, on a ship carrying indentured labourers. Soon after their arrival in the port city that was to become Durban, they were blessed with the birth of a son, whom they named Bhugwandass (meaning 'Servant of God'): my maternal grandfather. This marked a new beginning on African soil.

A few years after his arrival, Ramesar, now in his early thirties, contracted an illness and died. My great-grandmother, Sanjarie, served out the rest of her husband's contract, working on the sugar-cane plantations in Isnembe, near Tongaat, with her son Bhugwandass.

Sanjarie lived a frugal life and saved her meagre income. At the end of her contract she rented a small farm and planted vegetables. My grandfather attended the first four years of school, but had to forgo his education to work on the farm. The hardworking Sanjarie bought a sewing machine and made shirts and dresses for the indentured labourers, but eventually she continued with the traditional occupation of her *Ahir* ethnic caste – herding cows and working the land – thousands of miles from her Indian homeland.

My grandfather married Ethwaria, who grew up in Sophiatown and was the daughter of indentured labourers. Their marriage was arranged when they were both thirteen years old, only to be consummated at the age of seventeen. They worked with Sanjarie on the farm and had nine children: three boys and six girls. My mother, Geenamathee (a name that refers to the marigold flower), was the youngest child and is the last of that generation still alive today.

After Sanjarie's death in the 1930s, my grandparents continued to build on her resilient and enterprising spirit. Many of the indentured labourers used their limited agency to unshackle the chains of colonial exploitation and victimhood. My grandfather bought freehold property, the Spioenkop Farm in Isnembe, to which the family moved in the mid-1950s. He grew sugar-cane and participated actively in cultural, business and political organisations as a member of the Natal Indian Cane Growers Association and the Natal Indian Congress (NIC). He also donated one acre of land in Tongaat to the Divine Life Society of South Africa, which promoted the compassionate teachings of Swami Sivananda, a revered Indian sage. When my grandfather passed away in the early 1960s, my grandmother continued the family's charity, donating funds for building the Bhugwandass Primary School for the local Isnembe community and for the construction of the teachers' staff room at the Isnembe Secondary School.

My mother did not initially go to school. 'Girls could only wash the pots and clean the house,' she told me once. 'But not me, I wouldn't do that. My father taught me to read and write. I started school late and left in Standard 6.'

My father's first visit to my mother's family in 1956 went well. Bhugwandass liked Billy Haricharan (officially, Brijbehari; *Brij* referring to Lord Krishna and *Behari* to a person from Bihar); he was well mannered, a field worker and the secretary at the Riverside Area Care Committee of the Friends of the Sick Association (FOSA) working on eradicating tuberculosis, an endemic disease due to overcrowding and poverty. After this meeting, he often called my mother from a public phone box during his lunch break. On weekends, he visited my mother from Merebank in Durban, bringing *sev*, nuts and fried *gram dhal*. He was always well groomed and smartly dressed. After six months of courtship, on a rainy summer day, my parents married at my grandparents' home. Hundreds of family and friends attended. She was sixteen years old and he was twenty-nine.

Throughout my childhood, I looked forward to and enjoyed our visits to my grandparents' farm with its mango, banana and citrus orchards. I remember my grandmother, the benevolent and free-spirited matriarch, with fondness: her zest for life, her love for her family. I remember celebrating family events in grand style with live shows such as the popular Riverside dance group and *Nachanyas* with men performing dances dressed in women's clothing and jewellery. When my grandmother passed away in the early 1970s, so too did the family celebrations.

My paternal great-grandfather, Neera Dasruth, was from Patna in Bihar, a northern state in India. As a child of nine, he too journeyed across the Indian Ocean, arriving at the Port of Natal thirteen years before my maternal great-grandparents. He had travelled aboard the *John Davie II* with his parents, his two younger brothers and a sister.

Neera would have one son, my grandfather, Haricharan (meaning 'at the feet of Lord Vishnu'). Haricharan grew up to be a labourer who lived for music, playing the *sarangi* – a classical Indian bowed lute – at weddings and other social events. Both Haricharan and his future wife, Budhani, were born on a sugar-cane estate in Mount Edgecombe, near Durban. In the early 1940s, my father's family moved to Eagle Mount Road, off Duranta Road in Merebank, a mixed area with coloured and Indian people.

My father was forced to leave school in Standard 4 and he soon joined his brothers working shifts at factories. He realised that his destiny was beyond the life of an exploited factory worker, so he attended night school at ML Sultan Technical College, completing his Junior Certificate (JC).

I remember painful childhood stories of my grandfather Haricharan's violent death during the 1949 riots; he was killed on his way home from work during interracial attacks. These attacks came two years after the presidents of the African National Congress, Transvaal Indian Congress and NIC signed a declaration of cooperation. The apartheid regime realised the political and social significance of cooperation between two oppressed communities competing over scarce resources, and there was evidence of a white-led third force that stoked these attacks, exacerbating racial tension.

My father and his large family were saved by the bravery of their unflinching coloured neighbour who stood her ground against a ferocious group of men armed with spears and bush knives at the front door of my father's family home.

In the early 1960s, as a result of the Group Areas Act, Duranta Road would become apartheid's dividing line between coloured people on one side, in Wentworth, and Indians on the other side, in Merebank. I was the last Haricharan child to be born in the house on Eagle Mount Road, on 24 January 1961, eighteen months after my sister Shakila. My name, Shanildutt, was derived from Sunil Dutt, a famous Bollywood actor at the time.

When the Durban City Council started to build low-income houses in Merebank, my family moved to a semi-detached council house at 35 Rawalpindi Road. My younger brother, Sharan, was born here, four years after my birth.

I was five years old when my parents moved to Tongaat on the north coast of Durban, closer to my mother's family. We first lived in a small outbuilding and then in a flat. When I was six, we moved to a tiny cottage of no more than fifty square metres, made of concrete blocks. We had two bedrooms, a sitting room, a tiny kitchen, a pantry that we used as a bathroom, and an outside toilet. It was part of the Vishwaroop Primary School, where I started my schooling, and the Vishwaroop Temple and Dharamshala, where my father was later treasurer.

The town of Tongaat was home to the oldest sugar mill in the country, and was virtually owned by the Tongaat Sugar Company. The company's white managers and professionals lived in Maidstone and Westbrook, while the mostly Indian workers lived in sub-economic houses, distinctive because of their green roofs and doors and white walls. Neighbouring towns on the north coast, like Mount Edgecombe, Verulam and Stanger, were predominantly inhabited by Indian people. On the periphery of these towns, Zulu-speaking people lived in the Zululand homeland. Over time, they replaced the Indian labourers on the sugar-cane plantations.

In Tongaat, my father was a jack of all trades: a hawker, an insurance agent, a Singer sewing-machine salesman and a clothing salesman. We had some tough times during my childhood. In between jobs, or when he was unemployed, my father worked as a casual in shops and as a driver for the local cinema, Ajanta. Together with the cinema owner, Morgan Maistry, they travelled across southern Africa to acquire popular Bollywood movies. In lean times he borrowed money from Morgan. I worked in a clothing shop during the school holidays in my teens.

My father's last and most stable job was with the North Coast Regional Water Services Board in Umhlanga Rocks, initially as a water-meter reader, and later as a supervisor. He did his best to provide for our family. I admired his can-do attitude and his determination in overcoming difficulties in life, whatever the odds.

My mother was a housewife and a doting mother, doing her best to manage the household on a tight budget. We never had a shortage of her love and care. She told us stories of her upbringing and the sacrifices that our forebears had made, instilling their noble values in us. My parents valued respect, kindness, neatness, humility, and a strong work ethic.

The school I attended was built with support from the local Indian community. Initially, I hated school and I resisted attending Class 1 because I was fearful of the new environment and had no friends. But eventually I got used to it. I fondly remember my classmates and me lining up with our stainless steel plates to get *dhal* and brown bread.

My parents showed a keen interest in our education. My mother taught me reading, writing and the multiplication tables. As I progressed through primary school, I became confident and performed well academically. I also made many friends at school and in the neighbourhood.

Schooling in the 1960s and 1970s was highly regimented and punitive: corporal punishment was the order of the day. I had many encounters with this kind of punishment for a variety of offences, such as backchatting and 'rebellious' behaviour, both at home and at school. But what irked me most was the disrespect of the government imposing Christian national education on predominantly Hindu communities. It was farcical: our morning prayers were from the Christian Bible.

In the afternoon, after 'English' primary school, I attended Hindi school, where I learnt to read and write Hindi. My teacher and priest, Mr Panday, read from Hindu scriptures such as the Bhagavad Gita, Ramayana and the Upanishads. I loved the stories from these scriptures, and of Indian leaders, like Nehru and Gandhi, and also writers and poets such as Rabindranath Tagore. The stories taught us about good and evil, compassion, kindness, humility, service and forgiveness. I was drawn to the concept of *ahimsa*: the ethical principle of not causing harm to other living things. During my teens, I became a vegetarian and was drawn to Gandhi's pacifism. But while these values shaped my worldview, my life in an unjust society was at odds with them.

Education was given a high premium among the Indian diaspora and over time became a huge investment for families. Since the days of my great-grandmother Sanjarie, education was seen as the path to overcoming the indignities and hardships of migrant life. In my family, my parents' generation didn't include many professionals, such as teachers, engineers, accountants and doctors. Even in my grandfather's time, very few became farmers like him, and even fewer became professionals. Their destiny was to sell their labour cheaply as workers. My generation had greater access to education, so after completing primary school I went to Victoria School for Standards 6 and 7. I attended Tongaat High School for Standards 8 to 10 (matric). History was my favourite subject, although the curriculum was biased towards Western histories and their leaders, while the history of indigenous people and the liberation struggle in South Africa was absent or distorted.

There wasn't much political activism at my high school and the Soweto student uprising in 1976 had little impact on us. My daily interactions were with Indian people, though I was fortunate to visit my parents' friends in the nearby black township, Hambanathi. I had little contact with white people, except for my father's boss, Mr Shepstone. My political exposure was through attending NIC and civic meetings, interactions with university students and neighbourhood activists, and reading banned literature. My window into making sense of the political landscape subsequently appeared on Saturday afternoons.

My inspirational speech and drama teacher, Dr Muthal Naidoo, was a critical thinker and her classes gave meaning and creative direction to my rebellious and curious spirit. I began to understand how my realities and those of my forebears were intricately linked to the colonial and apartheid systems, and upheld by white, capitalist and Christian supremacy. Dr Naidoo freed my notions of theatre and art based on Bollywood, Hollywood and karate movies, encouraging and challenging me to write plays through the lens of my own reality in Tongaat and South Africa. I read protest plays by Kessie Govender, Ronnie Govender and others, and with fresh eyes I started to observe social and political injustices – the privileges that certain races and classes enjoyed and how this played out in a segregated society – which guided my own writing. The title of my first play was *Chill Penury*, from the line 'Chill Penury repressed their noble rage' in Thomas Gray's poignant poem 'Elegy Written in a Country Churchyard', which we studied at school. My play depicted the harsh experiences of the oppressed working class in Tongaat, and satirised Indian people's attraction to 'superior' white values and lifestyles while black people were treated with condescension, considered untrustworthy, related to as servants, and referred to in derogatory terms.

Steve Biko's writings on Black Consciousness came to have a particularly strong influence on my political awareness in the late 1970s. I was drawn to his provocation to black people to free themselves of the yoke of oppression. My second play – *Your Attention Please, It's Black Detention!* – was a tribute to Biko and, along with *Chill Penury*, was performed for the public in Tongaat. In this play, I aimed to draw attention to Biko's brutal death in detention, and the continued torture of other political activists by the security police. Little did I know that I would find myself in solitary confinement a decade later.

After matriculating, I was accepted to study for a bachelor's degree in pedagogy in the humanities at the Indian-designated University of Durban-Westville (UDW). Due to my fascination with the narratives of other cultures, my plan was to become a history teacher. This was not to happen. Our family dentist, who had studied in India, suggested to my parents that I study medicine or dentistry abroad. I was not interested in studying medicine, but my parents were excited about the option. I was becoming more politically aware and they had heard about UDW students being detained by police or quitting university. The dentist made arrangements with his friend in Bombay and my father borrowed money from Mr Shepstone for my flight, while the progressive Desai family from Tongaat generously provided a scholarship. My friend and classmate Vish Beeput joined me.

In early 1979, I was on another continent, the birthplace of my ancestors. Living in India was a major turning point in my life. At home, everything was segregated, but in India I found myself in a democracy, living in the bustling and vibrant city of Bombay where there was no racial segregation on trains, buses or in public spaces. During my first week, there was a huge march of workers with big banners; their flags and bunting bore the communist hammer and sickle, which was banned in South Africa. Every other week there were marches and protests. People exercised their democratic rights freely – a reality so different from the world I had known across the ocean. Soon, I blended in and became part of Indian society, cherishing my new-found freedom.

I had to complete a higher education certificate before being accepted to medical school, so I spent two years at Wilson College studying chemistry, physics, maths and biology, as well as French and English. I lived in Mackichan Hall, a hostel with students from different parts of Africa and Asia: Rhodesians who had fought in the liberation struggle or were escaping conscription, as well as students from Zambia, Tanzania, Kenya, Mauritius, South Africa, Iran, Iraq and Afghanistan. We interacted as equals and through them I had access to literature banned in South Africa. I still cherish the strong bonds and relationships forged then.

My experiences in India made me question my Hindu religion, however. I was shocked at the dismal lives of the poor, subjugated by their staunch religious beliefs and the dreadful caste system, forcibly or willingly accepting that their fate was ordained by the numerous Hindu gods, or their social status. The caste system reminded me of the apartheid racial order, but instead of black people being discriminated against and treated as inferior, in India it was the *Dalits* or the 'Untouchables' – the lowest caste. Even though India had political freedom and was regarded as the largest democracy, they had social and economic segregation.

In 1980, I visited the ANC Cultural Office in New Delhi to apply for a place at a medical school. The Cultural Office was allocated a quota of medical school admissions for South Africans by the Indian government. After the visit, I realised that my chances of getting a place at a medical school were remote, as few seats were allocated and private institutions' fees were expensive, so I returned home in early 1981.

Back in South Africa, I applied to UDW and the white-designated University of the Witwatersrand (Wits) in Johannesburg. I was accepted at both universities to pursue a Bachelor of Science (BSc) degree, and was excited that Wits offered me a full bursary. Then the reality of apartheid reared its ugly head: I had to get permission from the minister of education to study at a white university. This did not daunt me; I was determined to study at this prestigious university, so, I travelled to Johannesburg to register at Wits without receiving permission to study there.

I arranged to stay with Mike Maharaj, a friend and neighbour from Tongaat. He shared a flat in Branksome Towers, next to Joubert Park in Braamfontein, with other friends from Tongaat working in Johannesburg. A few janitors and landlords in parts of Braamfontein and Hillbrow turned a blind eye to the Group Areas Act, illegally renting flats at higher rentals to mostly Indian and coloured people. I vividly remember my first day in Johannesburg in early February 1982. There was a march to protest the death in detention of

Dr Neil Aggett, a medical doctor and trade union organiser. Mike was a UDW dropout and politically active, and we joined the march and attended the memorial church service downtown.

My hopes to register at Wits were dashed when I received a rejection letter from Minister Gerrit Viljoen's office. It sent me into a rage. I cursed Viljoen and the system he embraced as I tore up the letter, and I was downcast for days after that. Eventually, I decided to resist the minister and his discriminatory laws; after all, I was already breaking the Group Areas Act by living in a white area. I pleaded with the university to register me provisionally without the consent letter, lying that I had not received it yet. My gloom lifted when I was allowed to register with the provision that I submit the letter within a month. This was a gamble, and it made me anxious, but I suffered in silence and did not tell anyone about my predicament, especially not my parents.

Despite the fix I was in, I attended classes diligently and enjoyed physics, chemistry, botany and zoology. I moved out of Mike's flat, as there were too many disturbances and distractions, and shared a room with another person up the road. The living conditions were tough and our desperation was exploited. The police harassed us, taking our names and reminding us that we were living illegally. The white residents swore at us – 'Hey, *coolie*', or 'Hey, *Sammy, fok* off to Durban' – and we were not allowed to use the elevator, although our rental rate was higher than their rent-controlled flats.

In 1982, Wits's residences were predominantly white. I pleaded with the university officials for a room at one of the university's residences, despite studying illegally at Wits. A few other black students and I staged sit-ins at the administration offices, demanding that the residences be opened to all races. I joined the Black Student Society (BSS) and participated in their many protest and resistance activities on campus. Meanwhile, the science faculty continued to demand the consent letter, and I continued to be evasive. At times I was demoralised; my studies were demanding and it was tiring fighting the system at every turn. My living conditions did not get any better either. I fought back thoughts of quitting and returning home.

During this time, I remained on campus most evenings, studying in the library and then walking home to the flat after dark. It was safe to walk alone, but the police often stopped me to search my bags. In winter, the university administration finally offered me a place to stay: a tiny storeroom with a little window at the back of a white residence on Bertha Street. This basement storeroom did not get any sun, and I froze. It was my first experience of the bitterly cold Highveld winter, and I longed for the warmth of my subtropical coastal hometown.

The room had no bathroom, so I had to take the elevator to the roof of the residence to use the workers' toilet and shower. I avoided making eye contact with white students in the lift; I felt denigrated – a second-class squatter in the country of my birth. During one of these trips to the roof, I discovered that I was not the only squatter: three students of colour lived on the roof in what were once workers' rooms. When a room became available, I moved there, elevating my social status. Our resolve in resisting the racist laws regarding university and residence admission policies was finally rewarded when Wits allowed more black students into residences the following year. I subsequently took up residence at Ernest Oppenheimer Hall (EOH) in Parktown. I was now living in the affluent, leafy northern suburbs – a long way from my previous lodgings. I passed all my courses that year and received a bursary for my second year of study.

I did wonder why the faculty office stopped bothering me for ministerial consent to study, and I found out why when I was registering for my second-year courses: the university had intentionally or unintentionally reclassified me as white. I requested that my race be corrected on my registration form. I was proud that I had defied Viljoen and his laws.

Studying at Wits was a great opportunity to interact closely with people of all races. It was fascinating to observe and be part of emerging cultures and subcultures. Here and there, you could catch glimpses of a future non-racial nation, especially during protest action. However, I continued to experience racism at EOH: black and white students ate separately in the canteen, and the pub proudly displayed the Rhodesian flag, welcoming only white students. It was 1983 – Zimbabwe had achieved independence in 1980, and Rhodesia was no more! During my two years' residence, a few progressive white students joined us at meals. Over time, we formed a racially mixed group of friends, sharing similar worldviews, politics and music as well as booze and marijuana.

Early in my second year, I received news that my father was in hospital – he had suffered a severe stroke, paralysing the left side of his body. I returned to Durban to visit him and was devastated when I saw him. My father, who was usually full of energy and always busy, was now incapacitated, his speech slurred. He was not the person I knew. Worse, his work came to an abrupt end: he was medically boarded and unable to hold his job. It had been the first time he'd had stable work where he'd planned to remain until retirement.

My parents were very religious. They prayed daily and observed all the auspicious Hindu ceremonies. My father had dedicated his life to his religion through his work at the temple and serving his community. I was angry with his gods and I was angry with my father for not sticking to his diabetic diet. He'd had a difficult life, toiling to provide for his family and supporting our education, and now my working-class hero was yielding to illness. Nevertheless, my father did not give up.

This was an extremely low point in my life. I was disillusioned and started to lose interest in my studies. But I had to complete my degree: it meant a lot to my parents that I graduate. I persevered, half-heartedly and with many distractions, in a highly tense and vibrant social and political environment, and managed to pass all my second-year courses. I was fortunate to have met Rajes Chetty, a radiographer at the Johannesburg General Hospital, during this period. Her flat was a sanctuary for a number of students and activists. She was always available to offer comfort and was a positive role model when I was dithering with my studies. My caring sister Shakila was another role model, always supportive and motivating. She studied nursing at St Aidan's Hospital in Durban, and on graduating she worked there as a nursing sister. Her big heart and generous nature were lifesavers for the family.

The tide of popular dissent against the state heightened in the mid-1980s. The country was a cauldron of intensified resistance, with protests in townships and elsewhere meeting with the brutal might of the security forces. In 1984, the Tricameral Parliament election was held, the intention being to co-opt Indians and coloureds into the abhorrent apartheid political system, further alienating black Africans. Along with other students, I joined the 'Don't Vote Campaign' protests at polling stations in coloured and Indian areas. We were *sjambokked* and teargassed, then arrested and later released.

All around me was an impetus for change and this revived my spirit. There were many distractions from my academic studies: spiritual, social and cultural, as well as my growing political consciousness. I was discovering my identity, individuality and purpose. I bunked lectures, my grades fell, and I had to write deferred exams, which I did not attend. I had lost my zest for formal education by then – it had become meaningless in the broader scheme of life, and in the face of my personal inner turmoil and the turbulent environment in which I found myself. I was at a crossroads: despite my misgivings about formal education, my parents would be devastated if I quit university. In 1985, I decided to register to complete my outstanding courses.

That year was a tipping point for the nation. President P.W. Botha declared a state of emergency in July. Black townships became battlegrounds under army control. Visiting friends in townships like Alexandra and Soweto became difficult and dangerous.

My personal tipping point came on a hot, blue-sky afternoon in November. I was part of a huge group of students on Jan Smuts Avenue, protesting peacefully with placards against the presence of the SADF in the townships. The riot police were heavily armed, brandishing their *sjamboks* and batons. Suddenly, they charged at us, beating us wildly. We fled onto campus, hounded by the police. As I ran, a burning sensation spread across my back from a *sjambok*, fuelling my fury and my desire for retaliation. A few other victims of the attack shared the same vehemence. It was time for action, time to abandon passive resistance against a violent state.

That evening, some of us decided to make petrol bombs: Ernest Isaacs, a student from Namibia; Craig Mowat, a nursing student; Joe Nxusani, a law student; and a few others. Our target was the petrol station in Jorissen Street, opposite the university, that had allowed the police to park Casspirs on their premises, from where they had attacked us.

I found myself at another crossroads: having to challenge my dearly held principle of non-violence. That night I crossed the line of peaceful resistance and committed my first act of sabotage.

We were disappointed with our amateurish sabotage action, though. The damage to the petrol station was minimal, as its windows were fitted with safety glass. Ernest shared our disappointment and then, to our disbelief, told us of the dynamite that he'd brought from Namibia. His father used it in his farming activities, and a Wits student wanted it for some private non-political activity in East London. It was hidden at the swimming pool at EOH in Parktown.

We agreed to target the university as we resented the authorities' failure to protect students from police brutality and their reactionary position on student protests on campus. Our target was the office of the vice-chancellor (VC). We retrieved the dynamite and fuse, which were damp. As a precaution, we tested the fuse in the middle of the Wits rugby field and were alarmed by the acrid smell and then frustrated that the fuse only burnt a little before going out. Still, we placed the dynamite in a box containing steel nails, and late that night we reconnoitred the main Jorissen Street entrance and lifts to the VC's office. We were ready for the operation.

I drove to Jorissen Street in Craig's old cream-coloured Mazda 323 and waited down the road in the car. Craig and Joe entered the front entrance with the package. They first went up to the concourse to make sure the building was empty. It was now the early hours of the morning. They took longer than planned and my heart was racing. Then, in the rear-view mirror, I saw them casually strolling towards the car without the box, Craig with a cigarette in hand as if he was merely ambling around Zoo Lake. Suddenly, the silence was shattered by a thundering blast, and their casual walk turned into a sprint. Shaken, I shouted at them to get into the car. We had only made it a little way down the road before we began to panic, realising we wouldn't have time to get back to our base in Mayfair before the police were alerted. I remember turning down the next street and passing my former rooftop lodging. I pulled off in front of Dan Robbertse's house; he was a white drama student who had also been *sjambokked* during the protests, and he let us in without question. Minutes later the eerie silence of the morning was disrupted by police sirens.

The next day we received reports of the damage: a huge hole in the floor of the lift and shattered mirrors. It was years before the lift worked properly again.

When I was *sjambokked*, it was not just the physical pain that I felt – it was the pain of all the humiliating moments when my dignity was trampled on. I abandoned my strongly held belief that passive resistance would liberate us and picked up the spear of centuries of fallen heroes, imbued with their fighting spirit.

A month later, I successfully completed my BSc degree and bade a sad farewell to my close comrades and Johannesburg. I returned to my parents' home in Tongaat to ground myself and contemplate my next steps.

A few days before the end of the year, Craig Mowat visited me. We drove a few hundred kilometres to the Transkei, then a bantustan ruled by Kaiser Matanzima. During our visit in Port St Johns, I was moved by a local school principal's plea for maths and science teachers in the homeland. I always enjoyed teaching, having tutored high-school students from townships in Johannesburg on Saturdays. I also fell in love with the warm hospitality of this small town, the stunning Wild Coast and the tranquillity. On our return journey to Durban, we detoured to Umtata to visit the Department of Education, where I completed an application form to teach in the Transkei.

I did not hear anything back from the department until early 1986, and was already planning to return to Johannesburg when I received a telegram. To my surprise I had been appointed as a science, maths and biology teacher at the Maluti Senior Secondary School in northern Transkei, on the Lesotho border. Concerned for my safety, my parents did not share my enthusiasm to live and teach in a remote village in the homeland, but I was excited.

As you enter Maluti, the tar road suddenly disappears, leaving behind the white man's world of geometric agricultural fields and well-fed cattle for the kind of underdeveloped rural area where 70 per cent of the country's population lived: colonised and disenfranchised, relegated to bantustans governed by the white masters' autocratic minions.

I arrived after a day of travelling almost 400 kilometres on public transport from Durban, the last stretch completed in a liberal-minded white farmer's 4 x 4 bakkie. When I tried to find the school I'd been posted to, we mistook it for stables and drove past it. The community had built it using mud blocks and zinc sheeting.

I was welcomed by waving barefoot children carrying school books in plastic shopping bags. Ahead of me, against the backdrop of the majestic Maluti Mountains, were dusty gravel roads, mud rondawels painted turquoise, errant goats and lean cattle. Less than thirty kilometres away was the Lesotho border.

My new life began in a town with no electricity, under the dreaded emergency curfew, which forbade any movement away from your home after 10 p.m. The formal Maluti town centre nestled on a hill. There were two newly built hotels, a general dealer and bottle store, the magistrate's court, a police station and a post office. Below the sparse commercial hub was a sprinkling of formal houses for the professional class: teachers, nurses, lawyers, business owners and policemen – both isiXhosa- and Sesotho-speaking. I checked into the Maluti Star Hotel. The owner, Mr Khoatane, was very welcoming and gave me a discounted room rate; his son was in matric at the school. I was humbled by the appreciation the people of Maluti showed me for journeying to this remote town to teach their children.

Soon after I arrived, I befriended Sandile 'Sai' Nogxina, the smiling public prosecutor, and joined him for gin-and-tonic sundowners at the hotel pub. Over the next few weeks, we spent most evenings discussing politics and the liberation struggle. Sai had recently graduated from the University of Fort Hare in Alice. After sussing me out, he confided that he was an MK commander in the northern Transkei region. I gladly joined his unit.

Earlier that year, the SADF blockaded Lesotho and supported a coup to overthrow the government of Prime Minister Leabua Jonathan, an ANC supporter and critic of the apartheid government, installing their cronies to power. The SADF had previously launched attacks on MK bases in Lesotho, with MK and civilian casualties. There was an exodus of ANC members to other countries in Africa, and therefore MK soldiers were also infiltrating South Africa from Lesotho via Maluti. We helped MK operatives to infiltrate the country through the Transkei, providing them with false passports and safe passage.

Winter arrived and temperatures fell below zero, with snow covering the Maluti Mountains. I froze. There was no electricity at the school, and the many paneless windows let the chill into the classrooms. Nevertheless, it was encouraging to see children from underprivileged homes excelling academically. In between solving quadratic equations and explaining photosynthesis, I subtly shared my social and political awareness with my students.

Corporal punishment was customary at the school, and I took a stand against it. A young teacher, a family friend of Matanzima, aggressively told me: 'I will not spare the rod and spoil the African child.' I challenged this belief, sharing how I had detested teachers with a heavy hand, and how this had affected my learning. Victims of corporal punishment often became victimisers, reinforcing the vicious cycle of abuse.

Sai and I were living double lives: working full-time during the day and doing MK work in the evenings and over weekends. I travelled to Tongaat to buy a second-hand Toyota Corolla to support our unit's work, and we visited MK comrades in the northern Transkei towns: in Mzimkhulu, Raymond Conco and Justice Ndlangisa, a lawyer; in Mount Frere, Gantsho 'Gunman', the regional prosecutor; and in Mount Ayliff, Ndita, a prosecutor. A network within the Transkei government's justice system had been infiltrated by the ANC, even operating in Matanzima's office in Umtata.

In October 1986, Thami Maqelana from Alice in the Ciskei joined us. Once, I drove Sai and Thami to Alice to retrieve weapons and a box of banned ANC and SACP literature. There was heavy police presence in the area. There had been MK attacks across the Transkei and the Matanzima government was under severe pressure. The security police were becoming ruthless and we would soon experience the brunt of their wrath when we were arrested in mid-November.

I was at school when Sai and Thami were arrested. A teacher informed me that a number of security police were searching our house, as well as using metal detectors and digging up our vegetable garden. That evening I travelled to Mzimkhulu to inform the comrades of the arrests. I came hair-raisingly close to crashing into a black cow on a narrow, pitch-dark road just before the town, but otherwise my journey was without incident. The next morning I was off to Mount Frere and Mount Ayliff, driving through heavy mist along winding mountainous roads to receive instructions from the comrades based there. After lengthy discussions, we agreed that I should return to Maluti and monitor the situation. As I pulled into the driveway of our home in Maluti, I saw the security police waiting for me. I was not surprised. We all knew each other, so they were friendly, and I was asked to accompany them to the police station.

At Maluti Police Station they informed me that Sai and Thami were in custody and that I was being detained under the Public Safety Act. Their friendly manner soon turned serious as the interrogation began: 'What were you and the other two terrorists up to?' The mention of the word 'terrorist' sent a bolt of intense fear through me. I described my relationship with Sai using minimal detail, painting him as a friend and housemate. They impatiently probed me to tell them more. 'What activities were you involved in? Which places did you visit together and who did you meet?' I added a few unimportant details. They questioned me about specific incidents, and it became apparent to me that Sai, Thami or another comrade had given them information about some of our visits and activities. My agreement with Sai was that I would deny any knowledge of MK involvement, so I stuck to my legend, despite the threats. The interrogation continued into the night, back and forth, me denying any knowledge of Sai's MK membership and maintaining that I wasn't involved.

The police were civil towards me until later that evening, when their colleagues joined the interrogation. 'Take off your clothes,' they barked. 'Some exercises will help jog your memory.' I was put through a drill of tough physical exercises. When I faltered, I was repeatedly whacked on my knees with a baton. I was not given any food or water.

In the early hours of the morning I was taken to a police cell. The condition of the cell was dreadful: the blanket was riddled with fleas, the toilet stank and the wall was spattered with blood. The damp air seemed to smell of pain and suffering. My fear of what would follow the next morning kept me awake. I thought I had held up fairly well on the first day of interrogation, offering the bare minimum of information and doing my best to avoid betraying my comrades. Before sunrise I was served maize-meal porridge. I had to crawl to the steel gate to collect this much-appreciated meal, my body battered and bruised. Then the interrogation resumed.

The security policemen took turns questioning me. I sensed their impatience and smelt their breath, stale from cheap brandy. They jacked up the tempo, shouting at me, irate at my stubbornness: 'You said *fokkol* yesterday, you are *fokken* wasting our time. We know you were involved in many things. You told us you went to Mzimkhulu, you also went to Mount Frere and Mount Ayliff often, and to the funeral of Sandile's uncle in Redoubt.' As the day dragged on, the strenuous exercises and baton beatings fatigued me and I fell to the ground often, only to be taunted and forced to stand and continue the drill. I had heard about detainees who were suffocated with plastic bags over their heads, as well as other horrors, and I was scared of what brutality was still to come, but I held my ground. In the afternoon, as I was leaving the interrogation room to go to the toilet, I saw Sai and Thami getting out of a police car. At first, I didn't recognise them with their swollen faces, then I was utterly terrified by the realisation that both were showing signs of severe torture. I felt a surge of anger at the cops and sadness for my comrades. The fight left in me was rapidly draining. I thought of escaping, but knew that it would be both futile and fatal, as the police would then have reason to shoot me.

Things got worse that afternoon when two huge white security policemen from Kokstad entered the interrogation room. Earlier in the day I had been asked to write a statement, which I did, repeating what I had maintained during the interrogation: that I was not involved in MK activities. They read the statement and tore it up, raging, 'You *fokken* terrorist, you better start singing or else we will *donner* you good.' They reprimanded the Transkeian police: 'Why are you *fokken* holding back? Just *fokken donner* him!' Then one of them threw a punch at me. Fortunately, a Transkeian policeman intervened. Ironically, at that moment I was grateful that the Transkei was an independent republic, as the South African policemen had no authority in the homeland. If they had taken me to Kokstad, they would have shown no mercy. But after this incident, the Transkeian police were tougher on me. The interrogation continued into the second night.

On the third morning, I crawled out of bed, even more fearful than the morning before. I had hardly slept and I was physically, emotionally and mentally drained. For now, I was rescued from the *boere*, but a second horror would soon emerge in the form of Transkeian security police from Umtata. Just looking at them sent a chill down my spine: dark sunglasses, submachine guns and cowboy attitudes. They wasted no time in getting to the point. With a gun to my head, one barked, 'I read your statement. You are fucking lying. You haven't mentioned many things you and your fucking terrorist friends were involved in. Didn't you drive them to Alice in Ciskei to fetch weapons?' The local security police were livid that I had withheld the Alice trip, among other activities. Torture had undoubtedly forced my comrades to talk.

The security police demanded that I tell them where the 'weapons' I'd brought from Alice were. 'I don't know of any weapons,' I replied.

'You brought back a box!' one of the cowboys snapped.

'Yes,' I said, 'it was a box of books.'

They shoved me around, hitting me. 'We know you took the box of banned books to a shoe shop in Matatiele and that the owner hid it in the ceiling,' they said. I finally agreed that I had done so; there was no point denying what they already knew. Then they showed me a list of the books: 'You will get five years in prison for transporting banned literature; you are guilty of supporting a terrorist organisation.' I insisted I did not know what was in the box and they persisted in asking about weapons. In truth, there were no weapons – we had been unable to retrieve them because of the police presence in the area. After that, they showed me a stack of photographs. I denied having met any of the people in them.

I felt like a caged animal, baited by my torturers, the perverse pleasure of power visible in their eyes as they slowly chipped away at my fortitude. It was as if calling me a 'terrorist' justified the terror of the violent system they served. That week, hour after hour, day after day, my tormentors took turns breaking my spirit, but I resisted, denying them that victory.

I was unaware of the major crackdown across the Transkei during which seventeen MK comrades had been detained and interrogated, including the shoe shop manager in Matatiele. The police desperately wanted the weapons they thought we'd transported; banned literature was not good enough. I knew that there were caches of weapons hidden in the Transkei, but I did not know their location. I was forced to rewrite my statement a few times and I added what I had told them about the box, but stuck to my legend that I was not involved with MK, that I drove Sai to visit friends, and that I was a teacher.

During my first two weeks of detention in the police cell, the Maluti locals expressed their concern and demanded my release. They sent me fruit and milk, which was often denied by the police, and their support strengthened my resolve.

After the first week of intense interrogation, the police eased up on their demands for more information. At the end of the second week, something completely unexpected happened. I was taken to one of the police offices and the foreboding resurfaced – was my interrogation about to resume? Instead, I was shocked to see my parents, as well as my mother's nephew, Reggie Bhugwandass, and his wife, Premi. I later learnt that the security police had initially refused to let them see me, but Reggie had approached the magistrate, a compassionate colleague of Sai's, who granted them permission and repri-manded the police for denying my ill father access to me. My family brought me home-cooked food and assured me that Rabi Bhugwandeen, a lawyer and family friend, was aware of my detention and was trying to get me released. I was relieved to see them and felt reassured that I had legal support. The reunion was short and very emotional. I sensed their extreme anxiety, and I realised that it must have been a long journey for my father in his condition. He did not show his concern openly, though, and instead made a fatherly remark that once I was released, I should go to a barber shop for a shave.

Soon after their visit, with no explanation or warning, I was signed out of the police station and driven out of town, towards Matatiele. The dreadful knot in my stomach returned with the uncertainty of our destination. We left

Maluti, the mountains disappearing behind us, and the speeding police car turned towards Mount Fletcher, hooting at the donkeys in the road. We stopped outside the Mount Fletcher Prison.

I was transferred to one of six single cells, each not more than five square metres. On the steel door, visible under a thin coat of paint, were the words 'Isolation Cell'. There was a straw bed, a toilet and, high in the wall, a small window. I was relieved that the blanket was clean and not flea-infested. Outside the row of cells there was a narrow passage with high walls. A heavy door led to the other inmates. I was allowed to walk and exercise in the passage for an hour in the morning and in the afternoon.

I settled into a routine, although the uncertainty about my future was unnerving. I was completely cut off from the rest of the world. No one knew where I was. The warders were generally kind to me and I earned their trust. Thankfully the food was marginally better. For all three meals I was given maize meal, either as porridge or the firmer version, pap, sometimes served with spinach and beans, and once a week I got a small piece of meat. I was relieved at the reprieve from interrogation but the security police did not give up so easily and frequently visited to threaten me: 'You are now going to get a minimum of fifteen years, not five years.' 'Your name is on the list with seventeen other terrorists who will appear in court in Umtata.' 'If you tell us where the weapons are and who else was involved, you can leave at once.' I did not know whether I would actually be charged or whether they were just trying to scare me.

After the first week, with no contact with anyone except for rare visits from the prison officials, depression gradually set in. The thought of fifteen years' imprisonment distressed me. It was December and I was mentally preparing myself to spend Christmas and New Year in the tiny cell, but the uncertainty about how long I would be held in solitary confinement wore me down. I would be turning twenty-six the following month.

While I sat there, I was reminded of the previous year, when I had spent New Year's Eve in a Port St Johns police cell for breaking curfew. Craig and I had arrived in Port St Johns on 31 December, pitched our tent on a nearby farm in Lusikisiki, and spent the day in the small town. In the evening, on our return to Lusikisiki, we were stopped at a police roadblock and arrested for breaking the state of emergency curfew. We were held at the Port St Johns Police Station overnight, along with mothers with babies and small children, all of us thrown into dark, crowded, damp and smelly cells. On my release the next morning, I had been furious and had yelled at the cops: 'Matanzima's a bloody dictator!' The police had threatened to detain me. I had not imagined that I could be in a cell again within a year.

My isolation at Mount Fletcher Prison allowed me to reflect on my life: my childhood, my family, my journey of political consciousness, my joys and my regrets. At dusk, as the familiar sounds of the birds outside my cell window faded and disappeared, the depression would descend in all its darkness. I thought of my parents and their sacrifices, and I felt guilty that I had let them down through my political activism. My mother's tearful eyes as she bade me farewell the week before haunted me. I thought of my father's brave face, masking all the hours he would have sat agonising about my welfare, shedding his silent tears, and my parents' daily prayers for the Hindu gods to protect me – the gods I had forsaken for the revolutionary romanticism of Karl Marx's society where no one is born into a social class and everyone is equal in the common quest to be 'fully human'.

At other times I would be resolute and pleased with my decisions. I'd tell myself that a system that robs us of our full humanity must be destroyed, and that I would not allow it to break me down. 'I will fight it to the end,' I told myself. 'We will be free.' I also felt stronger when remembering comrades who had spent many months in solitary confinement, or decades in prison. Here I was in the Transkei, the birthplace of many ANC leaders such as Nelson Mandela, Oliver Tambo, Walter and Albertina Sisulu, and Chris Hani, as well as a line of Xhosa kings including the great Hintsa. Like his counterparts in Natal, King Cetshwayo and King Langalibalele, Hintsa had fought the British colonists 150 years before, and was executed for his dream of freedom. It was humbling to be on sacred ground.

After four weeks in detention, I was released and driven to Maluti. The mountains were a welcome sight as we headed to the police station. The police commander handed over my ID and reprimanded me for associating with terrorists. 'You are not allowed to work for the Transkei government,' he said. 'It is a pity we will lose you as a teacher. You are free to leave now.' The word 'free' had a strange and welcome ring to it.

With a heavy heart, I bade farewell to friends and students in Maluti. The long drive to my parents' home in Tongaat would have been a lonely one, but thankfully my brother, Sharan, had been willing to travel hundreds of kilometres to fetch me. I always knew I could trust his loyalty to the struggle and depend on him whenever I was in trouble or need.

I spent Christmas and New Year with my parents, and in January 1987 I returned to Johannesburg. With every trip it seemed I was growing more feet, like a millipede or *songololo* – a nickname I would soon be given.

In those days, many former detainees put on a mask of normality to hide the effects of their traumatic experiences. I joined their ranks. Detainees usually received legal aid after their release, but hardly any psychological support. Initially, I found it difficult to adapt, haunted by my experience. But instead of instilling fear, my detention fuelled my anger and strengthened my resolve to continue fighting. There was no middle road; I had no doubts about the path I had to follow.

I felt more comfortable in Johannesburg, as I knew the terrain and I could reconnect with friends and comrades. I also knew I could continue working in alternative education programmes and non-governmental initiatives for children from the townships. I moved into a place in Mayfair with Joe Nxusani, my comrade from university, his partner, Cecily, and their toddler son, Che. Joe had recently returned from a visit to Zimbabwe, where he had tried to make contact with the ANC. I shared my Transkei experience with him.

I was settling in well and felt grounded in Johannesburg. Then, at around 5 a.m. one morning, there was a loud banging on the front door. Cecily opened it. The security police stormed in and two others entered through the back door. They were looking for me. I was asleep in the back bedroom when the cops grabbed me out of bed and pushed me around. They fumed at the struggle posters on the walls – COSATU, End Conscription Campaign (ECC) and others – hurling abuse at the white ECC 'traitors'. Joe appeared, seething. 'Get out of my home, you fucking pigs,' he yelled, and was nearly arrested for interfering with my arrest.

A few cops searched the house frenetically and were jubilant when one found cassettes with struggle songs and the tricolours of the ANC that Joe had brought back from Zimbabwe. I was bundled into one of their cars. To my horror, seated in the car were the two security policemen from Kokstad who had interrogated me in Maluti.

I was taken to the security branch interrogation rooms at the notorious John Vorster Square. It was here in 1971 that the twenty-nine-year-old school-teacher and SACP activist Ahmed Timol was brutally tortured and thrown out of a tenth-floor window. After this tragic incident, the security police coined the phrase 'Indians can't fly'.

The security police informed me of a bomb blast in Matatiele earlier in the year, after I had left Maluti. They had information from people in Matatiele that I had been 'politicising' people to join the underground. I was guilty of recruiting, but I had not been directly involved in the blast. In the afternoon, the two policemen ended their interrogation and I was handed over to Indian security police. They arrogantly stated that I would now be working with them, providing information about the activists in Johannesburg. On my release, one of the policemen brazenly handed me a card with his name and phone number. A few days later, I moved to a flat in downtown Johannesburg, as it was unsafe to live at Joe's.

In March 1987, a chance encounter with Aneez Salie at Rajes Chetty's flat in Hillbrow propelled me back into MK. I had met Aneez at Rajes's flat a few years before and knew he was a political activist and unionist from Cape Town. We reconnected, and I told him about my MK involvement in the Transkei. There was some mutual connection between him and one of the comrades in the Transkei. After a few more conversations we gained each other's trust, and Aneez started the process of recruiting me into his Cape Town unit.

Soon, we were off to Botswana to make contact with an MK commander called Faiz, who turned out to be James Ngculu. I had been told that the police officers at the Bophuthatswana border post were open to bribes and, because Aneez's forged passport was of poor quality, I bribed the police officer with booze. For the next four years, I crossed the Botswana border several times via Ramatlabama and Kopfonteinhek, fetching weapons, communications and money. I had two passports, my own and another with a false name. I held on to my old passport with all the border post stamps in it and still have it today.

I was instructed to set up an MK unit in Johannesburg to act as the link and conduit between the Cape Town unit and MK Military HQ via James in Botswana. One of the reasons for setting up the Johannesburg unit was that the security police were tracing calls, and MK units were being detected through direct communication with Botswana. We used public phone boxes to contact each other and a system of codes to communicate. The Johannesburg unit also served as a contact point for comrades leaving or entering the country, such as Cape Town cadres Ismail and Julie Vallie, whom I took to Gaborone to meet James and fetch weapons. Anton Fransch, Mark Henry and Timothy Jacobs were also supported on their return to Cape Town after receiving training in Angola.

Over time, I recruited Joe Nxusani, who was then a labour attorney at Cheadle Thompson and Haysom; Mike Dearham, a Wits medical student who had dropped out; and Richard Ishmail, a former Wits classmate whom I knew well. Richard had been socially active at university and was the key driver in setting up the Club for Social Action at Wits, which organised social and cultural events on campus, creating a space for mostly black students to social-ise. I personally introduced Joe, Mike and Richard to James in Gaborone.

There were always roadblocks after Gaborone, and then again in the first town in South Africa – Zeerust – or just outside Mafikeng. 'Where are you coming from?' the soldiers and police would always ask. 'Do you have any weapons in your car?' My adrenaline would be peaking but I'd smile and calmly answer: 'No, officer.' Then they'd ask if they could search my car and I would have no choice but to oblige. Sometimes there were sniffer dogs and I was scared senseless. I really admired the comrades in Botswana who cached weapons in the cars we drove – they did a great job. Materials were generally cached in the fender, door panels, and behind the rear seat in a special compartment in the Nissan Skyline, and explosives in the spare tyre. While I always felt an overwhelming sense of relief after passing a roadblock, I had to remain vigilant, as there could always be another one before Johannesburg. There was no time to slack off.

Once, while Shirley Gunn and I were couriering weapons from Johannesburg to Cape Town, I saw a coloured soldier hitchhiking in Worcester. I mentioned it to Shirley, who told me to pull over and pick him up. 'He'll be a good cover,' she explained. I stopped, and the soldier jumped in. Shirley chatted away to him in Afrikaans. He told us about his family and where he lived, his army base and other details, oblivious to the fact that he was sitting in the enemy's car, carrying illegal Russian and Eastern European weapons that would potentially be used in attacks on the SADF. Julie and Ismail later told me about picking up a soldier en route to Cape Town from Botswana in a car loaded with weapons. The high-ranking officer drove their car for a good part of the trip, breezing through army roadblocks. Mike Dearham also had a similar story from when he couriered weapons from Botswana.

For the next two years in Johannesburg, I worked as a teacher and MK cadre. I received military training and couriered weapons, communications and money from Botswana to Cape Town a number of times. I also shared verbal briefings between the AKD commanders and James, who in turn communicated with the MK High Command. As in Lesotho, SADF Special Forces raided MK bases in Botswana, resulting in the fatalities of MK cadres, refugees and Botswana civilians. I had many encounters during this time, some of them disturbing. Once, in early 1988, I arrived in Gaborone after an SADF attack on ANC safe houses and found a distraught James. He had survived the attack; others were not as lucky.

I often visited my MK commanders, Aneez and Shirley, in Cape Town for briefings, debriefings and training in intelligence, reconnaissance, military hardware, priming limpet mines and using weapons such as AK-47s, hand grenades and Makarov pistols. In 1987, the security police had bragged that they had broken the back of MK in the Western Cape. The operations the AKD subsequently carried out totally undermined them. During a visit in early 1988, I reconnoitred a French bank next to Parliament. A few days after my return to Johannesburg, Shirley planted a bomb on the wall shared by the bank and the adjacent building in retaliation for the assassination of Comrade Dulcie September, who had been shot five times in the head outside the ANC's Paris office.

During another of my visits to Cape Town, Ismail Vallie and I were instructed to plant a limpet mine at the Cape Technikon in District Six, close to the city centre. I did not hesitate to undertake the operation. I was aware of the history of District Six and the significance of the target: the technikon had been built for white students on the very land from which people of colour had been forcibly removed by the apartheid authorities, despite the community's intense resistance. Ismail had deep emotional bonds to District Six: he was born there, had lived there with his paternal grandmother, his parents and siblings, and had been a victim of the Group Areas Act.

I primed the limpet mine in the car, and then Ismail and I walked down a steep grass embankment to a back entrance of the technikon, where I placed the limpet. It was a dark evening. My heart pounded as we clambered up the embankment to Ismail's car. My glasses fell off and, half blind, I groped around trying to find them. Ismail was agitated, telling me to leave them behind, but I could not – they would be evidence for the police, who would surely be on the scene soon after the explosion. Ismail then helped me search, found my glasses, and we hurriedly drove off into the night. We heard about the explosion on the news the following day.

In December 1988, I was redeployed to Cape Town to join Aneez and Shirley. They were hiding out in a secluded cottage in Constantia to await the birth of their child, so I settled into the hot summer in a small bachelor flat in Clifton, not anticipating the havoc that would soon unfold. On 10 January 1989, on national television, minister of law and order Adriaan Vlok framed Shirley for the bombing of Khotso House, the headquarters of the South African Council of Churches and offices of other anti-apartheid organisations in Johannesburg. Her face appeared in all the newspapers and on television. I had to vacate the flat in Clifton immediately: Shirley was renting it and she'd lived there long enough for neighbours to recognise her. She and Aneez abandoned the Constantia cottage.

The three of us moved to Shirley's friend Dr Roli Bloomberg's house on Princess Street in Mowbray, which he was sharing with Sue Kramer and Saaliegah Zardad. Because Aneez, Shirley and I were holed up in Roli's bedroom, which he kindly gave up, Saaliegah arranged with brothers Yusuf Sayed and Rashid Ahmed to share their flat on the same street. Thus began our sojourning from one temporary safe house to another, and it became my task to find safe houses for the AKD command.

The police had confiscated my Toyota Corolla, which Aneez had abandoned in Athlone after a hot pursuit from the safe house in Constantia. I was fearful that they might find my false passport hidden under the carpet behind the accelerator pedal. A few of my belongings were also in the boot, including my microscope and books. Until my car was impounded, the security police in Cape Town didn't know of my presence in the city. I grew a beard and wore Irish flat caps to disguise myself. However, I was still relatively unknown and could move around more freely, while Aneez and Shirley's faces had both appeared on TV.

Shirley was eight months pregnant when Vlok made the announcement, so I arranged clandestine evening visits to Dr Peter Roos, a sympathetic gynae-cologist practising at Vincent Pallotti Hospital. Dr Roos made arrangements for the birth at Somerset Hospital in Green Point.

A few weeks later, Shirley's contractions started, and we drove to Somerset Hospital from our safe house in Northpine, a coloured area near Brackenfell, thirty kilometres from the city. In the early hours of the morning, under cover of darkness, we entered the hospital through a back entrance. I acted as Shirley's husband, a fictitious Mr McKenzie, and completed the admission forms. At eight the next morning, on 21 February 1989, Haroon Gunn-Salie was born – a joyous and triumphant moment for us. He was named after Imam Haron, a Cape Town struggle activist killed in detention by the security police in 1969. I fetched Aneez and we arrived shortly after the birth.

It was fascinating to see how well Haroon adapted to the constrained underground conditions; not an ideal environment for a baby. His smile melted away the tensions of underground life. We developed a strong bond in the first few years of his life, and when he started to talk he called me Nene, which he still does. I remember shopping at the Brackenfell Pick 'n Pay Hypermarket for baby things. This was new to me, and kind, curious mothers would sometimes sense my uncertainty and come to my rescue in the baby aisle, sharing tips and advice. I deeply admired how Shirley continued to be Haroon's caregiver, breastfeeding him while actively engaging as a disciplined commander in our operations. Some evenings, under cover of darkness, Shirley and Aneez would leave the house to communicate with comrades. They always left separately and Shirley always wore a scarf. We read every newspaper in Cape Town, tracked news bulletins on radio and TV throughout the day and night, and performed routine route checks when we travelled. Security and constant vigilance were critical to our survival.

During 1989, I taught part-time at the Libra College in Observatory. I took a minibus taxi to Bellville Station from Northpine, then a train to Salt River Station, from where I would walk to Observatory, returning in the late afternoon, constantly checking over my shoulder. The money I earned went to the AKD unit. Shirley and Aneez had nicknamed me Songo, short for Songololo, the millipede, as I travelled so often between Gaborone, Johannesburg and Cape Town, as well as across the city, connecting with our comrades. I arranged secret meetings with Johnny Issel, Zubeida Jaffer and other UDF activists, who briefed us on what was happening on the ground. I had a few *noms de guerre*: in Cape Town I was Shafiek and Ben, and in Botswana I was Ismail. Like the rest of us, baby Haroon also had a code name: Tim, after slain activist Ahmed Timol.

I remained the link to the Johannesburg unit commanded by Richard Ishmail after my deployment to Cape Town, and I continued to travel to Gaborone, taking communications from the AKD commanders to James, providing briefings to members of the MK High Command and returning with communiqués. On one of these trips something catastrophic happened. I was rushing back from Botswana by rental car to Jan Smuts Airport in Johannesburg to catch a flight to Cape Town, carrying money, route sketches to cached arms, and communications. On the N14 between Ventersdorp and Krugersdorp, I was driving close behind a truck when it veered around a bend and onto the gravel shoulder. A hail of red sand and stones rained down on my windscreen. I lost control of the car around the bend, tried to brake on the gravel, slid across the road and rolled. My head was hurled back and forth and sideways, hitting the steering wheel. The car finally landed on its roof in the highveld grass. I lost consciousness.

When I regained my senses, I was lying outside the car in the blazing mid-afternoon sun. I must have crawled out of the driver's window. At first, I was unable to see, but after a few terrifying minutes I slowly recovered sight in one eye. The clear blue sky stared back at me. Relieved that I was not totally blind, I turned my attention to the throbbing pain in my right eye, through which I had no vision. A sharp pain shot through my neck and chest as I tried to lift myself and I became deeply distressed, wondering if I might be paralysed. Burning tears streamed down my aching, dusty face. Then the real terror hit me: where were the communications, the route sketches and the money that was cached in the car? Dreading that the police would discover them, I tried crawling back to the car but it was impossible to move. I was shattered, feeling completely vulnerable and stranded.

Finally, I got a grip on myself, bracing for the worst. I called on my fighting spirit for courage. A deliveryman on a motorbike stopped and promised to call for help. After many minutes, an ambulance appeared on the road. I could hear shouting – '*Hy's Indies*' (He's Indian) – then the sound of a vehicle departing. The ambulance had left because I was not white. I seethed with rage. This was just another reminder of why I had to stay alive and fight. Some time later, another ambulance arrived and I was taken to the Leratong Hospital in Krugersdorp, the closest black hospital.

I lay in the hospital passage on a stretcher, unattended but in severe pain. I cried out for medical attention, afraid that I had internal bleeding. Then I saw bloodied black youths streaming in and I was told that I had to wait: 'We have to attend to the gunshot wounds first.' Leratong was like a hospital in a war zone, in total chaos. Finally, at about 7 p.m., I was admitted into a ward. X-rays were taken and I was given painkillers. I had never experienced such intense pain before, nor such helplessness. I lay there at my wits' end, worrying about the illegal contents of the car and when the security police would walk into the hospital to interrogate me.

A kind hospital administrator finally called my sister Shakila, who was living in Hillbrow, informing her of my accident and passing on a message for Richard. He arrived at the hospital soon after and was shocked to see my condition. I told him about the items in the car and urged him to retrieve them at once.

I slept badly that night and had strange nightmares of wild creatures taunting me. It was, of course, my fear of the cops that summoned these demons.

Richard returned to the hospital the next morning with a big smile. 'I got them,' he said. He had been unable to find the car on the roadside, so he went to the police, who directed him to a tow-truck company. He then went to the tow-truck yard with a close friend, Andre de Jongh, but was confronted by two vicious guard dogs. Andre distracted the dogs while Richard jumped over the fence to retrieve the items cached in the car. Afterwards, he safely dispatched the contents of the car to the commanders in Cape Town. I discharged myself later that morning and Richard drove me to my sister's flat. Shakila, a nurse, knew the doctors at the hospital and covertly arranged check-ups with a physician and an eye specialist. I had dislocated a few ribs, and although my eye was not irreparably damaged, it would remain swollen and tender for some time. I needed care and rest to heal, so Shakila arranged with Richard that I would stay secretly with my parents in Tongaat until I recovered, as agreed to by my AKD commanders. My family was aware of my continued involvement in the underground struggle and respected that nobody should know I was there.

I was fearful of the security police, but glad to be home. My family were overjoyed to see me, although very concerned about my condition. My aunt, whose son Reggie had come to visit me during my detention in Maluti, insisted on preparing a hot poultice of aloes, turmeric and other herbs and bandaged it around my chest, despite the fact that I was on anti-inflammatory medication.

I spent about a week in Tongaat before I had to return to my fighting post in Cape Town – I knew that my commanders depended on me and that staying at my family home was too high a risk.

It was tough bidding farewell to my parents. They were unhappy that I had to leave, as I still needed to heal. Fortunately, when I arrived in Cape Town, Sue Kramer, a physiotherapist and activist whom I had met at the Mowbray safe house, treated me in secret for the whiplash injuries to my neck and back. Only decades later did I discover that the vertebrae in my neck had been damaged in the crash.

The AKD command's stay in the Northpine house was to be short-lived. Around Easter 1989, Anton Fransch and Mark Henry joined us at the house temporarily for briefings to prepare them for deployment to AKD units. Our aim was to build strong underground structures to sustain the armed struggle, as instructed by MK's High Command. I fetched Anton and Mark from the railway station in a kombi and drove them blindfolded so they were unaware of where we lived. I fondly remember the likeable Anton; he had a distinctive warm smile, and was always keen to help with domestic chores or play with Haroon. Mark was impatient and restless, itching for combat action in order to kill as many *boere* as possible.

One day, Mark jumped out of a window and deserted his post. All hell broke loose. This was insubordination and a major security breach: he knew our identities and where we lived. The command structure went into emergency mode once again, and I had to find another safe house immediately. Aneez, Shirley, Haroon and I moved to an isolated farmhouse on a small-holding near Kuils River. After a few months, due to security considerations, we returned to a second house in Northpine.

I blended in with the neighbours by establishing a similar routine – going to work, shopping, working in the garden and doing other everyday activities. My legend, for the benefit of my new next-door neighbour, was that I was waiting for my wife and baby to join me. The neighbours were unaware of Shirley, Aneez and baby Haroon, who also lived in the house at the time, as well as Richard Ishmail, who stayed there intermittently. Mike Dearham, who had returned from his training in radio communication in Zambia, joined us with his wife, Kim. I had known Kim from when I lived in Johannesburg and we would take Haroon for walks in his pram in the neighbourhood, masquerading as a married couple.

Anton moved to the flat in Clifton, and I joined him there for a brief time. In the evenings we would sit on the small balcony sharing our dreams for when we achieved liberation. He had a copper bangle from his girlfriend, Nicky Asher, and he spoke fondly of her. Mostly, he spoke passionately about his aspirations and how he would rebuild his Bonteheuwel community once we were free. Anton, who was in his early twenties, was politically mature, and I was encouraged by his youthful optimism for rebuilding our divided society. Our revolutionary cause inspired us and kept us going – a dream so powerful that youngsters like Anton were prepared to make great sacrifices, including the arduous and dangerous journey to MK training camps in Angola, in order to return to courageously continue the armed resistance.

After his stay at the Clifton apartment, Anton moved to a bedsit with a separate entrance in Athlone. I kept in contact with him, briefing him and reporting back to our commanders. One day, Anton met Mark in the street. He took him to his hideout and tried to convince him to return to the AKD. Soon after that, the AKD commanders heard that Mark had been arrested. We were afraid for Anton's safety and I immediately tried to call him to warn him to leave the house, but his landlady informed me that the lights in his room were off and he wasn't home. 'Please, this is an emergency,' I pleaded desperately. 'As soon as he arrives, tell him that his uncle has passed away and the funeral is tomorrow.' This was a red alert – code to vacate the place and remove the weapons cached there. I called many times until late at night, going out to different public phone boxes each time – a security precaution as there was a real possibility that the police may have tapped her line. I left urgent messages but the landlady repeated what she'd told me earlier – 'His room is dark, he's not in' – until her patience ran out and she told me to stop disturbing her. I begged her to give Anton the message as soon as he returned. At that point, I was desperate enough to go over to his place myself, but for security reasons, I didn't know where it was. I constantly briefed Aneez and Shirley on the situation. We ultimately decided that it was too risky to send anyone to his place, as it might already be under police surveillance.

Early the next morning, I drove from Northpine to Hout Bay, fifty kilometres away, and called the landlady from a phone box at the Hout Bay Post Office. 'It's you again! Who are you?' she shouted when she recognised my voice. 'The police shot at my house! My house is a mess! Your cousin is dead!' I slammed down the receiver, dazed and trembling, then slumped to the floor, tears streaming down my face. I felt rage building up within me, and I started cursing the police and Mark for selling out Anton to the enemy. I wondered how I should communicate this shocking news to the commanders.

We learnt later that Anton had arrived at his base around midnight, where he was confronted by the police. For seven hours this brave warrior had taken on the might of the security forces in a standing battle. He died on Church Street in Athlone that Friday morning, 17 November 1989.

On 11 February 1990, those of us at the Northpine house celebrated Nelson Mandela's release together. We watched the historic event on TV with tears of joy and sadness. Outside, in the distance, I could see the helicopters hovering over Victor Verster Prison. Later that day, Mandela's message during his speech was clear: that the armed struggle would continue. We obeyed our commander-in-chief: that night, the AKD carried out attacks at Newlands Cricket Ground, in protest against the English rebel cricket tour, and at the Parow Civic Centre and the Paarl Magistrate's Court. I visited Gaborone during this time, and our MK commanders instructed us to maintain the armed struggle. There were reservations about laying down our weapons, as we did not trust the apartheid regime's security forces. We moved house again, this time to a house in Zeekoevlei in the Southern Suburbs.

In June 1990, just seven months after Anton's death, the AKD was dealt another blow: Shirley was arrested with Haroon and detained for sixty-three days. The news of her arrest shocked us, and we were very scared and concerned for her safety in the hands of the ruthless security police. I was deeply disturbed and furious that Haroon had been detained and kept in solitary confinement along with Shirley, and then heartlessly removed from her while he was still breastfeeding and in need of comfort and security.

After Shirley's arrest, Aneez, Mike, Richard and I moved our safe house yet again, this time to Church Street in Athlone, not far from where Anton had heroically fought the security forces, and we stayed here throughout the initial political negotiations. The atmosphere in the house was more relaxed but still very uncertain, so we remained vigilant in the underground. Aneez and I were among the last to surface, as we were responsible for AKD's weapons and only received indemnity from prosecution for our MK activities in late 1991.

It was sad to leave Cape Town, where I had forged such close bonds with comrades in the AKD, people who'd been our support structures, and others. It had been demanding and daunting living in the trenches, involved in activities that tested one's resolve daily, living under fear of capture, torture and death. But there had also been many joyous and light-hearted moments. Ahead lay the 1600-kilometre road to Tongaat and my parents in my liberated old Toyota Corolla. Taswell Papier, an activist attorney, had collected my impounded car from the police after Aneez had been forced to abandon it, and had retrieved the cached false passport.

I left Cape Town in December 1991 with a small bag of clothes and a little money to tide me over for a few months, relieved to leave behind my bag of weapons – an AK-47, ammunition and hand grenades. I knew our struggle for freedom was still not over, but I drove back to Durban to regain my life as a civilian with a sense of transitory freedom.

I had always returned home for short periods to stabilise and ground myself, only to take off again, but when I returned to my parents' home in Tongaat this time, I realised that I'd come full circle. My parents were overjoyed that my underground days were over and I had returned safely. I reconnected with my brother, Sharan, and his family, and I was delighted to see my charming three-year-old niece, Shareesha, lovingly called Sasha, and my parents' 'adopted' neighbour's son, Prashen. My extended family and friends welcomed me, though only a few knew of my political activism. After six years in the underground, I was glad to be able to return to everyday life, although it was difficult at first. Comrade Chris Hani warned us not to trust the security forces after our indemnity and I continued to look over my shoulder for a while.

Once back in Tongaat, I connected with comrades Sagie Pillay, Shirley Raman, Logie Naidoo, Siva Naidoo and many others, and joined the local ANC branch and the Tongaat Civic Association. Former Robben Island prisoner Billy Nair, endearingly called Muna, took me under his tutelage. It was strange to openly associate with ANC members; when I joined the underground it was a banned organisation. After a year of locum teaching at a high school in Tongaat, I was employed by the Tongaat Child and Family Welfare Society (TCFWS), initially as a community development officer, working in informal settlements, and later as the director. I also participated in the transitional local government negotiations process, as part of the non-statutory team, and I helped to organise the South African Democratic Teachers Union (SADTU) march in Tongaat, with hundreds of teachers from all over the North Coast demanding teachers' right to join a union. This level of engagement assisted my integration into public political life.

My community development work in the expanding informal settlements on the periphery of Tongaat made me realise the depth of poverty and the huge challenges a democratic government would have to redress. The first settlement I worked in was Umbhayi, an ANC stronghold. Nearby was Gwala's Farm, an area aligned with the Inkatha Freedom Party (IFP). There were running battles between these two communities, with opposing ideologies competing for political dominance. After many discussions with the IFP leadership, I started working in Gwala's Farm. By building strong bonds of trust and service, irrespective of political affiliation, we supported peace-building and development. During this time I completed a postgraduate diploma in adult education at Natal University to equip me for my community facilitation and education projects.

An emotional climax in my life was casting my ballot at a remote voting station on the outskirts of Tongaat, in the country's first democratic elections on 27 April 1994. My heart was heavy as I drove towards Durban that evening to observe the vote-counting as an ANC party agent. I recalled the pain and suffering of millions of South Africans, over hundreds of years, to get to this day. Most vivid was Anton Fransch's charming smile, which brought me to tears. I also remembered the charismatic Chris Hani, whose funeral I had attended a year before at the FNB Stadium in Soweto. That day, standing in the middle of the football field as part of the funeral procession, in the traditional pleated blue Cuban shirt Hani had gifted me, I had felt the astounding force of people's power reverberate from the tens of thousands of people in the stands.

In May 1994, I journeyed to Pretoria with my mother and comrades from Tongaat to join the thousands of jubilant compatriots on the grounds of the Union Buildings for Mandela's inauguration, cheering and proudly raising our new flag.

Another memorable moment during this period was when Mandela visited Tongaat in October 1994, and I was part of his security team. When Mandela arrived at the hall, I greeted him and we shook hands. He walked straight to the large crowd of people that had gathered outside the hall, exuberantly shouting, 'Mandela, Mandela, Mandela!' The security team was in a panic, fearful for his safety due to the lingering animosity between the ANC and the IFP, but Mandela chided us in his authoritative voice: 'Let me meet my people', ruining hours of planning and detailed security measures. I was struck by his warmth, his authentic connection with the masses and his apparent lack of fear for the possible threat to his life.

Billy Nair officially welcomed Mandela to Tongaat, an emotional reunion of two struggle stalwarts who had spent many years together on Robben Island. Mandela spoke fondly of his memories of hiding in Tongaat as the 'Black Pimpernel' in the early 1960s, thanking the families that provided him with safe houses. He spoke passionately of reconciliation and peace-building to end the conflict in KwaZulu-Natal.

In late 1995, after almost four years of community development work in Tongaat, Songololo's itchy feet would yet again carry him to Johannesburg. During the next three years, I had the privilege to serve in our new democratic government as a senior manager in the Gauteng provincial government. I was responsible for developing policies in development planning to redress the segregated social landscape we inherited. I commissioned research and set up partnerships with progressive academics and NGOs, and led study tours with politicians and officials from provincial and local government, including the private sector, to learn from experiences in both developed and less-developed countries, such as India, Brazil, USA and UK in urban regeneration and people-centred development, planning and delivery. I also drew on my learning from the MSc coursework I completed in urban and regional planning at Natal University.

During one such visit to New York in 1996, my comrade from Cape Town, Zubeida Jaffer, introduced me to her Columbia University classmate and friend Hanne Jensen, whom I would marry in Johannesburg later that year. I cherish our loving relationship, which has provided me the stability and grounding I needed after years of moving around. Over the years, I enjoyed getting to know Hanne's large, warm and welcoming Danish family, and I proudly guided them on many travels across our beautiful country.

After three years in Johannesburg, my Songololo feet would transport me back to Cape Town, where I currently live. With the birth of our two beautiful children, Milan (which means 'sacred union' in Hindi) on 21 November 2000, and Anna-Malika ('gracious princess') on 12 July 2003, I would experience the joys of family life. Fatherhood is a precious experience, and children are excellent teachers. I remember having goosebumps watching Milan and Anna-Malika in primary school with their classmates from diverse backgrounds, proudly singing our new national anthem, devoid of the baggage of my seg-regated childhood schooling experiences. I shed tears for past torments and for a future filled with hope for our beloved country.

Over the past twenty years, I dedicated my energy to helping to build a capable democratic state with caring and competent managers. To under-stand the complex challenges in public service transformation and to gain new knowledge and skills to be an effective change agent, I completed an MBA at the University of Cape Town's Graduate School of Business in 2001. The rigorous MBA programme was a turning point in my academic pursuits. I was strongly drawn to courses such as government, business and society; strategy; change management; and leadership. Years later, recognising the knowledge gap in understanding public leadership behaviours and its impact on organ-isational culture, I researched senior public managers' emotional intelligence competence and their leadership performance, graduating with a PhD from the School of Public Leadership at Stellenbosch University. My studies were possible due to Hanne's support and understanding, especially managing the domestic front. Over the past five years I have taught on the leadership course in the master's programme at UCT's Nelson Mandela School of Public Governance where I am currently an adjunct senior lecturer.

My academic education over the years would guide my practice in management, leadership and organisational development as a senior advisor at National Treasury's capacity-building unit, the Technical Assistance Unit (TAU), and later at the Government Technical Advisory Centre (GTAC), for over a decade. I am grateful for the learning opportunities and the innovative space that Eileen Meyer, the visionary head of TAU, provided in transforming the post-apartheid state. I had initially worked with Eileen at the European Union–funded Parliamentary Support Programme supporting all nine provincial legislatures and national Parliament. One of my first projects at TAU was to support the Eastern Cape provincial government, which I did with sentimental enthusiasm due to my experiences in the former Transkei. I continue to work with this province, which has one of the highest levels of poverty and inequality.

My father bravely lived with his disability for twenty-one years, until the age of seventy-six. This was largely thanks to my mother's loving care and her strength over those difficult years, when she had little support. I continue to marvel at her compassion and community work in Tongaat, in the footsteps of her grandmother Sanjarie, and her parents. Another great loss was that of Richard Ishmail, my university classmate, close friend and committed comrade-in-arms. He was stabbed in his house in Woodstock in 2007. We continued to be close and shared many memorable moments after the dawn of democracy. He played a central role in sustaining the AKD's Johannesburg unit and, later, the Cape Town high command. I have always been in awe of his passion for life and his creative energy, which fuelled his many cultural pursuits.

I continue to admire my sister's determination and achievements, despite the many hurdles she had to overcome. She has lived in Perth, Australia, for over a decade, where she is a nursing manager at a private hospital. My brother lives close to my mum in Tongaat with his partner Julie and their two lovely sons, Aryan and Aditya. I am proud of my godson, Haroon Gunn-Salie, for his global artistic achievements that reflect the challenges of our post-apartheid society, overcoming the trauma of the first years of life in the underground and in detention – a profound example of the resilience of the human spirit.

As we mark twenty-five years of democracy I'm filled with mixed emotions and feelings. While we have made huge progress on many fronts since the dark, dreaded days of the apartheid regime, millions of dreams remain shackled by poverty, inequality and intolerance. The ANC's noble ideals, values and principles – which inspired many freedom fighters to take up arms against the former regime – have been tarnished by some senior party leaders. The greed of a number of politicians, state officials and their co-conspirators, at the expense of millions who don't enjoy a life of dignity, makes a mockery of the countless number that suffered through colonialism and apartheid, and the many freedom fighters who sacrificed their lives for the noble cause of the freedom struggle, such as Anton Fransch, Ashley Kriel, Coline Williams and Robbie Waterwitch, among many others.

My role as a MK cadre helped me to channel my anger into something constructive and noble, and to contribute to our country's liberation. Our struggle was not against white people; it was against the inhumane system that was dominated by white people. I realised early in life that race shouldn't determine how I behave towards people, and that everyone must be treated with respect and dignity. The struggle was about love during a time of hatred.

The AKD life story project provided me with an opportunity to reflect on my life. We talk about reconciliation and healing in South Africa; however, as former combatants and activists, we have not done much to reflect on our traumatic experiences. Expressing deeply held feelings made me realise that we have not had a time to grieve. Our feelings of betrayal, loss, sadness, guilt and hurt remain within us. The process of sharing my story has put me on a journey of healing past wounds. Our dreams of a democratic society start with us connecting with each other and sharing our multiple narratives. I dedicate this story to my forebears and fallen comrades, forever grateful for their spirit of resistance, courage and hope: the forces that nurtured my life's journey.

4

Melvin Bruintjies

No Time to Mourn

FIGHTING A HEARTLESS system turns your heart to steel. This dawned on me when close comrades died and I had no time to mourn their deaths. My duty was to pick up their spears and fight on.

In July 1985, Ashley Kriel, Gary Holtzman and I travelled by bus to Lingelihle in Cradock to attend the funeral of the Cradock Four – Matthew Goniwe, Sparrow Mkhonto, Fort Calata and Sicelo Mhlauli. The security police had intercepted them at a roadblock and taken them to Port Elizabeth, where they were brutally killed by the Civil Cooperation Bureau (CCB) on 27 June.

Cradock felt like a liberated zone. Hundreds of buses and cars lined the streets and thousands of people marched, singing freedom songs and shouting 'Aluta Continua' and other struggle slogans, united in our outrage and determination to bring the racist government to its knees. Attending the funeral inspired me and gave me renewed vigour to continue the struggle. On the same day, President P.W. Botha declared a national state of emergency. I did not really understand what the impact would be, but I knew that the killings, detentions and repression would intensify. It was the dawn of a new era in the liberation struggle.

A month after the funeral of the Cradock Four, I went back to the Eastern Cape and to the Northern Cape on a fact-finding mission with a group from the Western Province Council of Churches (WPCC). I felt honoured to be part of the team, meeting relatives of fallen comrades and bearing witness to the unprecedented repression people and organisations suffered at the hands of the apartheid security forces. It was evident that, long before the state of emergency was declared, the security forces were operating with all the powers and resources at their disposal to eliminate our comrades, instilling fear and thereby destroying community organisations.

During the fact-finding mission, a self-defence unit (SDU) escorted us, protecting us against possible attacks by the security police or their death squad operatives. Even so, on a deserted road between Noupoort and De Aar, the security police stopped us at a roadblock. We were ordered out of our Toyota HiAce, which was searched. We were also searched and ordered to unpack our luggage in the middle of the road. I had a UDF T-shirt in my bag and one of the security policemen held it up and said, 'So, you're doing church work for the communists.' Images of how the Cradock Four and other comrades had been assassinated flashed through my mind. We did not dare say anything reckless. After about an hour of answering questions and complying with the security police's orders, we were allowed to proceed to De Aar. Before we left, they threatened to arrest us if revolutionary action took place in any of the towns we were visiting.

Everyone in the armed struggle had a clear vision of the future South Africa we were fighting for. My career and what I wanted in life had become insignificant in the context of the many sacrifices my comrades had made. As the struggle intensified and my closest comrades lost their lives, my own life demanded introspection. What was my purpose? Answering this question left me no choice but to continue fighting for the principles for which comrades had died.

I was born on 19 February 1964 in Raapenberg, a tiny village of about twenty-four families east of Mowbray in Cape Town. My mother, Rachel Susan Bruintjies, was born in Raapenberg and grew up in the house where I was born. She raised me and my two older siblings, Abraham, or Abe, and Regina, on her own. She never married our biological father, Moses Davids, although she often talked about him when we were young. I didn't have a relationship with him, but Abe did. My maternal grandfather was a father figure to us, but he passed away in 1971. In 1976, my mother married Ivan Coker, a close family friend who was around from the time I was an infant, and everyone in the community accepted him as our father.

In the late 1960s, Raapenberg was declared a white area under the Group Areas Act, and the villagers were forced to move to the Cape Flats. Our family went to live with my grandfather in Taurus Road in Surrey Estate for a short time. Abe and I took early morning walks with my grandfather to buy milk at the dairy on sandy Klipfontein Road. Sometimes we'd board double-decker buses going to Athlone, where the cinemas were, and which was a hub of activity for shopping, business and recreation. Travelling further to Mowbray was a big outing for us, while going to town was a real event.

We moved to our own place in Manenberg when I was five, although my mother would have preferred to be closer to her sisters, who had moved to

Bonteheuwel. Our Manenberg house had two rooms and an outside toilet. Abe and I slept in the kitchen until we got bunk beds and moved to the bedroom. When Ivan Coker came into the picture and our sister Joan was born, we went back to sleeping in the kitchen.

When I was five, I spent my days alone at home. My mother was a domestic worker for white families in Pinelands, Mowbray, Claremont and Sea Point. Before she left for work, she'd make sandwiches and a flask of tea for me, then lock me in the house, where I stayed until Abe and Regina returned from school. This continued until I went to Portavue Primary, a government school in Greenhaven, in 1971. Eleven-year-old Abe enrolled me at school; my mother's long work hours prevented her from doing it.

Unlike Manenberg, Greenhaven was an area on the Cape Flats where people owned houses rather than renting them. It was about a two-kilometre walk from home to Portavue Primary, and Abe accompanied Regina and me to and from school every day. We had a morning and afternoon platoon system to accommodate all the children in the area. I stayed alone at home in the mornings and went to 'afternoon school', which started at midday and ended at 3.30 or 4 p.m.

Every year on 31 May, Republic Day, the school gathered in the quad and stood to attention while the orange, white and blue flag was raised, and we sang *Die Stem* and Christian hymns. There was no political education at home, so I didn't question this reality. I didn't socialise much with my Portavue Primary classmates because my friends went to schools in Manenberg. After school, I spent time with my Manenberg friends and we practised athletics together.

My family was among the first to move from Raapenberg; other families remained there until they were forced out. But the community stayed connected: on Boxing Day and New Year's Day we travelled by bus to picnic at Soetwater, Kommetjie, Kalk Bay and other beaches reserved for coloured people. The bus journey began by picking up former Raapenberg residents in Manenberg, Bonteheuwel, Kewtown and Bokmakierie, before picking up the remaining families in Raapenberg. When the bus hurtled down the steep slope as we entered Raapenberg, where City Lodge is today, everyone would scream. Picnics were an annual ritual for a long time after we moved.

One day, my mother mentioned that the council had started demolishing the houses in Raapenberg, and that the Black River had been rechannelled to make way for the N2. As I grew older, I better understood the devastating impact the Group Areas Act had on our family. We had moved from a small, close-knit community to the sprawling Cape Flats. My mother had previously been able to walk to work, but now had to commute to her employers in

Pinelands. I held on to memories of Raapenberg with its old pine trees, some of which are still standing today.

As difficult as it was in the beginning, we adapted to our new environment in Manenberg, and we had a lot of fun. Small wild rabbits roamed the bushy area where we lived and we enjoyed hunting them. We played and swam in a deep dam we called Coffee Dam, because of its murkiness. In winter, the heavy rains pooled on the Cape Flats, and by the September holidays we were able to swim in Castle Dam in Rylands. Castle Dam dried up as summer approached, but Coffee Dam remained. Boats on the dam pumped up the white sand, which was used to manufacture glass. We often swam to the boats, and sometimes Abe started the engines and the workers would chase us away. Later, a fence was built around Coffee Dam to protect the business.

There was an informal settlement next to Castle Dam, and many of the children from that community attended Portavue Primary. In the mornings, my mother prepared mealie-meal porridge and tea before setting off to work, but before school started I'd make a detour to have coffee made on the paraffin stove at a friend's house in the informal settlement. Meanwhile, my friend Shafiek Gafoor lived in Newfields, where the standard of living was higher, so I was exposed to different socio-economic realities from a young age.

After school, I'd play with my friends at the park in Greenhaven and then with Shafiek at his house, timing my return home to just before my mother arrived from work. Shafiek's father was a tailor and his mother a housewife and there was always lovely food for us. Shafiek always brought eight sandwiches and a flask of tea to school, which we'd share. We had a good friendship, but we went our separate ways after primary school, when I started high school in Bonteheuwel.

The schoolchildren I knew were motivated to excel in both academics and athletics. We had our own informal athletics competitions among friends before the big interschool competition held at Athlone Stadium every year, which I looked forward to. Our group ran marathons from Bonteheuwel to D.F. Malan Airport so that, when we competed at the stadium, we knew who the strong contestants were. From local interschool competitions, athletes progressed to an inter-district competition, and the winning athletes progressed to the Western Province team.

I first participated in the inter-district qualifier in 1975, when I was in Standard 3. I won the long jump and the high jump and came third in the running event. Abe and Regina were at the stadium watching me, but my mother was working.

When the competition ended that afternoon, I was so excited to tell my mother that I'd progressed to the inter-district competition that I couldn't wait for the bus; I ran all the way home to share the news of my victories. My mom was very proud of me. I didn't make it onto the Western Province team, but I came third in the long jump and received a certificate.

That same year, the Department of Coloured Affairs built two new schools: Surrey Estate Primary and Primrose Park Primary. I would have ended up at one or the other as they were closer to Manenberg, but we were given the benefit of choice and most of us stayed at Portavue Primary. However, we lost friends and many good teachers to these new schools.

That year, Regina had to repeat Standard 3 and we ended up in the same class. She wasn't at all happy about it, and it soon became too much for her. My mother insisted that we take the bus to school, but that didn't last long. Regina decided that we would walk to school instead, so every day we walked from Bonteheuwel, over the freeway into Welcome Estate, through Heideveld and Surrey Estate to Greenhaven – roughly five kilometres. At some point along the way, Regina would tell me to go ahead and she'd meet me at school. In class during roll call, our teacher would ask me where Regina was and I'd reply that she was on her way.

After many weeks of these disappearing acts, Mr Jansen, our principal, finally called my mother and Regina to a meeting. He asked Regina if she'd rather go to school in Bonteheuwel to take the pressure off her, but she didn't want to go back to school at all. My mother was very disappointed. She told Regina that she couldn't stay at home and had to find work, so Regina got a job at Val Hau, a clothing factory in Salt River. It made her happy and she quickly progressed from cleaner to machinist.

During this time, there was a constant influx of people into the area as the last of the residents who'd been forced out of District Six, Bo-Kaap and Harfield Village moved to Hanover Park and Newfields, and those with money bought property in Surrey Estate and other areas in the Cape Flats. Determined to move closer to her sisters, my mother applied to the city council for a house in Bonteheuwel, and we got one in 1976. It was a one-bedroom house at 49 Smalblaar Road, with a lounge, small kitchen, an inside toilet and a yard. That year my mother married Ivan Coker, who had lived with us in Manenberg. We already referred to our biological father as 'Daddy', so we called Ivan 'Pa'.

The events of 1976 did not pass us by, even as young primary-school children. Shafiek's family had moved from Bo-Kaap to Newfields and his older sister attended Salt River High School. She was detained and beaten by the police, along with other student activists. Black Power was in then – there was a strong belief that we were going to take back control of our country – and children reacted by pelting delivery trucks with stones on Settlers Way. I was caught up in this action on my way home from school on more than one occasion. Vanguard Drive separated Bonteheuwel and Langa by two narrow single-lane roads, and it was the only route that trucks could take to Epping Industria. There was a bridge over Settlers Way that the delivery trucks passed – the best place from which to stone them.

Many Bonteheuwel high-school students gathered on Vanguard Drive for the stone-throwing. The press would arrive and we'd make sure our actions were caught on camera, after which we'd run home to watch the early SABC news. We didn't fully understand the rationale behind our actions then, but we were inspired by the high-school learners and we believed that we had acted in the name of Black Power. I slowly became aware of the evil apartheid government and the way it was attacking, detaining and killing our people.

In the heat of the 1976 struggle, there was a lot of stone-throwing in Manenberg, Bonteheuwel, Langa and Athlone, but seldom in Greenhaven or at our school. Mr Jansen would dismiss us and send us home when stones were thrown on our school's roof, much like he did when there were heavy rains.

At home, our house soon became too small for our family. By then, the city council had started to build double-storey maisonettes in people's yards in Bonteheuwel. My mother was incensed. 'How can they build on top of us like this when we don't even have enough space?' she'd say. The Bonteheuwel Civic Association mobilised around the issue and organised protests at the Bonteheuwel Civic Centre, calling the maisonettes *muisneste* (mice nests), but the council's response was to continue annexing people's properties to build more maisonettes. My mother applied for a three-bedroom house, which was approved, and we moved from 49 to 67A Smalblaar Road. Our new house had a lounge, kitchen and one small room on the ground floor, and two bedrooms and a toilet upstairs. We didn't have hot water, but at least the bathroom was inside.

During school holidays, my mother took us to work with her and I was exposed to life on the other side of the railway line. She worked for several white families, one day here, another there. I remember two families in particular: the Thorpes and the Fishers. We were quite young when my mother worked for the Thorpes. Their daughter Elmay was raised by my mother, who took her to school in the mornings and saw to her needs while the Thorpes were at work and my siblings and I were taking care of ourselves. Much later, when Elmay got married and lived in Observatory, my mother worked for her too, although Elmay did not regard herself as my mother's boss or madam – they were friends. When she had marital problems, Elmay came to Bonteheuwel to speak to my mother and was often on the phone with her. She eventually divorced her husband, a panel beater who drove a Morris, and when she moved to a smaller place, she gave most of her household belongings to my mother. We fetched the furniture in a truck, and our garage in Bonteheuwel was crammed full. We sold the ex-husband's Morris to an old man in Bonteheuwel for R50.

As for the Fishers, he was an Englishman and she was an Afrikaner, and they proved to be very humane. My mother was accustomed to calling her employers Madam and Master, but they insisted we call them Mr and Mrs Fisher. They acknowledged the injustice of the apartheid system that segregated us and they had good hearts. The Fishers paid for my schooling, my uniform and a few other expenses, and they supported my mom through my primary- and high-school years. They were very worried when I got involved in politics in high school, yet they continued to support us. During the political uprisings, they constantly enquired whether it was safe for my mother to travel to work, and she was encouraged to stay at home when the situation was volatile. I knew of instances where domestic workers were treated as subordinates, but the Fishers were not like that. We played in their house, and when we went out to the shops with them in their car, I sat in the front passenger seat. Every Christmas we looked forward to gifts from the Fishers – the only gifts we received. In the mid to late 1980s, when the Fishers moved to Kilandini Residential Home for the Aged in Mowbray, they paid my mother to visit them as a companion. We were like family.

We were poor but we were well looked-after. My siblings and I never went hungry as my mother always had work and went out of her way to provide for us. She had started working when she was twelve, and died at the relatively young age of fifty-three, asthmatic and suffering from angina, high blood pressure and other illnesses, but she didn't complain about work and instilled in us an independence whereby we learnt to look after ourselves. She had the support of her siblings too, and they would contribute food so that there was always something on the table. My mother made sure that our uniforms were neat and clean and our shoes polished. Although she left early for work and returned home late, she kept our house in order. Despite her busy work schedule, she took us to St Mark's Anglican Church in Athlone, where Regina and I had been baptised in 1971. Later, I was confirmed at the Church of the Resurrection in Bonteheuwel. My mother was a spiritual person, but due to our circumstances we didn't go to church as a family every Sunday.

She planted the seed, though, and my siblings and I became deeply involved in the life of the church. In high school, the church played a pivotal role in exposing me to the struggle against apartheid.

My mother's brothers were always supportive. Uncle Domingo and Uncle Henry were self-employed, cutting wood to earn money, and I looked up to them. Uncle Domingo cut our hair when he came to visit and he took over my grandfather's role as father figure. They were my first role models, to be followed by leaders like Mahatma Gandhi, Nelson Mandela and Martin Luther King, whom I learnt about in high school. I admired Oliver Tambo, but I didn't know much about him, except that he was an ANC leader who had left the country and was mobilising international support against apartheid. I would also come to admire Desmond Tutu, Allan Boesak and other religious leaders.

I went to high school at Modderdam High in Bonteheuwel. My teachers played an important role in my political development, especially student teachers from the Zonnebloem and Hewat teachers' training colleges and the University of the Western Cape, who did their practice teaching at our school. I remember Ms Wilkinson from the University of Cape Town, who always had a progressive message that gave us hope that things would change. She was one of the few white people I came into contact with, besides my mother's employers. These student teachers were only a few years older than us, but they arrived with political knowledge that they'd developed on their campuses, and they passed it on to us.

I had been among the top ten achievers in Standard 6 and passed the exams in June and September of 1979. However, I narrowly failed one subject at the end of the year, which meant that I would have to repeat the year. I was devastated. My good friend Cliffy Morta also failed and we decided that this would be the end of our schooling. During the school holidays, the two of us had worked as casuals at factories in Epping, and we decided to find permanent work. It was not unusual back then for young people to look for work after finishing primary school. Abe had left school after Standard 5 to help my mother financially, and started his trade as a carpenter for a construction company contracted to build flats in Uitsig and Atlantis. By the end of 1979, I was the only member of my family still at school and if I left it would mean that none of us – not my siblings, nor my cousins of the same age – would have completed Standard 8, or Junior Certificate (JC).

Cliffy and I found casual work offloading sugar, chocolates, cooldrinks and rice from trucks into a huge storage room. We worked hard to impress the boss and move up the employment ladder, but after the school holidays, when everyone was going back to school, and my mother expressed her disappointment in me, I began to change my mind. Three days into the school year, when Cliffy and I were on the bus to work, we came to the realisation that we wanted to go back to school. The next day we were back in our uniforms. I repeated the year and excelled academically, once again becoming one of the top achievers in my class. Meanwhile, Abe went to night school in order to continue his education and matriculated in 1984, the year after me. On completion of his JC, he got work at the municipality, where he stayed for thirty years, occupying various positions and ending up as a foreman in the cleansing department.

During the 1980 school boycotts, as the struggle was intensifying, the state tried hard to undermine our unity. The Department of Coloured Affairs tried to divide teaching staff from the learners with threats of dismissal, but their strategy didn't succeed. The South African Police and South African Defence Force went on active drives to recruit young coloured men, and some accepted their offers of employment. We rejected those guys. The city council's Parks and Recreation Department also tried to divide us with its 'kom speel saam' (come play together) programme, which appeared attractive and fun, but was really a recruitment drive for the military. A few of my friends served on the border, but they hated it there and when they tried to desert and return to Cape Town, they were arrested. Contrary to the state's intention, these initiatives sharpened our consciousness.

Things changed dramatically after the 1980 school boycotts. There were many different political movements emerging and regrouping, and the ANC rose in popularity and became more prominent. We were beginning to visualise the future we strived for. For me, there was a great change in terms of my political consciousness. In Standards 7 and 8, our teachers established various student media, sports and art committees, and I got involved with the media committee. This became the start of the student movement and our mobilisation. The Student Representative Council (SRC) was another important platform to conscientise students.

We had a vision of where we were going politically, and we had the support of the teachers. Everyone was very excited. In 1983, I became head boy at Modderdam High School and chairperson of the SRC. The UDF was founded that year, and one of my tasks was to help organise the Bonteheuwel people, especially learners and church youth, to attend the UDF launch at Rocklands Civic Centre in Mitchells Plain on 20 August. We were issued with 20c tickets and filled many buses. Thousands of people attended the launch.

The Freedom Charter became our organising tool, and after the launch I got involved with the UDF's Million Signature Campaign, which mobilised against P.W. Botha's racist Tricameral Parliament elections in 1984. This campaign was an eye-opener for me. It brought together volunteers from white, coloured and African communities to work in areas such as Atlantis, Ocean View and Macassar over weekends, and I did door-to-door work for the first time. Some conservative churchgoers called our activities unchristian, but that did not deter me. I joined the UDF's media subcommittee in Bonteheuwel, where we were responsible for producing and distributing posters, pamphlets and newsletters, under the direction of Quentin Michaels, who was the UDF Bonteheuwel Area coordinator. We also learnt silkscreen printing and made our own revolutionary T-shirts and bags. At a later stage, I got involved in fundraising, and we organised events that were successful enough to cover our media campaigns, office rental arrears and *Grassroots* newspaper debts, with enough left over for the day-to-day running of the Million Signature Campaign.

I also became more involved in community politics by supporting the work of the Bonteheuwel Civic Association. My mother had attended civic activities in 1981, and I had been encouraged to assist. Civic work on the housing maintenance campaign was therefore a logical progression, and I distributed pamphlets among school learners and in the church. I also helped distribute *Grassroots* newspaper, which produced a free edition and a 5c edition. When selling the 5c edition, we had to motivate people to buy it. To counteract this problem, we made buying the paper compulsory at school; pupils had to have 5c when it was delivered every month. When a *Grassroots* edition was banned, Quentin, Ashley Kriel and I defied the ban and left copies in strategic places, such as the surgery, the pharmacy and in small shops whose owners didn't know that the papers were banned. This intensified security police surveillance on us, although we didn't know it.

I was also a Sunday school teacher in the Bonteheuwel Anglican church, the Church of the Resurrection. The Bonteheuwel Youth Movement was very active at the time and, along with other youths, we were encouraged and inspired to start the Resurrection Youth Movement. My involvement with the Inter-Church Youth (ICY), an ecumenical church movement that became part of the WPCC, also intensified. The ICY's mission was to mobilise all young Christians in greater Cape Town, including Macassar, Mamre, Malmesbury, Boland, West Coast, Hottentots Holland and Grabouw. By the mid-1980s there was an ICY structure in almost every township, and we managed to get the mainstream churches to commit to building an Ecumenical Youth Movement under the auspices of the WPCC. At the end of 1984, I went to a youth camp with Ashley and other Bonteheuwel activists at the Clarkson

Moravian Mission Station in the Eastern Cape. Our purpose was to conscientise and revolutionise the Christian youth.

May Day rallies became an integral part of our mobilisation strategy. We organised annual Workers' Day church services that highlighted the plight of exploited South African workers and the struggle for a living wage. In this way, workers in the church were mobilised to join the struggle for democracy and non-racialism, resulting in a strong activist force in Bonteheuwel. Comrades started calling me Jesus, because I'd walk from church meetings to UDF meetings dressed in formal church attire with a crucifix around my neck.

My involvement with the UDF Bonteheuwel Area Committee became an important part of my political life and activism. I helped mobilise sectors of the community under the banner of the UDF to oppose the Tricameral Parliament: Christians and Muslims; church youth groups and the Cape Youth Congress (CAYCO); sports groups affiliated to the South African Council on Sport (SACOS); students under the banner of the Bonteheuwel Inter-Schools Congress (BISCO); teachers and members of the South African Democratic Teachers Union (SADTU); workers affiliated to progressive trade unions; local businesses and members of the Western Cape Traders Association (WCTA); and residents and members of the Bonteheuwel Residents Civic Association (BRCA). We even managed to involve some of the more conservative residents and Black Consciousness Movement supporters. It was absolutely incredible, and I became progressively more active.

While all this was going on, I was enjoying school, particularly maths, biology, history, accountancy and geography, but not languages. I wasn't a keen reader and didn't have time to read all the prescribed books. I stayed in the top ten until matric and received awards for achievements in accountancy and biology. Cliffy had also continued with his schooling and was involved in school politics too. We both had bicycles and when one had a puncture we'd give each other lifts to Gatesville to repair the tyre. Along the way, we'd have serious discussions about how we were going to overthrow the white government. We were both interested in mechanics, which went contrary to the mainstream thinking and socialisation in our community, which saw teaching and social work as more desirable careers. In matric we both applied to Consani Engineering in Elsies River for job-shadowing.

We went together to take the aptitude test for the mechanical trade at the Bellville Training Centre for Artisans, situated on the Peninsula Technicon (Pentech) campus. I also applied at UWC and Hewat Teacher Training College. All three institutions accepted me with promises of government bursaries, depending on my matric results. I chose to be trained as a motor and diesel mechanic at the Bellville Training Centre. Cliffy and I had planned to start our careers together as mechanics, but he didn't pass the aptitude test and hadn't applied to any universities or colleges. It was a sad, abrupt separation. Cliffy ended up going into jewellery-making instead and enjoyed it tremendously.

While studying, I tried to keep up my political activism. The year 1984 was frenetic, with my involvement in the UDF's Million Signature Campaign, church, activism and studying. I felt isolated on the Bellville campus, and although I excelled in all the courses, they weren't challenging and I felt frustrated. For a time I considered becoming a priest – I was inspired by liberation theology and church was where I best expressed myself. However, I ultimately took the advice of people I trusted and finished my studies at the Bellville Training Centre.

I achieved my N3 National Certificate in 1985, the year Ashley was in matric and the big question was whether or not students should write their end-of-year exams. We didn't have final exams at college so it wasn't an issue for me, but it was for my comrades at school, Hewat Teacher Training College and other places of learning. Sidney Hendricks, who I knew through the church, was at Hewat and I remember that he decided not to write the exams.

On 25 July, President P.W. Botha declared a state of emergency in 36 of the country's 260 municipalities, and all political activities were banned in these areas. The Mass Democratic Movement (MDM) couldn't distribute pamphlets, except clandestinely, and couldn't hold public meetings. The movement of MDM leaders was restricted and many were detained. I had been helping with the banned SACP and ANC literature and pamphlets that Leon Scott and Cecyl Esau would hand over to us to print and distribute. Those of us involved didn't realise we were doing underground political work for the ANC; everything was on a need-to-know basis and you didn't ask questions. I got the shock of my life one night when a few comrades and I were preparing for May Day events at Cecyl's house in Wynberg. We were discussing the distribution strategy for our pamphlets when the security police stormed into the house with Quentin Michaels in handcuffs to arrest Cecyl for his involvement in MK. Only then did I realise that the two comrades were involved in serious underground activities.

The security police pulled the place apart, looking in the cupboards, under the beds and even in the ceiling. Then the police left with Cecyl and told us they would come back for us, having confiscated our bags and pamphlets. When the police were gone, we hurriedly left in a kombi. We knew that we had to go into hiding temporarily, so we drove to a friend's house in Kensington, which had a back room and space in the yard to park the kombi. We stayed there for the night.

Many activists went into hiding after the state of emergency was declared, living a dual existence above and underground in order to continue the struggle. Supporters offered their homes as sanctuaries for comrades, and many churches opened their doors too. Despite severe repression, the struggle not only continued but reached new revolutionary heights. However, with so many activists detained, underground, in hiding or forced to leave the country, the impact of the state of emergency repression and the leadership vacuum was acutely felt by the people on the ground, especially among the youth.

Then, in 1986, after the 1985 uprisings and with Ashley having gone into exile, the political terrain changed completely in terms of where I wanted to be involved. I was in the heart of Bonteheuwel UDF politics when P.W. Botha declared a countrywide state of emergency on 12 June 1986. Bannings and mass detentions intensified, and the state identified certain 'no-go' areas, including Soweto, Sharpeville and Orange Farm in Gauteng, and Bonteheuwel in the Western Cape, among others. The security forces employed a clandestine 'dirty tricks' strategy in these areas, mostly targeting individuals who could be turned against their communities. The Labour Party and Joint Management Centres in coloured neighbourhoods recruited informants to gather information on organisation leaders and safe house locations for the security branch, in an effort to crush these strong revolutionary communities. Their strategy was successful, creating paranoia and distrust.

Around this time, the state security apparatus began to take a great deal of interest in Bonteheuwel activists. The Joint Management Centres unleashed their repressive might to undermine and ultimately break the unity and revolutionary spirit in the area. As a result, a few comrades and I soon pushed our political work beyond Bonteheuwel, into the greater Cape Town area. My brother, Abe, was a shop steward for the South African Municipal Workers' Union (SAMWU) and was involved in strike action. He was delighted to be drawn into mainstream politics under the banner of the UDF, and although I didn't expect him to pitch up at the civic meetings, rallies and events, he always did and played a supportive role. He had a kombi, which he made available to transport Bonteheuwel comrades when they needed to get to meetings. The UDF worked very closely with the workers, especially municipal workers and those in the clothing industry, where most of our sisters, aunts and mothers worked. While I was angry at whites because of apartheid, I also had positive encounters with some white people: Shirley Gunn and Murray Michel, whom I met through the Clothing Workers Union; young white teachers; and my mother's employers. These encounters enabled me to understand that our struggle was about liberating and uniting everyone, irrespective of race, colour or class.

Also in 1986, during my final year at college, I resolved to study theology. The church offered me the opportunity and I started preparing, but first I had to go to Johannesburg to perform my final trade test at the end of the year. My qualifying as a diesel mechanic was important to my family: I was the first to complete matric and the first to get a further qualification. Working as a diesel mechanic was seen as a lucrative trade. Many friends who did the course with me went to work in the mines and at Sasol and they earned enough to enjoy fairly comfortable lives.

It was a thrilling moment when my fellow students and I left Cape Town Station for Johannesburg to do the trade test at Olifantsfontein. My mother, my Auntie Joan (or Noni, as we called her) and other family members came to the station to see me off. They cried with joy and pride.

Sixty of us from Cape Town occupied two second-class carriages. The first-class carriages were exclusively for white people, who were given bedding and had their meals in the dining saloon. In the second-class carriage, six people shared one tiny compartment and there was a small, restricted area where we could buy coffee. The third-class carriage was even more basic, and passengers had to sit and sleep upright on hard benches throughout the long journey to Johannesburg. I shared a compartment with Muslim students and we were fairly quiet, but some people threw a party and couldn't remember how they ended up in Olifantsfontein.

Once there, I was surrounded by people who were utterly different from activists in Bonteheuwel. At mealtimes, whites were seated on one side and coloureds on the other. The place was prison-like and cold, and we slept in barracks with a clear separation between whites and coloureds. I don't think they made provision for black people to do the trade test at all. Some Tswana guys assisted with passing tools to us during the test and we were advised to build relationships with them. If you failed, you had to repeat the practical test, and getting another appointment could take a whole year. We were given a week to complete the test, but I took two days and spent the rest of the week having good times in Johannesburg with one of my classmates. I received my test results about a month later, when I was back in Cape Town. I'd passed with a B. I was overjoyed.

The graduation ceremony was at Pentech, and once again it was an emotional moment for my family. I had qualified as a diesel mechanic and everyone thought I was going to make lots of money, but that was not my vision. I'd decided to focus on my work in the church and study theology at the Federal Theological Seminary in Pietermaritzburg, St Paul's College in Grahamstown, or whichever college the Anglican Church chose to send me to. I was advised to get some work experience before I started with the ministry and I applied for a job at the Churches Urban Planning Commission (CUPC). I started working there in 1987 as the convener of youth projects, and was soon involved in community work.

The CUPC office was in an old house in Observatory, but the organisation was about to move to Community House in Salt River. I experienced a great sense of community among the team of young CUPC organisers working under Nabawaya 'Nabs' Wessels' directorship. Charlie Martin, who had moved to Bonteheuwel to take over the Congregational Church parish in 1985, served on the CUPC board. It was Charlie who had encouraged me to apply for the youth organiser job. Johnny Issel was a consultant who gave political direction to the CUPC team. I had got to know Johnny very well a couple of years earlier. I realised I had a strong connection with him when he told me in 1985 that, despite opposition from the ultra-leftist movement and the political flack he would personally face, he was bringing Reverend Chris Nissen from Graaff-Reinet to speak at a meeting that was to be addressed by US senator Edward Kennedy. This was during the heat of things, when people were detained or in hiding, and South Africa needed to offer a positive image to the international community.

My relationship with Johnny deepened during my time at the CUPC. Not everyone knew his compassionate side, his Christian background and religious tolerance. Johnny and I travelled to the greater Cape Town area together and he engaged in discussions with a range of people, including prison warders. He once took me to Stellenbosch University, an Afrikaner establishment, and introduced me to some of the Afrikaners whom he knew and trusted, and I was forced to grapple with my own scepticism about what positive contribution they could make to change in the country. He inspired me and I learnt a lot about political flexibility and tolerance from him. When we talked about liberation and democracy, it wasn't confined to those in the struggle; he believed all South African people had to be set free, irrespective of race and class. That, he told me, was the ANC's message.

Johnny lived in Denchworth Road in Athlone. He had a lot of respect for Bonteheuwel activists and he invited us to his home. Ashley was around then, and I went with him to Denchworth Road, which is where everything seemed to be happening – politically and socially. In defiance of his banning order, Johnny would address us at meetings in Bonteheuwel. He came to get our support for the Release Mandela Campaign, and he once brought Aneez Salie, a journalist and activist, with him. Many high-profile comrades came to Bonteheuwel in those years. The political mood was extremely volatile – fertile conditions for the revolution, according to Marxist–Leninist theory.

I clearly remember the day we heard that Ashley had been killed. On 9 July 1987, the police released a statement that an ANC 'terrorist' had been killed in Athlone, and we heard that same evening that it was him. I hadn't known that he was back in the country. I was on a church youth camp in Strandfontein at the time, and a comrade told me the news over the phone. I cried and cried. I wasn't involved with MK then, nor was I part of any ANC structures, but I was consumed by feelings of guilt that we had deserted Ashley and failed to protect him.

I helped organise Ashley's funeral, and attended in the hope of finding closure. On the day, I couldn't reach his gravesite because of the interference of the police and the army, but I went a few days later. Shortly after Ashley was killed, while I was still devastated, I was driving in Athlone with Johnny and he said to me, 'Melvin, you must have a heart of steel.' I was taken aback and asked what he meant, but he didn't answer.

Soon after Ashley's funeral, we mobilised to celebrate Govan Mbeki's imminent release from prison, which was seen as a precursor to the release of all our imprisoned comrades. CUPC had seconded me to give my full-time support to the Release Govan Mbeki Campaign, which we saw as an opportunity to conscientise, prepare and mobilise the community, the church youth and activists in the Western Cape under the banner of the UDF. Johnny played a very important role in bringing people together to get this campaign off the ground and saw it as a testing ground for when Mandela and other leaders were released. My brief was to mobilise the church and youth structures in the Hottentots Holland area. We began at mainstream churches, like the Calvinist, Dutch Reformed, African Methodist Episcopal (AME), Methodist, Anglican and Catholic churches. We also managed to reach independent churches, as well as other youth through the Vereniging van Christelike Studente (VCS), a movement for young Christians at universities and high schools, which was particularly vibrant in the Western Cape. We were 'testing the waters' as Johnny put it, and the colours of the ANC – black, green and gold – were used in all the media we produced.

Johnny introduced me to key people in the church who were instrumental in identifying youth from Macassar, Strand, Somerset West and Firgrove whom I'd draw into the campaign. That's when I met Heinrich Magerman, a UWC student from the Calvinist Church, who was one of the first people I mobilised. Later, I recruited Andrew Adams, a Pentech civil engineering student who was also from the Calvinist Church. They were very willing to be involved, and organised venues in their communities where we could strategise. These meetings were followed by a highly successful weekend training camp at the Dora Falcke Youth Centre in Muizenberg. At the camp, we analysed the changing political context and the response of the church from a liberation theology perspective. We provided media training, and Debora Patta, a radio journalist and media practitioner, shared her skills in making posters and pamphlets.

At CUPC, Johnny and Nabs Wessels often sat down with all the organisers to discuss current political issues, after which we'd go out and do our work. We were given both biblical and Marxist–Leninist readings. Johnny encouraged us to get our own copies of certain banned books and I still have a copy of Lenin's *What Is To Be Done?*, which I continue to use as a reference. Lenin not only spoke about the time for revolution but also the time before and after it. It was very important for us to contemplate what could go wrong after the revolution. I didn't have any formal education in political studies, but my exposure to the struggle and the extensive reading Johnny encouraged me to do helped me to understand and articulate our vision for South Africa.

As we progressed with the campaign, the Macassar region emerged as one of the strongest church youth structures and even helped other areas in Cape Town. Having established this group, which was centrally involved in broader political issues at a student level and within the larger ecumenical movement, I left the project. The organisers were familiar with the WPCC and the CUPC office at Community House, where they had access to computers, typewriters, printers and a Roneo machine, and I knew they could carry on the work without me. I was moved to the Dutch Reformed church in the Wynberg region to start community projects. The church wanted to play a more active role in the community, not just setting up soup kitchens but also bringing Bible studies to the people. Soon after I started working there, I discovered that many farm workers from Constantia belonged to the church. A number of farms in Constantia were owned by Germans who treated their workers relatively well in terms of housing but paid them a pittance. They allowed us entry to the farms and we conscientised the workers and brought them into the church's community outreach programme.

I still had the desire to become a minister, and the Moravian youth invited me to preach at their Afrikaans services. I also preached contextual theology at the Dutch Reformed Mission Church in Ottery, and Charlie Martin invited me to preach at his Bonteheuwel Congregational Church. Around this time, the church also wanted my assistance with their newsletter, *Shalom*, and I drew in Fahdiel Manuel from *Grassroots* newspaper to assist. We put together a media committee that produced publications. I initiated and coordinated the project until 1988, when I handed it over to the church, which had established smaller groups to do Bible studies and media and continue with the soup kitchens.

My first direct encounter with MK was in the second half of 1987. Charlie Martin and I, along with two others, were drawn in to support a special operations unit that had been sent into the country. We met the comrades near Paarl and they made it clear that we were not going to be trained for military activities; our role was to assist with reconnaissance and provide safe houses. One comrade ended up staying in Athlone and the other in Old Crossroads. Both were armed with AK-47s and grenades, and I got to handle these Russian-made weapons for the first time. The comrades told us that they were in Cape Town to set up a unit, but did not elaborate. They trusted us, sent us on reconnaissance missions, and got us to help them retrieve weapons brought to Cape Town in Sipho 'Hotstix' Mabuse's HiAce. The two comrades only stayed for three weeks. Shortly after they left, a woman who we assumed held a high-ranking position in MK pitched up, and we handed over the bags of arms to her. We heard later that after the two comrades left Cape Town and returned to Soweto, one of them was killed in an ambush.

Around the time Govan Mbeki was released in late 1987, a woman came to Community House and gave me a note to meet someone at Muizenberg Station at a certain time. It was an instruction shrouded in secrecy, so I knew I had to be very careful.

The person waiting for me at Muizenberg Station was Shirley Gunn. The meeting took place shortly after Ashley's killing and Shirley got straight to the point: it was time for me to join MK. I agreed without hesitation. Soon after, I met the other Ashley Kriel Detachment commander, Aneez Salie, and he explained in detail what the AKD expected of me. Most comrades from other Western Cape MK units were on trial or had been sentenced and imprisoned on Robben Island. This had left a vacuum, and there was an urgent need to show the security forces and the people that MK was still operating despite the arrests, detentions, trials and prison sentences. It was a time of heightened repression, but people were committed and fearless in response.

My first military training session was at the municipal camping site in

Muizenberg, where Shirley, Aneez and I spent the weekend together. We covered the basics about explosives and military engineering. Many meetings and training sessions followed. Bonteheuwel was chosen as an area in which to expand the AKD and Coline Williams became our first recruit. Vanessa November, who was still at school, was the second recruit, and Sidney Hendricks was recruited soon afterwards. I think it came as a shock to Sidney when I approached him. He wasn't the type to seek the limelight or speak on public platforms, and that gave him the perfect profile for work in the underground. I saw great potential in Sidney, and I never feared that he would speak to anyone about his involvement in MK. I tested this over and over again and saw quite quickly that he'd be an asset in our unit. Coline was a perfect fit too. After spending a long time in detention, she had become involved in the community and really wanted to be part of MK. By early 1988, the Bonteheuwel unit was operational.

The AKD had to expand further and we believed the Macassar comrades were ready to form an underground MK unit. Andrew Adams, who was the chairperson of the Calvinist youth, was serious and committed, didn't talk much and always gave his best regardless of the risk. I knew Desmond Stevens had potential, as we'd become close friends, and the same applied to Heinrich Magerman. Initially, we wanted to recruit two people from the youth group without interfering with important political activity in the area. Andrew and Desmond, who were both studying at Pentech, were the first to be recruited. I took them through their first training in Muizenberg, which included explosives and reconnaissance. They were thrilled; it was what they'd dreamt of.

Our decision to recruit Andrew and Desmond was tested in our operations. In 1988, Desmond was detained and held at the Stellenbosch Police Station under the state of emergency regulations. We learnt through his lawyers that he was confused, not knowing if he was detained for MK activities or his community involvement. On his release, we feared that working with Desmond would be risky. We presumed the police would be watching him, so we restricted his involvement in the unit and he remained under my command. Our dilemma, though, was that without him Andrew was our only operative in Macassar, so we recruited Heinrich and Paul Endley. I trained them to support Andrew, who'd been carrying on the work alone.

During the time of the South African Breweries (SAB) strike in 1988, Andrew was sent to the Newlands plant undercover as a scab labourer to assess the situation and possibly respond as MK in support of the workers. He reported that workers were not searched, so it would be possible to take explosives into the plant. When the strike was called off and we aborted the mission he was very disappointed, as he'd risked a lot and laid a good foundation for an operation. In many ways he reminded me of Ashley – reserved and never seeking the limelight, but always saying something worthwhile when he chose to speak. It was no coincidence that his combat name was Ashley.

Sidney and I carried out the Bonteheuwel unit's maiden operation, at Woodstock Police Station on Tuesday 26 July 1988. After Yengeni Trial co-accused Suraya Abbas and Colleen Lombard were released from detention, they had to report to that police station daily, but we'd heard that the police captain was treating them badly. I did the reconnaissance, and at about 3.30 p.m. Sidney planted a bomb against the building in a side street close to the captain's office.

The blast threw Woodstock and Salt River into disarray. Clothing factories shut down and workers were sent home. Others were evacuated, so there was a traffic jam all along Main Road. It took ages getting away from the area by car. Sidney and I met up as soon as I got back to Bonteheuwel. He was very calm and our success made us confident about carrying out more operations. Our next few operations were at municipal buildings and magistrates' courts in Paarl, Goodwood and Parow.

By the time the 1988 municipal elections took place, Coline was the Bonteheuwel unit commander, working with Vanessa and Sidney. By then, the Macassar unit had grown, with Andrew, Heinrich, Paul and Desmond still involved. Paul was highly committed to MK work and participated in operations without difficulty. At one point, Desmond and Heinrich were detained, and Andrew and Paul continued the MK work on their own. They were responsible for caching the detachment's military hardware for long-term storage in the Helderberg Nature Reserve and on a hill in Macassar intended as temporary storage.

Initially, Macassar unit operatives took public transport to operations, as they had no vehicles of their own, and this put Andrew and Paul at risk on their first operation, at the Somerset West Magistrate's Court. After planting the limpet, they hopped on a minibus home. To their horror, the minibus made a detour past the court. When the device detonated, Andrew and Paul were close enough to feel the impact. Stunned by the close shave, they sat in silence, listening to people's remarks in the taxi.

In late 1988, the Mitchells Plain unit was getting off the ground. The first person I approached to serve in the unit was Desmond McKenzie, who was involved in the church youth with me. He was politically conscious and didn't have a high political profile, although soon after he was recruited, he became involved with local UDF activities, against my instruction. To expand the unit, Desmond identified Raphael Martin, a UWC student. Raphael was recruited and I trained them both. One night, the three of us were together placing a limpet at the Eastridge Rent Office. Desmond panicked and I had to take over, priming and placing the device. Desmond had a lot of energy but he became anxious when it came to operations, so although he had been recruited first, we made Raphael the commander because of his confidence and level-headedness. It was the correct decision; I learnt afterwards that Raphael did most of the work. There was also an occasion when a limpet mine placed at municipal offices didn't detonate and Raphael retrieved it the next morning, against instructions. He feared that early-morning commuters walking past might get injured, so he risked his life to retrieve the device. Nevertheless, he was severely reprimanded.

Raphael and Desmond carried out successful operations at the Mitchells Plain Magistrate's Court, the police barracks and a satellite police station. We continued to work with them, but believed we had to expand the Mitchells Plain unit, given the huge geographical area it had to cover. We spent months identifying and discussing possible recruits – politically mature and disciplined comrades who would operate under MK's code of conduct. We always gave operatives the opportunity to suggest names before anyone was approached, as they knew comrades in their areas. Raphael and Desmond identified Faiez Jacobs and Shane Oliver as potential recruits.

I had never met Faiez or Shane, so Raphael and Desmond were instructed to write up their biographies and submit them to me for scrutiny. After long deliberation, we agreed that the two would be approached but they'd only be exposed to the unit operatives, not to me. Both Faiez and Shane began the long process of preparation that precedes any active operational work, including political training and modes of operating in the underground, but, for reasons still unclear to me, they asked to be relieved of their duties before they were fully trained. Allowing members to leave was always risky. Redeployment was out of the question, so Raphael and Desmond were instructed to cut off all contact with Faiez and Shane. Although I had not been exposed to them, from an operational perspective we had to take a step back. Aware that we once again had to expand the unit, we recruited two student activists, Gloria Veale and Andre Bruce, but their involvement was also short-lived; they weren't trained and received no instructions to carry out operations. Andre later became an officer in the South African Navy.

I mainly used public phones to communicate with Shirley, Aneez and our units, and from time to time we used coded written messages. Our communication network functioned well. We always had back-up arrangements if we lost contact. After Shirley was framed in January 1989 for the bombing of Khotso House and the security forces were hunting her down, it became more difficult for us to communicate, so our communication was planned with absolute precision. If an arrangement was made, we honoured it. We went to extreme lengths to ensure the safety of detachment members, which was part of our intelligence and communications training. If someone didn't arrive for a routine meeting or call, we would know that there was a problem, as was the case on the tragic night of 23 July 1989.

By then, twenty-year-old Coline Williams was commanding both the Athlone and Bonteheuwel units. Anton Fransch, who'd joined the AKD in April 1989, was Coline's commander. I had recruited Robbie Waterwitch into MK to serve in the Athlone unit. We'd first rubbed shoulders when he and the Belgravia Youth Congress (BEYCO) assisted with the rally to host Senator Edward Kennedy in 1985. As a teenager, Robbie was very active in the political campaigns of the mid to late 1980s, including being central to the Save the Press Campaign. He was always ready to assist, regardless of the task. During our many discussions, I was exposed to his wealth of talent, intelligence and energy. Robbie worked selflessly during a turbulent period that made it very difficult to execute the tasks of the MDM. The apartheid regime was under pressure from all fronts, and in December 1988 Mandela was moved from Pollsmoor to a warder's house at Victor Verster Prison near Paarl, where he consulted with the political leadership.

As a keen reader, Robbie could engage in discussions on any number of aspects of our struggle, and he always had the latest banned literature. He understood the theory of the four pillars of the ANC's struggle – international solidarity, internal mass democratic struggle, the political underground and the military underground – and it was clear he had the qualities needed to serve as an MK cadre.

It took months to cultivate a relationship with him without compromising his role and relationships in the MDM. My connection to comrades in Athlone, ICY and campaign activities made it easier to approach him to become active in the military underground. Robbie had no connections with other underground structures and was excited to be part of MK, so I discussed his profile with Aneez and Shirley and he was recruited into the AKD without hesitation. We hoped that, in time, he would help set up the Athlone unit.

I trained Robbie in all aspects of military combat work, military engineering and firearms such as the AK-47 and Makarov pistol. All of his training was conducted in the greater Cape Town area at various safe venues. After a few months of this, Comrade Coline, his commander, took over. She was the main link to Anton and the AKD command.

The last time I saw Robbie was on Friday 21 July 1989, when he and Coline accompanied me to drop off ordnance at an arms cache in Strandfontein. We'd planned five simultaneous missions for the night of Sunday 23 July, to be executed by five units: Bonteheuwel, Southern Suburbs, Athlone, Mitchells Plain and Macassar. The plan was to target the courts and municipal offices in Athlone, Heideveld, Strand and Bellville, while the Mitchells Plain unit would target a satellite police station. I met up with Coline again that Sunday afternoon in a park on Klipfontein Road, to give her the materials for the Athlone operation. I was supposed to hand over a large SPM limpet mine cached in Mitchells Plain, but there wasn't sufficient time to retrieve it, so Coline was instructed to use two mini MPM limpets, joined together with one detonator. Robbie had temporarily stored these limpets in his house, intact in their silver packaging. After our brief meeting, I left, unaware that she still had to connect with Vanessa in Mowbray, as per Anton's instruction to them.

I was on the Bellville mission with Sidney that night. We had done reconnaissance in the Bellville precinct and initially decided that our target would be the Bellville satellite police station close to Bellville Railway Station. I dropped Sidney off close to the target, but he returned to report that there were too many civilians around, so we aborted that mission and changed the target to the Bellville Magistrate's Court around the corner. Once again, I dropped Sidney near the target and waited for him in the getaway car near Tygerberg Hospital. Just as Sidney had planted the limpet mine, a policeman at the court intercepted him. He ran, and fortunately the policeman didn't give chase. It was a frightening experience, but Sidney's agility saved him.

I dropped Sidney in Bonteheuwel and drove home to Wynberg, via the N2 and Jan Smuts Drive. On the way, I passed the Athlone Police Station, where I saw many red and blue lights flashing. I worried that something might have gone wrong with Coline and Robbie's Athlone operation. Back at home, I waited for the 10 p.m. news, where I learnt that casualties had been reported in a bomb blast in Athlone.

I didn't know what the follow-up to this devastating news should be. At the time, I couldn't believe Robbie or Coline had been killed. I thought it was a ploy to frustrate us, to get us to come out of hiding and reveal ourselves, as the security forces didn't seem to know who was responsible for these blasts. Later that night, news reports confirmed that two people had died, but their names weren't announced. I resolved to take reasonable steps to secure my own safety and that of others: I couldn't sleep at home that night and I had to secure the Makarov pistol and AK-47 I had with me.

I left my partner, Ruth Engel, at home, took the firearms, and drove to Silvermine, where we cached arms for short periods. By the time I was done, it was early morning and I'd still not had any contact with Shirley or Aneez. I started to panic. I drove to our flat in Clifton, knowing Anton was there.

I hadn't seen Anton since the night his image was flashed on SABC TV in the mid-1980s, when he was living in Bonteheuwel. We hadn't had contact since his return to South Africa, and he didn't know my whereabouts, although I knew his. When I arrived, the young comrade was reading *They Won't Take Me Alive: Salvadorean Women in Struggle for National Liberation* by Claribel Alegria. We hugged and Anton told me that he had arranged a late-night meeting with Coline, but she hadn't arrived. This implied that it must have been Coline and Robbie who had died, but we had to wait for confirmation. No one knew what had happened, but our two comrades were nowhere to be found.

We suspected the worst and made arrangements to share this terrible news with the Williams and Waterwitch families before the police told them. I met up with Vanessa and Sidney and was surprised by Vanessa's strength. I was still unable to internalise the facts and wanted to believe that the police were using this to cause disarray and get us to expose ourselves; they desperately wanted to kill us, not to arrest us. It was a very, very difficult time for me. Except for Aneez and Shirley, no one outside the unit knew that Coline was part of MK, and I was the only person who knew that Robbie had been recruited. We didn't know what had gone wrong.

During the week that followed, Shirley and Aneez confirmed that it was our comrades who had died in the blast. It was a huge blow, but as a soldier I had to recover quickly and make peace with this awful truth, as I had after Ashley's death. There was no time to mourn. We had to consolidate and support each other in order to continue fighting. The detachment wrote a pamphlet for distribution at Coline and Robbie's funeral, typed it up quickly in our traumatised state, and printed it under difficult conditions at CUPC's Community House office.

We believed Charlie Martin would be the best person to inform Coline's parents, while I instructed Geoffrey Brown to retrieve certain materials stored in the ceiling at Robbie's house, including an AK-47. Geoffrey was a friend of Robbie's. They belonged to the same youth structure, and Robbie had great respect for Geoffrey, although we trusted that Robbie did not share his underground military involvement with him. After I sent Geoffrey to retrieve the materials, however, we spent years trying to get him to hand them over to the detachment. This continued into the 1990s and throughout the demo-bilisation process, when MK was required to hand over all materials to the SADF.

I understood that Geoffrey had subsequently left for Johannesburg, and I didn't have any further contact with him. Much later, I learnt that Zayne Zemaar, Geoffrey's brother-in-law, had said that the AK-47 had been cached in the hills somewhere in Mitchells Plain but had disappeared from there. That was the last information we received about our stolen arms, and I got Zayne to write up a statement to that effect, which he did. I discussed this security breach with Shirley and Aneez in the 1990s. Zayne eventually relocated to Johannesburg and I've had no contact with him since then.

Determined to get to the bottom of the matter, in 1992 I traced the AK-47 retrieved from Robbie's house and found that it had ended up in the hands of a Mitchells Plain activist who was part of Mandela's unofficial security when he visited the area in 1990. This was where our investigation ended. We hoped that Jeremy Veary, then head of crime intelligence for the South African Police Service (SAPS) in the Western Cape, would be able to retrieve the weapons and provide answers to our questions, but we got none.

In the early 1990s, I discovered that the arms cache in Strandfontein that I had visited with Robbie and Coline the last time I'd seen them was still intact – evidence that they did not share their involvement in the military underground with anyone. They were faithful to the end.

As 1990 approached, things started going wrong in Mitchells Plain. In late 1989, we planned a collective operation to support the railway workers' strike by disrupting the railway service. The Macassar, Bonteheuwel, Southern Suburbs, Hottentots Holland and Mitchells Plain units were instructed to execute their missions simultaneously. Four blasts went off in Bonteheuwel, Athlone, Plumstead and Stellenbosch, but the limpet mine that Raphael and Desmond planted on the Mitchells Plain railway track didn't detonate, which we realised when there was nothing in the news. We began to worry, and after this aborted operation, we separated Raphael and Desmond, as we felt we couldn't trust them and needed a proper explanation. Through our enquiry, we established that Raphael and Desmond had involved one of the recruited student activists, Andre Bruce, in the railway line operation, which made us very suspicious of the Mitchells Plain unit, but we didn't have any concrete proof of the unit's fault lines.

We struggled to get the truth out of Raphael and Desmond about what had gone wrong with the operation, and when I met Desmond at Mnandi

Beach, I noticed I was being followed. The same thing happened later at Rondebosch Station, where I received Shirley's calls at a public phone box. I left my blue Toyota at the station one night as we suspected there might be a tracking device on it. Whenever I left the CUPC office, the security police were parked outside. It seemed as though whenever I met with Raphael and Desmond, I was being surveilled. Something was wrong, so the AKD command purged them, cutting all ties. Problems with the unit persisted: Raphael and Desmond had temporarily stored materials at a location in Mitchells Plain that only the two of them knew about, which we had to retrieve and ensure they were safely stored. Meanwhile, the police surveillance around me intensified.

Then, on 10 November 1989, a week after Ruth and I got married, Anton was killed by the security forces. We felt compelled to offer some explanation to our commanders in exile about what we thought went wrong and to get a briefing about what was going to happen post-1990, when political negotiations were to start. I was deemed the best person to meet Chris Hani in Harare and do the explaining. I felt honoured to go, although I didn't initially grasp the enormity of the mission. My legend was that I was on a short vacation, visiting a friend in Zimbabwe.

In a window seat on a small Air Zimbabwe aircraft, I had the wonderful experience of flying over the Limpopo River and leaving South Africa behind. I had been instructed to wear a white short-sleeved shirt in order to be identified by an old man with a briefcase waiting for me at the airport. He accompanied me to have my passport stamped and then disappeared. I was told to wait in town at the St George's Hotel, where I eventually met James Ngculu, our commander in Botswana. I spent the first night at the St George's Hotel, and the next day I was transferred to the Sheraton. There was an indoor swimming pool on one of the floors and I went there to relax. A strong, charismatic man arrived. I had heard about Chris Hani, but I didn't expect this man to be him. We greeted one another and spoke as if we had known each other for a long time.

Comrade Chris acknowledged that the recent past had been tough for us and he allowed me time to relax. He was well informed about what was happening in South Africa and thanked our detachment for the work we were doing. We talked about Ashley Kriel and Timothy Jacobs from Hout Bay. Chris asked if we would receive Anton Fisher into our detachment, as he wanted to go back home. He also enquired about the well-being of Shirley, Aneez and baby Haroon. Then he wanted to chat about me. I appreciated the way he introduced topics relating to the current political situation and what our responses should be. For example, there was talk in the media about the

English rebel cricket team coming to South Africa for a test match in 1990, and Comrade Chris gave clear instructions to us to make sure that the test was derailed. He explained that if the AKD were to expand, it would be to the Eastern Cape – to the Transkei and Ciskei – because of the support the ANC enjoyed in the so-called homelands and because accessing arms would be easier there. Despite the changed political landscape with the imminent unbanning of the ANC and other political organisations, Chris explained that Mandela was not going to denounce the armed struggle, and that our detachment had to remain in place in the underground and to be combat-ready. I had to internalise the long conversation so I could give a verbal report to my commanders, all the while saying to myself, 'What an honour this is.'

I had been instructed to take money back to South Africa, as we had materials but no cash, and I was given R10 000 neatly concealed inside a chocolate box. Some of the money was for our detachment and some was for other MK structures in our region. I had no problem with customs in Harare and flew home safely.

I returned to Cape Town in early January 1990 with renewed energy and hope that our struggle was going to move in a positive direction. I met my commanders to deliver the report and the chocolate box filled with money. Following Comrade Chris's instruction, we conducted an operation at the Avondale Cricket Club in Athlone, which Sidney executed, on 5 January 1990.

Then, on 2 February 1990, President F.W. de Klerk made the historic announcement that all political organisations would be unbanned and the restrictions on people and organisations would be lifted. Thanks to the efforts of those in exile under the leadership of Oliver Tambo, the ANC enjoyed international support and solidarity around the globe, and sanctions had put economic pressure on the apartheid regime. MK also played a powerful role: we were never going to be able to take on apartheid's highly resourced SADF, but we were a revolutionary army that used unconventional means to force the regime into peace talks. The racist government had no other option – they were forced to negotiate with the ANC.

News of Comrade Mandela's release led to national euphoria, and Ruth and I went to the Grand Parade on 11 February to witness his first public address. Mandela was only scheduled to arrive after his release from Victor Verster Prison at 3 p.m. on Sunday, but a mass of people had started gathering on the Parade on Saturday night. He arrived later than expected, and from the balcony of the City Hall he addressed the jubilant thousands patiently gathered on the Parade. We didn't know what was going to happen, but we could feel we were moving into a new phase of the struggle. Comrade Mandela made it explicit in his public statement that the armed struggle would not be abandoned, so we, as MK, decided to validate this announcement with three operations.

Our unit in Paarl was ready to execute a symbolic act that caused damage to state infrastructure. The target was the local municipality in Paarl, which we considered a symbol of oppression because it housed the combined facilities of the local municipality and the court. Charlie Martin had recommended Charles Chordnum, a second cousin of his from Paarl, as a potential recruit. Andrew approached Charles, and he was delighted to serve MK. He was recruited in late 1989, and assisted with the operation. I received instructions from Shirley and Aneez and passed the final instruction on to Andrew to proceed with the operation in Paarl with Charles under his command. The operation was successful, without any injuries.

I was involved in the other two operations that night. The first targeted Newlands Cricket Ground, where a rebel tour was due to take place. Andrew did reconnaissance at Newlands, and Sidney and I executed the operation, placing a limpet at the ticket office. As anticipated, the tour was cancelled as a result of mass protest and our military intervention. Next, we placed a limpet at the Parow Civic Centre, where a meeting by the right-wing AWB was scheduled for the following day.

As the transition from apartheid to democracy began, with negotiations between the government and ANC commencing in earnest, the National Party government moved to normalise the political climate. On 7 June 1990, at a joint sitting of Parliament, President de Klerk announced that he would be lifting the four-year-old state of emergency in all provinces except Natal. It was duly lifted the next day, and four months later, in October 1990, it was lifted in Natal.

We were aware that there were many comrades still in training camps out-side South Africa, waiting to come home to defend our country and bring about non-racialism and democracy, but the apartheid regime wanted Comrade Mandela to renounce the armed struggle. MK would have to hand over all its weapons. Mandela and the ANC were cautious to forgo military capacity, as the peace process was fragile. My meeting with Chris Hani affirmed that the ANC was not going to renounce the armed struggle. The apartheid security forces knew we were a threat because we had the revolutionary masses behind us, and this would be an advantage when our leadership discussed the question of the armed struggle at the negotiations. Hard bargaining had to take place and we were instructed to maintain the underground structures until further orders. There was still the question of whether the apartheid government would negotiate in good faith and honour signed agreements.

Throughout the year, Mandela travelled across South Africa, connecting with the masses. Politically, the country was still volatile. We didn't know exactly how negotiations would play out now that Comrade Mandela and other political prisoners had been released and those in exile, such as Chris Hani and Joe Slovo, had returned home. While the rest of the country was filled with anticipation and excitement, MK had to ensure that our weapons and operatives remained secure. Freedom seemed just a stone's throw away, but as soldiers we remained focused on our mission.

We were worried about the security of our materials in Mitchells Plain, so I met with Desmond McKenzie, whom we had previously purged, and I told him to tell Raphael to store the materials in a safe place. Soon afterwards, in March 1990, the police came in full force to arrest Raphael at his house. They found weapons and ammunition and he was detained under Section 29 of the Internal Security Act, which had not yet been repealed. He then led the police to one of our caches on the outskirts of Mitchells Plain. Pete Arendse, who worked closely with the comrades above ground in Mitchells Plain, alerted me that someone had been arrested with weapons. Neither Desmond nor Raphael was aware of Pete's role and Pete didn't know that the two were part of our unit.

After Raphael's detention, the next logical step was for the security police to come after me: I was linked to Raphael, the Mitchells Plain unit and, as the police would presume, to the command structure above me. My instructions were that if anything happened to any member of the units I commanded, I had to go deep underground. Mandela had been released, but the police were still intent on detaining operatives and rendering MK ineffective. We feared being detained and possibly killed.

When Charlie and I returned to my house from a meeting in Gugulethu in my blue Toyota station wagon, we saw a pale-yellow Nissan, popular among the security police, parked towards the top end of Broad Road in Wynberg, near the railway line. We parked outside my place and went inside, where I quickly explained to Ruth that I was being surveilled by the security police, that Raphael had been detained and that I had to go into hiding. Then I scaled the wall at the back of the house. Charlie drove off in my car to arrange for his wife, Helena, to stay with Ruth and Coline, our two-month-old daughter. Soon after Charlie handed over the car to Ruth that night, the police arrived in full force. They bashed down the door of the main house and came through to the back. They had guns and wore balaclavas. Ruth and Helena were in bed and Ruth began screaming, 'Leave my child!' They didn't even switch on the lights, but wielded their guns and torches, searching, pulling at the ceilings and asking for Melvin Bruintjies. They'd assumed I was there because my car was parked outside.

Meanwhile, I had joined my AKD commanders in an underground house in Zeekoevlei. Living in the safe house was a challenge at first, but I had no choice. Charlie was a great support during this time and nobody suspected he was also in the underground; they saw him solely as a priest and Christian activist. Being involved in MK put a lot of pressure on him, but he had passion and a commitment to the people's liberation struggle.

It wasn't easy leaving Ruth and Coline, and it also put tremendous pressure on our extended families. Things were supposed to be changing for the better, yet for us they seemed to be getting worse. I had to humbly face this contradictory political context, in which there were no guarantees that we'd survive. I accepted my new underground life with grace, just as I had accepted becoming part of MK to ensure that the objectives of our struggle were achieved. Not doing so would have been a huge disservice to all the sacrifices that we had made. Chris Hani had warned us that we would have to be combat-ready in the military underground. At no point could we let down our guard.

The double-storey safe house in Zeekoevlei had a large yard and swimming pool, both of which were out of bounds because we had to remain indoors. Shirley, Aneez and baby Haroon lived in the house, as did Richard Ishmail. Shanil Haricharan, who worked closely with the AKD commanders, also visited the house. A few months later, Ruth and Coline joined us. Little Coline was asthmatic and had eczema, but she was treated by the medical professionals supporting us in MK. We had everything we needed. During this time, the AKD continued working, as we still had units on standby in Bonteheuwel, Hottentots Holland, Macassar and Paarl. Richard was the only person who left the house during the daytime, as he had to go to work and do the grocery shopping. He left early every morning and returned at dusk, and I was impressed by his commitment. For the rest of us, our movements started after dark. On a number of occasions, Shirley and I left the house at night in Seiraaj Salie's beat-up old Peugeot bakkie, mostly to make calls. Richard would open the garage door when we were ready to pull out. When we returned, he was always there, ready to open it again, because the bakkie's silencer was damaged and it made such a racket he could hear it approaching from a mile away.

In June 1990, Shirley was arrested and detained with Haroon, drawing immediate public attention that threw us into disarray. For the sake of security, we were forced to hurriedly pack up the furniture, ammunition and everything else we had at the underground house. We couldn't find another safe house where we could all live comfortably under one roof, so we moved to a flat in Athlone for a short while, and then to Harfield Village, where the place was so small that we were forced to split up. Ruth, Coline and I moved into a house in Wynberg, and from there to a place in Bernodino Heights in the Northern Suburbs, then to Ottery, where we celebrated Coline's first birthday and Christmas. Although those of us in the underground were now living in different places, the command structure and security protocols were maintained, as was our communication with our units on the ground.

In 1991, when indemnity and amnesty were under discussion, we met with our lawyers, Essa Moosa and Taswell Papier. Chris Hani was back in the country by that point, and the political conditions seemed to be favourable for us to return home, but we were ordered to remain underground.

Towards the end of 1991, the legal indemnity process had been started and our stay in the underground finally ended when we were indemnified in October of that year. Richard, Shanil and Aneez were the last comrades to resurface. Ruth, Coline and I stayed in a self-catering unit at the Hansmann Hotel in Somerset West for a short while before Ruth and Coline returned home. I joined them as soon as my indemnity came through.

When I reintegrated into civilian life, Ruth and I agreed to regroup as a family, and just before Coline turned two, we moved into a small room at my mother's house at 67A Smalblaar Road in Bonteheuwel. My mother was ill at the time, but she was over the moon when we were reunited and we celebrated Coline's second birthday with the extended family and plenty of cakes and treats.

The next challenge was finding work. I hadn't earned much when I'd worked at CUPC, and the little that I had at the time I'd taken with me into the underground, so for a short while we had to depend on my mother. The people being released from prison or returning from exile were scrambling for work, and while the ANC had started to establish offices across the country, they never promised that those who had been part of the underground would be able to walk into employment. Many comrades thought they were going to come back and be treated like heroes. I didn't expect it to work out that way, and it didn't. Many of us started from scratch.

We had to build the ANC and continue with our lives. An ANC branch was established in Bonteheuwel, and I was fortunate to be part of that process. Quentin Michels and others had been released from prison and were back in Bonteheuwel, and we all found different ways of earning an income. Quentin went back to teaching, and I had to decide whether to work as a diesel mechanic for a private company or for myself. We weren't expecting charity to come our way, but we were fortunate to receive R900 every month for two or three months from the WPCC based at Cowley House in Woodstock to see us through while we got back on our feet.

Finding work was difficult. I explored opportunities at a few companies, but most were looking for people with work experience. I enquired at Golden Arrow Bus Services, but they didn't have vacancies for diesel mechanics, only bus drivers. 'This could be a small step forward,' I thought. 'My foot will be in the door when a vacancy comes up.' I got a Code 11 heavy-duty driver's licence, completed Golden Arrow's learner's programme and became a bus driver. After organising communities and then negotiating the dangers of underground life, I was suddenly in a rigid work routine. It was an anticlimax but that didn't bother me. What was important was putting food on the table at my mother's house and sending Coline to crèche. After a month or two, I landed a post as a diesel mechanic at Golden Arrow's main repair depot at Arrowgate in Charlesville. I was one of the most experienced mechanics there, so I was given specialised work and earned extra money working overtime and double shifts.

Although those of us who had been in the military underground picked up our lives and reintegrated into civilian society, we knew that the integration of different armed forces was going to happen at some point – an opportunity for those who had participated in the armed struggle to integrate into the new SANDF or the SAPS. I wasn't keen on integrating into either. I hadn't become involved in the struggle to become a policeman. Many MK members had already moved into the police force and others were attracted to the idea of joining Comrade Mandela's bodyguard. The second option didn't appeal to me either, although if instructed by MK to look after our leadership, I'd have done it. I was interested in working as a ship mechanic, however, so I considered joining the navy. I also felt I could fit into the air force, but I ruled out the army completely: I had a negative view of khaki troops.

In 1996, I received a letter reminding me that I was part of the non-statutory forces and had to decide whether I wanted to pursue a career in the SANDF or take a R22 000 package and demobilise. Several other comrades had already taken the money and demobilised, but I decided to integrate. Golden Arrow had been a means to earn money for my family and I was learning each day, but it wasn't really what I wanted to do. I briefly considered pursuing my interests in political or social studies, but in the end I accepted the invitation to the 19 April 1996 intake. I informed Golden Arrow that I was going to Pretoria to pursue this option and that I would let them know the outcome.

I completed the SANDF application and at 9 a.m. on 19 April, I reported to Manenberg Police Station, where two buses waited to take us to Fort Ikapa Military Base in Goodwood. The people in charge of the process offered little advice or time to prepare. I didn't even know what needed to be packed. On arrival at Fort Ikapa, soldiers checked the Certified Personal Register (CPR) to see if our names were on the list, and if they were we could board the bus to Pretoria. It arrived that evening, after a long wait.

At the Wallmansthal base, uniformed soldiers searched our bags thoroughly, took our luxuries, and asked us to declare any medication we had brought before we were medically examined. We were marched to the stores to get khaki uniforms, blankets and steel trunks and then taken to the tent where we'd live. It was very confusing, as we'd had no briefing, but it appeared we were going to be there for a while. I didn't know a single soul; all the other comrades were from black townships, and only myself and a comrade from Kimberley were from the coloured community.

Finally, we were given presentations from representatives from the various arms of service within the SANDF – the army, the air force, the navy and medical services. Personnel from intelligence, engineering, transport, logistics, management and the technical division spoke to us too. Two days were set aside for this and for us to consider where we could best fit in and how we'd be ranked. Members of a British military attaché were there to oversee the process, making sure that it was fair and we were properly looked after. Then our military backgrounds were profiled. I scribbled down that Shirley Gunn had recruited me and that I'd worked with her and Aneez Salie, and I presented this to the officials. A colonel from the ANC issued us with MK certificates after cross-referencing our IDs with the CPR details.

We were accommodated four to a tent and grouped into platoons. Besides being lectured on discipline and the military conduct of the SANDF, our platoon was taken for drills in the early mornings in the dark, and in the afternoons they put us through what they called 'tough drill' or the 'disciplinary drill' on a hill in the heat, until the group couldn't go any more. They didn't seem to take age into account, and some members of our platoon were senior MK veterans who made it very clear that they were not going to drill. Fights broke out. 'This is not right,' I thought. 'We are also soldiers. We are not here as new recruits.' We maintained this position and eventually succeeded: we only drilled when they wanted to teach us something new, and we did not tolerate being treated like new recruits, aimlessly running from one point to another.

I stayed in the camp for two months before I was taken to the air force gymnasium. A colonel in the South African Air Force (SAAF), who was a pilot and member of the ANC, advised me that, given my background and qualification, I'd fit into the mechanical environment of the air force, probably as a flight sergeant. My ranking would be determined by my age – I was thirty-two – and my experience, but he did not take my work in the underground into account. I could have gone into military intelligence, but I'd have had to study and start afresh and my rank wouldn't be guaranteed.

Before I was ranked, we were told that we had to undergo basic military training at the next intake to prepare us to be military soldiers, and another fight with the authorities broke out. We were *already* soldiers! I got a few recruits to oppose this and we succeeded: bridging training was introduced. I was ranked as a flight sergeant, the highest non-commissioned rank below warrant officer, and if I finished the functional courses, I'd progress to the rank of warrant officer. Another comrade, forty-two-year-old Thabiso Molaoa, who'd trained in Ireland and Canada on the Dakota aircraft used by the SAAF, was also ranked as a flight sergeant. When he agreed with this rank, I decided not to put up a fight and accepted it too.

The next step was finding out whether we'd be on short-term contracts or employed as permanent members of the SANDF. Many comrades made the mistake of accepting short-term contracts that they couldn't change afterwards, but a few of us fought to be part of the permanent force and petitioned the colonel and SAAF headquarters regarding our appointments, eventually succeeding in getting permanent engagements.

After a series of negotiations, I was placed at Air Force Base Ysterplaat in Cape Town. The instructors then looked at our qualifications and wanted to test our knowledge. 'Here are my qualifications,' I told them, 'I passed at Olifantsfontein, a nationally recognised institution!' We refused to do any written tests. They were unhappy with our attitude, but we were eventually given technical interviews, and afterwards the officers congratulated us on our excellent responses to their questions. I hoped that would be the last hurdle I'd have to jump.

This whole process took well over a month, during which I had not communicated with Golden Arrow Bus Services, so I knew I'd be fired. On my return to Cape Town, I explained to them that I was taking up the offer to work full-time for the SAAF. The company accepted my decision and, luckily for me, I received the money owed to me. I picked up my Unemployment Insurance Fund (UIF) card, completed some paperwork, and that was the end of my time at Golden Arrow.

I was well received at the motor transport workshop of the Motor Mechanical Mustering division at Air Force Base Ysterplaat. The warrant officer in charge of the workshop showed me around. I was told I would not work on vehicles; I'd be doing mechanical administrative work with the other flight sergeants, all of whom were supervisors in the workshop. They were all white, and there had never been a black or coloured person in the office.

There was a bridging and a mentorship programme, and I shared an office with a white Afrikaans guy, Flight Sergeant Douglas. Duggy, as we called him, was open-minded. He acknowledged that black people had been neglected and understood why we were being given opportunities through the integration process. He was a mechanic and a perfectionist, like me. He did quality assurance work, and because I had done an occupational health and safety course at Golden Arrow, he showed me how the SAAF were doing quality control. In a very short space of time, I was working independently. I got on well with Duggy, but our time together was short-lived, as he took a severance package two years later.

When Duggy left, I took over the workshop administration and completed my studies, obtaining a national diploma in engineering in 2002. Not everyone was happy that I was possibly going to be put in charge of the workshop, however, and they directed their anger towards me. Beyond my functional courses to become a flight sergeant, which I passed without difficulty, I did not have to do further development courses, so I was on the same level as them. I then completed the senior supervisors' course to be eligible for promotion. It was an intense written test on management courses that included subjects like military etiquette and military law. I completed the course successfully and was commissioned to the rank of warrant officer, second class. I was the first coloured person to be promoted to this rank in the Mechanical Transport Workshop in the SAAF, and I could see the other coloured members were excited: they now had hope of advancing too. After one year as warrant officer at Ysterplaat, I was accepted for the officer training course, and on completion of this course I was commissioned as a captain, and appointed as technical officer. By this point, I was the highest-ranked coloured officer in my technical environment.

I was then offered a post in environmental management, which had become an integral part of the Defence Force. I quickly developed a passion for it, despite not having any formal training in this field. I completed the ecological management course offered by the SANDF, and was subsequently utilised as an environmental officer at Ysterplaat. Shortly thereafter, I was given the opportunity to enrol at North West University to do further courses in environmental management. I completed modules in environmental law and environmental impact and risk management, and continued to work in environmental management for two years, receiving various regional and national awards during my time as the base environmental officer. While I was there, Ysterplaat received water management and energy efficiency awards too.

After serving for three years, I was promoted to the rank of major. I subsequently managed members who had been in charge of me when I was in the workshop, and we worked well together – even my previous section head accepted working under me. Being in the SAAF wasn't easy, but as I progressed I grew to love the environment. I saw potential in the people I came into contact with and was happy knowing there were opportunities for them, notwithstanding the resistance to change – as I moved up the ranks, I could sense uneasiness among some coloured members of the old SADF, and communication was strained. There was resentment among more senior members too, but my promotion wasn't a handout. No one from MK was walking around arrogantly in the defence force. In the military underground, we weren't given ranks as members are given in a conventional army. I had therefore accepted the rank given to me by the SANDF and had worked hard to get to where I was.

A highlight was being part of the SANDF's Respect for Cultural Diversity Programme. I went on a month-long facilitators' training course in order to present the short one- or two-week courses to new recruits at various SANDF colleges and training units. Its aim was to communicate the Department of Defence's Equal Opportunities and Affirmative Action Policy to members, especially those involved with basic training. Participants gained an understanding of the history of discrimination in South Africa and its negative impact, particularly on the lives of black people, and the importance of affirmative action and fast-tracking. The programme focused on discrimination, racism, sexism and sexual harassment, redress and support services. I could see that it was having a major impact on people's perceptions and helping to bring members from various backgrounds closer to one another. However, the programme was not well received by everyone and after two years it was discontinued for being too radical.

I am the only member of the AKD to integrate into the SANDF on a full-time basis, besides Charles Chordnum for a short period. In my twenty-three years of service I've progressed to the rank of lieutenant colonel.

My decision not to proceed with the priesthood was not easy, but it was respected and the church gave me the option to return to the ministry when I am ready. My faith was defined by a God of love and justice, and I am comforted by this.

NO TIME TO MOURN

Ruth and I met when we were young and full of energy and wanted to bring about change. We've now been married for almost thirty years. Our daughter, Coline, and our son, Daniel, who was born when Coline was nine, have been able to take advantage of higher educational opportunities.

During the Truth and Reconciliation Commission process in the late 1990s, the AKD felt it was important to approach the Amnesty Committee regarding the deaths of comrades Coline and Robbie. We gave our full cooperation, describing the conflict we'd had with the Mitchells Plain unit we'd purged and providing the TRC with information relating to our detachment. We hoped the TRC would do a thorough investigation, but the hearing we attended was more like an interrogation. It felt as though they thought we were withholding information. In reality, the detachment had gone out of its way to understand what went wrong the night Coline and Robbie died. We had even published a pamphlet at the time that explained three possible scenarios.

The TRC's report refers to the Mitchells Plain unit as being infiltrated. We'd explained in our submission that the Mitchells Plain unit members' behaviour was inconsistent and that we had purged operatives. Geoffrey Brown's role has caused so much confusion and has tarnished the public image of our detachment. Jeremy Veary reported in the investigation into Geoffrey that he was an NIS agent. The TRC summonsed Geoffrey to an in-camera investigation. He admitted that he was an 'unwitting' informant for the NIS, received large sums of money from them monthly, and that his handler was Johan Hattingh. I'd explained that Geoffrey had no link with the Mitchells Plain unit, as far as we knew, and although many suspicious things happened in Mitchells Plain long after the deaths of Coline and Robbie, I believe that the unit's issues had nothing to do with the deaths of our comrades, unless there are circumstances unknown to us. We only got Geoffrey involved because he knew Robbie well. Obviously we didn't know that Geoffrey was an NIS operative. Nevertheless, Geoffrey only became involved after the fact, and I don't believe Robbie would have shared his underground work with him. To date, no one has come up with another version of events and justice has not been done.

Another concern was the TRC's public hearing into Ashley Kriel's death. The hearing offered no closure for the AKD, Ashley's family or the community at large. The TRC found that Ashley was shot while allegedly resisting arrest. According to the police's version of events, Ashley had produced a small .22 pistol in the course of his arrest and Jeffrey Benzien, the senior police officer involved in the arrest, tried to disarm him. A scuffle ensued, during which Ashley was fatally injured by a bullet in his back fired from his own pistol. As with the inquest, there was a 'no blame' verdict.

There is also no closure regarding the death of Anton Fransch, nor Mark Henry's involvement in this incident. I didn't attend the gross human rights violation hearing into Anton's death held at UWC in 1997, but I read about it afterwards. Mark, who had changed his name to Yazir, spoke at the hearing, but the TRC inexplicably did not approach Shirley or Aneez to give more details about how he had deserted and compromised the detachment, actions that ultimately led to Anton's death. If they had, it might have helped get to the truth.

It was never the AKD's intention to harm civilians in our operations, and we went to great lengths to prevent any casualties by doing thorough reconnaissance before and during operations. Despite these measures, there was one casualty, Moegamat Nurudien Bartlett, at the Bonteheuwel Rent Office. Sidney, Coline and Vanessa had done the usual reconnaissance, and the device was timed to go off after 10 p.m., when the area would be deserted. It had been inconceivable to us that someone would walk past the rent office at that time of night and handle the milk carton in which the limpet was placed, but Bartlett did and it exploded. Sidney, Vanessa and Aneez testified to the Amnesty Committee about what had happened the night Bartlett was injured. We approached the Bartlett family before we went through the public TRC amnesty process, and when they heard the truth about what happened, they said in a statement that they had no regrets. The Bartlett family, and even Nurudien himself, understood that we weren't reckless killers and that our operations were in support of a political objective.

I'm constantly reminded of the sacrifices made by my comrades. We have buried so many of them: Chris Hani, Ashley Kriel, Anton Fransch, Coline Williams and Robbie Waterwitch, as well as Richard Ishmail, who was murdered at his Woodstock home in 2007; Andrew Adams, who passed on after a short illness in 2011; Paul Endley, who died of a heart attack in 2012; and Patrick Presence, who passed on in 2017. It is the thought of their contribution to the struggle that motivates me to continue working hard in the interest of social justice. We have achieved political freedom but not economic freedom. That struggle continues.

5

Mike Dearham

Divine Hand

'YOU KNOW WHAT we should do with you?' I said to Mark. 'We should take you to the road and put a bullet in the back of your head.' Mark Henry had deserted the Ashley Kriel Detachment, leading to the death of our comrade Anton Fransch at the hands of the police. I was at Richard Ishmail's restaurant, Off Morocco, in Cape Town, and Richard had pointed Mark out, because I'd never met him before. The discussion got heated and I told him to leave the restaurant. I felt like I was venting my anger at everyone who had abandoned the struggle during a time when cadres were sacrificing their lives in the fight for a just society. Why would a trained cadre, who had been through MK military training, choose to leave the unit? What had gone wrong? Mark had apparently deserted the AKD because he wanted to be out on the streets shooting the *boere*, but then he had sold one of us out to them. I thought back to my own experience of MK training, trying to understand it.

I left South Africa via Botswana in late 1988 and was away for a year. I spent three to four months in Lusaka, waiting in transit, and from there I was taken to Dar es Salaam. On arrival in the Tanzanian capital, I was met by ANC comrades, blindfolded and taken to a camp where I stayed for almost seven months. It was a small camp, deep in a forest, and there were maybe forty comrades in total, but it was all very secretive and no one divulged anything more to me. I was put through the standard intensive training: military combat work, political education, firearms training and military engineering.

There was so much discipline involved in living at the camp, and days in the bush were rigorous, starting with waking up early and fetching water from the river for cooking. I became a student again, and consumed Lenin's political teachings. We were taught to digest information and keep it in our heads, and we were not permitted to write notes. The instructors would teach us stuff over and over again and the next day we were tested on what we had learnt.

The camp commander was a charismatic man and I liked him a lot. My firearms instructor, Pitso, also made an impression on me. When we trained with the bazooka, a short-range rocket launcher fired from the shoulder, we aimed at a blanket hung between two pillars. I was adept at judging the wind speed and would generally hit the target three out of five times, which wasn't bad. I was a good student who trained well and in time I earned the name 'Mr Bazooka'.

The general feeling I had at the camp was that there was disparity between comrades. Many had been in exile too long, and desperately wanted to go home, but they had not been deployed. There was an underlying resentment that I could not understand at the time, and it troubled me that some comrades had this mindset due to endless waiting. Nevertheless, it was a great experience meeting comrades who hadn't been home in a long while and exchanging ideas with them. Our conversations were always about politics, never about personal matters. The experience had a deep impact on me. When I left the camp, I was completely changed.

My mom chose my name from my parents' interpretation of the biblical meaning of 'Michael the Archangel sent from God'. My dad, Wilfred – or Bunny, as his friends called him – was from Cape Town. He was not highly educated, but he had a creative spirit and was a quiet, contemplative man. He had a flair for the arts and painted beautiful murals of birds and wildlife on the walls of his family home in Claremont, where my aunt still lives today.

My mom's name is Sybil. Unlike my dad, she came from a very religious home that began as a violent one. My grandfather Douglas, known as Dougy, gambled, drank and gave his family a tough time. As the eldest, my mom spent most of her time looking after her four siblings. When she was in her twenties, she started corresponding with a pen pal named Wilfred in Cape Town. The correspondence went on for years, even when the family moved from Durban to Johannesburg.

In Johannesburg, things went terribly wrong for Dougy. He owed people money and was forced to uproot the family once again and move back to Durban. Then Dougy found Jesus via a black pastor from Umbilo Road Evangelical Baptist Church in Durban. Pastor Duma had a huge following and made such an enormous impression on my grandfather that he found salvation and became a devout Christian. He went from one extreme to the other in the way he viewed life, himself, his wife and his kids. The violence stopped, but he remained a very strict disciplinarian.

My mom continued writing to her pen pal in Cape Town. In one of his letters, Wilfred asked her to marry him. They had never met but had exchanged photographs. My grandfather put the matter to Pastor Duma, who prayed about it. 'Dougy,' said the pastor, 'this is a divine meeting of two minds. I give my blessing.' So Wilfred came to Durban to meet Dougy and Pastor Duma, and he and Sybil married soon afterwards. The pastor blessed their marriage, and as a result of this my grandfather always believed that the marriage was divine and that God ordained everything that came from it.

I was born a year later, the first of my parents' three children. The newly-weds moved into my grandfather's house in a mixed coloured and Indian community. I remember the house – it was like the one in the horror movie *Psycho*: to get to the toilet you had to go down a dark flight of stairs.

It was a very strict home. From the age of five or six, I had to get up at 6 a.m. for prayers. Reciting scripture was drilled into me, so much so that I can still quote many verses. My dad was passive in the marriage and was often forced into submission by his father-in-law's domineering character and powerful charisma. My mom was dominant in the relationship and always wanted to please her father, with the result that my poor dad's entire existence was confined to Sybil and Dougy's world.

The Indian community frequently called my grandfather to sort out family problems. He had a special attachment to me, and because of my father's passivity he co-opted me as his son. He was never close to any of his own sons, and I became the apple of his eye: 'Dougy's boy'. He took me into people's homes and I watched him solve issues and exorcise demons.

My parents had two more children in close succession, Gregory and Glenda, but I was the blue-eyed boy. All my mother's efforts were invested in me. Despite their strong Christian beliefs, there was deep-seated racism in our home. I was exposed to subtle racism from a young age, but I didn't understand it and it was never explicitly articulated at the time.

My grandfather's family was of European origin, but he happened to be darker skinned. All his brothers and sisters lived in Hillbrow in Johannesburg and were classified as white, but my grandfather was classified as coloured. Nevertheless, he believed that he was of a superior race. He admired white people, and missionaries in particular. At the time, white missionaries were often seen as demigods because they came with charitable gifts, such as huge boxes of clothing and medicine for the communities they wanted to convert. Dougy spoke to his white missionary friends with great reverence and respect but, strangely, he didn't see himself as their equal. He had an inferiority complex but tried hard to be on their level and was always going to great lengths to please them. My father reached a point where he couldn't tolerate this any more, and he decided it was time we moved out.

We moved to Greenwood Park, an affluent coloured area in Durban, where the five of us – my parents, my siblings and I – lived in a garage subdivided into rooms. We were dead poor. My father did painting jobs to sustain the family and we struggled to make ends meet. We were conscious of the affluence surrounding us, and my mother, in particular, always felt she deserved better.

There was a lot of pressure on my dad. He worked extremely hard with his small bakkie, ladders and stained brushes, and sometimes I went with him. My mother always wanted to improve the way he did things and she created promotional leaflets. The three of us would drive around handing out leaflets door to door so my dad could get painting jobs.

There was racism in Greenwood Park as in other parts of the country. Being neither black nor white, coloured people had a pseudo-identity rather than any real identity of their own. They perceived themselves as better than black Africans, and I grew up with this false sense of worth. Because the education system and communities were racially segregated, and Briardene Primary, which I attended, was a coloured school, we did not interact with children of other races.

I was obedient and hard-working and excelled at school. I received many awards from Standard 1 right up to Standard 5. I perceived myself as bright because I was told I was, and I always came first in my class. I was also considered good-looking, which drew people to me. My cheeks were always red because the aunties pinched them and said, 'Oh you handsome, clever boy.' Despite our poverty, I was favoured and spoilt. Because I was lighter skinned, had straight hair and was the firstborn son – an 'angel' – I was put on a pedestal. My siblings were not treated as well as I was, and my brother in particular carried a lot of pain because he was subjected to this form of favouritism.

I was an introvert as a child. I hated public exposure or being singled out. I remember being eight years old and forced to tell the story of Adam and Eve in the Garden of Eden at family gatherings – to the delight of the adults. 'Oh my goodness, he's so clever!' they would marvel. 'He reads the Bible on his own.' Pastor Duma saw me as a divine product. I saw myself as superior because everyone around me held that view.

My mother assumed the mantle of my grandfather. She tried to be everything he was and stood for, particularly a strict disciplinarian. Despite harbouring a deep-seated resentment towards him for abusing her mother, Hilda, she wanted to mimic him and was brutally strict. Our shoes had to be polished for school, our clothes had to be ironed, the bed in which we all slept had to be folded up, and dishes had to be washed in regimental style. Sweets were forbidden. She regimented church time, prayer time, homework time and bedtime with an iron fist. But, as the favoured child, I got away with murder. When I messed up I would be forgiven, but Greg and Glenda went through hell – someone had to pay when something wasn't done right, and *they* got the beatings. In line with the biblical philosophy 'spare the rod and spoil the child', we were disciplined with a stick or a belt. We would lie on the bed, bare-bummed, listening to my mother reading that verse while my dad, an unwilling partici-pant, administered the punishment because my mother told him to do so.

I saw very little of my dad's family, mostly because my mother was the stronger and more dominant personality in the partnership. I am told that my grandfather Arthur (from whom I get my middle name) was a handsome man, a Casanova, which was the reason my grandmother divorced him when my dad was very young. My grandfather played the saxophone, and was a long-standing member of the Salvation Army. He died from a heart attack when I was about fifteen. I never met my grandmother, Winnifred Dearham, who died from cancer when my dad was nineteen. My dad often spoke about his mother, and from what I was told they were very close. As a young man, my dad worked to put his brother, Terry, through medical school. I often got the sense from my mother that she expected some kind of payback from Terry, who later emigrated to Australia. He never returned to South Africa, even for a visit, and my parents did not have contact with him or his family. I found it very strange that he had emigrated and almost erased his life as a South African.

Then came my father's salvation. He was a Christian, but not as religious as my mother. He converted and his calling from God was to go to Bible School, so we moved to Bosmont, Johannesburg, a coloured working-class community near the mine dumps, separated from Soweto by a highway.

In Bosmont, I started high school at Christian Botha College. The pre-valence of gangsterism, drugs and crime in Bosmont was greater than in Greenwood Park and I spent the first year at Christian Botha with the wicked-est kids on the planet. To adapt, I became like them. I wanted to be the best at whatever I did, and so I became the leader of the pack. I was rebellious but bright. Teachers could not understand how I could fraternise with the worst of the worst, smoking *zol* and cigarettes, but always achieve distinctions. I was eventually moved from that school to Riverlea High, near Crown Mines and Nasrec in Johannesburg, in 1976.

Nothing eventful happened at Riverlea High. I reverted to being a good student. The school was a bit more integrated than my previous schools had been, and I met black kids for the first time. I had deep-seated prejudice against them because of the way I was groomed and the baggage I carried. I recall an incident at home when Greg, Glenda and I got a thorough beating from my mother for eating something that we were not supposed to. 'You spoilt brats!' she said as she whipped us with a belt. 'Don't you know what is happening in this country? The blacks are coming and this is how you behave.' The point was that we had to do our schoolwork and become educated because the blacks were going to take over and we would be left behind.

At Riverlea, I started meeting people who were politically conscious. I had teachers like Arnold Sckhady from Eersterust, who travelled daily from Pretoria to Johannesburg to teach us. In English classes, we read progressive poetry. Nevertheless, the 1976 student uprising didn't affect us. Other schools a few kilometres away went up in flames, but Riverlea High remained in a cocoon. We heard about current affairs in the news, but it was like it was happening in another world that had nothing to do with us. As teenagers, the last thing on our minds was the issue of Afrikaans textbooks. I did not ask questions.

When my father was called to attend the Evangelical Bible School, I changed schools again, to Chris Jan Botha High School. The Bible School period was another struggle. While my father was studying we were extremely poor, poorer than at Greenwood Park, and living on handouts. To earn a little money, my mother cooked for the other Bible students. This was the first time I was exposed to religious thought on another level. I talked to the students, who came from all over the country, and my interactions with them stimulated my thinking about spirituality and science. Until then I'd had a very scientific approach to life, but Christianity afforded me the means to tap into my own spirituality. In 1977, my father was called by God to go to Eersterust, a little *dorpie* near Pretoria, next to Mamelodi and Silverton, to spread the gospel to the non-believers there.

Coloured people had been forcibly removed to Eersterust from Marabastad in 1963 under the Group Areas Act. In Eersterust I underwent a cultural revolution. I was introduced to soul music for the first time and completely submerged myself in it, listening to groups like the O'Jays and the Temptations. Having only heard Christian music all my life, this felt like an explosion of sound. I was also exposed to a whole new group of interesting people thanks to the culture of gangsterism in Eersterust. The gangsters dressed smartly, were respected in the community and carried guns. Eersterust was a melting pot and precipitated an awakening in me. It was here that I experimented with drugs, rock 'n' roll and, later, sex. I thanked the Lord for having called my father to serve this community.

In Standard 9 I was caught with a joint during exams and taken to Westbury Police Station. I stayed in jail overnight and discovered an entire underworld. Meanwhile, my dad was summoned to bail me out. He had never suspected that I was smoking marijuana, and suffered great humiliation.

The morning after my release, Mr Veldtman, the school principal, announced that one of his pupils had been arrested with *zol*. He called me up on stage in front of an assembly of 600 students to make an example of me. His message was that if you did drugs you were going to fail. Soon after this, I wrote my exams and got straight As. This infuriated Veldtman and he repeatedly tried to make an example of me. If I came to school with long hair, he would send me straight to the barber for a short-back-and-sides schoolboy cut. I was victimised, but I had the respect of a huge following at school.

In the mornings when I went to school, I'd see this pretty young girl in the yard across the road, and I admired her from a distance. Her name was Kim Adams. Her brothers and mother were very protective of her, so at first I did not want to get involved. Nevertheless, I started dating Kim at the end of Standard 9, when she was in matric at Iona Convent, and she fell pregnant. My parents' response was to ship me off to my grandfather Dougy in Wentworth, Durban, and I went to yet another school to complete my education. It was then that my true political awakening happened.

There were school boycotts in many parts of the country in 1980, the year I was in matric. My uncle Peter McKenzie, a well-known photographer, had a big influence on me during this time. He was the rebel and radical in my Christian family. He talked to me about his struggle photographs and recommended books that I should read about Steve Biko and others. I had never really taken him seriously before then. Uncle Peter introduced me to the comrades in the hostel where Steve Biko had lived as a medical student. At night, we would visit Biko's comrades, mostly members of the Azanian People's Organisation (AZAPO) and the PAC. I'd sit in the corner while they discussed politics, listening to the debates and soaking it all up. A whole new world opened up. Books by Lenin were passed on to me and I read *Umsebenzi*, the Communist Party's quarterly newsletter.

I decided to participate in the schools boycott in 1980: pens down and no attendance. My school, Fairvale Senior Secondary School, and many surrounding schools came to a standstill. Trevor Tangling, Robert McBride and I initiated the boycott at Fairvale, and I assumed a leadership role. We only attended three or four months of class that year, and for the rest of the year we were usually to be found outside, addressing students from the school balcony. In between all this, I hitchhiked to Eersterust to see Kim and our daughter, Tracey, who was born in May that year. While I finished matric,

Kim held the fort and found a job. Even with all my philandering, I knew in my heart that Kim was my destination.

I was finding myself, and my radical side was growing. I wrote my final exams at the end of that year and did not do too badly, achieving a B average despite having been out of school for so many months.

In 1981 I was accepted at the University of the Witwatersrand and I enrolled to do a BSc degree, receiving a bursary because I had done well in maths and science in matric. However, I did not adjust well to university and made a complete hash of it. I needed to be self-disciplined and work hard, but there were too many things going on in my life: I was a father and madly in love. Kim and I got married the following year, and I dropped out of university and tried to find work. My first job was at LNB Motors in Durban. My mom proposed that I bring Kim and Tracey to live with us and that I enrol at the University of Natal. Kim and Tracey were subsequently shipped down. It was pure hell. My mother blamed Kim for my 'naughtiness' and hated her for supposedly messing up my career. She held church meetings, trying to chase out the devil in the house – in her mind, it was the devil that caused all these bad things. It pushed me over the edge and I became a complete rebel.

The following year, when my second daughter, Leslie, was born, I was rebelling in earnest. The responsibility was too much for me. Kim and I were so young. At home, my mother was forcing me in one direction and victimising Kim. Kim was miserable, and her parents took her and our baby girls back to Eersterust.

I got a job at an Indian motor spares shop in Durban. I bought a motorbike and started doing off-road trips with my cousins and friends, smoking marijuana, rebelling against the system and questioning the status quo, Christianity and everything it stood for. I hated what I saw around me – everything from church to family and politics was abhorrent and compromising to the extreme. I travelled all over South Africa, hitchhiking and motorbiking. The imbalances and injustices in the country became more explicit for me in that period. My resolve was slowly building, and I did everything to rebel against my family's expectations of me.

It was tough, though. I had two beautiful daughters who increasingly began to influence me, but as a young man in a turbulent state of mind, I wasn't honouring my parental obligations. Kim had to work, so much of the day-to-day parenting for Tracey and Leslie was thrust on to her parents, who provided the stability that the girls needed. When I spent time with them I tried my best to play a fatherly role, but I wasn't very present. Sometimes I vanished for weeks or months at a time, and no one knew where I was, not even my parents. Those times were an attempt to make sense of things, but the details are a void, blanked out. I liken that period to when Jesus went into the wilderness and spent days and months and years just contemplating and discovering people and things.

I knew I had to change and start playing my part in supporting my young family. Luckily, I knew my potential and believed in myself. Whatever circles I found myself in, among friends or family, people listened to and followed me. I knew I had influence. But then I lost my brother.

Greg was finishing high school in Pietermaritzburg at the time, while I was in Johannesburg doing some menial job. One day, he was walking home from a party with some girls, when they were stopped by a couple of thugs. The thugs started smacking one of the girls around and Greg, doing what he thought was right, stepped in to defend her. A knife was drawn, a scuffle ensued and he was stabbed in the heart. He was rushed to hospital, but efforts to resuscitate him were futile. He died in a brutal way at the age of nineteen. I was not as close to Greg as I should have been as a brother, and losing him compounded all the unresolved issues we'd had. I felt that I had not given him guidance because I was selfishly doing my own thing elsewhere, and I wished that I had been more present in his life. His death threw me into a spin and I couldn't process my emotions. I tried to suppress them, but went off the rails instead.

A good few years passed while I was in this state of mind. In 1985, I moved back to Johannesburg and returned to Wits. Kim and I drew closer to one another; our relationship strengthened. I also had time to bond with Tracey and Leslie. I shared my view of life with them in ways they could understand and spoke to them about the big picture: it wasn't only about South Africa but about the world – the Israeli–Palestinian conflict and the suffering of the Australian Aboriginals. The girls were thus exposed to the broader political and economic situation from a young age. I tried to give them knowledge that they wouldn't find anywhere else in their upbringing – not in a book, nor from my parents or Kim's parents. I remember them questioning whether they were good Christians according to the family's definition and I explained belief systems to them.

I enrolled for a BSc degree at Wits again. This time round, I did very well, achieving distinctions in maths, science and chemistry in my first and second years. I felt that I needed to prove to others that I was intellectually capable. I was first in my class in 1985 and 1986, and Wits offered me a scholarship to study medicine. It was rare for a BSc student to be offered the opportunity to go to the medical school in Parktown. I accepted the offer and started studying medicine in 1987. I was doing well, but soon I had an overwhelming sense that I should be doing something else to address the world's problems. I didn't see myself solving them as a doctor.

One of my professors came to my house twice, asking me why I had stopped attending classes. I replied that I wasn't interested in becoming a doctor and wanted to do something else. What I didn't tell him was that I didn't know what that was. Later, another professor called me to his office and tried to persuade me to pursue studies in anatomy because I excelled at the subject. I said I'd think about it. Soon after that, other lecturers came to my house. They thought Kim was putting pressure on me to provide financially for the family. I dropped out in third year and never went back to university.

Soon after that, Shanil Haricharan entered my life, as did Joe Nxusani and many others from a radical group of friends living in Mayfair. Shahiz, whom I knew from Riverlea High, was the link to Shanil. We got together at this little house in Mayfair where the political activists lived. I was initially not close to Shanil, but Joe Nxusani and I were both rebellious and we were very close. After I left Wits, Joe and I went to work on shutdowns at the Sasol refinery on a two-year contract, pretending to be pipefitters. I don't know how we did it, but we did.

People who worked on the shutdown were paid a fortune. Shutdowns happened on an annual basis and there was a migration of mainly coloured pipefitters to Sasolburg and to the platinum mines in Nelspruit and Brits. Hundreds of guys from Mitchells Plain, Wentworth and other parts of the country would converge at Sasol to work. It was like a prison system, but more sophisticated. We were all working in this place out in the sticks and sleeping in a dormitory. All hell frequently broke loose between the different factions from Cape Town and Port Elizabeth, and if you were not in a clique you were dead. I'll never forget the unbelievable violence that went on there.

Kim stayed with the kids in Mayfair, and Shanil, who lived nearby, would visit the family. Whenever Joe and I got leave for a few weeks, we'd go home to Mayfair and meet up with the guys. Joe was politically conscious. He had qualified as a lawyer and was very smart. On one occasion in Johannesburg, Shanil asked us what we were doing, wallowing in misery just to make a quick buck at Sasol. We were bright, he said, so why were we wasting our time and our lives? He told us that it was time to become aware of what was happening in the country, get out of our bad habits and contribute to the struggle in a meaningful way. We listened to Shanil; what he said made sense. He brought a fresh political perspective, neither rebellious nor anti-establishment, and he encouraged us to channel our energy in a constructive and organised way. Shanil was a stabilising force. Crazy, rebellious Joe says that he saved us.

Shanil did not hide anything. Once he had gained our trust, he asked me to go to Gaborone on a mission to transport communication for MK. I felt quite chuffed. Shanil trusted me, and I wanted to prove to him that I could carry out the mission.

I hit the road to Gaborone in Shanil's beige Toyota. It was about 2 p.m. when I overtook a car and, in an attempt to avoid another oncoming car, I hit the dirt shoulder. The Toyota spun out of control and rolled a few times. I was unhurt, but I was alone and in the middle of nowhere. 'Oh my God,' I thought. 'Now what?'

Shanil had instructed me that the communication hidden in the car should be destroyed if anything happened, so I took the papers out from the door panels, tore them into thousands of pieces and scattered them. I hitched a lift back to Johannesburg, leaving the car, which was registered in Shanil's name, lying on its roof. I got back feeling terrible and responsible for what had happened, even though it had been an accident. I reported it to Shanil and then didn't hear from him for some time.

During the weeks that followed, I was at home and unemployed. Then Shanil came to me about a second mission, a much more serious one. Seemingly unperturbed by my accident with his car, he asked me to be the driver again, and said I would be driving a bigger car, a hired Toyota Cressida. My legend was that I was Muslim and selling worker's overalls. This time I was much more clear-minded and focused on the mission. In Gaborone, I met James Ngculu, whom we called Faiz. We had a long chat and a couple of drinks. The Cressida was taken away. The next morning, the car was returned, loaded with weapons, and I drove back to South Africa.

On my way back through Koster in the Northern Transvaal, there was a massive roadblock. I was driving a car packed with arms, and I panicked at the sight of Casspirs in front of me. If they found the weapons in the car, I was dead. I stopped at the roadblock. On the seat was a big five-litre Liquifruit box, packed with detonators. I distinctly remember Shanil warning me that if I got into a situation such as this one, I shouldn't smoke, scratch my head or fidget. I must act normally, stay calm and stick to my legend. A policeman climbed into the car and began chatting to me. Everything seemed fine, but a big Afrikaner in the Casspir was watching my behaviour. I had been warned that there would be someone watching, so I didn't look at him. To my relief, I was allowed to pass through the roadblock. Soon afterwards, I picked up an SADF soldier hitchhiking on the side of the road, and I had no problems on the drive back to Mayfair after that. Once back in Johannesburg, I parked the car and informed Shanil. The car was taken away and I was not told anything more. So ended the mission.

Completing the mission was a revelation for me. I had a sense that I was contributing to something meaningful. All the turmoil inside me, the rebelliousness and anger, was being channelled into something constructive. For the first time I felt proud to be part of something – not that I knew quite what it was at the time, only that it was linked to the armed liberation struggle.

After my successful mission, I met Aneez Salie at our little house in Mayfair. In came this big guy with Shanil. It was not a long meeting; he just wanted to put a face to the name. That is how my involvement with the Ashley Kriel Detachment started. It was decided that I would go to Lusaka, Zambia, to be trained to support the AKD in more sophisticated methods of communication. I had mixed feelings about this: I was sad because I would have to leave my family behind, but I was happy because I had found a new purpose.

In late 1988 I was in Lusaka, staying in a brick house in a township with Miranda, James Ngculu's wife, a comrade named Gugulethu and a third comrade. Miranda was a lovely woman and Gugulethu was sharp as a razor and highly disciplined, but the other comrade was ill-disciplined; he womanised, going out and coming back very drunk late at night. Gugulethu made a deep impact on me. He spent a lot of time in his room reading and he educated me politically. We were not supposed to leave the house, so I spent all of my time with him and Miranda. I was eventually taken to Dar es Salaam and then on to a training camp.

My first stop after my basic military training was the Solomon Mahlangu Freedom College (SOMAFCO) in Tanzania, where I spent a few nights in a private room. Then I moved on to Zambia and stayed in a big house in the middle-class Roma district in Lusaka, where my specialised radio training started. There was a large gate, which was guarded, and a long driveway. We entered the house through the kitchen, and inside was a long corridor with rooms leading off it and a big lounge on the left with large windows. That was my world. There were washing lines everywhere outside. I asked why and was told that it prevented SADF helicopters from landing in the big yard. Our staple diet was *chima*, which is pap, and carpenter fish. A local Zambian cook prepared food for us daily. I only ever saw the cook and the radio instructor, but there were at least three others living in the house at the time.

I stayed in the house for several months. The comrade who trained me in radio communication was an expert in Morse code. The mastery is in the finger and it's all about rhythm: *ditata, tiditatata, tititida*. I am not a rhythmical person, so the comrade taught me rhythm by teaching me to dance, and we danced the Morse code in the room where I was confined. The Russian-made transmitter that we used was intended to send and receive encrypted messages to and from Lusaka, and decoding was done using codes contained in a combustible code book, which I was solely responsible for. The transmitter, along with other equipment, was later smuggled into South Africa to the AKD command.

Once, in my second month at the Lusaka house, I heard deep voices in the living room. I had just finished a training session and emerged to find Comrade Alfred Nzo in the corridor. I did not recognise him immediately, but my instructor introduced us. On another occasion, just before I returned to South Africa, I came across Chris Hani and Limpho, his wife, sitting in the lounge watching the Zambian National Broadcasting Corporation (ZNBC) News. Chris wanted to know how Shirley Gunn was, a question I could not answer. He clearly knew about me, what I was doing and why I was there, and which detachment I was linked to. We spoke about the current situation in South Africa and what I thought about it. He asked very general political questions, and nothing about what I was doing in Lusaka. I was guided by his questions, only saying what needed to be said and then keeping silent, demonstrating the discipline I had learnt.

In late 1989 I was sent back to South Africa to be deployed in Cape Town. I travelled by bus and stopped briefly in Johannesburg to visit Kim, just to tell her I was fine and that I was going to be deployed. I could not say more; I didn't know more. Then I was off again.

I suspected that I would be linked up with Aneez. I arrived in Cape Town where Shanil was waiting to take me to a safe house in Northpine. There, I met Richard Ishmail for the first time, before being ushered into a room where Aneez was indeed waiting. I briefed him on my military training and my specialised training in radio communication and informed him that the radio equipment was on its way.

I had come out of training with romanticised ideas of how I would tackle the enemy – going out guns blazing. But I soon learnt that life in the underground is about patience, analysis, timing and waiting for the right moment to act, as military action is not an end in itself but a means to an end. We had routines in the safe house: wake up, monitor and analyse the news, prepare food and engage in political discussions. The emphasis was on understanding what was happening in the country at a political level; as the military, we supported the political struggle, we didn't lead it.

We had planned to use my skills with radio equipment to communicate with Lusaka, but this proved difficult. Using the equipment created a security risk because comrades had to transport me to a suitable venue. Many of these safe houses had zinc or metal roofs, resulting in very poor transmission. The commanders were pedantic about the language used in our messages, as mistakes and misunderstandings had to be avoided. As a result I was severely stressed during radio sessions, while also remaining in a constant state of alert, even though I always had a comrade or two with me to ensure our safety and keep an eye out for the security police.

Kim joined us at the safe house a few weeks later. The real struggle for me was an internal one – to adapt to an underground lifestyle very different from what I had expected. I followed orders and performed my tasks to the best of my ability. All tasks, even washing the dishes, had to be done properly. I learnt that it was not the task itself but rather the approach to the task that was important. I still follow this practice, for which I am eternally grateful. Going through my mind while I was in the underground were the teachings of religion and preparation for the life hereafter. My experiences of self-sacrifice gave a new meaning to Christianity. I began to see religious practice as self-serving, and I developed a different approach. It was an important lesson. I saw the philosophy of Christianity as being about changing the system. At the time, my favourite essay was 'The Comradeship of Karl Marx and Jesus Christ' by Cedric Mayson.

After a threatening security scare in early 1990, Aneez, Shirley and Richard left the Northpine safe house immediately, while Shanil, Kim and I stayed on for a short while. Shanil asked if we knew anyone Kim and I could stay with, and the person who came to mind was Bruintjies, a truck driver who lived in Atlantis and who delivered fresh produce to Pretoria. Bruintjies used to visit our neighbour's house in Eersterust, and when I went home on week-ends to see the kids and my mother, he was there. Shanil and I reconnoitred his place beforehand to see if it was safe for us to stay there. Then, in the middle of the night, the three of us drove to Atlantis. I had to plead with Bruintjies not to tell people our real names because he was a flamboyant person, engaging with everyone in the street, and would have told the whole of Atlantis if he'd got a chance. Our legend was that we were there because Kim had a drinking problem.

It was bustling in Atlantis, and people were in and out of Bruintjies' home, so we soon had to move again, this time to stay with Amanda and Eugene, a couple living in Northpine. Amanda was from Namibia and had worked with Kim in Cape Town when she was temping. They clicked and Amanda often spoke to Kim about her husband Eugene, a trade unionist, so we felt safe with them. Eugene was a very quiet man, and the couple had a low-key social life, so we stayed there for some time. In exchange, we cleaned and did chores.

Staying with them was hard. We did not know what was going on, how long we were going to stay there, or the reason why we were being isolated from the rest of the AKD for so long. I'd go out in the dead of night to speak to Shanil from a public phone box four kilometres away, and he told me that if we lay low we would be fine. Everyone in our unit was on ice. Kim and I stopped talking about going home and reuniting with our girls and families; it was too hard. This period of isolation was one of the most difficult experiences for me to endure.

Our legend to Eugene was that we needed to lie low for political reasons, and he was very supportive. I think he would have harboured us there for as long as necessary, but Amanda was understandably afraid, especially after we returned to the safe house in Northpine to fetch bags filled with arms, which we then stored at Amanda and Eugene's house.

We tried to handle the tension with kindness and positive talk, but the house was small and it became claustrophobic. Over time, Kim and I felt an overwhelming sense of imprisonment. One night, Amanda told us there was a huge roadblock close to Northpine. We were dead scared and I stayed up all night preparing for an attack. I had an AK-47 at the ready because if something happened I had to put up a fight to defend us; we could not just be taken. Luckily, nothing happened and the next day we went back to our routine.

After Amanda and Eugene's house, we moved to Aneez's sister Ayesha's place in Belhar. Once there, I did not hear from anyone in the AKD for about three weeks. I was then moved to the safe house where the AKD command was based, but Kim remained with Aneez's sister. Kim was pregnant again and thought she was losing her mind. She started imagining that she could hear the voice of the Station Strangler, and that he was coming to get us.

Then, one day, Kim was brought back to the command safe house, where we had a sit-down with Aneez, Shanil and Richard when Shirley was still in detention. 'You probably wondered why we kept you there,' said Aneez, referring to the long period when Kim and I had been isolated. I had wondered. He explained that they had received intelligence that Kim was 'eating out of the hand of the enemy'. Later, they discovered that our informer had been referring to someone with the MK codename 'Kim'. I was told that Kim would be going back to Eersterust soon.

I then went to stay in Athlone, which was great because the comrades were all there and I had people to speak to. We also had some freedom of movement, with visits to the beachfront in the dead of night to breathe in the sea air. It was a huge relief. There was fantastic comradery in the Athlone house – when something happened, everyone gathered in the lounge and watched the television together. Nevertheless, when other people came to the house, we were not permitted to see them and they could not see us. We continued to exercise strict security measures within the unit even though the political environment seemed to indicate a positive negotiation process between the ANC and the apartheid government.

Kim was sent back to Eersterust on a luxury bus. On her return home, she discovered that her father had used her ID and incurred debt against her name. She had to find work to pay it off, support her family, pay school fees and buy school uniforms and clothing for the girls. During that time she was in weekly contact with Shanil via a public phone. It was a big adjustment for her to be reunited with the girls, the family and the noise of ordinary life. After Kim left, I knew I had to go home too. I had constant internal conflict: if one puts everything on a scale, with the struggle for change on one side and a family that needs you on the other, which holds more weight? I questioned whether it was right for me to be in Cape Town. Foremost on my mind was the birth of our third child.

I finally took a bus home in March 1991. I felt elated going back to my family and Aneez gave me a little money to tide me over. I arrived safely and was overjoyed at seeing Kim and the girls. Gugu was born in April 1991, and we stayed at Kim's mother's house in a room with a separate entrance.

Adjusting to civilian life again was a nightmare. I was completely lost and depressed. If it wasn't for Richard at that time, I don't know where I would have landed up. I'd completely misjudged Richard at first because he was very moody, but I came to understand him and I emerged from my underground life with deep love for him. It was divine intervention that he was there for me. He had a 'Mike Project' and ensured that he got me back on track. Kim had just given birth to Gugu, and she stayed in touch with Richard throughout this period. She told him about my depression, and Richard went beyond the call of duty to help.

Soon after Gugu's birth, Kim got another job and by June 1991 we had enough money to rent a flat. It was a period of trying to get settled. I needed to do something to help the family, but I had no idea what and there weren't many options open to me. On the other hand, I had come back to a community in dire need of politicisation. The ANC presence in Eersterust was non-existent, so the first thing I did was to coordinate with other comrades.

Together with Mandla Langa, Tessa Mitchel and a few others, I played a key role in forming the Eersterust ANC branch.

Eersterust was a deeply conservative community of National Party supporters, and they were very hostile to us. People hated me for being both an ANC member and a communist. I remember inviting the Mamelodi branch of the ANC to come to Eersterust. It was a war with the community to have such interracial meetings there, but we toyi-toyied at the hall and I led a march in the street.

During this time I still suffered from deep depression, but I tried hard to keep myself going by doing organisational work. I was overwhelmed by the sense of not knowing which direction to take, which was reminiscent of the feeling I'd had before I met Shanil. I became cynical and my relationship with Kim suffered. I felt a hopelessness that I could not shake off. Eventually, we moved to a flat in Lydiana, a suburb close to Silverton. It was our first little place together as a family, and I got a job at a sales company across the road. I hated the work, but I had to earn something to help support the family. Fortunately, I got into a managerial position quite quickly and the money was a little better.

In 1992, I received a call from Shanil telling me that I needed to report to the Wallmansthal military base to demobilise. Richard and I went together and we received R22 000 each, along with certificates that included our force numbers and stated that we were MK soldiers.

After we surfaced, Richard, Shanil and I maintained close contact, and Richard and I became like brothers. On weekends, my family and I visited him at his apartment in Hillbrow, and the two of us started scheming. Richard had joined a small NGO called the Film Resource Unit (FRU). I didn't know anything about film and struggled to get my head around what he was involved in, but he was passionate about it. All the principles that he fought for were there: films to free minds and educate people. In 1993, he approached me to join him at FRU and I applied for the position of distribution coordinator. The board interviewed me and I got the job.

I started in 1993 on Richard's birthday, 1 March, and found him waiting for me in front of the door to the little Kerk Street office. My experience at FRU launched me into the audiovisual field. It was just three of us – Richard, Muzi Sithebe and me. Kim joined a year later as the bookkeeper and project worker for the ANC. We launched an ANC History series, *Ulibambe Lingashoni* (Hold Up the Sun). Finally, I had a sense of belonging.

FRU had many projects and huge donor funding. The ANC and COSATU collaborated with us, as did many progressive organisations and movements. Kim became both human resources manager and finance manager. She developed an intricate system of tracking film producers' royalties and, with Richard's assistance, created a policy and procedural manual, which turned FRU into a dynamic roleplayer in the audiovisual sector.

FRU went from strength to strength and developed into an amazing NGO. It was very stimulating meeting new people and reconnecting with others. I even bumped into Pitso, my old firearms instructor. He was employed as a bodyguard to minister of defence Charles Nqakula, and he regularly came to FRU's offices with Charles, who bought a number of progressive political videos. This was the best period of my work life. It was meaningful, innovative, and we were making a difference.

We had focus, and FRU began to drive social change, fostering the idea that we should celebrate our own images on television, cinema and other audiovisual mediums, and not accept the endless Western images foisted upon viewers. FRU challenged the status quo. In those early years of our democracy, the SABC was very much an outdated structure, and was trying to redefine itself as a public broadcaster. FRU brought an African perspective to the SABC. Madala Mphahlele, who was the CEO of CCV, a unit in the SABC that would become SABC2, was a visionary. The two of us were the first to travel around Africa looking for broadcast content. From then on, SABC's African territorial policy changed.

In 1997, Richard and I launched Sithengi, the first South African television market, bringing broadcasters to South Africa to exchange ideas about content. We also pioneered the Rural Exhibition, which had a fleet of mobile units to take films to rural areas in Mpumalanga, Limpopo and the Eastern Cape, where people did not have access to audiovisual facilities, television or cinema.

Richard and I always saw our relationship as an extension of the AKD and we brought socio-political logic to the audiovisual field. The values, vision and mission of FRU were embedded in the work culture at the company. FRU was like a university in many ways. Employees were schooled in a whole new way of thinking and it opened doors for them – many people who came through FRU are in top industry positions today. The offices were always full of producers and filmmakers from Africa. Local producers came to talk about new narratives, styles and approaches to filmmaking. We were at the cutting edge of the promotion of cultural diversity. We wrote papers, spoke at conferences and were invited to Norway, Sweden, Germany, Japan, and Croatia, among other countries. We were elected to steer committees on cultural diversity, and ended up in Brazil with Gilberto Gil, then minister of culture, talking about cultural diversity. He launched the Brazilian Digital Culture Forum shortly after that. We even influenced the South African Department of Arts and Culture's policy, working with departmental senior managers Neville Singh and Themba Wakashe. They approached me to head the newly formed National Film and Video Foundation (NFVF), but I turned the offer down.

During the time Richard and I spent networking, Kim held the fort in the office and on the home front. She represented us at women-in-film conferences, and was sent to lobby and fundraise in Europe. FRU was a training ground for many of us. Even today, I receive messages from younger people whom we nurtured and trained and who are now in pivotal positions in the film industry.

Richard left FRU about six years before I did. He felt he needed to move on and joined United International Pictures (UIP) under the management of Roger le Combe, the representative of every big studio in South Africa. Richard wanted to get into the commercial sector and try new things. It was one thing to innovate in an NGO setting and quite another to influence corporate thinking. It was a deliberate strategy on our side: Richard went to UIP and I ran FRU until it was fully sustainable.

I spent ten years at FRU and was ultimately headhunted by M-Net to build the world's largest African film library. I was given a budget of $10 million. Many comrades saw this as a sell-out move, but I saw it as a chance to make a bigger impact, promoting African cinema to a new level. I finished building the library in four years, then launched channels such as Mzansi Magic, and headed the international sales department. I was later approached to join a Chinese-owned company called StarTimes and I am now a vice-president in charge of Africa. My decision to join StarTimes went beyond the bottom line. It was the chairman, Xin Xing Pang, a member of the Communist Party, who attracted me to the company. We share a political vision and talk a lot about politics and the need to democratise the audiovisual sector, which is dominated by a few powerful entities, such as MultiChoice. The mission of StarTimes is to bring digital entertainment to every African family. It's about access for the bottom of the pyramid – the working class. It's an extension of what Richard and I thought about and envisioned at FRU.

As my career developed, I earned more money and had more resources and disposable income. Kim and I moved to a two-acre property in Irene; we have three cars and very little debt. I travel extensively, flying business class, staying in five-star hotels and eating at five-star restaurants because the job requires me to entertain clients at that level. As a VP of a company, this is what I do. There is an awkwardness about it though, and I feel a sense of guilt that I am in a high class bracket while the class struggle is yet to be waged and brought to its conclusion. This is a dilemma other comrades face too. I justify what I do in terms of providing access to digital media, but the dollar is the bottom line of my work and I often ask myself: 'Is this corporate life it? Should I have been doing something else?'

Richard ultimately became completely disillusioned with the corporate world and left UIP after a few years. He bought Off Morocco, a restaurant on Adderley Street in Cape Town, intending to create a space where the cultural sector could come together, share ideas and have discussions. It worked well for a few years. Richard threw his heart and soul into Off Morocco, but he managed it less like a business and more like a creative refuge where he offered free food, drinks, music and even live bands. This matched his personality: Richard was one of the most generous people I've ever met and he always saw the best in everyone. Sadly, the restaurant was liquidated. Richard then began working for the *Big Issue* magazine and seemed happy there, but we later learnt that he had resigned from his position as CEO. He had told Kim that he would be working to support victims of human trafficking and homeless people in the Western Cape, but this dream never took off: on 10 January 2007, we received news that he had been stabbed and was on life support. He died soon after, when his family agreed to stop life support.

Towards the end of his life, there were ample signs that Richard was battling with existential questions. He mostly spoke to Kim during this time, but he sent me emails and called me from time to time. Sometimes his conversations didn't seem to have a point or purpose; he would just talk randomly about work, periodically mentioning that he didn't think he would live much longer. I deeply regret that we lived so far apart, and that our interactions were so limited. Richard was my mentor, my friend and even my guardian at times. He believed in me even when I didn't believe in myself, and I wish I'd had the time to be all that for him. When someone dies we ask, 'Did we love him well?' Did Richard know that he was my best friend besides Kim? I tried to support him as best I could, but in truth I never gave him the invaluable love and support he gave me.

Richard's death was never satisfactorily solved. From what we understand, he went to a bar with a friend and invited some people back to his home in Woodstock. There was a party, most people left, and in the early hours of the morning, there was a tussle with somebody and he was stabbed in the kidney. In his drunken stupor he didn't take the stab wound seriously and went back to bed. The landlord upstairs said that at some point he had called out: 'Mike, Mike!'

If I could rewind the clock, I would do things differently with Richard. I wouldn't give him the latitude to make stupid decisions and live recklessly. I would be more assertive in my relationship with him. It was a difficult relationship, but we trusted each other. Richard was always there for others. He called me to order and maybe I should have done the same with him, but I didn't. We got caught up in our lives. I could say the same about the AKD in general: we all got so caught up in our lives that we forgot about the imperative of caring for each other. I suppose it's understandable.

On the other hand, my family unit is tight-knit. Kim is my best friend, and we've been married for nearly forty years. Our relationship has matured and flowered and we are closer than ever. My children – Tracey, Leslie, Gugu and Gregory – are thriving, while my grandchildren – Ava, Arya and Seth – have become my motivation for rising every day. Kim's side of the family is now my family too. They have walked beside me throughout my life, and they will always have my eternal gratitude for caring for our girls while we were in the AKD. I could never repay them, but it is a pleasure and honour to help care for them in turn.

I still have a lot of unresolved feelings about my brother Gregory, about what I could have done better and how my not being there for him in his own early years of confusion affected him. He went through the same harsh upbringing that I did, if not worse because I wasn't there for him. If I had to live my life again, I would have been more present in his life. I believe that we all find a moment of realisation where we reflect honestly on our lives as young adults, and in the face of this honesty we begin to make changes to the way we view the world and ourselves.

When I think about it, I never really pursued a particular life path. I would never have dreamed of doing audiovisual work if it were not for Richard. I would never have gone into science or medicine if it weren't for family pressure. I would never have met Kim if my father and mother didn't believe that the Lord called them to Eersterust. I would never have joined MK if Shanil hadn't been my political commissar. It's as if there has always been some divine hand guiding my life.

6

Kim Dearham

Holding the Fort

I AM NOT SURE how it was decided that I would join the Ashley Kriel Detachment. All I knew was that I was going to meet up with my husband, Michael Dearham, who was part of an underground unit. Until the day of my departure from my home in Pretoria, I didn't know my destination or how I would get there.

I was told to meet a person at the Oriental Plaza in Mayfair, Johannesburg, where I was given a sealed envelope. Inside the envelope was a one-way air ticket to Cape Town, directions to the airport in Johannesburg, instructions outlining how someone would meet me at the Cape Town airport and a short note instructing me that I need only take one bag of clothing with me.

My flight was booked for midnight and I got a friend's husband to drop me off at Jan Smuts Airport at 9 p.m. Despite the instructions in the envelope, I'd packed a few extra things, including two additional outfits – one suitable for work and a cocktail dress – two extra blouses, earrings, hair accessories, jewellery, nail polish and lipstick. I had no idea what underground life would be like. I could not conceive of a situation in which everyday movements were choreographed down to the finest detail. In time, I would come to understand the need for the commanders' strict and meticulous planning.

Cape Town was not completely foreign to me, as my parents had taken our family there for Christmas holidays, but it was the first time I would be travelling by air. As the plane took off, I looked out of the window and felt my face wet with tears. I was not only leaving my life behind but also the most precious and important part of my being: my two girls.

When I arrived in Cape Town, it was rainy and dark and I wondered how the person I was supposed to meet would recognise me. I waited patiently and an hour later I was pleasantly surprised when Shanil Haricharan, whom I knew quite well, tapped me on the shoulder. (I was unaware that he had been surveilling the airport to see if I'd been followed.) I hugged him and, as we walked towards the parking lot, I chatted away, telling him stories about mutual friends, Mayfair, and life in general. He said very little but smiled politely from time to time. When we reached a panel van, he instructed me to get in the back and said that he would have to blindfold me. We drove for what seemed like ages and I talked incessantly, probably from nerves, until Shanil stopped me and explained that from now on I could not call him by his name but must address him by his combat name, Ben. He then told me how to exit the vehicle. I listened, fascinated, and memorised all his instructions.

The safe house was in Northpine in Cape Town's northern suburbs. Waiting for me in the kitchen were 'Lynn' and 'Sam' – Shirley Gunn and Aneez Salie – together with Mike, whose AKD codename was Abdul. They studied me from head to toe and I became self-conscious: my hair was streaked with blonde highlights and I was wearing a colourful patchwork waistcoat, torn jeans and bright red boots. My hair looked purposefully rebellious in those days and I must have appeared very strange in contrast to their deliberately conservative appearances. But Shirley was smiling warmly at me. 'Welcome,' said Aneez as I took in my surroundings. 'Welcome.'

I write my thoughts as I remember them. Some are likely coloured by my imagination, but I don't intend to distort or glamorise my story. My maiden name is Adams. My father named me after the actress Kim Novak, not because the Anglo-Saxon meaning of my name is 'noble and brave'. I was born on 28 August 1962 in a house on 8th Street in Marabastad, Pretoria. My father's name is Reggie and my mother's name is Iris. I was the second-born child and the only girl. Dino, my older brother, was two years old when I was born, and I have two younger brothers, Donny and Deon. Until the age of six, I lived with my great-grandmother, Ouma Johanna Lazarus. I called her 'Ma' and she raised me and my siblings until we were ready to go to school.

My mother's parents are of Indian and Griqua heritage, and my father's ancestors are Muslim and Malay. My father's people did not mix easily with my mother's people, and when my mother told me this I found it intriguing that even among communities like Marabastad, where my parents both lived, there was division and hierarchy based on the shade of one's skin and also along class lines. But the heart wants what the heart wants; my father was about twenty years old when he started making eyes at my mother. She tells me that she was wary of him because wealthier 'high-class' boys used girls like her for 'practice' and hardly ever married across the class line. However, my father was determined to follow his heart.

I was very young when the Marabastad community in downtown Pretoria faced forced removals. Coloured people were relocated to Eersterust and black people to Atteridgeville. My mother still tells stories about the Marabastad community, rich in culture, oblivious to their suffering and poverty. It was like District Six in Cape Town: a mix of cultures and ethnicities, and the kind of place where children played in the streets. Everyone knew the Chinese shop owner, who was known as Makulupan. Cooking dinner every night was a community affair. Children would run across the street and return with a tomato, or dash off to a neighbour for an onion. Only a few of the streets were tarred; most were dust roads. On Friday evenings, we ate fish and chips while jazz tunes spilled from people's homes. My warmest memory is of my paternal grandparents dancing, jiving and waltzing on their stoep on a Friday night, while my brothers and I clapped to the beat of the music.

My family was poor but the memory of my childhood is pleasant. I mostly remember the time I lived with my great-grandmother. She raised many children, some family, some not. She made her living by running a shebeen and selling marijuana. Once, during a police raid, I was tasked with sitting on a hole where a large tin of marijuana was buried. The sniffer dogs became excited and pulled on their leashes towards me, but I was not afraid and didn't budge. That evening, my great-grandmother rewarded me with a sixpence, which I promptly put into my mouth and swallowed.

I attended the Catholic primary school in Eersterust, which only had Sub A and Sub B classes. After that, I started Standard 1 at Eersterust Primary School. My younger brothers attended the same school, but my older brother attended the Indian school in Marabastad. My brothers and I had to walk to and from school every day, which took forty-five minutes. Juffrou Ollier was my Sub A teacher and lived a few houses away from us. My Standard 1 teacher was Juffrou Riene, who also lived in my neighbourhood. I remember them both fondly. They seemed especially nice to me, which I suspect was because they were afraid of my mother. One teacher, Juffrou Fortuin, was very strict. She didn't know my mother personally and I recall an incident when she caught me and a friend talking in her needlework class and tied our long plaits together to make an example – and spectacle – of us in front of the entire class. When I got home, I told my mother what had happened, and the following day she was at the school, shouting at and threatening Juffrou Fortuin. From that day on, I censored everything I told my mother, as I feared she would embarrass me again, despite her intervention having the desired effect: Juffrou Fortuin never humiliated me again.

I often got into physical scraps with other children when defending my brothers against bullies, but most of my childhood memories are of playing street games with the children in the neighbourhood. I was great at games like *kousie-kousie*, where we jumped over a piece of elastic stretched between two playmates. The winner was the one who managed to jump highest. We enjoyed playing *blikkies*, using cooldrink cans as musical instruments in group sing-alongs, squatting and jumping to the beat of the song and the rattle of the cans. *Angush* was similar to baseball, except that we kicked the ball instead of hitting it with a bat.

I was a happy child. I thought our family was rich because there was always food on the table, my brothers and I had decent clothing and the extended family would come to my mother for food or money. My father was the breadwinner and always made a plan, so we seemed better off than anyone I knew.

After primary school, I went to Iona Convent High School, an all-girls school that took in children of all races. We had excellent teachers – nuns from Ireland, who shared their own country's history and raised awareness among the learners about the struggle for justice and freedom in South Africa. I learnt about the abhorrent apartheid system and the suffering of the black majority for the first time. I first heard Nelson Mandela's name from Sister Claire, my history teacher. But when I tried to discuss these subjects at home, I was warned not to become involved in such things.

The Eersterust youth did not participate in the student protests against the apartheid education system in 1976. One friend told me that the SADF had come to the township to register young boys for military training. He said that the youth had very little career choice at the time: for boys it was either teachers' training college or the SADF, and for girls it was nursing. The apartheid government successfully convinced communities like Eersterust that the ANC and other liberation movements were satanic and communist and were trying to infiltrate our communities. Many churches warned their congregations against the evil onslaught of the 'terrorists'.

A few individuals joined the liberation struggle, but the community largely embraced and accepted the government propaganda as fact. They revered coloured leaders like Allan Hendrickse, who, I was told, swam at the whites-only beach in Port Elizabeth but later apologised to State President P.W. Botha for swimming in 'God's sea'. There was a stubborn belief in the system, and the '*swart gevaar*' was deemed a worse monster than apartheid. Most of us who broke away from this kind of racist indoctrination did so outside of Eersterust.

Meanwhile, I dreamed of being a nun or a writer, perhaps because of the influence of my schoolteachers, like Sister Claire, Sister Immaculata and Sister Brandon. They were my role models. I participated in many of the Catholic religious activities and believed that Gandhi's passive resistance philosophy could solve South Africa's problems.

The convent was situated in a suburb called Gezina, near Pretoria, and a short distance from Eersterust. During the youth uprising in 1976, Sister Claire and another teacher drove a few older students to Noordgesig in Johannesburg. We saw roadblocks and burning tyres, heard gunshots and smelled teargas, and were soon turned away and escorted back to the road to Pretoria. I was only fourteen years old, but I remember the fear, excitement and pride I felt in participating. I believed that this historic day would ensure that apartheid was abolished.

We heard later that young people had been killed during the protests. I felt strangely awakened, and realised that my philosophy of passive resistance was idealistic. My best friend, Lucrecia Seafield, was an ardent reader and well informed. She was the only person I could speak to about this, except for my cousin Debra, who was in love with a comrade who had left the country to live in exile.

My first boyfriend, Michael Dearham, lived across the road. He was the eldest son of the local Evangelical Bible Church's pastor. Most of the girls in my neighbourhood had a crush on him, but although I agreed that he was handsome, I didn't chase after him as they did. Mike seemed subdued and studious. Most days, I would see him through his bedroom window, sitting and studying. During school holidays, the neighbourhood children would play games in the street until late at night, but Mike stayed inside and continued to study and read. I was fascinated by him. One day he spoke to me and I fell head over heels in love – not so much with his appearance as his mind. He knew so much about our country. And so began my political education. He gave me banned literature to read in between all the smooching, and I specifically recall reading about Winnie Mandela's personal sacrifices as a woman and mother and how she became a revered icon.

Mike was a year below me in high school, but to me he was the most intelligent person in the world. I completed high school in 1979 with a matric exemption, already four months pregnant. Mike, who would start matric the next year, was shipped off to Durban by his mother, who wanted to ensure that his education continued. Our baby daughter, Tracey, was born in May 1980. At the time, all my friends were living a completely different reality at university. Anti-apartheid struggle activities were escalating and they found that their political consciousness was being raised to new heights. Although my formal education ended in 1979, the years to come would provide invaluable lessons.

Mike remained in Durban to complete his matric that year, and became involved in the nationwide youth activities against apartheid. He was at Fairvale Senior Secondary School, the same school as Robert McBride, and attended school rallies. Mike already had a gift for speaking and he became the orator at these gatherings. In June, when Tracey was two months old, I left Eersterust to work in Johannesburg. I rented a room with Mike's aunt and on weekends I went home to visit my family and my baby daughter. It was really difficult to leave my baby behind in Pretoria but I had no alternative; I had to earn an income to support her. I missed her desperately during the week, and Mike too.

I was working for a pharmaceutical company in Pretoria when Mike began his studies at the University of the Witwatersrand. He visited Tracey often. During one of his weekend visits he told my mother that he wanted to marry me. On the Monday morning, I received a phone call from him. 'What are you doing on Saturday?' he asked.

'Nothing much, why?' I replied.

'Let's get married,' he said.

After our conversation, I put the phone down in its cradle and dreamily told the four colleagues with whom I shared an office that I would be getting married on Saturday.

My mother arranged for the wedding to take place at my parents' home in Eersterust and immediately went out to buy me a wedding dress and a bedroom suite. My aunties hustled and bustled, arranging the meals and the decor, and my father supplied the drinks. My colleagues collected money and arranged a kitchen tea for me at work. I was dressed in a white lab coat, my face was painted like a clown's and I was given a feather duster as a bridal bouquet and a toilet-paper veil. I walked through the office and the canteen and down to the factory, cheered on by colleagues. At the end of the day, my boss sent me home in a company van with all the generous gifts I'd received.

On Saturday morning, I stood in my wedding dress surrounded by all my cousins and aunts. My mother was very emotional and kept herself busy with the food preparation. The ceremony was beautiful and traditional, and was conducted by Mike's father. My dad tried to speak but he cried so much that he could hardly get a word out. Later, we walked across the road to the church where Mike and his family had lived and took photographs in the garden. After the photo session, Mike's mother took us aside. 'I am not happy about today,' she said. 'But Michael threatened to live with you in sin, Kimmy, so I went along with this façade because I don't want any further scandal, but I assure you this marriage will never last.' She left soon afterwards with Mike's father, when the partying started in earnest.

We danced and laughed until the early hours of the morning. I woke up giggling. It was hard to believe Mike and I were a married couple. I was only twenty-one and Mike was twenty.

In 1982, I gave birth to our second daughter, Leslie. Mike was studying full-time, so I was consumed with raising the children and caring for my family. I participated in political rallies and was part of a community that held many late-night discussions about the intensified mass resistance in the country. During this time, we lived close to Mike's uncle Peter McKenzie, a well-known struggle photographer, and at his home in Mayfair I met many political activists, like Calvin Prakasim and Cedric Nunn. My awareness grew.

Mike spent many days making petrol bombs and attending secret planning meetings with student friends from Wits. When there was mass action at the university, I would leave work early to participate. I got caught up in the action many times, running from the police through a haze of teargas. On these occasions, I would arrive home and anxiously await my husband's return many hours later.

I met Shanil Haricharan during this time but was unaware of his underground activities and work with the AKD. At the time, our social circle participated in distributing posters and materials before rallies, and some acted in theatre performances about the Group Areas Act and detention without trial to raise awareness about these issues. Shanil was part of our group, but days or weeks would go by without any word from him. Nobody spoke about his activities, but we sensed that he was more involved in the political struggle than the rest of us.

I remained the breadwinner while Mike studied. His dream was to be a medical doctor. I was working two jobs at the time and believed that the sacrifices I made would benefit our family in the long run. I was always tired and had few friends during this period, and our social life increasingly consisted of spending Sundays with the children in a nearby park, taking train rides to Johannesburg and back to Pretoria, visiting museums or taking a taxi to Durban to visit Mike's grandparents. We also did a lot of walking in those days because we couldn't always afford public transport or fuel. Mike became restless. He started telling me that this dream we were working towards was nothing but a fantasy. He expressed his unhappiness about living within the confines of the apartheid system and obeying the inhumane laws of this country. He believed that we would never be free if we did not attempt to free ourselves from the chains of racist apartheid rule. His utterances made me feel anxious and I feared for us as a family.

Mike spent many days and nights with young men who shared his beliefs. They began to smoke marijuana as a form of escape. For some, this escalated into using harder drugs. Their relationships and marriages began to unravel, and some were dismissed from their places of work. I heard that one of these very unhappy men took hard drugs with his wife one night. When he woke up the next morning, she had died from an overdose of Welcanol, a synthetic form of heroin known as 'Pinks', which was injected intraveneously. I worried about Mike.

In late 1988, my husband left the country to train at the MK camps. I was not told his whereabouts. From time to time, Joe Nxusani, a close friend and lawyer, would visit to let me know that Mike was fine. I never knew what that meant exactly, but I kept telling our two little girls that their father loved them and would return one day. I explained that he was only away from home because bad policemen were harassing him. I told the rest of my family and friends that he had abandoned me and the children, as I could not tell them the truth.

Mike had officially joined MK and I was left behind, illegally renting a small house in a quiet street in the white suburb of Mayfair in Johannesburg. Many nights I would look through the window and see a vehicle with two men inside it parked outside. When I returned from work I would find the same vehicle parked there. I began to feel a deep loneliness. It was difficult to adjust to being alone with the additional demands of being a single mother and breadwinner. I battled against depression and feeling sorry for myself.

I owned a temperamental Mitsubishi Colt 1100 that needed to be pushed in cold weather. When it rained, the battery ran down completely, bringing the car to a standstill. Sometimes I'd be stranded on a highway with the children and our dogs. This was before the advent of cellphones, so every Friday evening when I visited my family in Pretoria, I had to give them my exact departure time from Johannesburg, even going so far as to telephone their neighbours. If it rained, my brothers would drive out to rescue me, the children and the dogs from the side of the road.

I continued telling friends and family who asked me about Mike that we were separated. At first it was difficult to lie to my extended family, but eventually this lie became routine. I was consoled by reading news about Winnie Mandela, Albertina Sisulu and other wives and mothers who found themselves in even worse situations than mine.

Shanil, who knew where Mike was, visited a few times and I received these visits with much joy. He revealed very little, but said that Mike was growing into an admirable man and that I might not recognise him when I saw him again, as he'd embraced a deeper meaning of life during his training.

This news was always uplifting but it saddened me that I could not share it, even with my parents, who held a negative view of Mike for apparently abandoning us. Sensing my deep sadness, young men constantly attempted to woo me into affairs. One friend, who was one of the few people who knew that Mike had gone for training, tried to exploit my worsening emotional state by harassing me until I finally stopped opening the door when he visited. His behaviour felt like betrayal.

In the early hours of one cold winter's morning, a year after Mike left, someone knocked at the door in a way that seemed familiar. I looked through my bedroom window for quite a long time, unable to recognise the person standing outside. I decided to check who it was anyway, and as I walked towards the glass door, I saw that it was Mike. He was wearing a trench coat, his hair was long and he had grown a beard. I opened the door and for a long time we just held each other without saying a word. I don't know how long we stood there, but suddenly I was overcome by a wave of anger. I pulled away, slapped his face and pounded my fists against him, silently sobbing. I realised then that there were times during his absence that I had believed he was gone for good, that he had died in exile and that I would never see him again.

Mike's visit was brief. He was gone before sunrise and I was once again left feeling displaced and afraid for him and for us. I continued to do what was necessary, working and seeing to my children, family and friends, but I felt disconnected from everything and worried that my life of isolation and secrecy was beginning to harm the girls. They missed their dad and they did not get to play with their cousins and friends or attend big family gatherings because of the risk that they might reveal something about Mike. Sometimes I'd send them to my parents' home in Eersterust, but they were bombarded with questions there and I had no easy answers.

Around this time it was decided that I would join Mike in the AKD. I would finally be with my husband, but being part of the underground detachment meant I would not see my children at all. I knew they would be safe and grow up in a more stable environment if they remained with my parents, but anticipating the separation from them was unbearable. I tried to stay focused on the present and the fact that the waiting and not knowing would come to an end, and that I, too, would be part of the struggle. Perhaps with more of us contributing, change would happen faster. It was a naive way of thinking and I did not fully understand the enormous repercussions of such a decision.

The days before I was to join Mike in Cape Town passed in a blur. As I despatched all our material possessions, I felt like I was packing up all my emotions in a cupboard to deal with later. I sold as many household items as possible and kept the cash for use in my new home. I sent some of the items, like kitchen utensils, via rail to an address in Cape Town as directed by the AKD. I tried to explain the changes to Tracey and Leslie and reassure them, even though I felt no assurance about the future. I felt simultaneously proud and sad at their remarkable ability to accept the move and look forward to living with their grandparents for a while. They enthusiastically packed their own belongings and I felt my heart break as I said goodbye.

It was still dark when my plane touched down in Cape Town. Shanil met me clandestinely outside the airport and I was driven, blindfolded, to the safe house, where I met 'Lynn' and 'Sam' and was reunited with Mike. Mike and I were left alone and he lectured me about how my appearance and behaviour had to change immediately. It took a few weeks of adjustment to better understand why I had to change to avoid drawing attention to myself and those around me. I became 'Patty', and I was secretly thrilled to have a code name.

Everyone at the safe house asked whether I knew who Lynn and Sam were. I am terrible with faces and even if I had seen or read about them, I was unable to connect the dots. I found out later that Lynn and Sam were really Shirley and Aneez – a couple who were the commanders of the detachment – and that they had appeared on TV as wanted 'terrorists'. I also met their little boy, Haroon, whose code name was Timmy, and who also lived in the safe house.

I was in awe of Shirley, whose discipline knew no bounds. She nurtured Haroon like a regular mom and always briefed me on what to do and what not to do for security reasons when it was my turn to babysit him or take him to the nearby park. I learnt new terms and ways of doing things from her, such as 'hands-free time', which meant focusing on only one thing at a time, balancing motherly duties and AKD duties. I was shocked that anyone had hands-free time; until then, I had mostly multitasked, such as cooking while talking on the phone and supervising the kids' playtime. This new way of mindful living impressed on me that the unit viewed safety as a priority and that unfocused attention, even if only for a minute on a seemingly unimportant task, could have a negative impact on the safety of the entire unit.

All the comrades in the house took me under their wing and demonstrated what vigilance meant. In short, it meant being 100 per cent aware of one's surroundings at all times. Meal preparation was a big deal in the safe house and everyone took turns to cook. I was a really bad cook, and once again Shanil came to the rescue; I simply helped when he prepared meals. Aneez was very pedantic about cooking, and I would watch him meticulously peel and cut potatoes, as if the act of preparation was a sacred ritual.

I also learnt to speak in a new way. Apparently, up until this point, I had talked without having anything to say. Despite being a chatterbox, I learnt to speak with great care outside the safe house, and guard against revealing anything about the unit.

One day, I was given permission to spend the day with a cousin who lived in Cape Town. She showed me photographs and we ate food that reminded me of home. I listened eagerly to stories about Eersterust and my immediate family, and specifically about my children. My cousin was disciplined about not asking me too many questions regarding my specific whereabouts. By then, my family knew that I was part of the ANC in some way and that it was best not to ask questions. She gave me a few letters from my girls in which they wrote happily about their lives with my parents and extended family, but also how much they missed Mike and me. 'Mommy, do you still sneeze funny?' Leslie asked in one of her letters. I was very sad when the sun began to set and I had to make my way back to the safe house.

My cousin gave me a lift to the taxi rank. On the way there, in Kuils River, we stopped at a traffic light. We were happily talking about life, love and the day we'd spent together when we noticed a car speeding towards us. We looked on in horror as it failed to slow down. I came to moments later and found myself on the side of the road, unable to stand up. When I looked down, my white pants were covered in blood and my leg seemed oddly twisted. I fainted. When I came to for the second time, I was in hospital, exiting the operating theatre. The next few hours were a blur, but I was somehow strong enough to make contact with the unit.

I was whisked away from the hospital and recuperated on painkillers. Duty called a few weeks later and, still on crutches, I got work via Kelly Girl, a temporary employment agency.

Underground life was not as glamorous as it looks in James Bond movies. I used minibus taxis and trains to commute, then walked several kilometres to get to and from work like most other working-class South Africans. At the safe house, we did daily chores like cooking, laundry, cleaning and buying groceries. But even these everyday activities were shrouded in tension, anxiety and fear, as we always had to be alert and vigilant.

After about a month in Cape Town, I was sent on an errand via the Bellville taxi rank. People who lived in the Northern Suburbs passed through this busy terminus on their way to the city. I came to love this meeting point – the smell of food, especially fresh snoek and chips, and the buzz of people talking. The taxi drivers shouted out their destinations: 'Belhar, Belhar', 'Northpine, Northpine' or 'Kraaifontein, Kraaifontein', conducting the smooth flow of taxis filling up and leaving. I found this strangely lyrical. While queuing for a taxi, I tried not to speak because my Pretoria accent might draw attention, and instead listened attentively to the Cape Town accents around me. The golden rule in the underground was to fit in as much as possible.

Inevitably, guys at the taxi rank would whistle at me, shouting, '*Kan 'n man dan nie?*' This was, I understood, a way of paying a compliment. At first, I hardly heard what they were shouting and just smiled politely, avoiding eye contact. One day, a lady sitting next to me in the taxi asked: '*Hoeko antwoert djy nie?*' (Why don't you answer?) I replied that I didn't know what the men were asking. The entire taxi-load of people burst out laughing. After much patient explanation, the lady said: '"*Djou tool is stomp*" is wa ek sou gesêret.' ('Your tool is blunt' is what *I* would say.) I never used this phrase, but who can blame me? I continued to smile shyly at the taxi men and went about my errands, faking normality.

My tasks for the AKD varied. I did temporary work through Kelly Girl to help sustain the detachment when outside funding was scarce or non-existent. I ran errands such as shopping, accompanying Shanil or Shirley. I took turns caring for Haroon. I cut and dyed Aneez's hair in preparation for an outing. Although my cooking was sometimes disastrous, I helped prepare meals. I cleaned common areas and did the dishes according to a strict schedule. Typing leaflets and posters was one of my tasks too. Nevertheless, I was not regarded as a fully fledged member of the AKD, but more as a comrade's wife.

I shared a room with Mike. In it was one mattress and a cupboard containing our few personal possessions. The way Mike and I related to each other had changed. He didn't tell me what activities he was involved in. He would go on errands with other comrades and I never knew where they went or exactly what these errands were. We had very few moments to share our thoughts about our children and, by that time, we had learnt to adjust our thoughts to the present and the tasks at hand.

Shanil was my shadow, patiently explaining anything that didn't make sense to me. I was still convinced of the peace-loving Gandhian approach to all things unjust in this world, but Shanil explained that we as a nation had crossed that line many years ago. I learnt about the four pillars of the struggle from him and he taught me the history of resistance to apartheid. In time, I began to feel deep pride and a sense of belonging. Life was still very difficult, particularly having to get up every day without my children, but understanding why we were in the AKD helped me to cope and remain positive. Shanil taught me so much, and years later I thanked him for being my permanent babysitter. 'More like a life coach and therapist,' he shot back, laughing.

During the time we lived in Northpine, Shanil and I posed as a married couple, with baby Haroon completing the picture. We spent a lot of time in the garden together, and during those times I mercilessly teased my pretend husband about his code name. 'Who'd ever believe your name is Ben?' I'd ask. 'Look at you! You look more like a fellow from Stanger.' 'Ben' seemed more suited to a conservative white man.

On 11 February 1990, Nelson Mandela was released from Victor Verster Prison. Everyone at the safe house in Northpine was standing in front of the television when it happened. We had hung up sheets to divide the room into separate cubicles, as there were comrades who had joined us for the occasion but who, for security reasons, we were not allowed to see. We toasted and cheered softly when we watched Madiba walk through the prison gates with Winnie at his side. Soon, we could hear cheering outside too – it sounded like all of Northpine was watching the same footage. We joined in – there was screaming and shouting, hooting and celebrating from across the neigh-bourhood and, we realised, around the world. I felt emotional and realised how close I had become to this group of brave people who had put their lives on hold to realise a new South Africa. I hugged everyone that day, laughing and crying. For the first time since arriving at the safe house, I allowed myself to dream of the day when I would see my children again.

In the first half of 1990 there was a security scare and everyone left the house except Shanil, Mike and me. Shanil asked us if we knew anyone who we trusted enough to approach about a place to stay for a while.

The cousin who had been involved in the car accident with me had returned to Pretoria, but there was always Bruintjies. Bruintjies lived in Atlantis on the West Coast and made a living as a truck driver, ferrying fresh produce between Cape Town and Pretoria. I had met him at my parents' home in Eersterust and he was like an uncle to me.

Bruintjies immediately welcomed Mike and me into his township home in Atlantis. He had five children and was married to a friendly, motherly woman whom we called Auntie May. They were a very poor family but always welcomed visitors, and there was a lot of laughter and storytelling. Mike had stressed to Bruintjies that he should make up a story about why we were there. Bruintjies told anyone who asked that I had a drinking problem, and that he was helping us start over again after my drinking had cost us our home and belongings.

Years later, we saw Bruintjies again and he teasingly asked: 'How's the drinking problem, Kim?' People like Bruintjies and Auntie May were guardian angels in the struggle. They asked no questions but offered their valuable assistance humbly and without hesitation. They've never received any recognition for their help, but I can see how proud they are when they relate the story of harbouring and feeding us, lending a much-needed helping hand.

Soon we had to leave Bruintjies and Auntie May's home. I had met a woman named Amanda through doing temp work with Kelly Girl, and I remembered her talking about the unjust apartheid system and her fears for her husband, Eugene, who was involved in trade union work. I asked for her help, and the couple agreed to let us move in with them in Northpine. During the time that we were there, I cleaned, helped with food preparation and did laundry and ironing. We only stayed with them for about two months but it seemed like a lifetime. It was very quiet during the day, so I did housework to occupy myself. Mike went to meet with Shanil from time to time but didn't report back to me.

In June, I was in the Pick 'n Pay in Brackenfell, and I got a huge shock when I saw in the newspapers that Shirley had been arrested and both she and Haroon were in police custody. The *Weekend Argus* had Haroon's beautiful face on the front page. I also read about them in the *Weekly Mail*. I felt deeply pained at what she must be experiencing in detention and angry about the life Haroon was forced to live. I knew, though, that Shirley would be strong, even in the face of systematic mental punishment and physical torture.

At some point during our stint at Amanda and Eugene's house, Mike and I were tasked with going to the Northpine safe house to collect a number of large Karrimor sports bags containing weapons. Shanil had befriended the neighbour, having gathered that he was sympathetic to the ANC, and confided in him in order to get his cooperation. We entered the safe house through the neighbour's yard by climbing over the wall, and carried the bags to Amanda and Eugene's home, where we stashed them under our bed. It took more than one trip. Soon after that, our stay with Amanda and Eugene became strained.

Amanda was unhappy and tense; I suppose she was afraid for their safety and wanted her normal, quiet life back. We had to leave.

I was taken to a house in Belhar, but Mike went somewhere else. I knew something was wrong but I was not sure what it was. I lived with a woman and her son for a few weeks. There, I had access to the bathroom and kitchen, but I couldn't go outside. When the woman received visitors, I remained in my room. She looked very familiar and, much later, I learnt that she was Aneez's sister, Ayesha.

The isolation was very difficult to bear. The Station Strangler was still on the prowl, and I read in the newspaper that he was possibly a teacher or an adult who worked closely with children. From conversations I overheard, I figured out that the lady of the house was a teacher. Once, a male teacher came to visit for dinner and he was, to my mind, the spitting image of the identikit the police had drawn up of the Station Strangler. I began to have nightmares about my own children and would wake up with the Station Strangler's voice in my head.

After a few weeks, I was blindfolded and taken to a safe house where the rest of the unit was based. At this location I met Melvin and Ruth Bruintjies, a couple with a baby daughter. Ruth seemed very anxious. I also met Richard Ishmail there. His code name was Rodney, and he later became my great friend and colleague. When I was introduced to 'Rodney', I remarked: 'Rodney looks like a Rodney.' I suppose I was thinking about how Shanil didn't look like a Ben. I spent ages explaining to some of the comrades why I said this. Later, Aneez called me to explain that I had been suspected of being an informer. Richard had been given information from a source who said that 'Kim is eating out of the hand of the enemy.' After some investigation, they'd discovered that the message referred to another comrade whose code name was Kim.

I went home to Eersterust in 1991, emotionally confused and pregnant with my third child. I'd been apart from my girls for a year, and when I saw them for the first time, I wept for an entire day. I spoke very little at first, and my family was concerned about my soft tone of voice and my refusal to leave the house or visit friends. The noise of the surrounding township terrified me. I sat in my bedroom tensing up at the sound of neighbours talking, tyres screeching, a vehicle backfiring or the odd gunshot. I found it extremely difficult to adjust and for a few weeks I stayed indoors, despite the fact that I had been tasked with finding reliable public telephones so that Shanil could remain in contact with me. During that time, I thought about my situation: living with my parents, in debt, pregnant and bearing the responsibility of looking after two children.

One Monday morning, I asked my father to drop me on the highway between Pretoria and Johannesburg. I hitched a ride to Sandton, where I checked in at Kelly Girl to sign up for temporary work. I worked until I was eight months pregnant, trying to save money while supporting the girls. It was very difficult, but I had no other choice. Mike came home one month before I gave birth to our third daughter on 3 April 1991. We named her Lynn, after Shirley's code name, but we call her Gugu, after a cadre who Mike had met at the underground house in Lusaka. After Gugu was born, I went straight back to work. I also found part-time work typing CVs and preparation schedules and selling cosmetics over the weekends. My brother fixed up a Volkswagen Beetle for me, so I had transport, and I found a part-time job for Mike across from our flat, managing a telesales team. I earned enough money for a deposit on a one-bedroom flat and we moved in.

For the entire year Mike struggled to adjust to ordinary life, and showed signs of severe depression. Our daughters Tracey and Leslie were already in high school and adjusting to family life was difficult for them too. Fortunately, my girls harbour no resentment against us for abandoning them. They seem to understand our reasons for leaving them with my parents.

Richard Ishmail had settled in Johannesburg and we remained in contact with him. He was working for an NGO called the Film Resource Unit at the time and when he told me about a vacancy, we broke into the telesales offices and I furiously typed up a CV for Mike. He was interviewed by FRU's board of directors and on the following Monday he started his new job. This was the beginning of a career for Mike. I joined FRU a year later and although I received no financial compensation, Mike received a decent wage and we tried to manage on one salary. Over the next eighteen years, Richard, Mike and I would work to develop FRU's vision.

FRU grew to be a pioneering blue-chip NGO that successfully brought African images to our screens, while providing a place for young people in the film industry to learn and be mentored by Richard, Michael and me. Many of these youth today describe FRU as a 'university' of sorts.

Mike and I cast our first votes in Lydiana, near Eersterust, in 1994. That afternoon, Richard and a few friends came over to our newly acquired flat and we celebrated the privilege of being part of this historic moment. Looking back, my expectations of the new ANC government were naive. I expected the dream of freedom and the political programme to unfold as we had hoped and planned.

My parents remained supportive while we found our feet in the early

1990s, and assisted us with food and by caring for the children after school. Mike and I struggled through our relationship, but developed an honesty with each other that had been strangely absent in our marriage until then. We finally felt complete in our lives together. We moved into our first home in Irene in 1997, when Gugu was seven years old. Our son, Gregory, who is named after Mike's brother, was born in 1999. Mike and I have now been together for almost forty years.

In 1998, I started working with trade unions through my work at the National Labour and Economic Development Institute (NALEDI), including COSATU and the National Union of Metalworkers of South Africa (NUMSA). During my four years at NALEDI, I realised that much still needed to be done on a national level on the labour front.

The post-democracy period has taught me that the culture of corruption and looting is deeply entrenched in all crevices of our society, and I now view every political party with scepticism. I believe the ANC theoretically embraces all that is entrenched in the Freedom Charter and the Constitution, but reality reflects a different story. Even the Economic Freedom Fighters (EFF), which once reminded me of a very young ANC, have been implicated in looting scandals. I believe, however, that from the fragmented movements born of current conflicts – workers reorganising, #FeesMustFall, #MeToo – we will see a body being formed to address past and present injustices. Sadly, this may not be the ANC to which we swore allegiance, the ANC that swore to fight for and represent the people all those years ago during the adoption of the Freedom Charter in Kliptown.

In 2015, Tracey gave birth to our first granddaughter, Ava. That year, I had an ischaemic stroke, or 'silent stroke'. It took a while for me to understand and come to terms with my illness, and the year of celebrating Ava was also the year of welcoming a new me. I always thought the term 'lifestyle change' was a cliché, but due to my illness, I found myself learning new ways of being and loving. In some areas it was challenging. My family had always viewed me as the glue that held everything together, but suddenly the one who held the fort had limitations. I had to teach myself to say 'no'. It was not easy for my family, and especially not for Mike, who became frustrated during the first few months of my recovery. I had taken care of everyone's daily schedules, family time and the financial management of our large family, as well as caring for our parents and dealing with issues in our extended family. But I had to learn to let others play these roles. It came as a relief tinged with sadness when I realised that my family was able to wake up every day and go about their lives without my help.

Over the last few years, I have had to let go not only of crucial leadership tasks within my family and extended family, but also in the workplace. This was a challenge. I found myself tempted to address any crisis that cropped up at work and often had to talk myself out of taking on new projects.

Healing takes time, and time was all I had, so I started on a gentle regime. I wrote stories and have since finished a collection, and I painted all the plant pots in my garden with the help of my granddaughter, Ava.

I learnt so much about myself during my time with the AKD. Being part of something so much bigger than oneself is a lesson, and this awareness is something most people never attain. I don't think of this time as a sacrifice and I have no regrets. I believe I am a better person for the difficult experiences.

During those years, I did not dwell too much on defining myself within MK and the underground work it carried out. Although I was a part of the AKD, I learnt that I was not quite a fully fledged member. I was like many women during the struggle against apartheid who lived this life by choice alongside their husbands – never as a cadre or comrade but rather as a helper, assistant and wife. I never saw myself as equal to the great Chris Hani, Joe Modise or Solomon Mahlangu. Nor did I liken myself to any of the other cadres in my detachment – Shirley Gunn, Shanil Haricharan and my husband, Mike – or the well-known wives of struggle icons, such as Winnie Mandela or Albertina Sisulu. I only hoped that my tiny efforts could speed up the process of liberation. I was determined to help the brave men and women in the struggle to dismantle an inhumane and unjust system. Like many people, I contributed to and assisted in this noble cause, believing that it was my duty to be part of making a difference.

There were thousands of people who were part of the wheels of resistance that finally broke the apartheid regime. If I am deemed a small bolt in this machinery, I am humbled. Through the AKD I met human beings who made invaluable contributions towards my view of the world. My children were affected by Mike's and my absence, but they have not grown into resentful adults. They respect the choices of the youth of the 1970s and the 1980s. Perhaps we were idealistic, but this is what pushed us to grow.

Ashley Kriel addressing a UDF rally in Athlone during the Don't Vote campaign before the Tricameral Parliament elections in 1984.

Johnny Issel and Essa Moosa after Johnny was released from detention through a court order in 1986. Johnny became a member of the Ashley Kriel Detachment's Regional Politico-Military Committee. Essa offered legal help to people involved in the struggle.

Ashley Kriel's funeral, Bonteheuwel, 20 July 1987. Ashley was shot and killed by security policeman Jeffrey Benzien soon after returning from military training outside South Africa.

Charlie Martin, in the foreground carrying Ashley Kriel's coffin, later became a member of the AKD.

This photograph of Shirley Gunn was taken by the police at Pollsmoor Prison in 1985. Shirley was detained for 112 days, and later became a commander of the AKD.

Shanil Haricharan as a student at the University of the Witwatersrand in 1985. Shanil later became the commander of the AKD's Johannesburg unit.

Shirley and Aneez Salie were married in Simon's Town on 12 October 1988. Top right: Aneez's mother Amina Salie, Imam Gassan Solomon, Aneez's brothers Seiraaj and Mogamat, and Zubeida Jaffer. Bottom right: Shirley, Aneez, Aneez's father Salie Salie, Imam Solomon, Seiraaj and Mogamat.

Melvin Bruintjies addressing the Anglican National Youth Conference in 1987. Melvin became the AKD's commander of operations.

Sidney Hendricks and Melvin Bruintjies at the Durban Youth Congress, 1987. Sidney worked with the AKD's Bonteheuwel unit.

Melvin Bruintjies with Heinrich Magerman and Allison Minnies at a youth training programme at the Dora Falcke Youth Centre, 1988. Heinrich was part of the Macassar/Hottentots Holland unit.

Vanessa November as a student at Bonteheuwel High School in November 1989. She was in the AKD's Bonteheuwel unit.

Brian Handel, Desmond Stevens, Clarence Syfers, Andrew Adams, Nicky Asher and Coline Williams at a Youth Drama Group in 1988. Desmond and Andrew worked with the Macassar/Hottentots Holland unit, and Coline worked with the the Bonteheuwel unit before becoming commander of the Bonteheuwel and Athlone units, reporting to Anton Fransch.

Robbie Waterwitch and Coline Williams were members of the AKD who tragically died when a limpet mine exploded during an operation in Athlone on 23 July 1989.

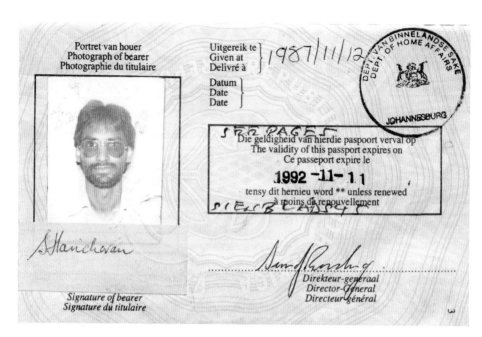

Shanil Haricharan made numerous trips to and from Botswana, couriering weapons, explosives and communications. His passport is filled with exit and entry stamps.

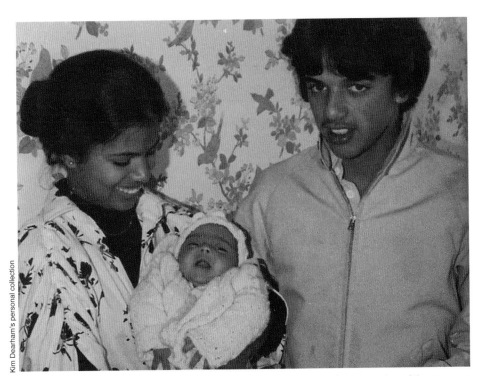

Kim and Mike Dearham with their first child, Tracey, in 1980. Mike served as a member of the Johannesburg unit before undergoing training in Tanzania and Zambia. He and Kim were then deployed to Cape Town to work with the AKD command structure.

Ismail Vallie on a boat trip to Seal Island in 1978. Ismail and his wife Julie couriered arms and explosives from Botswana to Cape Town, and later assisted the AKD in Cape Town.

Joe Nxusani in Alexandra township in 1986. Joe was a lawyer who was recruited by Shanil into the Johannesburg unit.

Anton Fransch was a student activist from Bonteheuwel who trained in MK camps in Angola before returning to South Africa. He commanded the AKD's Athlone unit.

On 17 November 1989, Anton was killed after a seven-hour shoot-out with the police at a safe house in Church Street, Athlone.

Shirley Gunn's personal collection

Shirley with her and Aneez's son, Haroon, at a picnic at Antoniesvlei in Wellington in February 1990 to celebrate his first birthday. This was a rare excursion during their time in the underground.

Did this woman cause this havoc?

SUNDAY STAR 1/7/90
P15

SHIRLEY GUNN . . . held for Cosatu and Khotso House blasts.   AFTERMATH . . . the blast tore a hole in the facade of Khotso House and showered shops opposite with rubble.   Picture: Karen Fletcher.

© *Saturday Star*, Independent Media

In January 1989, Shirley was falsely accused of bombing Khotso House and Khanya House in Johannesburg. She would be arrested in June 1990 and held in detention for 63 days.

Audrey Gunn, Ragmat Jaffer and Dorothy Boesak leading a protest march demanding the release of Shirley and all Section 29 detainees, Cape Town, August 1990.

Shirley with Chris Hani holding Haroon at an MK rally in Langa Stadium, 1991.

Charles Chordnum with his daughter Shastelle, soon after Charles received MK training inside the country in late 1989.

After leaving South Africa during his matric year for a year's military training in Tanzania, Timothy Jacobs returned to school in 1991. He is at the back, waving.

Shanil Haricharan in 1992.

Richard Ishmail with Nancy Sahib in 1993. Richard had first worked for the Johannesburg unit and then moved to Cape Town to support the AKD command base.

Aneez Salie receives the 1997 Henry J. Kaiser Award for Excellence in Health Writing from Graça Machel for his *Cape Times* articles exposing the *Sarafina II* scandal, the first such post-apartheid government corruption exposé. On the left is then *Cape Times* editor Moegsien Williams.

Haroon, Shihaam, Aneez, Shirley and Haanee with Nelson Mandela and Graça Machel at Genadendal in 1997.

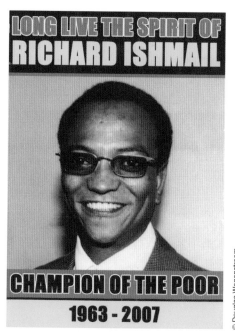

LONG LIVE THE SPIRIT OF
RICHARD ISHMAIL

CHAMPION OF THE POOR
1963 - 2007

© Douglas Wagenstroom

A funeral poster for Richard Ishmail, who was murdered in January 2007.

Dicki Meter and Patrick Presence at Johnny Issel's funeral in 2011. Dicki and Patrick were both members of the AKD's Hout Bay/Southern Suburbs unit.

Photograph by Shirley Gunn

Melvin Bruintjies with his daughter Coline in Kirstenbosch, February 2014.

Mike and Kim Dearham, Irene, Pretoria, September 2014.

Vanessa November with her brother Gori at an ANC anniversary event at Green Point Stadium, 8 January 2015.

Ismail and Julie Vallie, Rylands, 2014.

Photograph by Ruth Bruintjies

In Qunu, Nelson Mandela's resting place, 15 December 2013. Left to right: Coline Bruintjies, Carlito Mathews, Solomon Juries, Chris Frechas, Patrick Presence, Timothy Jacobs, Dicki Meter, Melvin Bruintjies, Michael September and Vanessa November.

Photograph by Haanee Gunn

Mogamat Salie outside a house in Claremont that once belonged to his uncle Achmat and family. Behind him is the house where Mogamat's family lived. Both families were forced to move from these houses in 1966.

An unveiling of a memorial to Coline Williams and Robbie Waterwitch, July 2014. Robbie's mother, Hettie, is in the wheelchair, and behind her is Robbie's uncle, Basil Snayer.

Members of the AKD in Cape Town in August 2019. Back row: Seiraaj Salie, Shanil Haricharan, Heinrich Magerman, Ismail Vallie, Charlie Martin and Aneez Salie. Front row: Shirley Gunn, Julie Vallie, Sidney Hendricks, Vanessa November and Mogamat Salie.

7

Ismail Vallie

Beyond the Skyline

'**M**Y GOD, WE are not going to make it. If they stop us now, we are finished.' This is what went through my mind when I saw the heavy police presence on the South African side of the border. My wife Julie and I were returning from Botswana, carrying arms and explosives for MK in a Nissan Skyline. We'd already avoided three roadblocks by taking a two-and-a-half-hour detour through dense bush, following an ANC comrade in a 4×4. Just before we joined the tarred road to the border, his vehicle got stuck in deep sand. 'You guys carry on,' he said. 'I will find my way back.' On we went, and now we were facing a huge roadblock. There were about forty men in SADF uniform manning it, supported by Casspirs. At that time, the South African government was at its weakest: bombs were going off everywhere, so they were intensifying vehicle searches, and commuters could be delayed for hours. The SADF had also introduced metal detectors, sniffer dogs, and mirrors on long rods to check underneath the cars. Our car was laden with explosives. I can't begin to describe the adrenaline rush. I wondered if I should turn around and attempt a getaway. It felt like we were driving into a deathtrap. Then my rational mind kicked in: 'Whatever happens, will happen,' I thought.

I was born in the winter of 1959, on 3 August. My paternal grandmother, whom we called Dadima, came to South Africa from India. My mother, Amina, was from Lourenço Marques (now Maputo) in Mozambique. I lived with them at 39 Selkirk Street in District Six, along with my dad Mohammed, and my siblings Abdul-Aziz and Salim.

My grandparents owned the house. In those days, people often didn't make wills, and when my grandfather passed away my dad lost the house, eventually having to rebuy it from the state at its market value.

My dad was very involved with the community. For years he was chairman of the Muir Street Mosque, and when there was a problem in the community, people consulted him as an elder and he gave them advice. My dad was well educated for his generation, even though he had been forced to leave school in matric and play the role of breadwinner after his father passed away, continuing the family's fruit and vegetable business and abandoning his ambition to become a doctor. We were what was then considered middle class.

In District Six, everybody knew everybody else and there was a wonderful community spirit. If a neighbour asked for sugar, no one hesitated to help them out. As children, my brothers and I used to play in the streets. If someone saw us doing something wrong, they'd give us a whack. We were children of the community.

My father and his two brothers, Suleiman and Moosa, owned Empire Farm Fruiterers. We had a number of tenders, supplying fruit and vegetables to hospitals, chain stores and restaurants. It was a fairly big business and we were busy. We had a warehouse in Chapel Street, close to where we lived and not far from the harbour. I had to wake up at four every morning to go to the Epping Market by truck with Uncle Suleiman to buy our fresh produce. During the closure of the Suez Canal at the beginning of the Six Day War in 1967, many ships came past the port of Cape Town, and because of the location of our business it was easy to deliver goods to the ships. Our business boomed.

If you went down Francis Street you'd find sweet factories where locals were employed. There was a cane factory too. Getting to work didn't cost anything, as the workers walked. At half past seven in the morning, we'd see the flow of workers leaving District Six, and at five o'clock in the evening we'd see a stream of workers walking back from Rex Trueform and other clothing factories in Salt River. We'd know what time it was by who was coming and going. In the afternoons, my brothers and I played soccer and cricket in the street, and I developed a keen interest in sport. I went on to play school cricket and was later selected for the Western Province school side. My dad wasn't particularly happy about my interest in sport – he said it wasn't going to put bread on the table and that I needed to give him good results at school. Nevertheless, I continued to play club cricket throughout my teenage years and afterwards.

Many good sportsmen came out of District Six, like the Abbet brothers. Because they could not go far in apartheid South Africa, one of the brothers emigrated and played cricket in the Netherlands. Eventually he became the coach for the Dutch national team; that's how good he was. Basil D'Oliveira left South Africa to play for the English cricket side, and when England toured South Africa, the government insisted that Basil be excluded from the English team because of the colour of his skin.

In District Six there was no class differentiation and race did not matter. The Minaars, who were all workers at Ensign Clothing, lived next door. A Chinese family, the Manleys, lived on the corner and owned a shop. A white Jewish family, the Schullers, lived next door. Mrs Schuller was very close to my mom. I remember one occasion going to town with them by bus. When a bus pulled up at the stop and Mrs Schuller climbed in, my siblings and I tried to get in too, but my mother pulled us back, saying, 'No, you can't get in that bus.' We had to wait for the bus for non-whites, and we met Mrs Schuller at the terminus.

I attended a formerly white school known as East Park Primary, which was renamed Chapel Street Primary after the apartheid government declared it a coloured school. We had a very nice playground compared to the other schools around us, and while those other pupils had to play in the streets, we had lawns and a rugby field.

One of our teachers, Mr Neethling, belonged to the New Unity Movement. I was in his class in September 1966 when Hendrik Verwoerd was assassinated. Mr Neethling was overjoyed. He talked to us about racism and how wrong it is to be judged by the colour of our skin, but we were young and did not fully appreciate how progressive he was.

That year, the government declared District Six a whites-only area. My dad and others took the Department of Community Development to court and Dullah Omar, who was our neighbour, was their legal representative. As the court proceedings went on, the houses around ours were bulldozed. Eventually ours stood alone, but we did not move. Our friends and neighbours, with whom we had grown up, left for Bonteheuwel, Belhar, Valhalla Park and Hanover Park, and moved into tiny sub-economic council houses, their dignity eroded. The Minaar family from across the road moved to Belhar, and we heard that their son became involved in gangs and was sent to prison for murder. It was hard to believe how negatively the environment they were moved to impacted their lives.

In the 1970s, I attended Trafalgar High, a politically active school within walking distance of our home in District Six. The SAP and the security branch kept a watchful eye on the school, and many of our teachers were arrested or banned. Achmad Cassiem, who later founded Qibla and joined the PAC, was a student there. When he was seventeen, he was arrested along with a teacher and several others and sentenced to five years on Robben Island under the Sabotage Act. We later learnt that Achmad planned to blow up a substation on De Waal Drive. His reasoning was that the people of Walmer Estate, an area just below De Waal Drive, were bourgeois. When there was a boycott call, like when Tramways increased bus fares, they would not participate because they were middle class and comfortable. Achmad and his co-accused wanted them to feel what it was like to live in the dark without electricity, just with candles, the way poor people suffered in District Six every day.

The government's strategy was to infiltrate schools, and it was understood that somebody had sold Achmad and the others out. There was a general air of mistrust. We had a large contingent of white teachers at Trafalgar High, liberals by and large, and some of them would engage us in debates. Through these exchanges we learnt that they enjoyed better salaries, even though they taught in a coloured school, because their salaries were paid by the white Department of Education, not the Department of Coloured Affairs. We wondered why they would leave their privileged schools to teach at our so-called 'non-white', underprivileged school, and suspected that they were planted by the government.

Those were very interesting years. Trafalgar had a long-serving teacher by the name of Mr Steenveldt, who belonged to the Teachers' League and its parent organisation, the Non-European Unity Movement. He used to bring the teachers' journals to us to read and we would engage him in debate. I noticed that the journals were written in highbrow, inaccessible English, yet the Unity Movement wanted to mobilise the working-class masses, so I challenged him about this. He was receptive to that sort of critical engagement and we developed a good relationship. Mr Steenveldt also introduced me to Antonio Gramsci, Paulo Freire and Karl Marx, and by reading them I developed an understanding of struggles besides the one we were fighting against apartheid. Another teacher, Mrs Wellbelover, gave me the communist viewpoint on different topics that we debated, and by my mid-teens I had developed a socialist–communist outlook.

In 1976, during the student uprisings, I experienced police brutality first-hand. At school there was a debate as to whether we should support 'education before liberation' or 'liberation before education'. The Student Representative Council was divided on the question. In the end, some pupils at Trafalgar High stayed in class while others, including me, joined the school's protest march. We marched down Adderley Street, joining students from Salt River High at Buitenkant Street. Together, we marched down Constitution Street and along Sir Lowry Road.

The police had cordoned off Buitenkant Street near Caledon Square Police Station, and we faced a line of police vans and policemen armed with wooden batons. We sat in the middle of the road chanting 'We will not be moved', stopping all the traffic across Buitenkant and Darling Streets. The police gave us two minutes to disperse. We didn't heed their warning, and they charged at us with their batons. Pupils were screaming, bleeding from head wounds. The protest action became very violent. I realised then how unscrupulous and merciless the apartheid government and its security forces were.

After the 1976 student uprising, the country became ungovernable. We were angry. Sometimes, we would spontaneously decide to stone cars and buses because of the frustration and anger we felt. Under these difficult circumstances I wrote my matric exams and managed to pass. I wanted to study law at the University of Cape Town, but because I was classified Indian, I was restricted to the University of Durban-Westville, which was designated for Indians. To study at a white university like UCT, I had to apply for a special permit from the minister of education. My eldest brother, Abdul-Aziz, was already studying at UDW, but my parents weren't happy about the extra relocation costs they would incur if I moved to Durban too.

Some of my friends had been accepted at UCT, so I looked at what I could study there. I walked from one faculty to the next, trying to find an opening. Eventually I found one in the architecture department. 'Why not?' I thought, and filled out the application forms and permit request. My application was approved in 1977, but I only received the permit at the end of the first term, and I soon lost interest in architecture because of having to play catch-up with the rest of the students.

Most of the time, my friends and I would laze on Jameson steps, talking politics instead of going to lectures. During this time we became highly politicised, and joined NUSAS, a predominantly white student organisation at UCT.

I found UCT to be largely conservative, but we discovered some liberals among the white students. My friends and I were influenced by the Black Consciousness Movement and challenged the white NUSAS students. We told them that even though they were progressive, they enjoyed privileges that blacks had never enjoyed. They could go back to their luxurious homes and lifestyles and so they were not oppressed. Black people couldn't move around freely, live wherever they wanted to or work wherever they chose. For this reason, we needed to unify all people of colour.

In June that year, some UWC friends and I decided that we needed to do something to commemorate the 1976 Soweto uprising. We came up with the idea that we'd print pamphlets for this occasion and make a bomb to disseminate them. We took a week to prepare the bomb from gunpowder we emptied out of firecrackers. Pamphlets were placed in a box, above and below envelopes filled with gunpowder, which were connected to a firecracker fuse. I placed the box at the Grand Parade opposite City Hall, lit the fuse and hurried off. A minute later there was a loud blast and all the pamphlets flew into the air.

There were some pamphlets left over, and because the pamphlet bomb worked so well on the Grand Parade, my friend Rudy Pierie and I decided to set off another at UWC two weeks later. This time the fuse failed to go off, so we distributed the pamphlets to commuters on the train from Bellville back home to Cape Town. We got off at Cape Town Station, not realising that we were being watched.

It was midday. As we walked past the Castle of Good Hope, I saw a black car approaching, then two well-dressed black guys walked up to me. My first thought was that they wanted to rob me. Rudy had stopped to light a cigarette, and when he looked up he saw the men grab me and force me into the car. There was a white man behind the wheel and Rudy instantly suspected that they were policemen. The railway police must have informed the SAP about students distributing pamphlets on the train. Rudy assumed I'd been arrested and immediately reported what he had seen to our friends. They were panic-stricken, but had the presence of mind to phone my parents from a public phone box so it would be difficult to trace the call. Rudy couldn't give my parents a detailed report; he just said that I had been taken away in a black car and that he thought I'd been arrested. Then my friends phoned the Caledon Square Police Station to ask if Ismail Vallie was being held there. They were told that there was nobody at the station by that name.

I was taken to the fourteenth floor of the Paul Sauer Building in Adderley Street, where the security branch had offices. They interrogated me throughout that night, until six o'clock the next morning, questioning me about the pamphlets and where they came from. I said that somebody had given them to me to distribute. From their questioning I realised that they had followed us on the train from Bellville to Cape Town. We were young and careless, thinking that the struggle belonged to us and that nobody could touch or stop us.

While I was being questioned, our family friend and struggle lawyer Dullah Omar phoned the security police to find out about me. After the call, my situation got worse. The security police started asking me if I was a communist. I replied that I was more of a sportsman than anything else.

'Hoe weet Dullah Omar jy is hier?' they asked. (How does Dullah Omar know you are here?) I told them I didn't know. They continued: 'What's your association with Dullah Omar?' I replied that we were neighbours. It became clear to me from their questioning that they assumed Dullah Omar and others close to him had organised the pamphlet bomb and that I was part of something bigger than radical student action.

From the Paul Sauer Building they took me to Caledon Square Police Station and locked me up in a dank cell. A day passed. It was June and freezing cold. While I was lying on a thin foam mattress, covering my head with the thin blanket, trying to get warm enough to fall asleep, white plain-clothes policemen entered my cell. It was about three o'clock in the morning. Then another policeman entered the cell and poured a bucket of cold, dirty water over me. 'Trek jou klere uit!' they shouted. (Take off your clothes!) I was made to strip and then ordered to jump up and down and do push-ups. The place was cold and wet, but my body slowly began to warm up. Then one of the policemen came with his big boots and stood on me, pressing my body against the ice-cold cell floor. It became apparent they were doing this because I was, in their words, ''n kommunis' (a communist).

The next thing they did was take me home and search my house. They were aggressive, throwing everything onto the floor, turning the whole house upside down. I had a copy of the ANC's Freedom Charter in the lining of my bedcover, and books, such as Gramsci's, in the cupboard. My brothers had got rid of my books when they heard I'd been arrested, but they didn't know about the Freedom Charter, and the policemen found it during their raid.

I was driven back to Caledon Square and they started torturing me physically all over again, playing good cop, bad cop. Then they took me back to the Paul Sauer Building, up to the fourteenth floor, where I was introduced to the notorious Hernus J.P. 'Spyker' van Wyk. 'Jong,' he said, 'ek het al baie mense by hierdie venster uitgegooi.' (Young man, I have thrown many people out of this window.) Then a huge security policeman took me to one of the big windows overlooking a parking lot. The cars parked below seemed tiny from so high up. I was dangled out of the window, holding on to the policeman's hand for dear life as he shouted 'Praat, jou donner!' (Speak, you fucker!)

I thought I was going to die. 'Okay, I am going to tell you!' I shouted, and they pulled me back inside.

'Praat!' they commanded. (Talk!)

I knew my friends probably had more pamphlets at their homes, and one of them had the Roneo machine that we'd used to make the pamphlets, so I gave the security police fictitious names. When they wanted to know where my friends stayed, I said I didn't know, probably somewhere in Bellville. In fact, they lived in Walmer Estate. The security police then drove me to UWC to point out the friends involved in the failed pamphlet bomb operation. I was petrified the security policemen were going to implicate us all. Fortunately, one of my friends saw me sitting in their car. He alerted the others, and they quickly got rid of the stencils and the Roneo machine.

It was a terrible experience. I was only nineteen years old and it was traumatic facing large men who were a law unto themselves. Added to that was the fact that they played psychological games with me. One policeman terrorised me by showing me pictures of people who'd been badly beaten. I could see the fear in the comrades' faces and imagined the torture they'd gone through. Afterwards, the policeman would remove these images, sit in the corner and Spyker would come in to continue the interrogation, threatening that if I didn't give answers to their satisfaction I'd get *moered*.

After the interrogation at the Paul Sauer Building, I was taken back to Caledon Square, and then to Sea Point Police Station. The sea breeze made it exceptionally cold and impossible to fall asleep. For breakfast they gave us *katkop* (half a loaf of stale bread) with jam on top. Initially, I could not get it down, but as time went on, I got hungry enough to eat it. This went on for some time. From Sea Point Police Station they took me to Camps Bay Police Station, where I was completely isolated. Then it was back to Caledon Square, where I was tortured. The security police attached electrical wires connected to a light-bulb socket to my fingertips and when they weren't satisfied with my answers to their questions they flicked the switch, electrocuting me. I was also repeatedly grabbed and thrown to the floor, while a policeman shouted, 'Stand up! Pick up the chair! Sit down!'

This went on for around fifteen days after my arrest. I think the security police were still hoping I would tell them who the guys involved with the pamphlet bomb were and where they stayed. I gave them a vague idea, but I did not pinpoint any of my friends. In the meantime, they went into hiding.

During this time I had no access to my parents and I became very demoralised and depressed. I had worn the same clothes for three weeks and was starting to smell, so I tried to wash them. There was no washing basin in the cell, so I used the toilet bowl. On one day I'd wash my jersey and squeeze it out to dry, the next day I'd wash my shirt, and the next day my pants. Eventually, I told a uniformed officer at Sea Point Police Station that I needed a change of clothes and gave him my home address. He made contact with my family and a few days later I received a single set of clothes.

In the meantime, Dullah Omar was pushing for the police to either charge or release me. After about six weeks, I appeared in the Cape Town Magistrate's Court, was charged with possession and distribution of banned pamphlets, and was released into my parents' custody.

About two weeks after my release, the security police came back and told me to hand over my passport. I became very scared. My passport was filled with Mozambican entry and exit stamps because my mother was from Lourenço

Marques and our family travelled there regularly to visit my grandfather and cousins. My cousins were FRELIMO activists and FRELIMO leader Samora Machel had grown up in the same village as my grandfather; the family knew him very well. Mozambique was known as an ANC training ground, and the police naturally assumed that I had ANC contacts. They wanted to know the purpose of my visits, how long I had stayed each time and who I had been meeting. They did not believe me when I told them I was visiting family there and persisted with their questioning, showing me photographs of ANC comrades and asking if I knew them. Eventually, I was released.

The first two years after my detention were very difficult. I became paranoid and suspicious, and I didn't want to get involved in radical activities, because I was scared that I was being watched. I panicked when anyone knocked loudly on the door, fearing it was the security police. I didn't think I could survive being tortured a second time and wondered whether being involved in politics was worth what I'd endured. My mother told me afterwards that she felt very resentful towards me. The whole incident was very traumatic for her too. When the security police raided the house, they'd been so aggressive that my mother had collapsed. She had not understood what was going on and had no idea what I had done.

After this incident, my parents told me that I couldn't go back to university – that I'd wasted their money getting involved in politics and that it was time I joined the family fruit and vegetable business. If I wanted to study, they said, I could do so through correspondence at the University of South Africa (UNISA). It took a long time for me to find my feet again, but I think it was good for me to spend time away from student life, in an altogether different environment cut off from radical politics. It provided some form of rehabilitation and I adapted well.

It took me two years before I enrolled at UNISA. My parents were always saying that an education is important. Everyone in my family is a professional – my elder brother studied computer engineering and my younger brother studied pharmacy. Some of my cousins are doctors. Studying part-time wasn't easy, but I was interested in studying law, so I enrolled to do a BA and enjoyed the courses I did, such as Latin, which would enable me to do an LLB later. I met many people through UNISA, especially through the orientation classes run by the South African Committee for Higher Education (SACHED).

After having spent time in police detention, I shied away from political activism and focused on sport. I played cricket for the Montrose Cricket Club and soccer for Stephanian Football Club, and I joined the South African

Council on Sport. SACOS leader Hassan Hawa, along with activist Frank van der Horst, led the opposition to South Africa's involvement in international sport under the slogan 'No normal sport in an abnormal society' and took on the issue of disparity between separate facilities and amenities for blacks and whites. Joining SACOS resulted in my involvement in politics on the sporting front.

As time passed, living in District Six became unsafe. There were empty plots all around us, and sometimes robbers jumped over the wall. Under these circumstances and pressure from the state, we decided to move to Rylands, which was classified as an Indian area. It was 1982 and we were one of the last families to leave. Soon afterwards, my dad's brother moved in next door to us in Rylands; he had also stayed in District Six until the bitter end.

Rylands and Cravenby were the two state-designated residential areas for Indians at that time, and because the Indian population was big, one paid a premium for land in Rylands. We were only compensated the municipal value of our properties in District Six, which turned out to be peanuts: my uncle was paid R1 800 for his house and we were paid about R1 600 for ours. When we were forcibly removed, we bought two houses in Rylands for R5 400. It wasn't a straight swap, and that set us back financially. The impact of the move on my family's fruit and vegetable business was immense. We were paid around R2 000 for the warehouse, yet building another would cost seven times as much, so we needed a loan. Our warehouse in District Six had had everything required to run the business, including three cold rooms and a hot room to ripen our bananas. When we started in Rylands, we only had one small warehouse. We had to rent a cold room, and slid further into debt. It also cost us more to travel to our customers, many of whom were based in central Cape Town and Sea Point. We had hardly any customers in the Rylands vicinity, as the area was still being developed. It was like starting all over again. All the money my dad had saved was put towards the deposit on the house, and he had to take out a bond on it too. Our new house in Rylands also needed to be furnished, so there were additional expenses.

In District Six, my mother could walk to Pick 'n Pay to buy groceries, but in Rylands she needed somebody to take her wherever she needed to go because the shops were not close by – another expense that we could not afford. Children couldn't play in the streets because the streets were narrow and the traffic was heavy. We didn't know our neighbours because of the high walls around their properties. Crime became rife as middle-class areas were targeted, and our house was not spared.

My Dadima was ninety-nine years old when we moved to Rylands. I clearly remember her saying to my dad: 'Don't move my stuff. I'll move it myself'; she insisted on arranging her furniture in her room for loading onto the truck. She had walked everywhere in District Six and everybody knew her, even the gangsters, and respected her because of her age. She lived to 107, but in Rylands she lost her zest for life. Her health steadily deteriorated, as she could no longer walk around freely. She was always complaining about the area. 'It's unhealthy,' she used to say. 'The air around here is not as it is in Cape Town.' She retreated to her room. Occasionally, she would sit on the stoep, but that was the furthest she would go.

The move broke me too. The environment I had grown up in had shaped my character and identity; it had given me a sense of belonging. When we were displaced, the soul of the community was destroyed. I have spent years piecing together the fragments of my fractured self.

By the time I met Julie Vallie, during the 1984 unrest, I needed a change in my life. I would pick her up from her home in Newfields and we'd go to political meetings and rallies together. We fell in love and got married a few months later. We moved to Harfield Village in Claremont and stayed there for four years until Julie's father became ill and needed to be cared for, after which we moved back to her family home in Newfields. All our children were born in the Newfields house: Raziya in 1984, Salim in 1991 and Nisreen in 1993.

I was sick and tired of the fruit and vegetables game, so Julie and I gave serious thought to the type of business we would go into and decided on packaging. We started the business with only R250 and slowly built it up. During the consumer boycotts of white businesses, we supplied packaging to companies in coloured areas. Township supermarkets became much busier at this time because if anyone was seen with Checkers, Woolworths or Pick 'n Pay carrier bags on public transport, the goods would be confiscated. With this development, our business boomed.

Julie and I were also active in political meetings and organising street battles during this time. I was approached to join the Azanian People's Liberation Army (APLA) and leave the country for military training, but I said no, because I disagreed with APLA's policies. Then Shirley Gunn approached Julie to courier parcels to Botswana. We knew Shirley through Julie's sister, Ghadija, who worked with Essa Moosa to support detainees. I had concerns about the contents of the parcels, and Julie and I met with Shirley to discuss what exactly we'd be doing. Shirley went into some depth about the mission, but she never said *what* we'd be couriering. Nevertheless, Julie and I decided to do it to advance the struggle. Over the next few weeks we stayed in contact with Shirley, who was in hiding at the time, and ran errands for her, bringing her newspapers on Sundays. Otherwise, we continued with our lives. One day Shirley informed us that we had to leave for Botswana the following day.

Our instructions were to meet a particular comrade, whom we didn't know, at five o'clock the following morning in Commissioner Street in Johannesburg. We hired a Citi Golf and left Cape Town that afternoon, driving right through the night.

We had been given a description of the comrade and how he would approach us. We were also given code names: Peter and Jane. The comrade's code name was Shafiek. We made it to Commissioner Street on time and waited. Then a person fitting the comrade's description arrived. He observed us, first walking right past us, before turning around and greeting us by our code names. 'Are you Shafiek?' we asked. He confirmed that he was and said we should follow him to a flat. Once there, he gave us breakfast. We were hoping we'd have a chance to freshen up, but the next thing he said was, 'Right. We are going to change cars at Avis and then we're going to Botswana.' 'My God,' I thought, 'there is no rest for the wicked.' Later, we got to know Shafiek as Shanil Haricharan.

We swapped the Citi Golf for a Nissan Skyline at Avis car hire and drove to the Botswana border. As we approached the border post, Shanil told us to stop. 'I'll meet you on the other side,' he said and got out of the car. We went through the border post and Shanil jumped into the car on the other side. We drove on and hit a roadblock. Our car was checked. My nerves were so frayed that I didn't realise that the engine was still on and tried to restart the car while it was idling. Fortunately, the policeman didn't notice, and we were allowed to drive on.

We booked into the Gaborone Sun, where Shanil introduced us to some ANC comrades. Then he left us. The comrades chatted with us in our hotel room and we were told to write our biographies. I did as I was told, but Julie refused to write hers despite my efforts to convince her, because Shirley hadn't given us that instruction.

We were in the hotel for about three or four days. On the second day we met the ANC comrades again. The Skyline was taken away and we were instructed to wait in the hotel room, as there were many suspicious people moving around the hotel. It was known that South African security agents operated in Gaborone. We intended to follow the comrades' instructions, but at some point we went down to the lobby. Out of nowhere, a drunken guy bumped into us.

'Hello, Comrade,' he said to me.

'His name is not "Comrade",' said Julie quickly. 'His name is Peter.'

We hurried back to our room, but the man followed us. We watched him through the peephole as he stood outside our hotel room, and the longer he stayed there, the more concerned we became. 'We're busted,' I told Julie every time we looked through the tiny peephole. An hour passed and he still hadn't moved. Questions ran through my mind: 'Who the hell was he? Why was he at our door? Did he know something?' And finally, 'Must I open the door and beat him up?' But that would have been foolhardy. We were in a foreign country. 'What would happen if he lays a charge against us?' I thought. 'They have our room number and I won't be able to get away.'

I began looking for an escape route in case the police came. We were on the third floor and I realised that I'd probably be able to make the drop if I jumped out the window. I asked Julie if she thought she would make it.

'Never!' she said, looking down. 'I can't make it. I'll die.'

'Well,' I said, 'I'm going to take a chance and jump if the police come, or if I hear a knock at the door.'

Julie maintained that she couldn't do it and we argued back and forth. Meanwhile, the guy outside our door was slumped on the passage floor, apparently asleep. By this time, he'd kept us hostage for three hours. He eventually left during the night. Needless to say, we didn't sleep very well.

The Skyline was returned to us the next day and a comrade explained the procedure to us. 'You need to memorise everything,' he said. 'There are limpet mines on the left-hand side and detonators on the right-hand side, and there are many grenades in the car too.' A woman called Pamela then gave us some basic training in detonators and different coloured lead plates and how explosives work. She told us there was nothing to worry about because the limpets were stored on one side of the car and the detonators on the other side. She reassured us that even if we were involved in an accident, the car would not explode, and that we had no need to worry.

Our cover was that we were doing business in Botswana. This was quite common, especially among the Indian business community living in Johannesburg. As an extra precaution, we dressed smartly and arranged a selection of packaging samples on the back seat. We memorised everything the comrades told us, operating on adrenaline – we still had to face the border, and roadblocks.

Our first roadblock was just before the Botswanan border post at Ramatlabama. The policemen were very nice, though, and we were friendly towards them, even going so far as to offer them cooldrinks. They opened our boot, checked inside the car and then let us through. On the South African side of the border, we took a detour off the main road. The ANC guys in Botswana had told us which route to follow. It was in the middle of the night, pitch dark, and there were no street lamps. There was nothing around us but open farmland, and livestock strolled across the potholed roads. We were extremely nervous, despite guarantees that the explosives were stored separately from the detonators, and Julie became increasingly paranoid. When I drove at 120 kilometres per hour, she insisted that I slow down, and it took us an extra few hours to get back to Cape Town. We handed over the Skyline to Shirley in Camps Bay, and that was the end of our first MK mission – our baptism.

Our second trip to Botswana was under the guise of a family holiday, and we took our daughter, Raziya, with us. We didn't have to meet Shanil in Johannesburg and instead drove straight to the Gaborone Sun, where we met up with the ANC comrades. Like the first time, they took the car away. That trip only took about three days and went well.

Our third and last trip was agonising. The struggle had intensified and the security forces had become aggressively vigilant. Julie and I went to Botswana in a Skyline, and the ANC took the car and returned it to us, as usual.

As we were leaving the hotel, one of the comrades said, 'There are three roadblocks on the road ahead.' What this meant was that we had to follow a comrade bumper to bumper through the bush, bypassing the roadblocks on the Botswanan side of the border. We managed it somehow and said goodbye to the comrade before continuing across the border into South Africa. Just as we thought we were home and dry, we hit a massive roadblock. I spotted about forty SADF personnel and a few Casspirs. They had sniffer dogs and were checking the cars with metal detectors. I was certain we were going to be caught and there was no way we could run. I kept driving, slowly drawing closer. Cars in front of us were pulled over and searched. 'My God,' I thought, 'we're not going to make it.' And then we were waved through! By sheer luck we had made it. I smiled and nodded to the police as I drove on.

As we were driving out of the town of Schweizer-Reneke, we saw a soldier hitchhiking and decided to give him a lift, as he would add to our cover – freedom fighters wouldn't be expected to assist the enemy. He sat in the front passenger seat next to me, and Julie moved to the back seat. As we were driving, he told us that he had just done duty at the border we'd crossed and that he was now going home on a short pass before reporting for duty again. I asked him where he stayed. 'Table View,' he said. It was almost too good to be true – a free pass all the way to Cape Town. I then asked the soldier whether he didn't mind driving, as I was feeling very tired. He got behind the wheel, wearing an army beret that signified his senior rank. With him driving, we breezed past two huge roadblocks, one in Kimberley and another in Worcester, where cars and trucks were being thoroughly searched. 'All's fine, I'm going home,' he'd tell the soldiers, and overtake the line of vehicles waiting to be searched. He drove the whole way from Kimberley to Cape Town, telling us stories about what it was like on the border. He strongly believed that the ANC was a terrorist organisation and a communist threat. We dropped him off right in front of his Table View flat.

We kept in contact with Shirley for about two years after that, and she and Aneez Salie taught us how to cache materials – how to mark the landscape with a rusted nail and how to describe the surroundings – as well as giving us intensive training in logistics and reconnaissance. Once, Shirley instructed Julie and me to retrieve a cache of weapons in Franschhoek using a route map. We searched for the cache but couldn't find it and had to return later with a metal detector that Shirley had hired. We looked everywhere, but couldn't locate the cache, even with the metal detector. I still don't know what happened to the weapons. On another occasion, I took a pick and shovel and dug up a cache near Silvermine, stashing the weapons in my red Mazda, which we then delivered to the detachment. The only other trip we had to make was to Essa Moosa's office to collect a pram for baby Haroon.

In the second half of 1988, Julie and I did reconnaissance of targets, including the Cape Technikon, the Bonteheuwel Rent Office and the Tokai area close to Pollsmoor Prison, where Mandela and other comrades were imprisoned. I was involved in three operations, but the last one was aborted. The first operation was in September 1988. Shanil and I were instructed to sabotage the Cape Technikon. This technikon, which was for white students only, had been built on District Six land from which my family had been uprooted. Julie and I did the reconnaissance, paying particular attention to people's movements to ensure that no one would be injured. We monitored the movements of the security guard around the building and arrived at the decision that the best time to plant the bomb was at night. Shanil flew down from Johannesburg and spent the day with us, and it was decided that he and I would be the ones to sabotage the building.

That night, we parked on the road above the back of the technikon, where there was a slope leading down to the door where we were going to plant the bomb. Shanil primed the limpet and placed it. As he was running back up the slope to the car, he lost his glasses. It was dark and he could hardly see without them. 'Leave the glasses!' I hissed, starting to panic as he groped around in the dark. 'We have to get out of here!' But Shanil was adamant that we couldn't leave evidence. I scrambled down to help him look and by sheer chance I found them. We hurriedly jumped into the car and headed straight to Newfields. Shanil left for Johannesburg that same night.

The next morning, the explosion at the technikon was headline news in the *Cape Times*. It was on the radio too. The police were under the impression that the bomb had been planted on the inside of the building, because the door had blown out and not in. From that operation I learnt that if explosives were placed in a certain way, a bomb would blast outwards. The police thought that somebody had come into the building, planted a bomb, and then left. It was a victory for us, as the police forensics team was totally fooled.

The next operation was at the Bonteheuwel Rent Office, as we needed to respond to rent increases in the area. Julie and I did thorough reconnaissance, monitoring the place continually for about a week. We observed the rent office at various times of the day and night and again established that the best time to plant the limpet was round 11 p.m., when the place was deserted.

On the night of the operation, Julie and I took a Salticrax box containing the limpet mine from our grocery cupboard and drove to Bonteheuwel, where we planted the limpet at the bottom of a door at the rent office. Once again, the police thought that the bomb had been planted inside the building and not outside, and suspected it was an inside job. It was another victory for us.

The third operation was in 1989, in response to the call to intensify mass resistance and the armed struggle and to support the 'Free Mandela' march. Mandela had been moved to Victor Verster Prison near Paarl the previous December, but most of his fellow Rivonia trialists were still being held at Pollsmoor Prison, and we planned to have an operation nearby to coincide with the planned march to Pollsmoor for their release. We hoped that they would be able to hear the explosion. I was tasked with carrying out that operation on my own. I did reconnaissance for about a week beforehand. It was nerve-wracking. I planned to place the limpet in an empty rubbish bin on the outskirts of the Blue Route Mall parking lot facing Pollsmoor, mindful of any potential casualties.

On the day I was supposed to plant the bomb, I drove along Tokai Road and saw that the area was abuzz with a heavy police presence and people waiting to join the march to Pollsmoor. But things were not going as planned: the march had started in Thornton Road in Athlone but had been stopped by the police in Kromboom Road. Many people had been arrested. I was not aware of this when I parked in the Blue Route parking lot.

I was busy priming the limpet mine when the police began chasing a group of journalists and photographers gathered on Tokai Road. I'd put the lead plate in my mouth while unscrewing the detonator when Rashid Lombard, a friend and struggle photographer, suddenly banged on my car window. He opened the door, jumped into the car and shouted, 'Drive!' I turned to see a police van right behind us. In the commotion I dropped the detonator and swallowed the lead plate, with the limpet still under my thigh. Rashid didn't know what I'd been up to or that I was an MK cadre.

My adrenaline was pumping. I sped off and when I glanced in my rear-view mirror I saw the police van pursuing us. I took side roads towards Bergvliet, trying to evade the police. Eventually, I pulled into a sloping driveway and we sat there, waiting. Rashid cautiously got out of the car to see where the police were, and I took the limpet out from under my thigh, put it back into the Salticrax box, sealed it, and put it under my seat. When Rashid got back into the car, he told me it was safe and that we could go.

As we were driving, he received a message on his pager that Jimi Matthews and a few other journalists had been arrested. Jimi was a close friend of Rashid's and Rashid naturally wanted to get him out of police custody. I drove to the Retreat Police Station, all the while thinking about the limpet in the car.

The police gave Rashid the runaround: from Retreat Police Station we were sent to the Athlone Police Station, but the police there couldn't confirm where the comrades were being held. We eventually gave up and I dropped Rashid off at his home and left the area immediately. I wondered whether I should try to complete the mission, but by then Belgravia and Thornton Roads were ungovernable. Tyres were burning and the police had fired teargas at the marchers. The whole of Athlone seemed to be on fire.

I took the limpet home and put it back in the kitchen cupboard. Later that night, I had intense stomach pains, so bad that I couldn't sleep. Julie and I went to Groote Schuur Hospital and my stomach was X-rayed. Miraculously, the doctor did not pick up the lead plate I'd swallowed, but informed me that I had a bleeding ulcer, which was treated. After that I seemed to be fine, but as time passed both Julie and I suffered from a number of health problems. Julie was diagnosed with Parkinson's disease, which is now at an advanced stage. Doctors detected a large malignant tumour in my throat and insisted that I have it removed, followed by radical chemotherapy, but I decided not to undergo the operation, as it could affect my larynx and my ability to speak. The consultations and treatment were very costly and we struggled to pay the bills. Instead, I treated myself with hemp oil, which has significantly reduced the tumour. Fortunately, in late 2013, both Julie and I were able to register as military veterans at 2 Military Hospital in Wynberg, and we receive free health care.

*

I sometimes look back and ask myself: 'Was it worth it?' People died in the struggle: Ashley Kriel, Anton Fransch, and others. MK comrades and their families continue to face enormous hardships.

When the Land Claims Commission was set up in 1995, my uncle, Suleiman Vallie, submitted a land claim application on behalf of our families to reclaim our property in District Six. After his death, I pursued the claim, as I felt compelled to rectify the injustice of the forced removals that inflicted horrendous suffering. Some people do not begin to understand the impact of the forced removals and the enormous costs that District Six residents and other affected communities had to bear. Given the opportunity, I would love to move back to District Six. It won't be the same mixed-class community, and the community spirit won't be what it was, but at least it's close to the CBD and there is easy access to highways. It's also relatively close to our family-owned garage in Maitland.

The ANC's Freedom Charter says 'there shall be houses, security and comfort', yet many are worse off than they once were. People gave everything to the struggle, for the ideals enshrined in the Freedom Charter, only to find that they have been sold out by politicians.

The legacy of apartheid is still alive. I stay in an area that is predominantly Indian. When we stepped outside our home in District Six, we saw our Christian and Chinese neighbours and the white family staying further down the road. I experienced no cultural and racial divide until we moved to Rylands, which still remains a segregated community.

8

Julie Vallie

Where It All Started

W HEN YOU'RE YOUNG, you dream. You don't really understand the consequences of your decisions yet. Perhaps you don't care because you are so angry. Our freedom was being crushed by apartheid, so we dreamt of all the good things that would come out of our revolution. All we wanted was to overthrow the government, and we thought it would be easy. We were very idealistic.

When Shirley Gunn approached me in 1987 to fetch arms and ammunition from Botswana, I said yes without hesitation. Agreeing to be recruited into Umkhonto we Sizwe and to fetch weapons to defend our people was easy. I felt it was the least I could do, but I was young and very green when it came to understanding anything about the armed struggle. I thought someone would put the stuff in the car and we'd come back home, end of story. When I told my husband, Ismail, that Shirley had approached me and that I'd agreed to a mission, he had a blue fit.

I sulked. 'It's a nice opportunity for a break,' I said.

'A break?' Ismail cried. 'Julie, you don't understand what you are getting yourself into.'

My idyllic childhood with my family and friends in Newlands will always have a special place in my heart. What remains of that pleasant episode in my life are shattered images of loss – of my community and of my sense of belonging.

I was born on 4 February 1960 in a semi-detached cottage at 5 Thicket Street, on the corner of Hemlock Street in Newlands. I lived with my parents; my brothers, Shafick and Moosa; and my sisters, Muneerah, Fatima and Ghadija.

My father came from a fairly well-off home. Horses were stabled on our property in Thicket Street, and I loved riding Domino, a very tame brown horse. These weren't ordinary horses, though; they were show horses that my uncle Ranie looked after, and which were entered into dressage and other competitions. We also had chickens, which Auntie Minnie, my father's older sister, was in charge of, and which we slaughtered and ate. We had cats too. In our big yard there were many fruit trees – pomegranates, figs, plums, and different types of apples, as well as grapevines. A number of trucks also stood in the yard; that was the nature of my father's business – providing a trucking service. He had contracts with big furniture retailers and he'd deliver the furniture to the buyers. On weekends, he drove people to sporting events, or to outings on the beach or the mountain, such as Tweedetol in Bainskloof. On Saturday nights, he packed our big family in his Chevrolet and we would go to Sky View in Ottery, the only drive-in open to blacks. Often, the neighbour's children wanted to go with us, and I hated that because I wouldn't be able to see the screen over their heads. My favourite trips were the Sunday afternoon drives to buy ice cream in Sea Point or at Spotty Dog in Retreat.

Newlands Rugby Stadium was around the corner from us, and as children we charged rugby fans for parking in our yard. That entrepreneurial spirit was nurtured in us from a young age, and was perhaps a family legacy: my maternal grandfather had owned taxis in Port Elizabeth, but due to the Depression he lost his business and moved to Cape Town. Once there, he bought a fishing boat and opened a restaurant on Kalk Bay beach.

My grandmother outlived my grandfather, and although she struggled to run the business alone after he died, she was a darling among the fishermen because she always made time to help them out. In return, they would bring her fresh fish off their boats. She adored and spoilt me, buying me clothes at Duncan Taylors, an exclusive outfitter in Wynberg, and I was very attached to her.

My mother's eldest sister, whom we called Sisi, also had a restaurant in Kalk Bay. She had no children, so she worked hard to run the business on her own, and I remember her as a very vibrant character.

I don't have memories of my paternal grandparents, but from what I've heard, my grandmother ran a soup kitchen for homeless people from her home in Newlands, and she provided meals for the truck drivers who worked for my grandfather.

My mother was a quiet, reserved and dignified woman, and took pride in how she dressed, always wearing gloves and taking a handbag whenever she went out. I maintain that she was the best confectioner on earth. There were always lovely smells coming from our kitchen. She used to bake for weddings and functions, seldom charging people; they supplied the ingredients and paid in kind. We had stacks of fabric in the house that she had received as payment for her cakes, more than we could ever use. That was the spirit of the community.

We lived parallel to the Newlands railway station and there was a shop on the corner where we bought our bread and milk, as well as a fruit and vegetable shop on the opposite corner. Other shops, such as OK Bazaars on Claremont Main Road, were close by. Auntie Janey, the wife of Abdur Rashied, my mother's brother, lived on the other side of the bridge in Claremont. She was a dressmaker and made most of our clothes.

In our small Newlands community, we played with all the children in our racially mixed neighbourhood. We didn't know about apartheid then. We played with Marie, whom we called Marie Biscuits, and her brother – they were white and lived in the railway cottages, as their father was a South African Railways employee. We played with black children too. Colour made no difference to us; poor or rich, black or white – we played with whoever was nearby.

My father, Dawood Vallie, also had many friends in Claremont. I particularly remember Boeta Salim, our Madressa teacher; Ebrahim Davids, Boeta Salim's brother, who worked at the Stegman Road Mosque; and Imam Haron. Imam Haron used to visit us and always brought us chocolates, since he worked for Rowntree's at the time. We longed for his visits. When I was much older and my father fell ill, his old friends visited him and they reminisced about what they'd got up to during apartheid. It was only then that I discovered that my father had worked in the underground with Imam Haron.

I was about fourteen when my family was evicted from Newlands because of the Group Areas Act, and we moved to Carwell Road in Lansdowne. We had managed to stay in Newlands longer than others because my grandfather owned the property, but we were eventually forced out and our house was demolished. Moving to Lansdowne was a big adjustment for us. My siblings and I asked why people who had lived around us, and those who lived in houses belonging to my grandfather, all had to move, and my father tried his best to explain why the white government wanted white people to live on our properties.

After Lansdowne we moved to Newfields. It was 1976; a time of protest and fear on the streets. I was sixteen years old and a student at Livingstone High School. One day I saw students marching and I wanted to know what was going on, but my mother forbade my siblings and me from getting involved. 'Don't you dare go to town!' she said. 'You don't know what is going to happen.' Disappointed by her response, we turned to our father. 'Go,' he told us, 'but be careful.'

I got a lift to town with our neighbour, but I was not prepared for the chaos in the streets there: students running, adults running, teargas burning our eyes and throats, and police charging and beating up everyone with batons. It was petrifying and I wondered what I had got myself into. There was complete chaos and confusion. I ran into a men's outfitters in Darling Street to hide, and regretted not listening to my mother. I hid there in terror for some time and, to my relief, the shopkeeper locked the doors. I had lost my friends in the confusion and felt vulnerable and alone, but I eventually managed to make my way home. When I related the experience to my parents, my mother shook her head. 'That's because you don't listen,' she said. This became her mantra.

It was around this time that my father became very ill. He had a brain haemorrhage, and when he was discharged from hospital he couldn't even remember his name. The stroke also affected the left side of his body and hence his mobility. He was the breadwinner so it was a very difficult time for the family. We all had to pitch in. I left school and did a short secretarial course at Todds Commercial College in Athlone so I could find a job and earn an income for the family. My eldest sister, Muneerah, did a dress designer course and then went on to work for Elzbieta Rosenwerth, an exclusive fashion designer in Newlands. All of us sacrificed our education.

My mother nursed my father until he was able to walk again. Uncle Dawood, who was married to Zuleiga, my father's youngest sister, would bath him every Sunday. Fortunately, he made an exceptional recovery and eventually he could drive again.

My mother's passing from cancer seven years later was, in a way, even tougher than my father's illness. She was our pillar of strength, and then she was gone. Muneerah and I nursed her until the end, and Fatima assisted when she returned from work, while Ghadija took her to hospital for her chemotherapy and radiation treatment.

I found an administrative job in Philippi at Cape Machine Movers and Engineering and worked there throughout the early 1980s. Mr Seeley, the owner, fetched me in the mornings, and after work I either took a ride home with him or with Amina, who worked opposite me. I didn't belong to any organisation or political group, but I was part of the Mass Democratic Movement, supporting the struggle where I could by pamphleteering and attending rallies. Ismail Vallie and I got married in 1984. Our families were closely connected, as our forebears were from the same region in India and both our parents and grandparents spoke Gujarati.

In August 1985 we attended the march to Pollsmoor Prison. A group of us, including my sister Ghadija and my cousin Zubeida Vallie, who was a photographer, arrived at the assembly point in Athlone in Ismail's yellow kombi, which we called the 'People's Casspir'. I always seemed to be the one who got lost in the crowd, and during the march down Thornton Road I lost Ismail, Ghadija and Zubeida. Then the police arrived and attacked the marchers. Clerics such as Charles Villa-Vicencio were there, and many people were arrested and detained. I managed to escape somehow and ran over Kromboom Bridge, seeking refuge at Adile Adams's hair salon on Kromboom Road.

Very soon after that, on 15 October 1985, we experienced the Trojan Horse Massacre. We were marching on Thornton Road in Athlone, near the Hewat Teacher Training College, when an orange railway truck pulled up and policemen hiding in boxes on the back jumped up and began shooting at us with live ammunition. The bullets missed us by inches, but three boys were killed. The following day there was a protest meeting at St Athens Road Mosque close by, which was called because the police were holding the bodies of the boys who had been shot dead, and it wasn't known whether or not they were Muslim. The protest meeting demanded that the police immediately release the boys' bodies to their families for burial. The police arrived en masse to break up the gathering and shot teargas through the high glass windows of the mosque, where hundreds of people were congregating. A youth outside the mosque was shot by the police, and he died in hospital a few hours later. It was mayhem. The crowd then defiantly marched from the mosque to Hewat Teacher Training College, before we finally dispersed amidst a hail of rubber bullets fired at us at close range. As per usual, the security forces wanted to teach us a lesson and remind us of their might and that they were in power. They were trigger-happy and didn't care about the people they shot at. Ultimately, their strong-arm tactics didn't work in their favour, and street protests intensified as our fear gave way to anger.

During the state of emergency that year, Ghadija worked at Essa Moosa's law firm for the Western Cape Relief Forum (WCRF), which provided support to detainees and their families. In terms of the state of emergency regulations, a member of the police force, railway police or the South African Defence Force could detain any person in a prison or police cell if the person was perceived as a threat to the maintenance of public order or the safety of the public. Thousands of activists were detained indefinitely. Many children were detained too.

Along with Swalia Abrahams and Faizel Moosa, Essa's son, I helped the WCRF collect money for the funerals of fallen comrades and food for families whose breadwinners were detained. We also made large pots of soup to give to mourners and bereaved families. It was around this time that I met Shirley Gunn through the work I was doing for the MDM, and when she needed a safe house in 1986, my sister Muneerah provided one.

Despite helping in these small ways, I felt angry and absolutely defence-less. Living in a police state made us want to pick up arms and shoot back at the cops. I had this pent-up anger that had built up inside me over the years as I saw innocent children killed and mothers and fathers treated like dirt. This was the reason why I didn't hesitate when Shirley approached me in 1987 to fetch arms and ammunition in Botswana.

I was already a mother by then. Raziya, my daughter, was three years old. Fortunately, my support system at home was strong, and Muneerah was able to take care of Raziya while I was away. After convincing Ismail to meet Shirley, we had a considered discussion and agreed that we would both go on the mission.

Ismail and I made three trips to Botswana to collect arms. Our legends for the first and third trips were that we were going to Botswana to do business selling plastic packaging. Our legend for the second trip was that we were on a family holiday, and we took Raziya along.

The trips were nerve-wracking. I was a very nervous passenger in those hired cars loaded with weapons. I remember shaking, telling Ismail that he was mad to drive so fast, but he would always reply that everything would be fine.

'Even if I drive at 180 or 200 kilometres per hour nothing is going to happen,' he'd say.

'How do you know?' I'd shoot back. 'Maybe the ANC made a mistake, maybe they did not pack this stuff properly and we are going to be blown up in this car.'

And he'd carry on reassuring me that nothing of the sort would happen, back and forth all the way to Cape Town. It's quite funny when I think about it now – how scared I was and all the crazy things that went through my mind about what might happen – but I also think that's where my health problems began; that's when the Parkinson's disease started.

Ismail and I also helped Shirley cache and retrieve arms in Franschhoek, and for some time we'd meet her every Sunday on a bench at the top of Clifton, overlooking the Atlantic coastline. Shirley was stuck in the underground at that point, and we'd sit with our backs to the road so no one could identify us. Ismail and I would bring her the weekly newspapers and occasional treats. We'd chat about what was going on and share news of the outside world.

Ismail and I had two more children in the years before the first demo-cratic elections: Salim, our son, was born in 1991 and our second daughter,

Nisreen, was born in 1993. We voted in 1994 and felt that we had achieved freedom. By then I was shaking badly and was referred to Dr Gardner at the Constantia Medical Centre. He diagnosed me with Parkinson's disease. It is very difficult to explain what it is like living with Parkinson's because one moment I feel perfectly fine and the next moment I don't know who I am; one moment I am happy and the next moment I feel utterly miserable. With what feels like the flick of a switch there can be absolutely nothing going on in my head, and my mind's a complete blank. I won't know who you are, I won't know your name, I won't know anything.

When Ismail was diagnosed with cancer in 2013, we went to 2 Military Hospital in Wynberg and were able to register for free health care because we had military veteran force numbers as former members of MK. Ismail says he's not stressing, but I fear he has to pretend that he's fine because I'm so sick and our kids are around us. He doesn't tell anyone if he's in pain and stays strong for me, for them and for everyone else around him. I don't know if we are managing with our finances; Ismail deals with that and keeps the details away from me as much as possible so I don't worry about that too. Thank God that he does! It's our religion, and it's part of life to look after one another.

My children and Ismail have accepted my condition and have been exceptionally wonderful about it, even though it's very difficult for anyone to understand what it's like. Parkinson's is a progressive disease; slowly my muscles are becoming weaker. They bunch up when they are supposed to be relaxed and when they bunch up, it pulls and pulls and it's excruciatingly painful. The unbearable pain is the scary part for Ismail. When I had a severe attack recently, he said to me: 'I can't leave you alone any more.' I told him not to talk nonsense, but it's true; my mind switches on and off and I can be a danger to myself. A side effect of the prescribed medication for Parkinson's is psychosis. I hear voices, and this condition also has to be managed. However, I'm not giving up on life and I try to do as much as I can every day.

In 2002, I did a six-month oral history and media training course with Shirley at the Human Rights Media Centre. For my practical assignment, I focused on the forced removals of the Claremont community. This assignment got me thinking about my own family's trauma of forced removals from Newlands, and the vast suffering so many people were subjected to when their homes and livelihoods were stolen from them. For most of us, this wound has not healed and will not heal until the land is returned or people are properly compensated for their homes. I often wonder how our lives would have turned out if we hadn't been forcibly moved from Newlands.

9

Mogamat Salie

Claiming What Is Rightfully Ours

IN 1985, my brother Aneez was profiled on the SABC as a wanted man with a ransom on his head. Comrade Johnny Issel was also profiled at the same time. Everybody was shocked, but my brother Seiraaj and I were better informed and knew that what the police were saying about Aneez and Johnny was untrue. The SAP, with the cooperation of the SABC, was setting them up and the police could now do what they wanted with them, even shoot them dead. Everybody knew that being profiled in this way was an ultimatum. Aneez had to get out of the country, where he would be safer.

The security police and SADF came to my parents' Crawford home many times after that, and sometimes SADF soldiers would surround the place to intimidate them. If they came on Fridays, my father handled the situation by saying that he didn't have time for them just then, as he was going to mosque to pray.

Aneez had been staying in Bresee Avenue in Crawford when he was forced to go on the run. Certain that the cops would come looking for him, Seiraaj and I fetched his books, magazines, documents and photographs – anything that would incriminate him – and we took the boxes to Moegsien Williams's house for safekeeping. Later, we had to collect the boxes again because the Williams family became anxious about having them at their home, and we destroyed them. It took us two days to get rid of everything.

My parents didn't receive any news about Aneez once he'd gone underground and for them that was devastating, especially for our mother. Seiraaj and I consoled them, but we could not tell them where Aneez was or what he was doing; we didn't know either. Later, we received messages from comrades letting us know that Aneez was alive. For many years, my mother kept a rose that she picked from her garden in a little vase on the kitchen windowsill in remembrance of him.

*

I am the eldest of my parents' seven children, and I was born on Boxing Day in 1944. Ibrahim was born two years later, in 1946, and every two years after that my mother had another baby. Seiraaj came after Ibrahim, followed by our sisters, Ayesha and Tourhiera, then Aneez and Adenaan.

The eldest son in a Muslim family is often pressured to fulfil a fatherly role, and I took on that role even before our parents passed away. This was particularly evident when Aneez was wanted by the SAP in 1985 and Seiraaj and I rallied to protect and support him. This support intensified when he returned to South Africa in 1987. I did what I could, because he is my brother.

My parents were both from Cape Town: my mother from Claremont and my father from Bo-Kaap. I was born in Bo-Kaap and the house in Buitengracht Street is still standing, but it has been renovated into loft apartments. When I was six months old, my parents moved to Mark Road in Claremont. My siblings were all born at home in Mark Road. Our house had a big stained-glass front door that I won't forget, because when I was older and I came home late at night, I had to open it slowly and carefully so as not to wake my parents. There was a little lobby that was the reception area and a front bedroom with a fireplace that was my sisters' bedroom. Down the passage was my parents' room and a small lounge. Off the lounge was the boys' room and the kitchen. My father built a big bathroom and a toilet off the kitchen. From the kitchen door, we could see the mountain. When clouds came down over it, we knew it would rain, and after the rains we could see beautiful waterfalls cascading down the mountainside.

We had a few fruit trees, and my father planted vegetables. We also had a little chicken run, and turkeys that my grandfather bought at the market in Cape Town, which was held where the Good Hope Centre stands today. In the mornings and during school holidays, I went to the market with my grandfather to buy greens for his shops.

Mohamed, our maternal grandfather, was Indian. He had two shops in Claremont: one on the corner of Ralph Street and Main Road and the other at the top of Station Road and Main Road. From when she was in Standard 5, my mother worked at his shop, Suburban Fruit and Veg, with her sister Hajira. We called Hajira 'Auntie' and she lived opposite us. Our grandfather was unusual in that he encouraged his daughters to work, he didn't believe in arranged marriages and he didn't force his daughters to marry Indians. My mother and Auntie continued to educate themselves; they belonged to the Claremont Library and they read the daily newspapers.

I don't know much about my paternal grandfather, Mogamat Salie Salie, but he must have been a philanthropist of sorts, as his photograph hangs in

Somerset Hospital. He was educated, although he did not complete his degree, and he was a community leader, serving as the first secretary of the Cemetery Board. My grandfather was reasonably well off, but when he passed away, the extended family needed support and my grandmother gave most of the inheritance away. Because of her worsened financial situation, she started a laundry business next to their house at No. 2 Orange Street in Cape Town. The business did well, as people did not have washing machines then, and my father delivered their washing on his bicycle. He had to play the role of a father at a very young age, taking responsibility for his sisters, Mariam and Asma, and his brother, Abdulla. Sport was popular in Bo-Kaap, but my father didn't have time for it because of his responsibilities. However, he made time to serve his community as secretary of the Boorhaanool organisation at the Longmarket Street Mosque, and he later served on the Livingstone High School Committee and at the Stegman Road Mosque, where Abdullah Haron was the imam.

My father had left school in Standard 5. He didn't want us to follow in his footsteps and go into the building trade, which is where he had ended up, because it was hard work for little pay. He wanted us to become educated and find good jobs. But the Group Areas Act spoilt it all.

Schools were already racially segregated when I started school at the age of six in 1951. I attended Stephen Reagan Primary in Claremont, a co-ed school for coloured children. Our teachers motivated us to be neat and tidy and to read in order to educate ourselves about what was happening in South Africa, thereby planting the seeds of my political awareness.

My father attended political meetings, and my political awareness grew as he brought discussions and ideas from the meetings home with him. He would also invite Malaysian and Indonesian seamen to our house. This was during or just after independence in Indonesia – the anti-colonial period – and there was a strong political element to their conversations. My uncle Achmat, who lived next door to us, was politically aware too, and associated with Barney Desai and comrades from the Communist Party.

I started at Livingstone High School in 1960. One Monday morning in Standard 6, our science teacher, Mr Abramse, passed around a newspaper. On the front page were images of the Sharpeville massacre. He then told a boy by the name of Nigel Schreuder to stand up. Nigel's family were light-skinned 'try for whites' who acted superior. 'You, your brothers and your family want to be white,' Mr Abramse said, 'but this is what the white people are doing.' In Clare-mont, we fought with the 'try for whites'; they had their gang and we had ours.

Livingstone was a politically inspired school. The revolutionary Dr Neville Alexander was twenty-four when he came back from Germany with his doctorate, and he taught us history. I was his favourite pupil and he was my favourite teacher, and history was the only subject in which I achieved an A grade. I won't forget what Dr Alexander told us about the history he taught: 'You must look at history at this school as two railway lines,' he said. 'The line I am giving you, you must stay on; the other line is what you must write about in exams.'

When I was in Standard 9, Dr Alexander was arrested and we went to his trial at the Cape Town Supreme Court in our school uniforms. The police bullied us and tried to chuck us out, but we returned the next day to show our support. The following day, there was a photograph of us on the front page of a daily newspaper. Dr Alexander was charged with conspiracy to commit sabotage and sentenced to ten years' imprisonment on Robben Island. Livingstone High lost an excellent teacher, someone who had made an enormous impact on us and who was impossible to replace.

When my siblings and I were in our teens, we started going to madressa at Stegman Road Mosque. Our teachers were Imam Ebrahim Davids, whom we called Sep, and his brother Imam Salim Davids. Imam Abdullah Haron was the principal. When the sports boycott started in the 1960s, Imam Haron explained their position in the mosque each week, trying to make everybody understand his mantra: 'Let us stand together against the South African government and their collaborators.' Sep Davids and others spearheaded the anti–Newlands sports grounds campaign, and although Claremont had many talented sportsmen and coloured people who went to the Newlands Rugby and Cricket Grounds, we began boycotting these facilities.

Although Claremont seemed politically backward compared to other areas, like District Six, we had the Claremont branch of the Muslim Youth Movement (MYM), which Sep and his comrades started at Stegman Road Mosque. I was too young to go inside and listen to the men, but my father and others did. I sat outside with the other youngsters, where our job was to flatten the tyres of the security police who came to spy on and disrupt the meetings. It was great fun.

The Progressive Party (PP) also had a small following in our Claremont community. Imam Allie Gierdien and his friend Mr Toefy, a teacher at Tafalah Primary School in Draper Street, called people together to attend meetings. 'I told them there is no use in talking,' my father said to my mother when he came back from one of these meetings. 'It's better to go underground.' I didn't understand what he meant by 'going underground', but later I understood, and realised that he was right.

When I was nearing the end of high school, in 1962, Claremont and Newlands were declared white areas under the notorious Group Areas Act. The apartheid government wanted to move coloured people to far-flung areas, like Faure and Macassar, which was a topic of discussion at home. I attended Boy Scouts at St Saviour's Anglican Church on the corner of Bowwood and Main Roads in Claremont, and when the scoutmaster, Mr Peterson, resisted moving, the authorities burnt down the Scout Hall. They burnt down the Orpheum Bioscope on Main Road, Claremont, and the Avalon Cinema in similar operations.

On Thursdays and Fridays, Sedick Isaacs, a politically active teacher, tutored Ibrahim, Seiraaj and me. He tutored black students too. One day, Sedick told us to go to the MYM in Hanover Street for lessons. At the MYM meetings, we took part in discussions and were exposed to many more politically active people, and we became more politically aware and broad-minded.

When I learnt that Sedick taught karate, I was excited because I had wanted to learn karate, but there were no facilities nearby. I joined the karate club at St Marks in District Six. Activist Frank van der Horst was an instructor at the karate club too. I made it to brown belt, the second-highest level before black belt, but then my family was thrown out of Claremont and I lost touch with the club. However, I kept in contact with Frank van der Horst.

In 1964, Sedick was sentenced and jailed on Robben Island with Achmad Cassiem and others. He attempted to escape five times and was the only political prisoner to get an extra year added to his sentence for bad behaviour. He also attempted to poison the water, for which he was flogged.

I was always conscious of apartheid, and it became more apparent to me as it was systematically formalised. We were forced out of our homes and paid very little for our properties. My siblings and I were relatively young when this happened, so I don't think it affected us as negatively as it did our parents and older people. They were not the same afterwards. I remember this very clearly. Mr Dolly, the tailor who lived in Mark Road, had to move to Hanover Park. He had done uniform alterations for Herschel Girls' School nearby, and the girls came for fittings at his house. Mr Dolly always dressed formally, complete with a bowtie. He died soon after he moved to Hanover Park, and two other people we knew also died within three months of leaving Claremont.

My mother's suffering was deep, as she had been evicted from her birthplace, but she was pragmatic and tried to adapt to our family's new circumstances. My father could not adapt easily, and after our eviction he became strongly anti-establishment.

We moved from our Claremont home in 1966. We first moved to Auntie's house across the road, then to her house in Ottery Road in Wynberg, before eventually moving to Crawford. We never saw our neighbours and friends from Claremont again. The government evaluated our houses in Claremont and offered a cash price for them, well below market value. We got R4 000 for our big house on Mark Road, while the house in Crawford that my father bought cost double that. It was much smaller than our Mark Road house – there was only a front room, two bedrooms and a kitchen – so my father had to extend it to accommodate our large family, incurring more expenses.

We were lost in Crawford. It was safe, but we didn't know anyone in the neighbourhood. In Claremont we could walk everywhere we needed to go, but in Crawford we had to use public transport to get around. I remember going to house parties in District Six and Bo-Kaap by bus and then walking home to Crawford afterwards because the buses didn't run late at night.

District Six was very vibrant. Gangsters stood on the street corners, but unlike gangsters today they didn't interfere with ordinary people and only fought among themselves. There were many house parties in those days. It was the time of The Beatles and rock 'n' roll, and because the people in District Six and Bo-Kaap were not yet affected by the Group Areas Act, their lives went on as usual. When evictions started in Claremont, Imam Haron and a delegation went to Cape Town to ask the residents and religious communities in those areas to support us, but they refused because they didn't think they were going to be evicted. I get upset when people speak of District Six as if it was the only place affected by the Group Areas Act and as if the people there were forerunners in the eviction struggle. They were not.

The year we moved out of Claremont, Dimitri Tsafendas killed Prime Minister Hendrik Verwoerd. Uncle Achmat managed my grandfather's shop in Ralph Street then. Two shops away was a restaurant. One side was for coloured people and the other side was for white people. The owners, Mr Martin and Lulu, were Portuguese and we were friends. Dimitri Tsafendas used to go to Martin's café, and he visited my uncle's shop to buy fruit and chat. Marie, a domestic worker, used to bring her madam's child with her to the shop, and Uncle Achmat, who talked a lot, mentioned that Tsafendas had been there. I think the child must have told her mother, because after Hendrik Verwoerd was killed, the police came for my uncle. Luckily he was not at home, but they called him to report to Caledon Square Police Station.

At Caledon Square, my uncle told them *'Tsafendas het net daar gekom om goeters te koop.'* (Tsafendas only came to buy things.) Then the security police took out a file. *'Jy gaan rond met Imam Haron en Barney Desai,'* they told him.

(You move around with Imam Haron and Barney Desai.) This was true, and my uncle realised that the police were watching him.

This wasn't his first run-in with the *boere*. He had a big lead police baton that he'd got from accompanying Dr A.H. Gool, Cissie Gool's husband, to political meetings at the Woodstock Town Hall. The police used to hire the Globe gang to break up these meetings, and after the Globe gang assaulted Dr Gool, those at the meetings started to retaliate and defend themselves. Uncle Achmat and others fought the Globe gang, and during one of the scuffles he managed to take a baton from a policeman.

Imam Haron was detained in 1969. A flower seller named Amina had a stand opposite Auntie's shop on Main Road, and she knew someone senior in the security police. She would ask him simple questions, using her shrewdness as a hawker to fish for information. She asked him about Imam Haron, who was detained at Maitland Police Station at that point, and she got permission to take the imam food, which she did every day. One day, the imam was gone and Amina raised the alarm.

When people came to tell us he had died, everybody in our house in Second Avenue was crying. On the night of Imam Haron's funeral there was an earth tremor. I was in the kitchen at my fiancée Fatima's home and I could hear the wind, and then felt the tremor. Fatima's mother was sleeping and woke up and said: '*Wat was daai? Wie het die deur so gekap?*' (What was that? Who banged on the door like that?) The next day we heard that it was an earthquake in Tulbagh that we felt as a tremor in Cape Town – the most destructive earthquake in South African history. It was as though the gods had spoken.

I clearly remember the imam's funeral. Thousands of people attended the procession. We were up from Sunday night because the funeral was on Monday at 3 p.m. We walked from City Park in Crawford, timing it so that by rush hour we got to the highway at Red Cross Children's Hospital and the procession blocked traffic. I was in the middle, and I could see mourners in front and behind me, spread across the road. We walked along Main Road to the Mowbray Cemetery, where Imam Haron was finally laid to rest. As I walked with the massive crowd of people snaking down the road, I thought, 'To hell with this. No more discussions. I will join the first person to approach me to take up arms.'

Years later, when Aneez approached me to join MK, I was fully prepared. Experiences like Imam Haron's funeral had prepared me.

My first job was at Old Mutual in Pinelands as a filing clerk. A filing clerk was a big thing in those days. There was a counter and rows of files, and when we worked at the counter we wore roller skates because we had to go back and forth fetching files from the shelves. Some guys from the University of the Western Cape who worked at Old Mutual started to talk about going on strike, and we did, but the strike was crushed, and we were taken to Langa Police Station. Old Mutual could not fire us because almost all the staff had come out on strike, but we were given warnings and we received threats.

I left Old Mutual after that and got a job at a pharmaceutical company, sugar-coating the tablets and making them shine with beeswax. The work in the other section was more specialised – the guys there pressed the tablets using formulas for how much powder had to go in each capsule. I could see that they had all sorts of ailments as a result of their work, like chest problems from working with the powders. One guy who did the sugar-coating had problems with his hands.

My experience at Old Mutual, where we had exercised our rights as workers, prompted me to explain to a colleague that we were doing skilled work but getting labourers' wages. I disliked the manager, an immigrant from England, and I gave him a hard time. As a result, I was deemed an agitator and given warnings. Eventually I told them to shove their job and left.

My next job was at the library on the corner of Wale and Burg Streets in Cape Town. The library was on the first and second floors of the building and all the other floors were occupied by government departments, such as the SADF. At first, they wanted to give me a labourer's job and make me work my way up, but I refused. I ended up as a library assistant, sorting and packing books on the shelves. I read a lot while working in the library. Frank van der Horst advised me on which books to read, and when we wanted books that were about to be banned, I took them out, never to be returned.

At the library I met Mrs Rust, who was from Claremont. Both she and her husband were members of the South African Communist Party. She told me to organise a study group, and that we must have discussions and keep the group active. I subsequently started the Young Africa Group along with my brothers Ibrahim and Seiraaj, Nigel Abrahams, Allie Dollie and Abdullatief Dawood. We met every week to discuss different topics and educate ourselves politically. We were young, aware and unafraid, and we had heated discussions when we presented topics for discussion. One of my topics was *Expand or Explode: Apartheid's Threat to Industry* by Ralph Horwitz. Horwitz wrote about South Africa, explaining that the apartheid economy was made up of haves and have-nots, and would not last long. He explained that paying workers starvation wages meant that they couldn't contribute to the economy and therefore the economy would never grow.

When the library wanted to send me to Bonteheuwel and Bridgetown to run the coloured libraries, I told them to shove their job. A friend who worked for a clothing outlet got me a job as a canvasser, and for a couple of years I went door to door selling clothes. It was alright. No job was really viable in those years because of the low pay, but at least I could move around freely.

My first car was a bright yellow 1200 Volkswagen Beetle. It cost R400 and my father had to buy it in his name. One day, Mr Naidoo, an older friend of mine who was quite a character, told me that he could get me a brand new Mazda van for R1200. I laughed and said that he was talking nonsense. 'I will get it for you,' he said. 'Ask your auntie to buy it in her name. They have just started importing those vans to South Africa.' I approached my Auntie Gabiba, whom we called Auntie B. I could afford the deposit with the licence, which was R150, and Auntie B kindly helped me out by buying the van in her name. In 1968, I became the owner of a brand-new, turquoise Mazda van, purchased for just R1195.

Soon after this, Mr Naidoo organised a part-time job for me with the *Telegraph*, a tabloid newspaper similar to today's *Daily Voice*. The newspaper was printed in Observatory on Mondays and then delivered to Johannesburg, Durban and Port Elizabeth (PE). My route started at Salt River Station, through to Milnerton and right down to Ascott Café, back through Woodstock to Cape Town, up Kloof Street, around Sea Point and Hout Bay, and my last stop was at Alphen Supermarket in Constantia. Every Tuesday I did the Wynberg, Claremont and Rondebosch route. I worked for the *Telegraph* for R75 a week, a lot of money considering that petrol cost only 32 cents a gallon. I kept that money for myself, and the money I got from selling clothes I gave to my mother.

In 1970, the *Telegraph* had problems in PE, so the boss, Mr Kaptein, called me in with a proposition: would I like a new job in PE where I would be in charge? He knew I had a van and he insisted that I move there immediately. I was engaged to be married, but the wedding date was not yet set, and Uncle Achmat advised that I tie the knot and take Fatima with me to PE. Two weeks later, Fatima and I got married, left for PE and settled in Gelvin Park.

Faatigh, our son, was born in Livingstone Hospital in PE later that year. The woman we boarded with had a doctor boarding with her too: Dr Faatigh Fatar, who worked at Livingstone Hospital in the casualty ward. He was very good to us as newcomers to PE and our son is named after him.

Soon after settling in PE, I was approached to work for the *Clarion*, where I was introduced to the circulation manager, Patrick Henry. We clicked instantly. 'If you stick around we'll have work for you,' he told me, and subsequently gave me the job of delivering voucher copies of the *Financial Mail*,

Sunday Times and *Sunday Express* to the homes of big company bosses on Sunday mornings. I saw the beautiful places where these big shots lived; the boss of Ford drove a gold Cadillac and had security guards at his gate, which was quite unusual then. I was paid R20 per delivery, of which I gave R2 to the guard. That was good money then.

Patrick Henry gave me many jobs after that, such as taking the *Financial Mail* from the airport to the post office and picking up the *Sunday Times* magazine from the railway station. It was during one of these jobs that I encountered the South African Railway Police (SARP), who had a reputation for assaulting people. It was a windy day and some of the magazines I'd been carrying blew onto the railway line. The SARP told me to pick them up, which I refused to do because it was dangerous. They arrested me, pushed me into their charge office at the station and kicked the door closed. Luckily for me, the commander from the police station came along and Patrick Henry arrived soon after, wanting to know what was going on. I was released some hours later.

In PE I met Frank van der Horst again. He told me that I should help organise the people in PE to resist apartheid. I told him that it was difficult for me because of the state repression and, as an outsider with a young family, I felt vulnerable. The security police were ruthless. Nevertheless, I saw that people still resisted. In New Brighton, people had erased the street names so that those unfamiliar with the area couldn't navigate their way around the place.

By the mid-1980s, it seemed as though everybody was politically aware, and the Mass Democratic Movement was doing a great job of mobilising the masses. There were a lot of debates, and schoolchildren and students were becoming more radical and vocal. They were fearless. After Aneez left the country in 1985 after being profiled on the SABC, Seiraaj and I continued attending mass meetings, but we kept a low profile. We certainly did not want to draw attention to ourselves.

When Fatima and I moved back to Cape Town, we lived in Auntie's house in Ottery Road in Wynberg. By then, Auntie had set up a new shop in Mitchells Plain, having lost the one on Claremont Main Road. One day, the notorious Frans Mostert and other security policemen pitched up at the shop. Mostert was incredibly arrogant, and as he walked around the shop he told his colleague, '*Dis die ANC se winkel.*' (This is the ANC's shop.) But Auntie wasn't afraid, and fortunately Auntie B was also there, so she wasn't alone. '*Waar is jou man?*' Mostert demanded. (Where is your husband?) '*Ek het nie 'n man nie,*' Auntie replied. (I don't have a husband.)

The security police harassed her, wanting to know where I was and where Aneez was. '*Mogamat is nie my man nie, hy is my nephew,*' Auntie explained. (Mogamat is not my husband, he is my nephew.) Then she showed Mostert her framed shop licence, which was in her name. He got such a shock he went red in the face – he obviously had the wrong information and had humiliated himself.

I was selling chemicals at the time, but I was not earning a lot, and much of what I earned I spent assisting Aneez, as he was on the run and staying with different people for short periods of time. I was running around for him, unable to settle my debts and dodging the sheriff of the court.

Things got worse early one morning in December, when Frans Mostert and other security policemen came looking for me at our home in Ottery Road. Fatima told them that I wasn't there, so they asked her what car I was driving. She told them I was driving a Fiat. Then they came looking for me at Seiraaj's house in Mitchells Plain. They searched the house, even in the ceiling, and when they were leaving they spotted my father's old Fiat standing in front of the house without an engine. They assumed then that Fatima had been lying, so they went back to our house to arrest her. Amina, our second child, was very young, but the policemen showed no concern when Fatima asked what would happen to her. She decided to leave Amina with Tourhiera, my sister, who was living next door. The security police accompanied Fatima to Tourhiera's house and then drove off with her.

Because I was evading the debt collectors, I was staying at my cousin Faldie Hanslo's flat in the Bo-Kaap. Seiraaj sent me a message to say that Fatima had been arrested. To my relief, she was released later that afternoon.

On 19 December 1985, the messenger of the court got me for my debt. I was sentenced to 120 days and locked up at Pollsmoor Prison, but my father settled my debt and bailed me out. Soon after my release, on New Year's Eve 1985, two security policemen came to the garden gate, demanding to know about Aneez's whereabouts. 'I know nothing,' I said. Then they took me to Caledon Square Police Station to interrogate me. They wanted to know why I was running and hiding from them, but luckily I had my Pollsmoor admission card on me as proof that I was not evading them. I was released the same day.

Aneez returned from exile in 1987, disguised with an afro and beard, and Seiraaj and I started to move around with him again. He trained us in the military work that he had done in Angola, and we stopped going to public meetings and kept a low profile. We also helped find safe accommodation for him in Woodstock, then at Faldie's flat in the Bo-Kaap. Soon after, he stayed with a very kind auntie in Elsies River, Ma Betty. Ma played a big role in keeping Aneez safe. We took him to stay there a couple of times. Our legend was that he was my brother-in-law from Johannesburg, but I'm sure that if Ma had known who Aneez really was she would still have accepted him. I think she would have done anything for us.

On a number of occasions, we had to pick up a car cached with weapons and take it to my house in Wynberg. I would get my family out of the house, and then Aneez and Seiraaj would strip the car in the backyard, taking out the spare wheel and panels to retrieve cached arms. Aneez had already given us some training and I recall having to buy Vaseline, cotton wool and a plastic bin because after retrieving the weapons we'd have to bury them securely in a properly sealed container. We knew what tools were needed and we took all precautions to avoid leaving fingerprints on anything.

Our lifestyles impacted heavily on our family relationships. In addition to that, I struggled with financial difficulties as much of my time was spent supporting Aneez rather than on my business, but I didn't think of it in a negative way. If I have money and someone needs money, I will give that person what I have. I also spent a lot on petrol and helped Seiraaj out too – neither of us could work full-time because we were called to assist the Ashley Kriel Detachment at odd hours.

I had many connections from when I'd travelled backroads, going from small town to small town across the country to sell chemicals. Sometimes, Aneez and I would travel on these backroads to Calvinia in the Northern Cape via Carnarvon, on a dirt road coming out through Prieska and Kimberley, and we'd land up in Johannesburg. I had an Opel Kadett then. The first time I saw Shanil Haricharan was in Kimberley when he had a meeting with Aneez.

Seiraaj and I operated together, although we got our instructions independently. We never asked questions – we just did what we were instructed to do. The scariest moment for me was one Saturday night when I was instructed to go to Sea Point on my own. 'Yoh,' I said. 'Alone?' I was very worried. But I had to follow orders. I drove to Sea Point, all the while asking myself why I had to complete this mission alone. I drove up the road towards the mountain, where there were many blocks of flats. It was dark, cold and eerie. 'My God,' I thought, 'if the security police take me here, no one will ever know.'

I had to fetch Shanil and another comrade. The two were packed and waiting by the time I arrived. I drove them to Heathfield Station, where they were to be fetched in a blue car at midnight. There was a blue car waiting there, but it could have been anybody and when the driver approached us, I had a gun at the ready. The thought crossed my mind that we might have to shoot our way out if anything went wrong. Then Shanil recognised the driver, who was a comrade, and got out of the car to greet him. I relaxed.

My firearm was a lifesaver. If you had a licensed firearm, the cops didn't search you or your car too thoroughly because they assumed you were one of them. I got a licensed pistol when I started delivering the post in the early 1980s. I had found out that the post office was looking for somebody to take post from Franschhoek to Huguenot Station, so I applied. It was mostly Afrikaners who worked for the post office then, and to get the job I buttered them up with some biltong I bought in Oudtshoorn on one of my trips upcountry. After that, I got a contract to deliver post to Atlantis and had a brilliant idea for using the post office to get a gun. It was very difficult to get a firearm licence, so I told them I needed protection because I was carrying pensioners' money. They laughed, but gave me an official letter and I subsequently bought a licenced .38 special in Cape Town. The gun-shop owner said the cops used it. I still have it.

I remember the first time Seiraaj and I saw a Makarov pistol. Aneez wanted to make a call from the public phone box in Claremont, where we received our instructions at the time. There were two phone boxes on Lansdowne Road, but we used the one on the corner of Second Avenue, close to Claremont Police Station. Seiraaj and I went to do some reconnaissance and saw that there were two suspicious Afrikaners there, one on this side of Lansdowne Road and the other on the opposite side. We returned to my place in Wynberg to tell Aneez, but he was anxious to make the call so we took him to the phone box anyway. Afterwards, on the drive back to Wynberg on Rosmead Avenue, I noticed him fiddling with something: a Makarov pistol. I knew then how determined he had been to make the call.

On another occasion, Seiraaj and I helped Shirley Gunn dig up arms in Franschhoek using a metal detector. I won't forget this mission. The two of them were digging on one side of the road while I stood guard behind a tree on the other side with my little .38 pistol, thinking that the *boere* would shoot us to pieces if we were caught. When Shirley and Seiraaj had retrieved the arms and deposited them in the boot of my car, we drove to the Shell garage in Northpine and used a small screwdriver to rip open the metal box. Shirley packed the arms into bags and then we set off again. Close to Hartley-vale, Seiraaj and I were instructed to get out of the car and Shirley drove off in the Kadett with the arms. When she returned, she instructed us to dispose of the empty metal-framed box.

*

Aneez and Shirley got married in 1988, near Boulders Beach in Simon's Town. The house where they held the ceremony belonged to an English admiral. There were submarines drifting by in the bay, and when we arrived Aneez said, 'Come inside, we're having the wedding in the lion's den!' Johnny Issel and Zubeida Jaffer, Imam Gassan Solomon, Seiraaj, our parents, Shirley's mother and I were present. My father had paid for Shirley's wedding ring, made by Boeta Latief, a jeweller from Steenberg, and Zubeida brought a wedding cake iced in black, green and gold: the colours of the ANC.

Soon after that, Shirley was framed for the bombing of Khotso House. We laughed because we knew that it wasn't true, but we had to reassure my mother that it wasn't her. We also understood that framing Shirley gave the security forces licence to kill her – as simple as that. They had set her up, and we strongly believed they were not intending to take her to jail; they were planning on killing her. By then we were so hardened that it did not even touch our nerves.

Mandela and De Klerk were having 'talks about talks', and then came the unbanning of political organisations and Mandela's release. I overheard something on the Parade in Cape Town in 1990 that still haunts me more than twenty years later. I was there, waiting for Mandela to address the crowds, along with Seiraaj and many other comrades such as Shahieda Issel, June Esau, Theresa Solomons and Elizabeth Erasmus, when this remark was passed: 'You better be quiet, you've got no qualification.' They were talking about the new ANC leadership, the exiled leadership, and I did not realise it then, but those without qualifications were sidelined.

After 1990, I started focusing on my delivery business. I got a contract to take the *Argus* to Somerset West in 1992. I started getting more work and my business was doing well. Then my marriage hit the rocks. There were no fights before Fatima left, but she had made up her mind. Maybe I had been too preoccupied with the struggle and did not pay my family enough attention, but Fatima had never said a thing, so I assumed everything was alright. She left me and took her heirloom imbuia table, on which Seiraaj and I had had our training with limpets, grenades and firearms. Faatigh had just turned twenty-one. I think the fact that work was picking up saved me mentally. There was enough work to keep me busy around the clock, and it meant that I had to carry on with my life, despite struggling with depression in the first few months after Fatima left.

Seiraaj and I demobilised in 1997. We went to the military base in Faure, but we did not really understand what the soldiers from the British army who were facilitating the process were saying. I had no ambition to join the army, and I was unaware of the option to join the Protection Unit as bodyguards for the ANC leadership. I was an excellent driver and I would have liked to drive Mandela around, but when he was released from jail and for some time afterwards, the AKD had continued to keep a low profile; that was our instruction. The guys who got positions in the Protection Unit had been free to move around.

We received R22 000 as part of the demobilisation package. It was sacred money, so I went to Mecca with it, and I took my daughter, Amina, and Soraya, my second wife, with me. Soraya's father organised the trip. The people in Mecca said that we were Mandela's people – not South Africans, but Mandela's people.

When the land claims process started, I represented my family. Most of the people from Claremont didn't know about the land claims process or their rights – some only heard about it later. When I went to the land claims meetings, there were no people from Newlands, yet I knew about many coloured families who had lived there and were forced to sell and move out of the area. Julie Vallie's grandfather, for example, had owned large properties. As children we played rugby in her grandfather's yard. Mr Allie Abdurahman, an outspoken Claremont resident, was vocal about this at a land claims meeting at the Claremont Civic Centre one night. He told the officials that most of the Claremont and Newlands people didn't know about the process. Former residents were scattered across the Cape Flats like wind-borne seeds, and we'd lost contact with one another.

My family had owned four large semi-detached houses. Uncle Achmat's house was attached to ours, and Auntie and Auntie B's houses opposite us on Mark Road were attached. When I went to the Land Claims Commission office in Cape Town, the project coordinator, Patrick Mthembani, told me I couldn't receive my claim because it was not on their system. Eventually, he came back and said my claim *was* on their system but that we couldn't claim for our house and Uncle Achmat's house because the houses had been on one plot. I was upset. 'Keep the claim!' I told him. 'I don't want it. We were robbed by the Group Areas Act then, and we are being robbed again by you!'

Some time later, Patrick got back to me to discuss whether I wanted a flat or money as compensation. 'What am I going to do with R40 000?' I told him when I went to the commission's office. 'That amount must be shared among seven of us.'

Auntie had claimed for the two semi-detached houses in her name, and left the claim to me in her will when she died in 2012, but Patrick told me that there was no property attached to her claim. I challenged him on this, and then he contradicted himself and said there *was* a claim for Auntie. But what about the claim for my grandfather's houses in Newlands? He had houses there too; a whole street belonged to him. I was told that the claim was null and void because the family had been paid out for the properties at the time.

The land claims rest on my shoulders and it is a heavy burden to carry. The commission is not working as it should, and I sometimes feel despondent. But we must fight for what is rightfully ours in our new democracy, and I won't give up.

10

Seiraaj Salie

Brother in Arms

J ACOB ZUMA, FORMER commander of Umkhonto we Sizwe, once stated that all the trouble in South Africa began with the arrival of Jan van Riebeeck at the Cape. In my case, all the trouble started in 1948, the year I was born, because that was the year the National Party was voted into power in a whites-only election and brought apartheid and chaos to South Africa. Two years later, the Group Areas Act, the Suppression of Communism Act and the Population Registration Act were implemented, forcing us to live as second-class citizens in the country of our birth.

My family lived in the coloured part of Claremont in Cape Town, at 23 Mark Road, not too far from the foot of Table Mountain. When I was in high school, Claremont was declared a white area. We had to relocate immediately, no questions asked. Parents, uncles, aunts, grannies, cousins and friends left for areas that the white government had designated for coloureds – the worst parts of Cape Town on the windy Cape Flats, where they didn't want to live. Even the *bergies* had to move, though I don't know where those poor souls ended up.

A few years after the forced removals, a friend asked me to accompany him to visit someone in Claremont. The house we went to was on Frederick Road, parallel to Mark Road, where my family and I had lived. Inside, a bunch of young, boisterous white hippies were having a party, obviously very drunk and drugged. Music blared from the house but it was practically bare, devoid of furniture. I sadly remembered the coloured Christian family who were forcibly removed from that home and who were decent and religious. I left in disgust, deeply traumatised and angry.

Claremont was a perfect place to grow up. It had a long-established community of Christians, Hindus and Muslims, and it was a place of natural beauty. It only took me, my friends and my siblings a few minutes to run to the unspoilt Liesbeek River with its trees, birds, squirrels, tadpoles and flowers, to play. As we got older, we'd walk through the parts of upper Claremont and Newlands where white people lived, raiding the fruit trees along the way, then through the countrified Protea Village with its white-painted cottages to the magnificent Kirstenbosch Gardens. As teenagers, we spent many happy moments there and in Claremont Gardens with the pretty neighbourhood girls. In high school, we regularly walked from Kirstenbosch up Table Mountain. There was no entrance fee then.

The coloured section of Claremont stretched up towards the mountain, from Main Road to Frederick Road, and down from Main Road past Rosmead Avenue. The community was essentially working class and did not display excessive signs of wealth – a sharp contrast to the surrounding white areas. The neighbours were always kind and my siblings and I had lots of friends, all attending the same schools. Everybody knew each other and we could come and go as we pleased between the neighbours' houses. My mom, Amina, had two sisters, Hajira and Gabiba, and a brother, Achmat, who lived in Mark Road too. Uncle Achmat, or Ummie, as we called him, lived right next door to us with his five children.

When I was in primary school, I enjoyed accompanying Ummie in his big Fargo lorry when he transported the local rugby team to their matches. But my favourite outings were when I joined him and his friends on fishing trips to what then seemed like far-off places – Cape Point, Betty's Bay, Harmony Park, and Laaiplek on the West Coast. I learnt a lot from him about the coastal environment, the influence of the tides, wind and seasons on fishing, where the best fishing spots were, and various common fish species. I became efficient at collecting different types of bait for him, including prawns, *rooiaas*, moonshine worms, wonderworm and bloodworm. One thing I liked about Ummie and his fishing trips was his insistence on having enough *padkos*. His wife, Auntie Mariam, had to make sure that we had more than enough pies, samoosas, koeksisters, sandwiches and coffee.

I was very young when Ummie was detained and interrogated by the security branch in connection with the assassination of Prime Minister Hendrik Verwoerd by Dimitri Tsafendas. Tsafendas had frequented a small restaurant in Ralph Street, Claremont, around the corner from my grandfather's shop. Afterwards, he would pop into the shop to chat to Ummie. The security branch was questioning everybody who had come into contact with Tsafendas, and we were traumatised by this.

My maternal grandfather owned two businesses on Main Road, within walking distance of our house. Sometimes, at dawn, I accompanied him in his lorry to the market in central Cape Town to buy fresh produce for his shops. The early morning market was fascinating to me as a young boy, with its fresh vegetables and fruit straight from the farms in Philippi and Constantia, and the loud bidding between buyers and sellers. There were still horse-drawn carts then, selling fruit and vegetables door to door, as well as a fishmonger with his trumpet, selling fresh fish. These hawkers sold to housewives on credit, or on the *boekie*, as we called it, on very lenient terms with no interest.

My grandfather also owned other properties in Wynberg and Newlands. This was an amazing achievement for a man who had arrived in South Africa from India on his own with no formal education and hardly any money. He married our grandmother, who was racially classified by the colonial government as Malay, before the start of apartheid.

My aunts, Hajira and Gabiba, lived in their own semi-detached houses opposite ours, owned by my grandfather. They were very involved in our family life, with the result that my siblings and I had many adults supervising us and there was no way we could step out of line. Hajira, known to the neighbourhood as Auntie, proved to be a good businessperson and took over my grandfather's shops when he passed away. Gabiba – Auntie B – loved life, baking cakes, dancing and dressing up in fancy furs, jewellery and high heels. She introduced me to Western music, something frowned on by our father, who thought it was both frivolous and unworthy of a good Muslim. She loved her record collection though, and from an early age I got to know Ella Fitzgerald, Count Basie, Nat King Cole, Duke Ellington, Billie Holiday and many others. Auntie B patiently tried to teach me *langarm*, a popular dance performed with a partner, but I was hopeless.

I never met my paternal grandparents, who were both classified as Malay. I've heard that my grandfather was an educated man who, together with Salie Dollie, were two of the first black students to enrol at the South African College, forerunner to the University of Cape Town. Salie Dollie owned and ran the first chemist in Hanover Street in District Six. I've heard that there was once a portrait of my grandfather displayed at Somerset Hospital, but for what reason I do not know.

My siblings and I all went to Stephen Reagan Primary, a school for coloured children on Campground Road, from which many coloured families and some of my school friends were later forcibly removed. The retail magnate Gus Ackerman, father of Raymond Ackerman, had his first Ackermans shop opposite my grandfather's shop in Main Road. They bought their vegetables from my grandfather.

Most of the coloured children of Claremont and Newlands went to Stephen Reagan Primary School. After the forced removals, the school building was used as a training school for white cadets. Mr Hammer was the principal at Stephen Reagan during the time I was there. He was a strict man and I had to be very creative with my excuses whenever I was late, as corporal punishment was rampant in those days, and he knew I didn't have far to walk to get to school. During winter, my mother and other women in the community made pots of soup for the children, as many came to school hungry, while the school provided brown bread, peanut-butter sandwiches and milk. At that point I was unaware that I was being taught a watered-down curriculum.

At home we all got on well with each other and did our duties in the house. My brothers and I took it in turns to clean the yard, and we chopped firewood for our Dover stove. We had chickens, ducks and turkeys, and on special occasions a community member would slaughter them according to Muslim rites. He recited a special *duah* (prayer) and was compensated with tea and a *slaawat* (gift). There was always great excitement and consternation among us children when things got out of hand with the slaughtering and a headless chicken ran wild in the yard.

My father had a tough life, but he was very disciplined and took great pride in his work as a builder. Before I was born, he worked in Simon's Town dockyard during World War II. He often took us to admire the ships in Cape Town harbour and he regularly befriended and entertained Malaysian and Indonesian sailors who had docked there. Whenever he asked my mother for tea, he would proudly use Malaysian language. Once, he entertained Malaysian delegates who were en route from England after signing an independence agreement for Malaysia. This was around the time of the historic 1955 Asia–Africa Conference in Bandung, Indonesia, which charted the way forward for most African independence struggles.

The early years of my parents' married life were filled with tension and uncertainty due to the *kragdadige* (forceful) policies of the newly installed white Nationalist government. My parents immediately became second-class citizens, disenfranchised by law. The world, South Africa included, had hardly recovered from World War II and Nazism, yet in South Africa the Nationalists were determined to follow a path of racial exclusivity and separatism.

As a consequence, from 1950 to the early 1960s, there was unprecedented political upheaval and oppression in the country. It was the time of the Coloured People's Congress (CPC) and the breakaway Pan Africanist Congress, a time when people felt that the ANC was not radical enough in opposing apartheid. There was the rise of the Non-European Unity Movement, which preached non-collaboration as a form of protest. The PAC's anti-pass campaigns took place, as did the shooting of black protesters at Sharpeville. The Defiance Campaign was launched. The ANC adopted the Freedom Charter. The ANC and the Communist Party were banned. Umkhonto we Sizwe was born and the armed struggle began. The Rivonia Trial took place and Nelson Mandela and the ANC high command were incarcerated.

My father spoke to us about these events at the dinner table, as well as about the injustices he encountered in his working life. He also told us about the people he admired, such as Cissie Gool and Bennie Kies. Even though he had little formal education and did not belong to any political organisations, he was strongly influenced by the revolutionary spirit of opposition sweeping through South Africa and the continent in the early 1960s. At the same time, his generation felt helpless and fearful for the future, and we could sense that.

It was natural for my father to commit himself to community work. Besides sitting on the school board at Livingstone High School, he acted as secretary of the Longmarket Street Mosque in Cape Town for over twenty years, and he served on the Mowbray Cemetery Board for many years, sharpening his reading and writing skills along the way. As secretary of the mosque, he had to send out regular notices to the congregation, and from Standard 5 onwards I had to address hundreds of envelopes, which I hated doing. I only realised later that he was trying to teach me to be civic-minded. My father also served on the executive of the Building Workers Union for decades. As a result of his community involvement, especially during the 1960s, he naturally came up against all South Africa's discriminatory apartheid laws affecting black lives, education and workers' rights. There was even religious discrimination against Muslims, and he fought to get permission for new mosques and cemeteries, and recognition and upkeep of shrines. There was a minefield of new discriminatory laws that he and his compatriots had to contend with, and he spoke to us of all of these.

My father was the proud owner of a little black Austin car. We would pack into the Austin and head off to the Bo-Kaap to visit his sister Asma in Buitengracht Street, where he was born, and his other sister, Mariam, or Ammatie as we fondly called her, who lived in the flats there. Auntie Asma was married to a tailor who made all our suits for *Labarang* (Eid). Another relative, Boeta Latief, who lived in Gympie Street in Salt River, was also a tailor and he made some of our clothes. He was well known because he made the uniforms or 'gear' for the big minstrel troupes from District Six and Bo-Kaap. I don't know how my dad managed to clothe all of his seven children, but I suppose he took it in turns with these two tailors, making financial arrangements that were handled with dignity and discretion. Perhaps there was some bartering involved. That's how things were done in those days.

It was always exciting going to town to visit family and friends in Bo-Kaap, District Six, Woodstock, Walmer Estate, Salt River and Hout Bay. We visited these places on an almost weekly basis, and while the grown-ups had tea, koeksisters and cake inside, we played ball games outside in the street with our cousins. Most coloured families in Claremont had family and friends there. *Labarang* was especially exciting – the hand-tailored suits, new shoes, keffiyehs, food and cakes. Best of all was the monetary gifts we received – the *Labarang* box. We loved counting the pennies when we got home, each trying to outdo the other.

After completing primary school, most children from Claremont, including my brother Mogamat, went to Livingstone High School in Lansdowne Road. The school, like the shops, mosques, barbers and everything else, was conveniently within walking distance, but by then things were segregated. Mogamat, Ibrahim and I attended the Boy Scouts, which was for coloured boys only and was held at St Saviour's Church. It had been a shock for me when I first entered the beautiful church to see coloured people sitting on one side and whites on the other. There was a municipal swimming pool for coloureds only, while the newly built Olympic-size Newlands swimming pool was for whites. I remember leaning over the wall when no one was looking to see what it was like inside. Similarly, the Newlands Rugby Stadium had a small and inferior segregated section for coloured spectators. Activist Hassan Howa campaigned tirelessly for black people to boycott sports games played there. We also could not play at the Claremont Cricket Grounds, even though we lived only four houses away from it. Nevertheless, Ibrahim and I were paid to keep score for the white teams who played there every weekend. I still don't know how he managed to arrange that. The public gardens were also segregated with separate benches and toilets, and even the local dentist had segregated entrances and rooms – I remember him having to run back and forth between them, but the business was profitable so he probably didn't mind.

Some black families had houses in Lower Claremont, among the coloured families, but they were excluded from most of the amenities unless they were working as labourers, domestic workers or petrol attendants. It was here that I first experienced the brutality of 'influx control' when I saw Afrikaner cops harassing black people for their *dompas*. This happened frequently, often in front of the exclusive, whites-only Vineyard Hotel, which we saw as a symbol of British colonialism. Many Africans were arrested on the spot in the most degrading manner and manhandled into the back of police vans.

Of course, the white patrons inside the hotel were spared these sights, or they turned a blind eye. These violent confrontations left an indelible mark on my young mind.

My whole family attended the Longmarket Street Mosque in the Bo-Kaap, where my father was the secretary, as well as the Stegman Road Mosque in Claremont run by Imam Abdullah Haron. In the afternoons after school, my brothers and I had to attend the Stegman Road Mosque for our Islamic schooling. The imam edited *Muslim News* and played a leading role in the anti-apartheid struggles, especially the resistance to the forced removals under the Group Areas Act. Mogamat remembers that Imam tried, but failed, to get the support of District Six residents in his campaign against the Act. Apparently they believed that District Six would never be declared white.

I remember Imam as a humble man fully committed to the upliftment of all. He must have been brave to do what he did during that repressive period. When this gentle teacher, preacher, editor, salesman and foremost community leader was tortured and killed while in the custody of the security police, the brutality of his death shocked us all and had a lasting effect on me.

After primary school, Mogamat went to Livingstone High on Lansdowne Road (now Imam Haron Road), while Ibrahim and I went to South Peninsula in Diep River. The principal was Mr de Villiers, a dignified man who always tried to maintain high standards. This was a period of intense agitation against 'gutter education', an inferior education dished out to all who were not classified white – which amounted to 80 per cent of the South African population. Many teachers became docile and despondent, but some were brave and tried their best to make us think positively and critically. Our English teacher, Richard Rive, opened our minds to black literature in South Africa, the rest of Africa and America. He was an Oxford University graduate, and he regaled us with his experiences of travelling to literary events all over Africa and the rest of the world. He also talked about ideas like Négritude in America, and about writers such as Chinua Achebe, James Ngugi, James Baldwin, Langston Hughes and Nadine Gordimer, as well as the *Sestigers* – anti-establishment Afrikaner writers like André Brink and the poet Breyten Breytenbach. Some of these authors' books were banned, even the ones in Afrikaans. Richard Rive was a writer too, and all his works were banned at the time, but I read and enjoyed his novel '*Buckingham Palace*', *District Six*, which captured the vibrant multicultural atmosphere of the area. I also remember Mr Lesch, a superb maths teacher and versatile pianist who played great piano classics and jazz for us. But I especially liked our Latin teacher. He'd always make a very dramatic entrance, put down his case and start discussing the book he was currently reading, passionately reading excerpts until the period was almost over, leaving hardly any time for Latin or homework.

It was in Standard 8 at South Peninsula that I experienced my first protest. Initially, I didn't have a clue what we were protesting, but I soon learnt that it was against the Coloured Affairs Department's insistence that the orange, white and blue national flag be raised at school on 31 May to commemorate Republic Day. The school was in turmoil.

That year, my father arranged for my siblings and me to take extra private lessons with two committed democrats: Sedick 'Dickie' Isaacs and Dr Achmat Davids. Dickie was later convicted of sabotage, sentenced under the Terrorism Act and sent to Robben Island, where he spent many years with Nelson Mandela and other political prisoners. Achmat Davids became a historian and prominent UDF activist. His father was a well-known but controversial figure among the conservative Bo-Kaap Muslim *ulama* (religious leadership) for his progressive views and interpretations of aspects of Islam, and was a childhood friend of my father's.

At first, we were taught at Achmat's house in Longmarket Street, opposite the mosque, but as the number of students grew, Achmat and Dickie established an educational organisation in Hanover Street in District Six. Being quite young then, I did not really understand the context in which they were operating, but I enjoyed taking the bus with my brothers on a Saturday morning to attend classes there. Mogamat also started taking me to house parties in District Six, Walmer Estate, Woodstock and Salt River. This was a great time for us, but everything changed when we were forced out of Claremont.

Fortunately, our grandfather had houses in Wynberg, so we went with Auntie to live there while Auntie B went to stay in Belgravia Road in what was to become Crawford. Ummie went to open a shop in the Steenberg housing estate.

After much searching, my dad found a house for us in Second Avenue, Rondebosch East. It was a predominantly white area with a small pocket for coloureds. This pocket was then renamed Crawford, to distinguish it from the white section.

Moving was exciting because I was young and it seemed like an adventure, but the reality of it soon hit me hard. We had to adjust to our new environment and the surrounding Athlone area, where we knew no one. Everything familiar that had defined my identity and brought me happiness as I grew up was taken away overnight. My youth and innocence were stolen, and I lost all contact with my friends.

We had owned a fully paid-up house in a prime area of Claremont, but in

Crawford we had to add extensions to our new house to accommodate our large family and, at the age of fifty-two, my father had to take out a bond to finance the renovations. This was part of the moving costs that my parents had to carry. Meanwhile, some people were making huge profits from forced removals. Only a brave, progressive liberal minority raised objections to this. There was a huge human cost that is impossible to quantify yet is still easy to see in some of the coloured and African communities that were uprooted and where dysfunction is now endemic.

During the removals, my brother Ibrahim was trying to overcome official hurdles so he could continue his education in India. He had to be interrogated and then cleared by the security branch before he could get a visa to study, as the government considered India to be a hostile country. He eventually went, and returned many years later with a science degree. I completed my matric in 1967, the year the Terrorism Act came into effect. I did not achieve the best results, but considering the upheavals in my life I was glad that I had passed.

In the early 1970s, a new and radical spirit of resistance appeared in the form of the miners' strikes in Durban. Black Consciousness and liberation theology were sweeping through the predominantly black universities and seminaries. Led by people such as Steve Biko, black students broke away from NUSAS to form their own organisation.

I started working, and in 1973, when I was twenty-five, I married Faika. A new chapter in my life began. We stayed with my parents for a few months while searching for a place to live, and then moved constantly with our two children for a number of years until we finally found a house in Portlands, Mitchells Plain. It was 1976, the year of the Soweto uprisings, and student protest spread to Western Cape schools. A year later, Steve Biko was brutally killed in police custody, just like Imam Haron and Ahmed Timol, who was thrown to his death from the tenth floor of the security police headquarters at John Vorster Square in Johannesburg in 1971. Many others also died in police custody as a result of the security force's brutality.

During this time, my younger brother Aneez got his first job at *Muslim News* as a photographer and reporter under the editorship of the prominent struggle poet James Matthews, who had taken over after Imam Haron was killed. Aneez covered many protests, especially the response to the bulldozing of squatter settlements by the apartheid authorities, who were determined to keep blacks out of the urban areas and trapped in their homelands or Bantustans. I was proud of his spirit.

In Portlands, a few of us tried organising at a grassroots level around bread-and-butter issues to break the cycle of despondency and fear in the community. But we needed a campaign. A small group of committed comrades started canvassing door to door and discovered that people in coloured areas always complained about the cost of electricity, among other things. There was no prepaid electricity then, and the electricity payments in coloured areas were due a week before payday, a time of the month when people had no money. Most people paid late, incurring interest charges. However, in affluent white areas, the payment date was conveniently set seven days after the end of the month, so they were more likely to pay on time and were never saddled with interest. Our first campaign highlighted this as another example of apartheid exploitation – the white City Council made millions of rands in interest from the coloured community, and then spent this money on white areas.

We took our message and our pamphlets door to door throughout Mitchells Plain, organising house meetings in different streets in all the surrounding suburbs. We were surprised at the support we got and we relentlessly drove home the fact that dormitory suburbs like Mitchells Plain were designed to be a gold mine for white industry in the grand apartheid plan. The campaign went on for many months and led to the formation of street committees, rallies in civic centres and, eventually, marches to the City Council. At some point, the security branch became interested in our activities. One day, after marching to the civic centre with our petitions and placards, demanding to be heard, we were led to an auditorium. On the stage sat a number of Cape Town City Council officials, or so we thought. Marcus Solomons, who had recently been released from Robben Island, recognised two of them as members of the feared security branch and immediately objected to their presence. Everybody loudly added their voices to the objection and the men eventually left the building. The mighty security branch had been forced to retreat! We were stunned.

After much campaigning, the electricity due date was changed and everybody in Cape Town paid on the same date. As a result, people were galvanised and more civic organisations sprang up in other areas.

From then on, I spent a lot of time at rallies. School protests continued on a daily basis and I witnessed a young schoolboy being killed by riot police in Hanover Park. Aneez was working at the *Cape Herald* by then and he led a strike action against the newspaper, which was staffed by black people, who were paid far less than their white counterparts would earn. He was a founding member and national vice-president of the Media Workers Association of South Africa. The *Cape Herald* eventually folded. During this time, Aneez and I had become very close, and it was at his granny flat in Athlone where I met MK cadre Leon Meyer. Soon after that meeting, Leon and his wife, Jacqueline Quin, were assassinated in Maseru in a raid by death-squad operatives. I had to recover Leon's documents, which were hidden in Aneez's flat. The whole episode shook me because it felt so close to home. Not long after this, pictures of Aneez and Johnny Issel appeared in the newspapers and on television – they were wanted by the police. They both went into hiding. I knew that the two of them had been operating from a house in Belgravia, Athlone, with Zubeida Jaffer and Shirley Gunn, but I had assumed that they were doing political work, not actively involved in the armed struggle. None of us realised the extent of their involvement, but a lot of friends and family rallied to my parents' side in solidarity. I was working at a computer company in town at the time, and it wasn't long before Aneez made contact with me through intermediaries.

I had to liaise with Advocate Dullah Omar at his house in Rylands a few times regarding Aneez. The house was a hotbed of activists, and although it was my first time meeting Dullah and his wife, Farieda, he didn't hesitate to confer with me privately. The family arranged funds that I passed on to Aneez through Moegsien Williams, a media colleague of his. One of the many places where we met Aneez was in the Longmarket Street Mosque. My brother Mogamat and I then had to arrange various safe houses and material support for Aneez. The people who sheltered him were amazing, as they never raised any doubts or misgivings about the dangers involved. We acted as intermediaries between him and the people he needed to contact. As this went on, Moegsien confided in me about the tremendous pressure the security branch was putting on him regarding Aneez's whereabouts. After a few months, Dullah advised me that it would be best for him to leave the country.

Aneez left Cape Town in late 1985 with a close family friend, Ebrahim Vallie from Claremont, who owned a trucking company. After that, Mogamat and I played a lesser role in Aneez's activities and we got on with our lives. The disturbing part was that we did not know what had happened to our brother. Despite this, we had to visit our parents and other siblings regularly to keep morale high. It was a difficult time. I got stuck into my work and did not get involved in any grassroots activities or attend any political rallies, preferring to keep a low profile until we heard from Aneez again. Shirley was detained during this time, but soon after being released in December 1985 she also left the country.

Around the time Ashley Kriel was killed by the security branch in 1987, Aneez returned to the country and contacted me. Mogamat and I were overjoyed, but many MK cadres and political activists were on trial, so for obvious reasons we could not tell our parents, siblings or even our own wives that Aneez was back. He looked healthier, fitter and more determined, and this time he had his own means of support and did not have to rely on us so much.

The first time I met Aneez after his return was at a Sea Point beachfront hotel, well away from the political upheaval on the Cape Flats where the security branch had their focus. He had brought a large number of weapons that had to be cached immediately. From then on, Mogamat and I met daily. There were a lot of things that we could do to support him, and it wasn't something that we deliberated; Aneez was our younger brother and we had to do everything possible to help him.

The 1970s and early 1980s had prepared us mentally for what was to come. Mogamat had already been detained by the security branch and interrogated about Aneez's whereabouts. On a different occasion, his wife, Fatima, was also briefly detained. Police came to my house in the middle of the night looking for Mogamat, but they were ordinary local police from Mitchells Plain and just looked under one bed, then left. By this stage, Shanil Haricharan, the MK cadre working closely with Aneez, had visited me at work and I had met with him when he delivered a consignment of weapons. Meanwhile, armed soldiers surrounded my parents' house while the security branch intimidated my elderly mother and father, demanding to know where Aneez was. My father, who had great strength of character, refused to be intimidated. Then my son Ashraf was shot by riot police at Spine Road High School in Mitchells Plain during a student demonstration, and charged with public violence. I was at work when this happened and my boss immediately sent our driver to take me to Mitchells Plain Police Station.

Ashraf was covered in blood when I collected him. The police at the station stared at their desks and did not once look me in the eye. They were not part of the riot squad and they looked ashamed. Lawyer Taswell Papier was representing all the students. Taswell was young, but he had already become known for his pro bono work in political trials, especially representing students in public violence cases. The trial lasted some time but eventually the case was dismissed. Increasingly, I realised that it was young people who bore the brunt of the state's violence.

After this incident, I went to work for Mogamat. This proved very convenient. Mogamat was his own boss and had a fleet of vehicles delivering newspapers all over Cape Town, as well as in Port Elizabeth, the Eastern Cape and sometimes Johannesburg, so we could move around freely and legitimately, even at night.

The next few years became more dangerous for us as Mogamat and I became more involved in MK work. It was not that we were very brave; we just could not turn back when people's lives were at stake. We no longer questioned things when we were called on to perform tasks for the Ashley Kriel Detachment. Many people were involved in the struggle then, on different levels, and other combatants in the detachment conducted very brave operations and sacrificed even more than we did.

I regularly met with Aneez and Shirley, as well as Shanil, who helped tutor my daughter Zulfa in biology and science while she was studying dentistry at the University of the Western Cape. Richard Ishmail taught me the intricacies of spreadsheet formulas to assist me in my daily work. All of this teaching was done as part of their revolutionary duties in keeping with the ANC motto of 'each one, teach one'. I discovered that Aneez had become a highly skilled cook during his time in the underground. Because of their circumstances, the comrades maintained strict diets, as they could not afford to let any member get sick.

I had to be in almost daily telephonic contact with the AKD, using public phone boxes at prearranged times. This was to ensure that the security branch never got near them. The number of telephone numbers I had to memorise was mind-boggling, and they changed constantly over a long period of time. I was also regularly taken to various safe houses, always in a very professional and clandestine manner, and I still don't know where those safe houses were. Besides this, and ordnance, liaison and intelligence gathering, I did repairs on the vehicles. This came as a welcome distraction, although it was also quite stressful because transport was a critical part of the AKD's operations and I had to ensure that their vehicles were safe and reliable. I think I also acted as a morale booster at times, because living deeply underground for years and being disciplined at all times was mentally strenuous for the AKD members, and they needed to touch base with the lives of ordinary people from time to time.

I was always amazed at the disciplined manner of the leadership as well as their deep commitment to the just democratic struggle. They, in turn, gave me tremendous confidence and I sometimes think that my parents could sense this when I went to visit them, even though I could not tell them anything.

The death of the courageous Anton Fransch in 1989 was very disturbing and traumatic. I had to meet with the detachment the next night, when everyone was on high alert. The AKD command obviously could not attend Anton's funeral, but I did. As a member of a detachment that the police were determined to eliminate at all costs, I went out in broad daylight, surrounded by dozens of armed police, and threw a spadeful of soil onto Anton's coffin, saluting him as a hero while a lone comrade from the township honoured him by sounding the Last Post on his trumpet. When I reported this to the leadership that same night, I could see that it gave them some peace.

There were happy moments too, including Shirley and Aneez getting married and the birth of their son, Haroon. The logistics of their wedding were impressive and taught me how creative people can be in the most extreme circumstances. The ceremony took place in an admiral's house next to the Simon's Town dockyard, virtually in the enemy's lair, and I realised then that support for the armed struggle reached deep – even within the state's military forces. The place was decked out with wedding cakes, tea and lots of delicious food. Shirley looked radiant and happy. Imam Solomon performed the *nikah*. My parents, Shirley's mom Audrey, Mogamat, Johnny Issel and Zubeida Jaffer were present. To add to the celebrations, the navy unintentionally honoured the occasion by conducting a sailpast right in front of the house with a flotilla of naval ships and even a submarine!

The breakthrough came in 1990, when F.W. de Klerk unbanned the ANC and other banned organisations, which was followed by the release of Nelson Mandela and other political leaders. In 1994, what we fought for was realised: South Africa became a democracy. I felt honoured to have played a role in the AKD, however small. Mogamat and I demobilised at 9 South African Infantry Battalion military base at Faure in Cape Town. We received our demobilisation certificates and R22 000 each. We now receive a special pension and free medical care at 2 Military Hospital in Wynberg, although this is only for those whose salaries are not great or who are retired or unemployed, and not for our dependants – a privilege enjoyed by former SADF and SANDF personnel.

I am not bitter about the slow pace of change, in spite of the disillusionment I see all around me. I am at all times mindful that many comrades made extraordinary sacrifices for the struggle, and some gave up their lives. I am proud that, through these sacrifices, some of our objectives have been achieved. The armed struggle is over. Apartheid is dead forever. The baton has been passed on to the new South Africa to genuinely work towards the main goal of the Freedom Charter that states that South Africa belongs to all who live in it.

Meanwhile, in Mark Road, Claremont, the semi-detached house with a small yard at the back still stands exactly as we left it more than fifty years ago.

11

Sidney Hendricks

An Unusual Suspect

'I THINK YOU ARE ready for Umkhonto we Sizwe.'

I was taken aback. Usually, when Melvin Bruintjies came to me it was because he needed help distributing anti-apartheid pamphlets, putting up posters, or finding people to fill buses to the rallies. He could always count on me. 'Yes,' I told him. 'I am ready.'

I was made commander of the Bonteheuwel unit, and the first members I met were Vanessa November and Coline Williams. Melvin trained us for the most part, but Anton Fransch took over after July 1989. Melvin taught me how to prime and detonate a limpet mine and how to dismantle and reassemble firearms, specifically the Makarov pistol and AK-47. We never did target practice, but I kept a training kit at home and practised arming a limpet on my own to gain confidence and skill. Once I was ready, I went through the procedure with my unit members.

In July 1988, Melvin came to my house. 'We are going to go on an operation,' he said. 'The target is Woodstock Police Station.' I was not familiar with Woodstock, but Melvin assured me that the reconnaissance had been done. I would be dropped close to where I would place the limpet, and then we'd leave together.

On 26 July, the day of the operation, Melvin went through the procedure with me one last time: 'This is your detonator. These are the lead plates for the timer. Put one in and be very careful that it does not fall out.' I had often practised putting my finger at the back of the lead plate to keep it in place. 'Then put the cap back on and pull the pin,' he continued. 'Never pull the pin while it is in the explosive. If something goes wrong only the detonator will go off, but if something goes wrong while the detonator is in the explosive you could blow yourself up.'

As soon as the operation was under way, I ran into difficulties because I didn't know Woodstock. I was dropped a block away from the police station, the pin of the detonator already pulled. I walked right past the station and had to double back with the timing device burning away in my hands. As per Melvin's instructions, I placed the limpet against a side door of the police station and left. I walked down the street and when I'd turned the corner I started running towards Woodstock train station. Once there, I realised that I did not have a blue cent on me so I couldn't buy a train ticket. That was the second mistake I made that night. I got on the next train home to Bonteheuwel anyway, and as it was pulling out of the station I heard an almighty *BOOM!* Luckily I wasn't caught without a ticket, but it taught me a lesson, and after that I always kept some money on me, just in case.

I had followed my instinct and got away as quickly as possible, but it was unclear where Melvin and I would meet after the operation. He eventually found me at Bonteheuwel Station. 'I was waiting for you,' he said. 'I went up and down looking for you.' Not clarifying our exit strategy was another mistake.

According to the newspapers the following day, we had damaged the door to the office of a high-ranking detective. Unfortunately, it was speculated that he'd been targeted because of a criminal matter he was investigating, rather than the blast being politically motivated. From that first operation, I learnt how critical reconnaissance is and the importance of being familiar with the environment in which we operated. I also realised that I needed to be on top of my game and committed to doing the job properly, to the bitter end, because this was serious work and we could inflict unintended harm if anything went wrong.

I was born on 26 June 1965, ten years after the ANC adopted the Freedom Charter. The Charter instilled in me a passion for the struggle and gave me a vision for South Africa that we would fight to realise. I thought that I would die in the struggle, like Moses failing to reach the Promised Land, but I survived.

My parents married soon after I was born. I was named after my father. My mother's name was Louisa Martha Jameson. Jameson wasn't my mother's original surname: her mother married an African man from the Eastern Cape whose surname was Motshega. My uncles struggled to find jobs during apartheid with that surname and, being fair-skinned and able to pass as coloured, they changed their surname to Jameson.

My grandmother was originally from a farm near Kimberley, but she joined her brothers and sisters when they moved to Johannesburg. I remember going from Johannesburg to the farm in Kimberley with my grandmother twice by train: once when I was six years old and again when I was eight. After that, we lost contact with our family on my mother's side.

I'm the eldest of my siblings. I was born in District Six and have vivid memories of the house in Mount Street, where I lived with my mother and grandparents. My father lived with his mother around the corner from us, opposite the Peninsula Maternity Hospital, where I was born. I remember the day my grandfather died in our house: I was sent to buy a sachet of milk at the little shop around the corner and when I returned, carrying the milk on my head, I saw people milling around the house and sensed that something had happened. When I was told my grandfather had died, the sachet of milk fell and burst open.

I started attending a crèche in central Cape Town, as there was nobody to care for me during the day. My mother worked long hours as a machinist at Cape Underwear in Hope Street, and my grandmother worked for a Jewish family in Oranjezicht. On one occasion, however, nobody came to fetch me at the crèche due to some miscommunication between my mother and my Uncle Hennie. I remember being alone and thinking: 'I can climb over that wall but I don't know the way home.' Eventually I was fetched, but to avoid the recurrence of what my mother perceived as a traumatic experience for me, she sent me and my younger sister Georgina to live with our aunt, Marina Petersen, in Bonteheuwel. Auntie Marina lived in a two-bedroom house with her nine children in an area known as 'die kak jaart' (the shit yard), as the toilets were outside.

I started my schooling at Boundary Primary School in Bonteheuwel, and continued to commute to District Six on weekends. My mother would put Georgina and me on the bus to Bonteheuwel to Auntie Marina's house on Sunday afternoons, and we bussed back to District Six after school on Fridays. We have a strong matriarchal family. Auntie Marina became my other mother and I called her Ma; I called my mother Mummy, and I called my grandmothers Mama. They were all strong women.

The following year, my mother was forcefully moved out of District Six as a result of the Group Areas Act. She and my father moved to a one-bedroom house at 10 Lambert's Place in Hanover Park on the Cape Flats. The house had a living room, a kitchen and a bathroom with an inside toilet. There was no more travelling for Georgina and me after that: we moved to Hanover Park and stayed there for six years before moving to Bonteheuwel, where the rest of my mother's family lived. My other two siblings, Karen and Michael, were born in Hanover Park.

My father was a contract worker at the docks, loading fruit on the boats. When we moved to Hanover Park, my grandmother moved to Oranjezicht to stay with the white Jewish family for whom she worked. As a sleep-in domestic worker she stayed in the garage, which was renovated into servant's quarters. Sometimes I went with her to work, and while she cleaned the large house, I played downstairs with Carol, the madam's youngest child.

My grandmother was a chef extraordinaire. She could bake anything and she made the best cheesecake. The madam had a catering business and employed my grandmother and other members of my family when there were large functions. Ma was roped in as a waitress, my uncles were involved, and later all the children were roped in too. I assisted by washing the glasses and dishes and helping to pack up.

I remember what a treat it was when my grandmother brought delicious leftovers from work. When she became too old to do housework, she moved to Hanover Park, but continued working in the catering business until she was knocked down by a bus and broke her leg. Her employers were good people and had paid everyone well, especially my grandmother, who was the madam's right hand in the business. I think the madam knew that without our family's support, she wouldn't have had a successful business, and it actually collapsed after my grandmother stopped working. However, they remained good friends and the madam sometimes visited my grandmother in Hanover Park.

It was my responsibility to see to my grandmother after she broke her leg. I walked from one side of Hanover Park to the other every day to ensure that she was comfortable and had everything she needed, like bread, milk and other food. I even offered to stay with her in her one-bedroom house, as she was lonely, but she did not accept.

At home, we played in the street with the neighbourhood children every day. It was safe. The gangsters didn't bother us; they fought among themselves and no one got injured in the crossfire.

When we moved to Hanover Park, I changed schools a few times. First, I went to Number Seven School, which had an *oggendskool* and *middagskool* (a morning and an afternoon school platoon system) due to overcrowding. I attended *middagskool*. By the time I reached high school, the Department of Coloured Affairs had built Number Six School, next to Number Seven School, on the boundary of Hanover Park. The high-school learners from Number Seven School moved over to Number Six School. After Number Six School I attended Mount View High School.

We lived in a poor area in Hanover Park. The man opposite us worked for a movie rental shop, fixing broken reels. He had a projector and showed reel-to-reel movies every day, occasionally allowing some neighbourhood children to watch the movies, depending on who was in or out of favour with him. My mother could sense our frustration when we weren't allowed to watch the movies, and one day she'd had enough. 'This is nonsense,' she told us. 'You are not going to stand there at his house hoping to be let in. We're going to buy our own TV.' She bought a black-and-white TV that she perched on top of her wardrobe, and my sister, our friends and I would sit in the bedroom watching *Haas Das* and other children's programmes. We were the first family in the street to own a TV.

My family had a very small house, yet my mother took in both her brothers. One uncle was a drug addict and dealer, and the other worked for a fruit seller. They slept on the couches in the living room and my three siblings and I slept in the bedroom with my parents. Georgina and I shared the fold-up bed, and when we grew bigger my mother bought a bunk bed. I slept on top, Georgina and Karen slept below, while Michael slept with my parents.

We had a very traumatic family life because my father was an alcoholic. He drank every day and, when he was out of work, he fought with people. He would first go to his family, get drunk, and then he'd come home and fight with us.

The fighting stopped after he stabbed my mother. My siblings and I tackled him – one sister went for his leg, the other sister went for him with her teeth, and I attacked him too. We screamed at him that we would not let him hurt our mother and he broke down crying. After that incident, he never laid a hand on her again.

My parents eventually divorced and my father moved out. Because the house in Hanover Park was in his name, my mother moved with us to her own two-bedroom house in Candlewood Street in Bonteheuwel. I was in Standard 6 when we started a new life there.

When we first moved to Hanover Park, my mother had left the clothing factory in Cape Town and joined an underwear factory in Lansdowne. She walked to work every day. Sometimes we would meet her at the factory on Friday – payday – and she would take us to Claremont and buy each of us our own platter of chicken and chips at OK Bazaars. Other times, we would run to meet her on her way home because we knew she was bringing us chocolates.

My siblings and I mostly had to look after ourselves, even though both our uncles lived in the house. Our mother prepared our sandwiches before she left for work, and we'd listen to the radio until the news was over at 7.30 a.m., which was time to walk to school. The last one out had to lock the house and put the key in the letter box. We were never late or absent, despite having to see to ourselves every morning. As the eldest, it was my responsibility to ensure that the place was neat and organised when my mother arrived home from work.

I was a strange *boeta* (boy) because I was something of an outsider. My three siblings were very close and played together, but I played with my friends. Sometimes I teased them. Occasionally they'd get cross and fight with me, even though they were no match, as I was stronger. My siblings are still close-knit; I think the struggle robbed me of a close relationship with them, but they followed in my footsteps, joining the youth movement and getting a tertiary education.

My Hanover Park friends attended church on Sundays and I thought I should go as well. My friend Richard de Bruyn attended the Catholic Church, so I went with him to Mass. He also belonged to the Boy Scouts, so I joined the Scouts too. My mother explained to me that we were not Catholics but Anglicans, and from then on the two of us started going to Anglican services. I went to Bible classes and Sunday school too, and my mother and I went to confirmation classes at St Dominique's Anglican Church in Hanover Park. We were confirmed at the same time. When we moved to Bonteheuwel, we went to the Church of the Resurrection. That was when contact with close primary-school friends, like Richard, was severed. I saw him only once after that, when I visited my old friends in Hanover Park in my new school uniform, but after that I didn't see him or any of my other friends again.

Our living conditions changed dramatically when we moved to Bonte-heuwel. My little brother slept with my mother and my two sisters slept on the bunk bed in her room, while I had the second bedroom to myself. Uncle Hennie slept under the stairway on the same folding bed that my sister and I had slept on as children. When I got home from school, he'd help me with my homework. He was very intelligent, particularly in mathematics. He'd even skipped a standard at school and his teachers said he was going to be a doctor one day, but he never followed a professional career. Later, Uncle Hennie moved back to Hanover Park to be closer to his place of work. He became an alcoholic and eventually drank himself to death.

My grandmother joined us after that because she didn't want to stay on her own in Hanover Park. She could have stayed with any of my uncles and aunties, but she wanted to stay with us. Mama moved into my room and I moved back to the top bunk with my sisters on the bottom, and my brother in my mother's bed.

My father didn't support the family, so my mother had to pull one of us out of school to work and help her make ends meet. Mama found work for me at a radio shop owned by her former employers, and I was told to go to Shop 143 on Main Road, Sea Point, where I would learn how to fix TVs and radios. When I got to the little shop, I knew I didn't want to work there, so I turned around and went home. I told my mother that I wanted to go back to school. She accepted my decision and took Georgina out of school instead. When she was in Standard 4, at the age of thirteen, Georgina started working at the same clothing factory as my mother. To help supplement my mother's income, I worked at Pick 'n Pay during the school holidays, seeing to the trolleys.

I started at Modderdam High in 1979, when I was in Standard 7, and that's where I met Melvin Bruintjies. Melvin and I weren't in the same class that year, but we were together in Standards 8, 9 and 10. In 1983, the year we matriculated, the UDF was launched in Mitchells Plain. The event was breathtaking, and was my introduction to politics.

Melvin and I both went to the Church of the Resurrection, and I joined the youth movement there. We attended rallies, distributed pamphlets and put up posters, with Melvin making me run from pole to pole from Woodstock to Gugulethu. Our poster crew was very efficient. Each poster had to be individually stamped by the city council at a fee (if not, the police could stop us from putting them up), but we learnt to deceive them by keeping a stamped poster on the top of the pile. If we were stopped, we told the police that we had permission to put them up – 'Look!' we'd say, holding up the top poster, 'They're stamped.'

To get the job done, Melvin deployed those who were eager to work. Afterwards, he'd take us camping as a reward. These camps included a programme of plays, reading groups, discussions and debates intended to liberate us and make us more conscientious so that we could participate in the struggle in a useful way. The pie-in-the-sky Christians at the camps always said that we shouldn't worry about what was happening around us because one day we would be rewarded in heaven. We told them that was rubbish and that God should empower us to do something about our situation *now*. We needed to fight for our own liberation.

My real radicalisation began when I enrolled at Hewat Teacher Training College in 1985. That was the year of the Mandela march to Pollsmoor Prison, the Trojan Horse Massacre, and numerous school boycotts. Friends and I were already openly stoning buses on Belgravia and Thornton Roads, and sometimes our attacks were so vicious the police would storm the college campus and randomly beat up students. There was an exam boycott that year, and as a result of the police brutality and our radical activities, I didn't write all my subjects and failed. In 1986, I was back in first year and I worked harder at everything – the church youth movement and studying to be a teacher – but two years later I failed again because of my involvement in the struggle.

Melvin recruited me to MK in mid-1988, when I was in third year at college. Soon after I agreed to be part of the military underground, he took me to meet other members of the Bonteheuwel unit. He parked opposite Bergsig Primary School, and Vanessa November and Coline Williams got in the car. Melvin told us that we would need code names: mine was Steven, Vanessa's was Tania and Coline's was Tessa. He told us to write our biographies for the ANC and added that the first training we would receive was in military engineering. Melvin then handed me a book. The pages were cut out in the middle and inside the cavity was a limpet mine training kit. He explained that we were going to blow up carefully selected targets after thorough reconnaissance had been done.

Melvin informed me of a planned attack on the Bonteheuwel Rent Office. He always explained the choice of target and we would discuss it. The rent office was part of the apartheid machinery: residents were paying high, escalating rentals but our people's circumstances were not getting any better. We would hurt the apartheid government by sparking a rent boycott in Bonteheuwel. Hitting the rent office would also make things difficult for the government. I walked Coline and Vanessa through the procedure and told Coline that she would carry out the operation, but she said that she didn't feel ready. Melvin instructed me to take them through the steps once more, but said I should carry out the operation myself. I placed the limpet at the rent office and it detonated successfully, but caused minimal damage to the building.

We were always trying to be more inventive when carrying out operations, and after the poor result at the rent office, we asked Melvin how we could do more damage. One method was to pack additional shrapnel around the charge and another was to use thermite, a highly flammable powder.

Coline and Vanessa carried out the next operation – a second attack on the Bonteheuwel Rent Office on 28 September 1988 – but I was part of it too. I gave them the materials that I had received from Melvin, and I packed the limpet with thermite. Coline and Vanessa had to put the lead plate in the detonator, pull the pin, put the detonator in the limpet mine and place the limpet so that the building, and all the records inside it, would burn. We had done careful reconnaissance of the area, and knew the street would be completely deserted when we placed the charge.

That night, I accompanied Coline and Vanessa as they carried out the operation, then rode home on my bicycle. On the way, I saw a friend from church standing on a street corner. As I stopped to talk to him we heard the blast. By then, people in Bonteheuwel were used to the sound of explosions and he didn't flinch. '*Jy hou daarvan om Bonteheuwel op te blaas,*' he joked. (You like to blow up Bonteheuwel.) We laughed together, but I was unsettled by his comment – did he know where I'd just come from?

It was one of my darkest moments when I heard that Moegamat Nurudien Bartlett had been injured in the explosion. We had done such rigorous reconnaissance, which is why I took his injury so hard – for three weeks we had reconnoitred the area at night, until we were sure that nobody walked past the rent office at that time. But Moegamat Nurudien did. He had picked up and dropped the milk cartoon in which the limpet was concealed and it had gone off. He lost an eye, some fingers and one leg, and sustained extensive burns.

In October, we targeted the Bishop Lavis Magistrate's Court. Melvin fetched me, gave me the materials and drove me there. I always tried not to look suspicious by blending in with my surroundings as naturally as possible, but this time it was difficult – I had to swing myself over a one-metre-high fence to place the limpet at the court. I activated the limpet, placing it against the door facing inwards, where it would cause maximum damage. I then jumped back over the wall, walked down the road for about a hundred metres, then started running. Melvin met up with me at home. We reflected on the operation and our getaway strategy, and then he took me to a family braai at Monwabisi Beach. On the way there, he drove over the bridge past the Bishop Lavis Magistrate's Court and turned towards me, smiling. The operation had been successful.

The explosion made front-page news. The door of the court had been blown open and the police had scoured the area for evidence, but apparently found none.

In December 1988, Melvin approached me again: 'Listen, Sidney, we have a heavy schedule,' he said. 'The three of you in the unit are going with me to Mamre, then to Paarl and Parow.' We went in his car, and took a cooler bag with us on the pretext that we were going to a braai. I did the Mamre operation, using a thick lead plate, and Coline and I did the operation at the Paarl Magistrate's Court. I walked Coline through the process and we posed as a couple taking a stroll. Vanessa and I carried out the third operation at Parow Magistrate's Court. We parked some distance away and walked to the target. When we approached the building, we saw that there were pillars obstructing access to the windows, and I was unsure where to place the limpet. I ended up putting it behind the pillars, facing the building, so that it would explode towards it, causing maximum damage. I walked Vanessa through the process, and after completing the operation we went to Goodwood Magistrate's Court, where Coline and I planted the limpet. We performed four operations that night, using lead plates of varying thicknesses so that they would go off simultaneously. Of the four operations, three were successful; the limpet in the Mamre operation did not detonate. According to newspaper reports, the police had defused it.

During the railway strike and the stay-away in late 1988, we began looking for committed people to expand the Bonteheuwel unit. Vanessa introduced us to Neil Bartlett and we recruited him. The railway line bombing I performed was to be his first operation. We agreed to meet at 9.30 p.m., when the people of Bonteheuwel had not yet gone inside for the night. It was a good time to meet without attracting attention, and then by 10 p.m. most people were indoors. On the night of the operation, I waited for Neil on the corner at Bramble Way Primary School with the SPM limpet mine on me. After thirty minutes, I decided I couldn't wait any longer, so I went ahead with the operation on my own. I approached the railway line from the primary school, climbing through a hole in the fence that workers had made as a shortcut to Epping Industria, then walked about twenty metres down the track, away from Bonteheuwel Station. I placed the limpet where it would cause damage to as many lines as possible, but far enough away from the houses facing Epping.

The bomb blast brought many people outside, including Neil. I asked him why he hadn't met me as planned. He told me that he was worried about working with explosives and that this line of work was not for him. I was disappointed, but I had to accept his decision and I immediately retrieved the eight grenades he'd stored at his house. My unit later hid the grenades in the roof of the Catholic church.

Things were getting tough – besides my MK work, I had my studies to think about, as well as my involvement in the church youth. By that point I was responsible for all the Bonteheuwel unit operations and the pressure was getting to me. I told Melvin that I no longer wanted to be commander of the unit and suggested that Coline be made commander, as she had our respect. Coline was happy to take over and carry out operations, and I was relieved to relinquish the position.

Around the time of the municipal elections in July 1989, Coline phoned me. 'Listen, Sidney,' she said, 'Major operations are going to be carried out simultaneously. Everybody is going to be involved.' I asked if I could be excluded. 'No,' she said, 'everybody is part of it; we must be disciplined. Everything is planned and the reconnaissance has been done – you must just slot in.' I agreed, but hesitantly.

On the night of the operation, Melvin picked me up and informed me that we'd be targeting Bellville Police Station and the Bellville Magistrate's Court. I had never been to Bellville, let alone the Bellville Police Station. On top of that, the target turned out to be a mobile police station at Bellville Railway Station. I was ordered to place the limpet at the side of the flimsy structure, but as I was placing it, a sudden mass of people exited the station – workers coming home from a late-night shift. I ran back to Melvin and said I didn't think it was wise to put the limpet at the side of the mobile station because civilians might get injured. He asked why I hadn't placed it under the police vehicle – limpets are magnetised and stick to metal. 'That was not the plan,' I said, and argued for aborting the operation. Melvin eventually agreed and we continued to the operation at Bellville Magistrate's Court on Voortrekker Road.

Melvin suggested I take the Makarov with me this time because it might be dangerous and I had to be prepared to defend myself. Bright lights lit up the courthouse and I tried to stick to the shadows, but as I was busy placing the limpet on the side of the building where I knew it would cause maximum damage, I inadvertently stepped into the light. Just as I placed the limpet, someone shouted, '*Staan stil of ek skiet!*' (Stand still or I'll shoot!) It was a policeman. I faced a decision: fire at the policeman with the Makarov, or run. My instincts kicked in and I ran. A car approached me, and to my relief I saw that it was Melvin. It took a second to open the door and get in, then we were gone. The policeman didn't give chase. Apparently, he suspected that I had placed a bomb and called the bomb squad to defuse it. The limpet went off though, damaging the court.

I knew of three operations that were meant to take place simultaneously that night: Bellville Police Station; Athlone Magistrate's Court, which Coline and Robbie Waterwitch would carry out; and the voting tent in Heideveld, which Vanessa and new recruit Shamiel Isaacs would undertake. Vanessa and Shamiel's mission in Heideveld was aborted. Coline and Robbie's led to them being killed.

Anton Fransch became my commander after the tragic deaths of Coline and Robbie. He reintroduced me to the AK-47 and Makarov pistol, showing me how to dismantle and assemble them confidently. Anton was an expert in handling firearms and he was happy with my progress. I cached an AK-47, a Makarov pistol and SPM and MPM limpets in my room. At night, I would retrieve the AK and Makarov to practise, going through the procedures Anton and Melvin had taught me.

My next operations were with Vanessa and Shamiel, who was the driver. In October 1989 we attacked the BP Centre on Heerengracht Street in Cape Town. Anton had explained that we had simultaneous operations targeting BP that night; the others were BP petrol stations. I was familiar with the target; the pension office was in the same building as the BP Centre and I'd been there a number of times.

Anton's orders were that we should wait for his final instruction, but if we didn't hear from him we should go ahead with the operations anyway. We waited for Anton's call at a phone booth in Mowbray, but no call came. Despite his instructions to carry out the operation regardless, I felt unsure – something might have happened to him. We followed the usual routine that night: I took Vanessa through the procedure and we walked around the building together. To effect maximum damage, we placed the limpet at the back of the building so that it would blow out all the windows from below.

The next operation was at the BP petrol station in Woodstock. We didn't want to blow up the pumps because we feared it might cause a massive explosion, so we placed the limpet against the garage offices. The limpet damaged a number of vehicles parked there, including a police detective's car. The third operation on a second BP petrol station was aborted because the pin of the detonator broke when we pulled it.

We read in the newspapers the following day that the police had linked the Woodstock petrol station bombing to the previous operation we had carried out at Woodstock Police Station, and suspected that it was intended to stop a criminal investigation that was at a crucial stage. Melvin and Anton were both at the debriefing afterwards and I gave them the report. Although the outcome of the Woodstock bombing was not what we had hoped, the damaged BP Centre building was sold and BP withdrew from South Africa in line with the call for sanctions, which we saw as a victory.

Sometimes Vanessa, Shamiel and I trained with Anton at Blue Waters camping site. On one occasion, Shamiel went AWOL. We were all very worried, not knowing if we should leave the campsite immediately, because if Shamiel were to tell the police anything, we'd all be caught. We didn't see him for some time after that and didn't get a chance to ask why he'd left the unit.

Anton was killed in November 1989, and I heard what happened on the radio. My first thought was that MK should have retaliated to defend Anton and get him out of the situation. That was probably what the SADF and the police thought MK would do, so it would have been suicidal and ultimately we couldn't save him.

A month later, my unit targeted the railway line in Athlone during a railway strike. Melvin did the reconnaissance and I carried out the operation. I took the Makarov. At some point during the operation the magazine went missing; it probably fell out of my pocket when I climbed over a fence. Fortunately, this did not have any serious repercussions: we were always extremely careful about not leaving our fingerprints on materials.

In January 1990, we attacked a number of sports complexes because some clubs were continuing to host sporting fixtures despite the sports boycott. We were still trying to grow the Bonteheuwel unit, so we recruited Mark Naidoo, a close friend of mine from the Church of the Resurrection. I spent a lot of time training Mark and preparing him for the Avondale Cricket Club operation on 5 January 1990, but when the time came to execute it, he didn't feel ready, so I walked him through the procedure and did the operation myself.

On 11 February 1990, the day Nelson Mandela was released, Melvin informed me that we were going to pull off an operation at Newlands Cricket Ground that night. He said the reconnaissance had been done, and I trusted him. Melvin gave me the materials and dropped me close to the grounds. The target was the ticket office and the operation was relatively simple as the place was deserted. I got out of Melvin's car, walked to the ticket office, planted the limpet, got back into the car, and we drove off. I thought we were going home, but Melvin drove to Parow. He told me that, in response to Mandela's release, the right-wing AWB was planning a mass meeting at the Parow Civic Centre the following day, so we were going to blow up the building. We placed a limpet without difficulty and got away safely. These were our last operations and the least complicated of the ones in which I'd taken part.

When Melvin informed me that Vanessa and I had to appear before the South African Truth and Reconciliation Commission's Amnesty Committee in 1999, I thought about what he, Charlie Martin and the Anglican youth workers had once preached: we must live, work and learn with the people and not leave until our work was done. 'I am part of a community and I don't want to expose myself,' I said defiantly. 'My colleagues and my family don't know I was part of MK. Let the commanders face the Amnesty Committee.' My whole family was in the dark; my wife, Cheryl, was the only person I had spoken to about my underground activities. But I was ordered to go. I felt vulnerable, because I feared my school and community would judge me. It was a traumatic experience.

I appeared before the TRC's Amnesty Committee on 28 October 1999 to apply for amnesty for the bomb blast at the rent office in Bonteheuwel that had injured Moegamat Nurudien Bartlett. I was the first applicant, Vanessa was the second applicant and AKD commander Aneez Salie was the third applicant. Taswell Papier was our lawyer. I was a teacher at Easter Peak Primary

School in Manenberg then, and I was extremely worried about what the principal would say when I told him that I was taking a day off to appear before the TRC. Fortunately, he did not listen very carefully and subsequently did not remember the reason I had not been in that day.

At the TRC hearing, the commissioners asked serious questions about what happened the night of the explosion. The more I listened to them, the more I felt that they were implying that we had been irresponsible in recruiting high-school students – Vanessa had been in Standard 9 at the time. When I was directly addressed, it felt like my testimony was pulled apart. The chairperson asked Taswell whether he had prepared us for the hearing, because we were divulging much more information than was necessary for our particular amnesty application.

The hearing was reported in all the local daily newspapers the next day, but the articles were short, and only one of them included a (blurred) photograph of Aneez, Vanessa and me. Thankfully, nobody from my community approached me about appearing before the TRC, but as a result of the hearing, I withdrew my application for the head of department at Arcadia Primary School, despite knowing that I was a strong candidate for the position. Moegamat Nurudien Bartlett lived next door to the school and I feared that, if the story got out, the community would see me in a negative way and wouldn't want me to hold the post. I felt personally responsible for Moegamat Nurudien's injury and believed that my career had been dealt a blow because of this.

When Melvin brought me some forms and told me that I could either demobilise or get a job in the army or police, I told him I wasn't interested. 'I'm a teacher,' I said. 'Teaching is my passion and my calling. I don't want to fill in any forms. I don't want to be remembered as a hero. I don't want any of this!'

Nevertheless, I asked Cheryl's opinion. I told her I had an opportunity to integrate into the army, but if I accepted I would have to go to Koekenaap, a base on the West Coast three hours outside Cape Town. Cheryl told me that if I wanted to go, I must forget about her, so I demobilised at the Faure army base and took the package of R22 000. Heinrich Magerman, Pete Arendse and Andrew Adams demobilised at the same time as I did, but I had no idea that they were from the Macassar unit of the AKD. Afterwards, I heard that Vanessa had demobilised and many others as well. During this time, Shamiel Isaacs appeared again and I felt like he was pressurising me. 'Remember me?' he said. 'I was an MK soldier.' *Who went AWOL,* I thought. To be fair, though, Shamiel, Mark Naidoo and Neil Bartlett had kept our secret, despite leaving the unit. They knew we had ammunition, AK-47s, limpet mines and grenades.

At the time, we'd been worried that exposing ourselves to them had compromised our safety, but they kept their mouths shut.

When I think back on it, the main reason I kept out of the crosshairs of the security police during those years was that I was an unusual suspect. I was a member of the church, the church youth, and the Inter-Church Youth. Even though I associated with people who were deeply involved in the struggle, I remained unobtrusive. I was also introduced to the struggle later than others; I only started becoming politicised in matric, and more seriously at college. Mostly I could be found playing cricket, climbing the mountain and going to the beach with friends.

When the armed struggle came to an end, I rejoiced because I had survived. But I feel that the struggle might still take my life. I'm fighting on a different front, trying to liberate the children of Manenberg so that they can rise above their circumstances and make something meaningful of their lives. The school where I teach is in a gang-ridden area and we are forever caught in the crossfire. Enrolment fluctuates every year. When children in Bonteheuwel and Manenberg go to schools in their communities, they rarely have the chance at a better future because of the prevalence of drugs, violence and gangsterism. But take the children out of these areas, put them in better resourced areas and schools, and you will see them blossom. I maintain that if I sent my daughter to a school in Bonteheuwel I would decrease her chances of succeeding by 50 per cent. To try to combat these challenges, I started an extramural programme to keep children off the streets and got a feeding scheme off the ground. I worked in collaboration with a woman called Michelle India Baird at the Department of Justice who was involved in writing the Children's Act and children's rights policy, and we focused on creating opportunities for young girls. One project, the Rock Girls Foundation, constructed safe spaces, peace benches and gardens. We now have more than thirty-two benches across in the Western Cape. One bench in Cape Town honours Krotoa, the first indigenous person to communicate with Jan van Riebeeck when he arrived in South Africa and who became an interpreter. Another bench honours the memory of Amy Biehl, who was killed in Gugulethu during the unrest in the early 1990s.

I fought for a democratic South Africa that has been paid for in blood, and this is what drives me. Nobody is going to squander that because it would mean that my comrades – Coline, Ashley, Anton and Robbie – died in vain. So I work with children, teaching them one by one, hoping that I make a difference in their lives.

12

Vanessa November

Young in Arms

Between 1985 and 1986, the security police frequently pitched up at my family home in Bonteheuwel, hunting down my brother Gori, a politically active student leader. If they came at night, they wore balaclavas and shone their torches in our faces, shouting 'Where is your brother? Who are the leaders at school?' at me and my siblings. Sometimes they questioned my mother and father, threatening to shoot Gori and his friends if they caught them. Gori was young, but the police called him a terrorist. During the state of emergency curfew, when they spotted me walking in the street, the security policemen would call out: '*Vanessatjie, waar is jou broer?*' (Little Vanessa, where is your brother?) There was no place to hide, and the anger that I felt towards the police grew because of the torment they put us through.

On the few occasions when Gori and his comrades couldn't find a place to sleep, they would come home. They slept in their shoes so that, if the police came, they could get away quickly.

Gori was on the run for two years before he left the country in May 1987. I remember the weekend he left clearly because it was the day after my uncle's funeral. It was a Sunday and I rode my bicycle to the Holtzmans' house to visit them. Most students involved in the struggle knew the Holtzmans' house as a safe haven, and many comrades were assisted by Mama Evelyn Holtzman. Gori was there with his girlfriend Verna, bags packed, waiting for Melvin Bruintjies to take him to Cape Town Station. It was sheer chance that I was there to see him leave. I didn't see him again for many years.

After school the next day, I found my mother in the kitchen, peeling potatoes. I was helping her when I realised I could not keep it in any more. 'Gori has gone,' I said. 'I don't know where he went, but he is gone. We won't be seeing him, so you shouldn't keep supper for him any more.'

She burst into tears. We both cried and held each other. My mother told me that she had sensed that he had left the previous day. A sadness had come over her while she was cooking Sunday curry for the family.

On 1 June 1990, my mother received a letter with a Namibian return address. It was our first letter from Gori. He had sent some photographs too, and he looked well. I told my mother to keep the letter and photographs to herself, but she could not contain her excitement. Seeing Gori's letter and pictures really lifted her spirits, and she felt she needed to share the good news with others close to her, especially the mothers of other Bonteheuwel activists.

A month after receiving Gori's letter, my mother had a heart attack and passed away. Thinking about how the apartheid system and all those things we were subjected to had affected her health made me extremely angry. A consolation, at least, was that she had known Gori was alive.

After the death of my mother, I went to lawyer Essa Moosa at his Athlone office. Essa was well connected in the ANC and I asked him if he could get a message to Gori about her passing. He said he would try and that his office would get back to me, but nobody did. A year later, in June 1991, my family received another letter from Gori from a Namibian address. 'How is mom and everybody?' he wrote. I went back to Essa's office and angrily asked him why Gori had not received the message I had asked him to send.

I decided to go to Namibia myself. I did not tell anyone where I was going, not even the Ashley Kriel Detachment, which I had joined two years previously. I had a lot of pent-up anger towards everything and everybody. Nobody was going to stop me from trying to find Gori. I got on the bus to Namibia with a backpack, a sleeping bag, Gori's photographs and the letter with the Ondangwa address.

When I arrived in Windhoek, I asked an old lady where I could get a ride to Ondangwa. She kindly took me to the taxi rank and I sat in a taxi for a long time, waiting for it to fill up before we set off. I was sitting next to a girl called Janet, who offered me a place to sleep and accompanied me to find a detective at Ondangwa Police Station. The police seemed suspicious of my mission at first, but I showed a photograph of Gori to Ivan, one of the detectives, and he agreed to help me. I was taken to the address in Gori's letter, which was in an informal settlement, and I asked the people living there if they had seen the person in the photograph. 'This person is long gone,' one of them said. There was nothing further I could do, so I left. Ivan took me right to the country's northern border.

'You can walk over to Angola,' he told me.

'I'm going home,' I replied, and I went back to Cape Town by bus.

When Gori finally returned to South Africa in 1992, comrades went to meet him at the airport and took him to Cowley House in Woodstock, where exiles had to report that they had returned. I was overwhelmed with emotion at see-ing him again. He was one of the lucky ones; many comrades who left didn't live to see democracy.

Like many young people in Bonteheuwel, I became involved in the struggle at a young age – I was only fourteen. Strong student leaders, teachers and com-rades from the area where I lived made an indelible impression on me and shaped the decisions I have taken.

My mother, Enid Davids, provided a strong foundation in my life. Her mother, Sophia, was Muslim but married an Indian Christian and they had a big family of thirteen children. They lived in Harfield Village, a racially mixed area in Claremont, but were forced out by the Group Areas Act. They then moved to District Six. My father's name was Paul John November. His parents were from Tulbagh and Saron, but they moved to Cape Town to find work.

I was born on 24 April 1969 in Netreg, or 'Kreefgat', a small area at the far end of Bonteheuwel, where we lived until I was four years old. Our home in Oliehout Road was a one-room terraced house with an outside kitchen and toilet that we shared with our neighbours. Our large family had no option but to live with the indignity of overcrowded conditions in a sub-economic council house built for poor working-class families. The struggle for survival built my character and taught me many valuable lessons.

My mother's first seven children were Fatima and Juleiga, who embraced the Muslim faith when they married; the twins, Henry and Linda; John; Charles and Elaine. After her first husband died, she raised her children on her own with Grandma Davids' support.

When she met my father, they married and had six children: Nolan, Paul, Patrick, Andrew – better known as Gori – and me. There was also Caroline, but she passed on at an early age. Some of my older siblings, and four of us from my mom's second marriage, stayed in Netreg. We grew up together, so we were close. Because our one-room council house in Netreg was so over-crowded, some stayed with Grandma Davids in District Six. They started working at a young age to assist my mom financially. In 1973, before I started primary school, the Council allocated my family a larger three-bedroom house with an inside toilet in Essenhout Road in Bonteheuwel. My brother Patrick was born in this house.

I have fond memories of our visits to Grandma Davids in District Six. All of us called her Ma van die Kaap (Grandma from Cape Town). She lived in a flat above Allie's Grocery Shop in Sackville Street, accessed via a narrow stair-way. She was a soft-spoken, humble and caring woman, and she told us stories about Java in Indonesia and St Helena Island, where her family came from. When we visited her on weekends, we would catch the early train to Cape Town, and we'd take the last train back to Bonteheuwel.

By then, one of my sisters had her own three-bedroom flat in De Villiers Street in District Six. There was a square in the centre of the apartment block where we could play safely. The Group Areas Act forcibly moved them all. My sister was allocated a flat in gang-ridden Valhalla Park and others were scattered across the Cape Flats, to Bonteheuwel and Manenberg, and later to Mitchells Plain where they eventually settled. When they moved, we missed the outings and visits to our family and to the Plaza opposite the Good Hope Centre.

My mother worked at a laundry in Cape Town, but when she married my father she stopped working and became a housewife, caring for us while we grew up. When my dad was young, he worked as a caddy at the Rondebosch golf course, carrying Gary Player's bag and running after his golf balls. When he met my mom, he was working for the Cape Town City Council, and he later worked for Tramways. He was a hard worker and strict, and he was the breadwinner until he became ill and was boarded, after which he received a state disability grant (DG) until he died.

It was a struggle growing up in Bonteheuwel, and when my father became ill, things got even tougher. I was in primary school when he had to stop working and that's when the real hardship began at home. Our neighbours and friends in the area supported us as best they could. The Flynn family always gave us their children's old clothes, so we grew up with hand-me-downs. We had to wear our school shoes for the whole year, even if they were broken. Christmas time was very special because we got brand new outfits.

My mother also received a DG because she had heart problems and high blood pressure. She was an outpatient at Somerset Hospital in Green Point and was in and out of hospital for angina treatments. She spent so much time there that everybody there knew her. Like my grandma, she was a soft-spoken, caring and humble woman. Our door was always open to strangers. My mother would help whoever came to the house, giving them a plate of food or a place to sleep. There were extra enamel plates on the table every night. 'You never know who is coming in from the road,' she often said. As a result, our modest house in Bonteheuwel was always crowded, and there was always something for those who pitched up at mealtimes. Neighbours would also come to my mom with their problems. Netreg was poverty-stricken, as very few people had work, and life there was about survival. My mom was essentially a social worker to the families around us. As such, we grew up very closely connected to our neighbours: the Ebdens, the Phillipses, the Frederickses, the Jardines, the Hendrickses and the Flynns were like family to us. We couldn't afford a TV, so we would watch TV at a neighbour's house. Eventually, after many years of saving, we got a small, portable, black-and-white Blaupunkt TV that brought joy to the household.

I attended Pioneer Primary School, the closest school to home. Initially, my eldest sister took us younger kids safely across the busy main road, but later we walked with a group of children from the neighbourhood. I enjoyed primary school because my friends from our street attended the same school, and we played together at school and at home. I learnt to stand up for myself at an early age, trying to sort out my problems without involving my parents. I also stood up for my friends when they were bullied or got into trouble. When I was in trouble and punishment was being dished out with a long ruler or bamboo cane, I would defiantly stand with my hand closed instead of open. When my nieces got in trouble at school, they would call me to come to their defence, and I often got into trouble for doing so.

Mr Jones, a caring teacher at our school, often visited our home. He would compliment Gori on his good behaviour and good marks and complain bitterly about my stubbornness. Mr Jones also developed a close relationship with my youngest brother, Patrick, and introduced him to pigeon racing. At one point, we had a big pigeon cage in the backyard where Patrick tended to his birds.

Late one night, my brother Paul, one of our cousins and a few friends were coming home by train after visiting our aunt in Manenberg. They didn't have tickets so the conductor chased them through the carriages. As they were running, Paul was accidentally pushed out of the train, and the next morning the police came to inform us that he was dead. He was only eleven.

The tragedy of my brother's death caused a dramatic turnaround in our home. The Friday-night drinking stopped, and my parents, especially my mother, became very spiritual. Our neighbour, Auntie Annie Flynn, who had always been there for us, introduced her to the Baptist Church and things started changing for the better. The whole family began going to church, and my siblings and I started Sunday school and joined the junior choir. My mother would do her testimony with song, making trumpet sounds with her mouth, to everybody's amazement. Our lives improved; at least until we became politically active.

My mother was a strong person who did her best to support us, and my older siblings did their bit too. My brother John, for instance, worked at the Cape Town dockyard and brought us fish and hessian bags of rice and spices from the ships. We put the spices in little packets and sold them door to door for twenty cents, and we only came home when they were all gone. Most of my sisters left school at a young age to work in clothing factories. Nolan, Paul and Gori went to town very early in the morning to sell the *Argus* and they came home late. That was our destiny as working-class children. Some of my sisters were single mothers, but others married, and they helped my mother support the younger ones where they could, while seeing to their own survival and raising their kids. That is what I remember of my older siblings: always working and assisting our household.

With the positive changes at home, I started ballet at the Eoan Group in Athlone in the last few years of primary school. My mother's friend Mrs Bruckner, who sold meat in Bonteheuwel, introduced me to ballet because her daughter Simoné took ballet classes. I travelled by bus every Tuesday afternoon and on Saturday mornings to the Eoan Group. I enjoyed ballet tremendously, especially because it gave me a chance to get out of the area and use my imagination. I danced in many performances at the Eoan Group and I loved Lydia, my ballet teacher.

I finished primary school in 1984, and in 1985 I started at Bonteheuwel High, a five-minute walk from home. A few of my friends from primary school went to the same high school and we always walked to school together.

Ashley Kriel was a student leader at Bonteheuwel High School the year I started there. He was the Che Guevara of Bonteheuwel. He formed a Student Representative Council with a group of senior students, and Gori was also at the forefront, attending meetings and organising students to be part of the SRC. They introduced awareness programmes in the school quad, trying to teach us about what was happening in our community with the high rentals our parents were forced to pay and the problems with apartheid's gutter education.

I have vivid memories of seeing the damage caused by barricades and burning tyres on the main road that we crossed on our way to school, and of having to close our windows when the police threw teargas at protesting students in the 1976 uprisings when I was in Sub A. In high school, the political situation captured my imagination, and I started following our student leaders to see what they were up to. I tried to attend meetings, but Gori and his comrades told me I was too young to join. I didn't yet understand the dangers of getting involved.

A teacher, Miss van Driel, taught us about Steve Biko, and the Black Consciousness Movement emerged at our school. Along with a group of friends, I began to participate in marches and attend political education programmes organised by the student leadership. In 1985, we had the schools boycott in Bonteheuwel. The student leaderships of the three high schools jointly formed the Bonteheuwel Inter-Schools Committee, which later became the Bonteheuwel Inter-Schools Congress (BISCO). They organised many student rallies to discuss the situation in our schools and the changes we wanted in education. The other high schools came to Bonteheuwel High for meetings and protest action, and we went to their schools for meetings too. We also met at the Bonteheuwel Civic Centre, which we called 'Freedom Square' because it was a central rallying point for action, such as the rent boycotts, which Ashley spearheaded. I recall a student protest at the civic centre when the police charged at us. We all scattered, fearing for our lives, but Ashley stood his ground and smacked a policeman in the face.

Bonteheuwel had been rich in student resistance since 1976, which we learnt about when we became student activists in 1985. I got to know about students being shot with live ammunition and rubber bullets in 1976, and again in the 1985 and 1986 uprisings. I attended weekend workshops to gain knowledge of the political situation in South Africa and about struggles in other countries. One workshop I recall was at Kijk in die Pot in Stellenbosch. Students from all over the Cape Flats were invited. At the workshop, Cheryl Carolus, Graeme Bloch and Trevor Manuel gave us leadership training on how to organise awareness programmes in our schools. We also had to read a lot of banned literature that we couldn't take home. It was hard to digest the information all at once. Nevertheless, we enjoyed the workshop tremendously and students from different communities got to know each other, which helped to strengthen the student movement.

The 1985 unrest distracted me from my books, so I had to repeat Standard 6 in 1986. From that year onwards, we had annual summertime picnics for the activist youth, away from the volatility of the area and the threat of the police. Ashley and the other student leaders were coming to school less and less often because of police harassment, and when they did it was only to run awareness programmes or facilitate protest action. It was very tense in Bonteheuwel during that time and eventually the student leadership, including Gori, had to leave their homes and families and go on the run. The security police visited our home frequently that year to harass us about the whereabouts of Gori and his comrades.

Ashley sometimes surprised us when we had a mass rally at school, pitching up on a motorbike to address us, covered up to hide his identity. He was a fearless and dedicated leader, always giving political guidance to students in the area. When we held the rent boycott that year, we met at Freedom Square with dirt bins we'd collected on our way from school and we pushed our way into the rent office and dumped the trash inside. That, as well as other protest action, all happened under the leadership of Ashley, Gori and student leaders from Arcadia High and Modderdam High, including Coline Williams and Anton Fransch, among others. These experiences gave me courage, which I needed because policemen often chased us with dogs and *aapsterte* (short whips). If we got away unharmed it was sheer luck. Many students were badly beaten and progressive local doctors tended to them free of charge.

There were occasions when we had protests at school and barricades burning outside on the road. The police would come onto the school grounds with Casspirs. My friends and I often closed the school gates, preventing them from entering, and then we'd run away. They'd come after us, searching for those who had closed the gates and organised the protests, but we'd change our clothes and hide.

One day, the police surrounded the school and came into our classroom. *'Ja, ons sal al die vrot appels uitroei. Wie is die moeilikheidmakers hier in die skool?'* they said. (Yes, we are going to root out all the rotten apples. Who are the troublemakers in the school?) We all sat there without saying a word and eventually they left. They were determined to break the students' morale, but their actions only made us stronger and more determined.

During another protest that year, the Casspirs chased and provoked us, and we threw stones at them. The protest was eventually broken up and we scattered. I ran into someone's yard and knocked on the front door to be let in, but no one was home, so I lay in the garden, hiding from the *boere* while my friends Henrietta and Berenice got away. The Casspirs parked right in front of the house and two policemen got out. They shouted at me to come out, and I was so terrified I almost peed in my pants. They took me into the Casspir; there were lots of other students inside and the police questioned all of us, wanting to know who the leadership was and who stayed where. They were looking for Gori and other committee members, unaware that Gori was my brother and that his real name was Andrew.

The policemen insisted on taking me home. Just as Henrietta and Berenice were coming down the road to tell my mother I'd been picked up, they saw the Casspir in front of our house and ran the other way. The policemen escorted me inside because they wanted to know who lived in the house, which was a big shock for my mother. She demanded to know what was happening and why they were bringing me home. They said I had participated in a protest but that they would let me go because I was underage.

Things became even more hectic from 1986 onwards, with my growing involvement in the Bonteheuwel student organisations, and the following year I was elected secretary of BISCO, which joined the Western Cape Schools Congress (WESCO) and later the Congress of South African Students (COSAS). We attended meetings in Athlone, Heideveld, Gugulethu and Langa, where we met students from other schools. WESCO also had a branch in Bonteheuwel. I attended meetings there and my political awareness grew through pro-grammes that introduced us to other struggles in countries such as Cuba, Namibia and Algeria. We read *Grassroots* newspaper and assisted with its distri-bution. There was a wide range of political books and pamphlets going around that we read and shared, and we had access to videos about the apartheid struggle and struggles in other countries through the older Bonteheuwel youth who were members of the Cape Youth Congress.

By then, the state of emergency was in place and many student activists from our area were arrested and detained. Forty-one BISCO students were arrested at a meeting in Bonteheuwel and became known as the BISCO 41. We organised and mobilised in protest against these detentions. Bonteheuwel became ungovernable: buses and businesses were targeted and barricades were burnt for the release of our comrades. Some youths were arrested, tortured and then sentenced on charges of public violence.

Coline Williams was one of the forty-one students arrested, but she served longer in Pollsmoor Prison than other students from Bonteheuwel. It was tough for us without our leaders around, and we had to communicate with caution because everyone was being watched. One night we held a candlelight vigil on Settlers Way. It was supposed to be peaceful, but cars were stoned and the police arrived in full force. We scattered. That night a rumour spread that we all had to leave our homes and move to other areas or face arrest. A friend and I were taken to a house in a white suburb. We were told we could eat *anything* in the fridge and we feasted on a whole leg of lamb.

Bonteheuwel had a support group for the parents of detainees, which Coline was involved in. Some parents were angry and blamed the comrades for misleading their children and getting them into trouble with the police, but others became involved in the struggle through their children's activism. Many residents attended meetings of the Bonteheuwel Civic Association, an affiliate of the Cape Areas Housing Action Committee.

Being involved in student and youth activities in Bonteheuwel meant that high school wasn't easy. We did a lot of organising in our area to make people aware of the struggle, and we started to get to know the trade unions and unionists. Many parents worked in clothing factories and joined unions, and at one stage we students were brought in to assist the Clothing Workers

Union (CLOWU) in their fight for better wages and working conditions. Early in the morning before school, we pamphleteered at Bonteheuwel Station with June Esau and Shirley Gunn, whom I knew only as a white activist working for CLOWU, and we protested outside Cape Underwear in Epping, the industrial area next to Bonteheuwel, in solidarity with the striking workers. We helped make posters and pamphlets at the Community Arts Project (CAP) and we were trained to silk-screen T-shirts. Many of the T-shirts we produced were banned. We also assisted CLOWU with poster-making at their Woodstock office. I remember going by bus from Bonteheuwel to Atlantis to help organise the clothing workers there. We pamphleteered in Atlantis too, and it was sad to see how neglected and poverty-stricken the community was, and how people struggled to survive. Fundraising discos and *gumbas* were organised at the Copacabana Club in Athlone Industria and at the Tavern in Bonteheuwel. With all this going on in my life, there was hardly any time to study, although our student leaders encouraged us to continue with our schoolwork.

Around 1987, I started working at The Groove nightclub in Athlone Industria with a few of my school friends and comrades. We all had to bring in some money because there was often not enough to make ends meet at home. Coline, Charnel, Melanie, Selina and I were close. We were all in high school, and mostly from single-parent families, or with parents who were unemployed. Our shifts were from Wednesday nights to the weekends, from 7 p.m. until the club closed the next morning, and we earned R25 a night. On weekends, the club closed at 3 or 4 a.m., so we worked very long hours. But we met people from all walks of life, so it was an eye-opener, and we all learnt to be independent at an early age. Alcohol was readily available to us as bartenders and waitresses, but we'd seen too much hard drinking to be interested in it. Coline was extremely protective and watched over us.

Gori left school and went into exile in May that year, as the security police were hunting him down. He'd had many narrow escapes with Anton Fransch, trying to avoid arrest, and security policemen Harris, Abels, Van Brakel, Mostert and Odendaal were familiar faces to us. On more than one occasion, they took my brother Nolan to the police station when they didn't find Gori at home. Nolan was married and working by then, and he wasn't involved in politics, but that was how they harassed the family. A few times the cops came when Gori or Anton were in the house, but they would be out through the toilet window at the back before the police even knocked at the door. After one of these escapes, the only place Gori and Anton could find to rest was at Gori's former primary school. Fortunately, they always managed to avoid arrest.

In July 1987, Ashley Kriel's death at the hands of the security police dealt a major blow to student activists in Bonteheuwel and the Western Cape. People were really angry. We all rallied around Auntie Ivy, Ashley's mother, and his sisters, Michel and Melanie, to show our support and solidarity, and we all threw our weight behind organising Ashley's memorial service and funeral the next week.

Ashley's funeral procession started at his family home and proceeded to the New Apostolic church. After the first service, the coffin was carried to the Bonteheuwel Anglican church while the SADF and the SAP chased the comrades from one church to the other. The pallbearers held on to Ashley's coffin, which was covered with an ANC flag, until they reached the Anglican church. It was packed to capacity with activists and church leaders from all over the Western Cape.

After the second memorial service, the procession to the Maitland cemetery was interrupted. The security forces tried to take the flag off Ashley's coffin, but the comrades held on to it, so they chased us with batons and teargas, preventing the large procession from reaching the cemetery.

I have a clear memory of the day I was recruited into MK. It was 1988, and I was in Standard 9. Coline came to visit me at home one afternoon and said we needed to talk. We left the house to find a quiet place to have the conversation. She told me about underground military work and asked me how I felt about taking the next step. I did not hesitate. I believed MK's work was necessary, considering all the brutality we experienced with the army and police patrolling our streets and taking over our communities while our leaders, brothers and sisters were in exile or in hiding. It was the call I'd been waiting for. I wanted to contribute to change in our country, bringing the apartheid regime down, and moving forward. 'Yes!' I unhesitatingly replied.

When Coline said we would be meeting the commander, I expected it to be Gori, but it was Melvin Bruintjies. I was surprised; Melvin was one of our church leaders and a member of the local church youth. For the meeting, Melvin picked us up at Bonteheuwel Station, and from there we went to the chosen location. I was given an introduction to the armed struggle, told about plans for taking the struggle forward, and given banned *Sechaba* and *Umsebenzi* magazines to read, which I hid at home later.

Coline was already a good friend of mine, but when she became my commander we became even closer. We did our AK-47 training together, disassembling, reassembling and cleaning and oiling the weapon. Being introduced to the AK-47 was a big moment, as were my later introductions to hand grenades and limpet mines.

The first operation was carried out by our unit commander, Sidney Hendricks, at the Bonteheuwel Rent Office in early September 1988. It was successful but caused minimal damage. We targeted the rent office again on 28 September, this time with Coline and me more directly involved. Sidney exercised great patience with us in the field. The operation took place during the rent boycott. People were angry and protesting about the high rentals charged by the Cape Town City Council, as well as municipal rates and services imposed by the House of Representatives, so the operation was also directed at the racist Tricameral Parliament. Coline, Sidney and I did extensive reconnaissance around the area for three weeks before the operation.

After 9 p.m. that night, when people were at home, Sidney, Coline and I placed the limpet at the door of the rent office and left the area as quickly as possible. I was at my neighbour's flat when the blast went off. The next day, everyone in Bonteheuwel was talking about the explosion, but no one knew who was responsible for it. We then heard that a man was injured and had been taken to hospital. For security reasons we couldn't do much to get more information and had to depend on newspaper reports. We read that the police were guarding the man at his bedside, and that he was later taken into custody and interrogated because the security police wanted to know what had happened and why he was in the area at that time of night. We later learnt that he had handled the milk carton that the limpet was in and it had exploded. It was a terrible accident. I felt a deep sadness, but we had to keep our emotions hidden, and we couldn't speak to anyone. In MK, we were told that the safety of citizens came first, so it was very hard on all of us that this had happened.

My next operation was with Melvin, Coline and Sidney on 16 December 1988, the anniversary of the formation of MK. The target was the Paarl municipal building. We drove to Paarl, did reconnaissance in the area, considered safety aspects, and carried out the operation, which was successful. We also carried out an operation at the Parow Municipal Court that night.

After that, I carried out an operation with Sidney at the Goodwood Magistrate's Court, also in December 1988. He was in charge of that operation, and he planted the limpet. We posed as a couple and I dressed up in a polka-dot skirt. Sidney calmly placed the limpet in position and we left immediately. Late that evening it was confirmed on TV that there had been an explosion at the court. The operation had been successful. However, there was always the fear of being identified, and we were alarmed to see that in the newspapers the next day there was a description of a young couple seen outside the building.

*

One warm Sunday morning in July 1989, Coline visited me at my house for a briefing. She went over how to prime a limpet mine in preparation for the evening's operation at the Heideveld Rent Office that I was to undertake with Shamiel Isaacs, another comrade from Bonteheuwel, who I had recruited and trained. I popped in at her house that afternoon to discuss where we were going to meet later, and Coline put a Makarov pistol in her handbag. She left the house with it, and in the early evening we met up at one of our regular meeting places, a small café with pool tables near the station in Mowbray. Coline handed me the limpet wrapped in a towel inside a bag. We spoke briefly about what needed to happen that night, wished each other luck and said our goodbyes. Then I went back to Bonteheuwel by taxi with the limpet.

Later that evening, I met up with Shamiel and we walked across the footbridge to Heideveld together. There was not much street lighting in the area and the streets were quiet. We chose an open dustbin at the bus stop on Heideveld Road to prepare the limpet, but in the dark we lost the lead plate that would delay detonation. While searching for it, we suddenly heard a loud bang. I was aware that other explosions would be taking place at the same time as ours. We still couldn't find the tiny lead plate, and eventually decided to abandon the operation and head back to Bonteheuwel. I went home, hid the limpet in a safe place and waited to hear from Coline.

She never came home. I did not know who had done the operation with her, and was waiting for a phone call or some kind of confirmation that she was safe, but nothing came. First thing the next morning, I went to look for Sidney to hear if he had any news regarding Coline. We then waited on Melvin for information. When news of the blast appeared in the papers, we were still trying to find out where Coline was. The newspaper reported fatalities, but we did not know who had died. As the day wore on, I realised that the explosion I'd heard the night before had come from the Athlone direction.

I went to look for Coline at different comrades' houses, hoping to find her or hear whether anyone had seen her. A comrade, Anthony Diedricks, accompanied me to activist June Esau's house in Woodstock, but she hadn't seen Coline either. After we left June's house, Anthony stopped at Don Pedro's and bought me an Irish coffee, which he said would help me sleep, then he dropped me at home. I did not sleep. Instead, I experienced a rollercoaster of emotions that night. Deep down, I feared my comrade was dead. We were the only two women in our unit, and now I was all by myself.

On Tuesday morning, Coline's family went to Essa Moosa's office in Athlone, and from there to the Athlone Police Station to report that Coline was missing. Later that day, we discovered that it was Coline and Robbie

Waterwitch who had died in the explosion. It was the longest, saddest day of my life. My heart was broken into pieces. I had to be disciplined and keep my composure, but I was devastated, choked with emotion. Other comrades who I worked with, like Sidney, were as well. The two of us spoke about what could have happened and met with Melvin, knowing that word would soon reach the Williams family. The news that two of our most humble comrades had paid the ultimate price for our freedom spread quickly. I remember running into Shamiel, my unit member, on Jakkalsvlei Avenue. He had been on his way to work when his mother called him to tell him that Coline and Robbie were dead. When I saw him he broke down crying and we hugged each other.

Security protocols meant that our unit could not get close to the Williams family; the security police were in and out of the Williams' house, searching it. We had to be strong. Two days after the incident, the AKD approached the family via the clergy. I was not part of the group that met the family. Our instructions from the AKD were to stay calm and stay put. Melvin told me that we had to retrieve any arms and ammunition cached in Coline's house and, because I could not be seen going there, we asked Anthony Diedricks to retrieve the weapons.

The week leading up to Coline's funeral was very tense and emotional. I was part of the team of comrades organising the funeral and putting up posters. The AKD also produced an A4 pamphlet with the MK logo that honoured our two fallen comrades and explained what could have gone wrong on that fateful night. We distributed these at the funeral.

The memorial service was held at the Bonteheuwel Civic Centre and it was packed to capacity with people from all over Cape Town expressing their deep sadness. It was harrowing losing a close friend and comrade, and I never got to speak to a psychologist. We had to deal with our emotions on our own, put them aside and move on. That's how we lived then. We couldn't trust many people. It was very tough.

After Coline and Robbie's deaths, I did a few other operations with Sidney and Shamiel, including the BP Centre in the city centre in October 1989. Sidney and I planted the limpet, and the operation was successful. We did another operation that night – a BP garage on Main Road in Woodstock.

This all happened in my matric year. I didn't really want to be at school any more. Losing Coline was too much for me to deal with. She had finished school and always encouraged me to study hard and pass, but without her I felt lost and alone. It was not easy going to class every day and doing my schoolwork. My work at the nightclub kept me sane, but I found it emotionally difficult to pick myself up every day and carry on. There was no time to recover and rest. Students in the politically active Bonteheuwel area were busy organising the community, so I had to split my time between my schoolwork, my aboveground work and my underground work. It was hectic juggling all these commitments, trying to survive while getting through the trauma of loss on my own. Family life had to continue as well. Gori was in exile, and I was the family's spokesperson in the community.

As the end of the year approached, some of my teachers realised that I was struggling to concentrate on my schoolwork, and they talked me into continuing my education. All they knew was that Coline and I were close friends and that Gori had left the country; I couldn't really speak to them. I had to keep my emotions to myself.

I didn't have the energy to sit with my books and I wrote two matric subjects without studying much. I failed matric that year. Melvin and the unit were very concerned about my well-being. We continued with our briefings and training sessions and we received words of encouragement from the detachment, but we were not as operational from that point on.

We continued with our lives. On 16 November 1989, on Evelyn Holtzman's birthday, I helped a bunch of comrades throw a surprise party for her. We made a big banner and put out the word to the comrades in Bonteheuwel to gather at her house. Many comrades came and we had a wonderful get-together, reminiscing about old times and the people no longer with us. Lots of happy and sad memories were shared, and we went home glad to have done that for Evelyn, as she'd been a great support to us over many years.

Very early the next morning the home phone rang. It was June. 'Did you hear the news?' she asked. 'It's all over the newspapers and on TV. There was a shoot-out in Athlone.' I was suddenly wide awake. My mother had an uneasy feeling after the phone call. I did not tell her that there had been a shoot-out, but she could sense that something was wrong. I got dressed and went out to find out from the comrades what had happened. By then, the news of a seven-hour shoot-out between the army and a trained comrade was everywhere. My first thought was that it was Gori. It was traumatic waiting to hear who had died and what had happened. Only later that evening did we learn that it was Anton Fransch who had been killed. It was another enormous blow. I had so many questions and so much anger. Another one of us was dead!

Losing Anton and Coline made me more determined to continue the struggle. We helped to organise Anton's funeral, and on the day I could see the pain our mothers felt. My mother held Anton's mother and said, 'Dit kon my kind gewees het.' (It could have been my child.) It was very difficult for my family having a son and brother out there somewhere, not knowing when bad news might come our way.

After Anton's death, Melvin explained an incident that had happened during a training camp at Blue Waters Resort in Strandfontein, when I was first recruited to MK. Melvin, Coline and I had been in his car. He was driving and I was sitting in the back seat when he suddenly told me to lie down and cover my head with a blanket. I wondered what was going on but, being a disciplined soldier, I did as ordered. Melvin drove on and eventually we stopped at the resort, where I was allowed to uncover my head. I asked Melvin and Coline what had happened but I was told: 'It's none of your concern. The less you know the better.' Melvin now revealed that the reason I'd had to cover my head was that Anton had been there and had been looking directly at us. I wasn't supposed to know he was working with Coline.

I later learnt that Anton was one of the comrades who had trained Coline. I was also told how worried Anton had been about me and that he had often enquired about my well-being. I was pleased to know that he had been watching out for me. I often thought about an evening before Anton and Gori left for exile when both of them, along with Coline, Melvin and I, had gathered at a safe house belonging to a guy from the Anglican Church. We'd had such fun together, listening to jazz and making jokes. We were the young in arms. 'If only I'd had a glimpse of him,' I thought when Melvin told me about the Blue Waters incident. 'If only my commanders had given me the chance to see him one last time before he died.'

When the news broke about the release of Nelson Mandela in February 1990, the mood in Bonteheuwel was one of jubilation. The comrades in the Western Cape ran around organising the mass rally on the Grand Parade, and all our parents wanted to be part of this miraculous moment. My mom and I took a train to Cape Town with a big group from Bonteheuwel on the day of Mandela's release. We were all very excited, but there was also an emptiness inside me because Coline was not there with us. She had fought so hard for change, and the thought of her not being part of this moment made me very sad. Mandela's release was a breakthrough for our struggle, but I missed my comrades who had died and I missed Gori.

After Madiba's release, we had to work tirelessly to raise awareness in our communities in preparation for the upcoming elections, and we pamphleteered every day. At the time, I babysat for some of my teachers and their friends, as well as working at the club. One night Aneez Salie came to see me. I had met him before, but I could not remember where. Many months later, I made

the connection: Aneez was Shirley Gunn's husband, and they were commanders of the AKD. He had come to enquire about my well-being.

After my mom passed away, I moved out. I was twenty-one. My mother
had kept the family together, but after her death most of my siblings got their
own places. I moved in with friends in Bonteheuwel and tried to get on my
feet, working at the nightclub and babysitting. I eventually found a room in
Crawford, and from there I moved to Rondebosch East and then to Fairways,
sharing a flat with my comrade Nicky Asher.

In Fairways, I connected with many comrades, as I lived close to Johnny
Issel and Zubeida Jaffer. I visited their house often and ran into comrades who
had come to Bonteheuwel in 1985 and 1986. They encouraged me to remain
active in Bonteheuwel. There was much to be done to build an ANC branch
there. I did door-to-door pamphleteering and was involved in organisational
and community work, coming face-to-face with poverty in our area. I finished
matric and, after receiving a small bursary, I did a two-year Educare course at
the Cape Town Vocational College, and I worked at various Educare centres
in 1993 and 1994. I continued to work at the club, waitressing and cashiering in
the bar, and I continued babysitting. Each and every time an opportunity
to earn money came my way, I grabbed it with open arms. I pushed myself to
work at night and then be in class the next day. It was rough, but I managed.
It was the first time I started focusing on myself.

In 1994, I counted votes for the Independent Electoral Commission. I felt
immensely proud that my small role had contributed to our first democratic
election. Nevertheless, I worked tirelessly to save enough money to leave the
country. I wanted time out to discover myself and meet new people in new
contexts without worrying or watching my back all the time. I bought a
plane ticket for Amsterdam to work as an au pair for Mr and Mrs Klein
Essink, a wealthy couple with one child and another on the way. I stayed in
the Netherlands for thirteen months.

Dutch society had what we hoped to see in South Africa: many cultures
lived together harmoniously and there were plenty of mixed marriages. The
experience broadened my mind. Back home, we read bad news every day.
When I stayed with my Amsterdam family and the newspapers arrived, I
didn't want to read them. I didn't want to hear the news, I just wanted to be
myself and experience normal, everyday life.

During the months I was with the Klein Essinks, I had no worries about
food or rent. When I arrived, the family told me to ask for whatever I wanted,
but having come from a humble home in Bonteheuwel, I couldn't ask for
much because I had my pride. I told them that everything I needed was there:

a roof over my head and more than enough food. I was also spoilt with birth-day presents and holidays abroad; what more could I possibly want?

I got to know other South Africans while doing au pair work that year. I stayed in the centre of Amsterdam, and when new girls arrived from Durban, Johannesburg and Cape Town, they phoned me up. They were from different cultures and it was great getting to know them. I was like a social worker, giv-ing them advice. When communication between some of the girls and their parents broke down, their parents would phone me and I would reassure them that their daughters were okay.

Whenever I got the opportunity, I travelled. I went with an Irish friend, Nicola, to County Dublin one Easter. We went to clubs and listened to Irish folk music. Nicola's brother was a folk musician and singer and I, the girl from Africa, would toyi-toyi for them. I could be myself, have fun and laugh. I travelled to Greece, as well as the UK and Belgium. Money was never an issue with Carolien Klein Essink. She encouraged me to go out and she gave me pocket money and sometimes booked and paid for my travels. For some time, she was a mother figure in my life. I was treated very well and felt like part of their family.

I could have stayed with them for longer, but I wanted to see other parts of the world, not only Europe. In my last two months there, I searched for jobs in other countries and got one in San Francisco in the USA with a Dutch couple I had met. The husband worked for Shell International and the fam-ily was being relocated, so they needed an au pair to look after their two children. I was on holiday in Greece when this job came up, and on my return to the Netherlands I hastily got all the paperwork together on my own because I knew I had the job. I went to the US embassy in Amsterdam, but my appli-cation for a work visa was rejected. I was devastated.

I had two options: return to South Africa on my open return ticket or stay in the Netherlands. I decided to go home, apply for a new passport and reapply as a visitor to the US. Soon after I arrived back home, I went to the US consulate in Cape Town to reapply, but my application was rejected yet again. However, I was glad to be in the country. My father had become very ill and I was able to be by his side during the last few months of his life. He died in December 1995, on my mother's birthday. Not long there-after, Clive Mettler and I started dating. I had known Clive, who was from Elsies River, almost all my life. We had reconnected in September 1995, soon after my return from the Netherlands, when he came to visit my father. We moved in with friends of mine and later found our own place in Brooklyn. Our small, intimate wedding was at John Fredericks's place on Hanover

Street, opposite the Castle. Clive had a good job as a manager with Dos Santos Transport.

In 1996, a year after I returned to South Africa, I received a message stating that I had to attend a demobilising session. I stayed at the army base for three nights and a British colonel briefed us and told us we could choose to stay in the army or demobilise. If I integrated, I'd be ranked as a corporal, the lowest rank in the new South African National Defence Force, so I decided to demobilise. The fact that I had fought against apartheid and survived despite all the risks was enough for me. I took the R22 000 package. I was unemployed at the time, so this money came in handy.

Later, I completed the Special Pension application, but it was rejected. Applicants had to have been thirty-five years old in 1996, and I was only twenty-seven. This was very frustrating for me: I had not been too young to take up arms to bring the apartheid system down, so it seemed unfair that I was rejected on the basis of my age. I had been a dedicated cadre. I had been prepared to give my life. I never expected that we would be compensated; all I prayed and hoped for was that one day we would be part of the changes that some of my comrades didn't have the chance to see.

During this time, I tried to connect with comrades, as I had decided that I wanted to study further at a university or college. I went to the ANC Veterans' League office in Athlone to find out about possible bursaries. I was directed to Robert McBride in Johannesburg, but I did not have any luck and eventually gave up trying to get assistance. I realised I was on my own and had to find work and pursue a life without help from other people.

Clive and I were renting a small house in Brooklyn, which was where our daughter Austen was born on 2 June 1997. Just before Austen's birth, Clive became very sick with a lung infection and was hospitalised for a few weeks in the Intensive Care Unit at Somerset Hospital in Green Point. He was discharged and home again just before I gave birth at the same hospital. It was a very stressful period, as he never recovered fully, but he was very supportive, bringing me food and caring for me after Austen's birth.

Initially, the doctors could not figure out what his ailment was, but he was eventually diagnosed with heart disease as a result of dermatomyositis, a rare condition that affects the muscles. Over time he had to be fed and washed like a baby; he couldn't do anything for himself. It was a very tough period. A month after Austen's birth, I went back to my job as an office manager at the South African Institute for Race Relations (SAIRR) in Mowbray to earn some money to help us get by. One of our neighbours looked after Austen two or three days a week and in between Clive also looked after her, even though he was sick. He was a positive person and always pushed himself to recover, but every two years he'd relapse.

We moved from Brooklyn into a garage in Ravensmead that we made homely before moving into a small Reconstruction and Development Programme (RDP) house in Delft that Clive qualified for. Our son Clive was born there on 22 November 1999. The twenty-four-square-metre houses were freestanding and ours was on a reasonably sized property so we could extend it. We built a kitchen and a bathroom with a toilet. I was still working at the SAIRR and Clive was self-employed, as he was boarded when he relapsed. He received a DG from the state for a while. I nursed him back to health after each relapse. I don't know how I got through that time, but thankfully our family and our Delft neighbours helped us.

At that stage, we had a Husky van and Clive transported children to and from crèche. He'd push himself even when he was unable to drive, and sometimes he'd ask our neighbour Marie Dirks to assist. She'd help him get into the van, pick up kids and open the door for them. Clive would always postpone going to hospital until the last moment. He persevered, trying his best to continue living a normal life each day. He'd been self-employed for some time when the owner of a security equipment store offered Clive the job of running, managing and maintaining all the company's buildings, and also building a large storage plant from scratch. Clive put in lots of late hours, explaining to me that he was doing it for us. I also began working for the company, doing office administration. We moved to a rental house in Wesley Street in Observatory, five minutes from the office. Clive loved his job and his clients depended on him. Old and new clients always phoned him specifically because they knew that he would sort out their transportation and storage problems.

We stayed in Observatory for a few years and felt as though we were moving forward in life. In 2004, we got a bond of R200 000 and bought a house in Rondevlei, where my children and I live today. Clive had been diagnosed in 1997, and he died in 2005. Towards the end he had deteriorated, but he wasn't bedridden.

A month after Clive died, I was told to leave the company. At the meeting with the director I explained that I had to continue working to support my family, but they had already employed a new manager after Clive passed away, and I was tossed out like an old rag. I felt that it was very cruel of them considering how much Clive contributed to building the company. When I asked about the benefits that Clive had always spoken about, I was told that there was nothing for me. I was on my own again, having to find a way to make ends meet.

I was at home for almost a year after that, trying to get odd jobs, such as taxiing people around, or doing renovations and painting with the assistance of Desmond Simons, who had worked for Clive. I pushed myself to create work and earn an income to pay outstanding school fees. Eventually, the school governing body told me that if I could not afford the fees I would have to take my children out of the school. I replied that I would not take them out. In the struggle we fought for good education for our children, and I felt strongly about their right to stay in this school. I kept them there and qualified for a partial fee exemption.

I then got a job as an administration clerk at Whiteheads, a paint company. I was trying to get back on my feet and I enjoyed working for this small company. The staff was very supportive and helpful, and I felt hopeful that my life was taking a turn for the better. After two and a half years there, in 2008, the company had to reduce the staff due to the economic slump, and I was retrenched. Once again, I was unemployed, staying at home and receiving benefits from my Unemployment Insurance Fund.

Then, in November 2009, Comrade Desmond Stevens, who was working at the Department of Agriculture, Forestry and Fisheries, contacted me about the department's anti-poaching presidential project, which provided employment to military veterans who were part of the armed struggle. The project kicked off with sixty of us that year. We received four months of training and a R2 000 stipend. I worked hard and got a certificate for best female student.

Gradually, we were employed on the project. We worked stints of two weeks away from home, followed by two weeks' rest. Some members of our group were inspectors from the old marine guard or the South African Police Service. They didn't readily accept us. From their perspective, we were intruding on their turf and taking over their jobs. Eventually they relaxed and realised we were all there to work and we all needed employment.

We mainly operated in the Overberg area, as there was a lot of abalone poaching going on there. Local people living in informal settlements told us that poaching had been their livelihood for years and that they ate from the sea, but we had to apply the law and stop illegal poaching, as they also sold abalone to the Chinese. We patrolled the coast day and night. It was dangerous work, as there were many incidents with armed poachers.

We worked in the Overberg for about four years. Spending two weeks away from home every month was challenging for me as a single parent. Thankfully, my friend and comrade Estelle Holtzman came to live with us and was a great help taking care of my kids while I was away. I hated not being there for them and having to deal with trying to be in two places at the same time.

When there were school functions and I had no money because we earned so little, I would sometimes hitchhike to Cape Town to be there.

For the first two years we earned R4 000 per month. Conflict arose when we discovered that we weren't paid for overtime. Time off became another conflict. We knew we had rights, and joining the National Health, Education and Allied Workers' Union (NEHAWU) could have helped, but only a few of us wanted to join, so it was hopeless. The living conditions at the base were also terrible. We slept in double bunks in an old police base with three dormitory rooms. There was no privacy whatsoever. Because one group stayed for two weeks while the other went home, we shared beds and facilities. The toilets and showers were outside and everybody had to use the communal kitchen to cook meals. Sometimes meat was provided for us, but communal cooking didn't work, so we decided to see to ourselves. A further challenge was that on payday the men in our team socialised in the township, and when they came back to the base they were rowdy. There were language barriers too. The isiXhosa-speakers made the effort to speak to us in Afrikaans and we were rightly asked why we couldn't learn isiXhosa. Racial tensions flared up from time to time. Coloured people were in the minority, and only around fifteen of the sixty team members were women.

We were not insured, which we found out when Gerard Waterwitch, Robbie's uncle, died after being swept off the pier by a huge wave and his family weren't compensated. Another colleague also died in the line of duty when his patrol bakkie rolled. That family lost their breadwinner and didn't get compensation either. We had several meetings with the department, but they refused to concede to our demands because we were not permanent staff. A few employees were unfairly dismissed and had to take up their matters through the Commission for Conciliation, Mediation and Arbitration (CCMA).

Over the next five years, our salaries increased by only R1 000, to R5 000. The permanent staff earned three times more. When we started, we'd been told that when we finished our training, our salary would be about R8 500, but that was an empty promise.

In 2013, the contract suddenly came to an end and we were left unemployed for six months. At the time, a contract with the Passenger Rail Agency of South Africa (PRASA) contract came up for security officers patrolling Metrorail trains. Some of our comrades took the opportunity. They didn't earn any better, and they didn't get the permanent positions they were promised.

After being home for six months, a few of us tried to hold meetings with the South African Military Veterans Association (SAMVA) to find out if they could help us resolve our employment issues. Some of us took the initiative to form a committee, and swore not to leave without a resolution. On Thursday 19 December 2013, the day before the department closed their offices for their end-of-year holiday, thirty of us went ahead with a march and held a sit-in in the office boardroom of the Department of Agriculture, Forestry and Fisheries. Representatives from the department came to see us, and we explained that we had tried to communicate with the department with no success, so this was our last measure. Our comrades on the ANC's Regional Executive Committee (REC) approached us too. 'You can't do this to our comrades in the department,' they complained. 'Disciplined comrades wouldn't do this.' But we were headstrong and steadfast.

'We came to Cape Town for a purpose,' we said. 'We are going to stand firm, because we haven't earned anything for six months, yet department officials earn lots of money and have secure posts.' We refused to move until we got our contracts. Officials called the police. They couldn't remove us, but they made sure we didn't damage anything. Finally, we were informed that Desmond Stevens and officials from his department were going to see us at noon the next day. We stayed in the boardroom all night and slept on the floor. The next morning we were served tea, coffee and biscuits, and had a meeting with Desmond and a few of the directors and comrades from the ANC REC and PAC leadership. They agreed to pay us part of our salary and we walked away with R4 000 each. They also said we could start work on Monday 6 January 2014. We demanded another meeting to see the contracts and talk about our salaries, which was agreed to.

At our first meeting in January 2014, Vernon Jacobs from the Department of Military Veterans' Skills Development for Job Creation was present. They urged us to start a cooperative because they wanted us to take over the project. We formed the Anti-Poaching Western Cape Military Veterans Association and took over the project as requested, but eventually failed, as we didn't get the support that was promised. We went back to working for a service provider, and we are still at the bottom end of the salary scale, with the company benefiting from the profits. After this ordeal, I realised that the struggle for benefits, health care and good free education rests on our individual efforts, when it should be a right for all who can't afford it. All of this took an emotional toll on me.

In March 2015, I barged into a meeting at which deputy minister of defence Kebby Maphatsoe was present. I had met him in December 2014 at the Coline, Ashley, Robbie and Anton (CARA) Memorial event, where I had approached him regarding the anti-poaching presidential project. I was finally granted a meeting with him a few days later to raise all the issues I had raised with the

SAMVA office over the years: our housing bonds, medical assistance for our dependants and for the mothers of those who died in the struggle, scholarships and the problems with the SAMVA office in Cape Town. I had all my issues lined up and raised them one by one. It was a big personal success for me. The department said it would assist me with housing benefits, and other matters are also being addressed. It has taken so long to sort out my grievances, but I finally got to the right people at the top, and there has been some progress. I stood up for my rights and I was successful.

We continue to remember our fallen comrades through the CARA memorialising project, which I started, with Gori's support, with the Williams, Fransch, Waterwitch and Kriel families when I returned from the Netherlands. The project fundraised to erect headstones on their graves at Maitland Cemetery. I hope that one day the doors will be opened for all combatants, making their life struggles easier; they fought for a long time and found that freedom wasn't free.

13

Dicki Meter

The Sentinel

Y OUR FIRST OPERATION is always nerve-wracking. Mine was the Southern Suburbs railway line. The South African Railway and Harbour Workers Union (SARHWU) was in a protracted battle for higher wages, and they had embarked on a strike. By blowing up the Southern Suburbs railway line, we would be sending a message to the government that MK supported the workers' struggle, forcing them to negotiate an acceptable settlement. I took Patrick 'Patty' Presence with me. The date was 15 December 1989, the night before my family and I were to go on holiday.

That night, I slipped away, picked up Patty, instructed him to get into the driver's seat and gave him directions. I had done reconnaissance throughout the week, so I knew exactly where to place the mini limpet mine, as well as my approach to the specific section of track that I would access through some broken fencing. When we got to Wittebome Station, there were people up and down the platform, so I moved the operation about a hundred metres further down the track.

I climbed over the fence and planted the limpet on the track, then climbed back over the fence and returned to the waiting getaway car. I had timed the limpet so that we'd have a few minutes to get out of the area, and I thought we'd hear the explosion as we drove away, but we didn't. That night, I was too worried about what might have happened to close my eyes, but in the morning we discovered that the operation had been successful; we'd just got out of there too quickly to hear it go off. After that, I felt a lot more at ease with the Russian-made weapons we used in MK, and was ready for the next assignment.

I was born on 5 December 1958 in Hout Bay. My family lived in a small house that had one bedroom, a lounge and a kitchen. Ten children and our parents lived in that three-room house. We had a number of fold-up beds, and at night every available space was used for sleeping. Although we were living like sardines, it had its benefits: being forced to share a small space and minimal resources brought us closer together.

My mother, Annie, was a factory worker. After she contracted TB, she stopped working. My father, Soma, was born in Hout Bay. He started going to sea from the age of fourteen and worked as a fisherman all his life. He was employed by a company called Oceana, which owned the house we lived in. The houses in our community were subsidised by the apartheid government to accommodate, control and enslave workers. As I understood it, if workers left Oceana's employment, they had to vacate their houses, so they had to accept whatever salary was offered to them to avoid being evicted. I believe the company also abused their power to force workers' children into employment on the factory floor or on the boats after they left school: if they found employment elsewhere, the family had to move out.

I never met my grandparents, but I've been told that my paternal grandfather, Rouche, came from India on a ship called the *R. Morrow* to work. The ship ran aground in Table Bay and the wreck was sold to someone who took it to Hout Bay, where it was later converted into a crayfish canning factory. My grandmother on my mother's side was born in Hout Bay and was of Khoisan descent. My maternal grandfather was Muslim, from the Bo-Kaap, and also a fisherman.

Before the Group Areas Act, in the years when my grandparents and parents grew up, people lived in zinc and wood houses in what would later become the Hout Bay central business district, close to the beach. The economy consisted mainly of fishing and a little farming, and the people were tradesmen and craftsmen, such as tailors and builders. The Group Areas Act disrupted the way people lived. Oceana built a hostel for black men on the beachfront in Hangberg – the only way black people could 'legally' live in the area.

My father was only fifty-five when he died; the life of a fisherman is tough. He raised eight daughters and two sons, and his one hope for us was that we'd empower ourselves through education so that we could sustain ourselves.

My father did not administer punishment; my mother did. She would grab the girls by the hair and stamp on them if she had to. Being a middle child had a lot of advantages: I was shielded by the older ones and I could hide among the younger ones, so I escaped most punishment. My father was strict, though. '*Ek praat net een keer*' (I only speak once) was something he often said, and when he said 'No', he meant it. My siblings and I had a more distant relationship with him due to his being away at sea so often. However, I have fond memories of him regularly taking us for walks in the mountains. In summer, we'd pick sour figs. While on the mountain, my father would teach us which roots and berries we could eat, how to harvest different kinds of flowers at different times of the year and how to care for the environment.

While growing up, I knew only a few white people. There was Sister Kraus, a Roman Catholic nun, and the white shop owners I encountered at the shops in the Hout Bay business district, where I went shopping with my mother. There were no supermarkets then, and the grocery stores were owned and managed by white people. There were also a few white people who worked with my father. They came to our house often, as my father was a skipper and therefore a paymaster, because Oceana gave the skippers the crew's wages to dole out. Most of his crew were coloured and black, though. Black fishermen stayed in the hostel, but two or three black skippers had family housing from Oceana. Their children went to my school, so there were isiXhosa mother-tongue speakers in my class, although they also spoke Afrikaans fluently.

When I was confronted with racism for the first time, I really could not understand why white people thought they were different and better. Race did not enter my mind except as an understanding that white people controlled everything – people and resources. We would see whites driving trucks with blacks in the back and an empty passenger seat. I could not understand how they could do this. Later on, when the state got tough about enforcing pass laws, I saw young white policemen chasing old African men in Hout Bay for their *dompasse* (pass books), and beating them up. These acts sparked an awareness of the injustice of what I saw around me.

My family belonged to the Anglican Church. We had a very strong spiritual foundation, which is still the case today, and we were raised without room for uncertainty: there *is* a God and we need to find His favour. We were expected to participate in all Sunday school activities. I had special shoes that I wore on Sundays, and these later became my school shoes.

St Peter the Fisherman, the Anglican church in the Hout Bay village, was donated by a settler family and was built from stone in the late 1800s or early 1900s. We did not go to the stone church, because it was reserved for white congregants. Our Sunday services were held at a crèche until St Simon's was built between the flats in the harbour, a measure used by the government to keep us in our segregated community.

Later, as a result of my activism, I joined the Methodist Church. The Anglican Church ran relief services for the homeless, but they would not open up their churches and facilities to people whose informal homes had been destroyed by apartheid officials under the pretext of squatter control. Only the Methodist Church did, so I stopped attending the Anglican Church and joined the Methodists.

Hout Bay was a very poor working-class community and people were not well educated. However, I think poor people tend to look out for one another. There was a lot of caring and sharing; mothers in the community were mothers to all children. Hout Bay was very safe. Everyone knew each other. The area was rich in its own culture and in the natural environment too.

When I was growing up, the community had access to lots of seafood. When my father came home from the sea, he always brought fish with him. My mother cooked every day. She made the nicest soups and curries, and did roasts on Sundays. The fish heads would be steamed with vegetables and spices to make *viskopsop*. For the lean season, we cured snoek in layers of salt to prevent it from perishing. The salt snoek was called *moetjies*, and my mother would cook a very tasty pot of food made with *moetjies* and cabbage. When snoek was in season, we dried it like biltong in rows and rows on the washing lines for about three weeks, and then we would store it. Every household had dried, salted fish that would last the whole off-season. We could trade the *moetjies* too, for vegetables and canned fruit from the farmworkers who came to the harbour from Wellington, Paarl and Ceres.

I met my lifelong friend and comrade, Patty Presence, at crèche. We started school at Hout Bay Primary at the age of five. The principal, Mr Richard Manuel, was a radio presenter who was involved in the arts and various community activities. He started the Boy Scouts in the harbour community, and I became an active member. While I was in primary school, a brand new school called Sentinel Secondary was built. It went up to Standard 8. Our primary school was turned into a playground, which was later developed for housing. I attended Sentinel Secondary School and then went to Wittebome High in Wynberg.

I remained a member of the Boy Scouts throughout high school, and in 1975 I went to the 14th World Scout Jamboree in Lillehammer, Norway. It was my first opportunity to travel overseas and be away from home. Going overseas right before the big conscientising of 1976 was an eye-opener. We travelled from Cape Town to Johannesburg by train, where we linked up with the rest of the Jamboree contingent – scouts from across the country. On the train trip we were confronted with apartheid laws when we could not use the same facilities at the stations. In London I saw multiracialism for the first time – racially mixed groups engaging socially and mixed couples walking hand in hand – and I was amazed. It made me aware that apartheid was wrong. I am so thankful that the Jamboree took place in 1975, as I probably would not have gone if it was in 1976, due to my political activism that year.

I matriculated in 1976, a very troublesome year for the schools. Four students from Hout Bay became student leaders at Wittebome High. After that, the school was not keen on taking more students from Hout Bay. The four main 'troublemakers' were William Stevens, Wally Johnstone, Kariem Ibrahim and me. There was also Edward Damons, from Graaff-Reinet, and Kenny van Zyl, who both operated with us.

With the student uprisings, we were really pushed to understand what exactly was happening in our country. We went to meetings at Oaklands High School in Lansdowne, and Alexander Sinton and Belgravia High School in Athlone. We became part of an interschools committee and we regularly addressed the students at our school, taking over assembly on Monday mornings to report on political developments in other schools.

We began defying the teachers, dictating what time the school closed and the programme for the day. In September 1976, the principal suspended me, and student leaders mobilised the school in solidarity. Incidentally, 80 per cent of the students who participated in the 1976 schools boycott passed matric – due to our determination to get an education – while many who didn't participate didn't pass.

During the December school holidays, the security police visited one of our Hout Bay comrades. Word reached us that the security branch were looking for us as well. We wondered if the principal of Wittebome High was working with them. The next day, Wally, William, Kenny, Edward and I decided that we couldn't stay in Hout Bay. We thought it would be best to leave the country, so we packed our bags and collected what little money we could get. A teacher took us to Worcester, where we slept for one night, and the following day – Christmas Eve – we hitchhiked to Uitenhage, heading for the border.

That night, a patrol van pulled up next to us and policemen searched our bags, which were covered with stickers sporting human rights slogans. They loaded us into their van and took us to a police station, where they phoned Snyman, a security policeman they bragged was responsible for pushing an activist out of a fifth-floor window of the Sanlam Building in Port Elizabeth. Snyman pitched up to interrogate us.

We were taken outside one at a time and they were very abusive and aggressive. When they questioned me on my school and my background, I told Snyman that I often took these kinds of trips with the Boy Scouts and that the stickers on my bag were environmental slogans. It turned out that Snyman was in the Boy Scouts too. We started talking about scouting, and I took the opportunity to use this common ground to get my friends and me out of the fix we were in. When he brought me back to the others, he said we could go.

We were very surprised and grateful, but the other policemen were not at all happy. Snyman took us away in a police van and, to our relief, we were dropped on the road outside Uitenhage. We thought we were being tricked.

That night, we stayed in the bush, and on Christmas Day we set off to Graaff-Reinet. We had no food or money, and when we arrived in the town we were told to go home. We'd met up with some guys who seemed to know what was going on and why we were there, and one of them said, 'This mission of yours is unplanned; no one outside knows you are coming, so it's best that you go back home.' He was right. We didn't know how to make contact with the ANC outside of South Africa, we didn't know anyone in the ANC and, in fact, we knew very little about the ANC, period. All we knew was that we had to do something and that the ANC camps were outside the country. Despite having come so far, we decided to turn back.

Fortunately, our hosts in Graaff-Reinet knew of a guy who was driving to Cape Town, and we got a lift home with him. We had to cook up a story as to why we'd left in the first place, as we didn't want to say that we thought the police were after us. My parents were relieved to see me, and I was happy to see them too, but they were furious that we had left.

On our return from our adventure, my friends and I were very unsure about what we wanted to do. There was no structured community life in Hout Bay besides what the churches, the school and the senior citizens' club offered, and there was a lull in political activity in the area during the three years following the 1976 uprisings. With our parents unable to afford much in terms of tertiary education, I became involved in sport. We formed the Blue Birds Rugby Club, as well as soccer clubs.

When these clubs were founded, we had no sports field. We played barefoot on sand dunes. We only played on grass when we got invitations to play away, but other than that we didn't know what it was like to play on a proper pitch or wear football boots. There was cohesion and unity in these clubs though. They offered a structured way for young people to get together and live out their talents for the first time. By participating in these clubs, members also learnt how a democratic organisation should operate, which served as an introduction to organisational work in the community.

While I was growing up in the late 1960s and early 1970s, people classified as coloured were forced out of the areas in Hout Bay that were proclaimed 'white', and as a result, our harbour community doubled in size. With this new state of affairs came drugs. At first it was just marijuana, which did not pose a big problem, but when the harder drugs came in, users engaged in crime to feed their habits.

There were other social challenges too. When the government moved people to the Hout Bay harbour community, it put pressure on the limited housing owned by the fishing companies and the Divisional Council of the Cape. The Divisional Council only built flats for the people forcibly removed from the rest of Hout Bay to the harbour area, and had no development plans to accommodate the growth of existing families. Before the flats were built, everyone lived close to the beach and along the Disa River, as far as Orangekloof. Young families found themselves doubled up in parents' houses, and eventually every housing unit had two, three or even four families living in it. The lack of privacy contributed to an increase in domestic violence and child abuse, and the youth were often forced out onto the street, where they were exposed to gangsterism and drugs. In one instance, twenty-seven people were living in a two-bedroom house. They explained that the 'corridor family' and 'kitchen family' could only go to bed after the 'lounge and bed-room families' had gone to bed. The corridor and kitchen families had to be up early in the morning to make way for the four families to cook.

There was change in the fishing industry too. More factories sprang up. The indigenous people's economy was destroyed and taken over by Afrikaners assisted by the National Party government. Fishing licenses and quotas were allocated only to whites as part of apartheid's affirmative action plan, which ensured that whites owned and controlled the industry while using indige-nous non-white people as cheap labour. In this way, and with the control that white-owned businesses had over housing allocations, they were able to expand rapidly. Oceana owned the biggest stake in the fishing industry and raped our fishing resources. After the boom, the industry slowed down. With white affirmative action opening up many new opportunities, smaller fishing companies sold their businesses to bigger ones, causing many factories to close down. More than 700 fish-factory jobs were lost and many more were lost on the boats. This was a huge contributor to the social ills experienced at that time, which continue today.

In 1980, I read my first *Grassroots* newspaper. I was very surprised to learn that civic protests were happening in communities such as Steenberg, Elsies River and Lotus River, as well as other areas. I don't know how *Grassroots* reached Hout Bay or how it got into my house. The only local newspaper then was the *Sentinel*, which we picked up in the white business area and which covered activities, events and social issues in the white community. After the arrival of *Grassroots*, my Wittebome friends and I got together. 'Did you see this paper?' we asked each other. 'Things are happening out there!' At the time, Shirley Gunn was a community worker for the National Institute for

Crime Prevention and Rehabilitation of the Offender (NICRO), and, as a result of our curiosity, we ended up meeting her.

One of our first real engagements was when Shirley introduced us to the General Workers Union. From then on, serious consideration was given to how we should organise ourselves. Shirley scheduled a meeting at the Methodist church and invited all local organisations, including representatives from the Food and Allied Workers Union (FAWU), the Pippa Duffy Drama Group, and us. After that meeting, the Hout Bay Youth Movement was founded, and in 1981 the Hout Bay Action Committee (HBAC) was formed to deal with housing issues. At that time, the pro-state Hout Bay Civic Association, which claimed to represent the people of Hout Bay at Divisional Council Management Committee (MANCOM) meetings, was operating and chaired by the principal of the primary school. Looking back, I think principals were probably expected to act as extensions of the security police, whether by choice or force. MANCOM did everything in its power to keep progressive organisations out, and we believed that it had been formed to pacify local residents. HBAC was formed in opposition, as an alternative community voice. That was the beginning of the end for the apartheid-puppet Hout Bay Civic Association.

The formation of HBAC and the youth movement set me on the road to activism. For the first time I was linking up with other anti-apartheid activists, discussing politics and holding workshops to find solutions to certain issues, as well as coming up with visions for South Africa. I was in a critical stage of my life, becoming a young adult, and was finally among people who shared my values, striving for the same goals of openness, sharing and caring. However, it also isolated me from some friends and family who were not willing to take a more active role in the struggle.

I found myself being pushed to take the lead. When I got involved in youth, civic and other progressive organisations, this work replaced all other activities, and activism became my life. All my spare time was devoted to building community organisations through which members could take control of their lives. My priority was to build people's political consciousness – within my family, among my friends and in the community – in order to take the struggle forward. I engaged with people everywhere I went – on public transport, in church, on the sportsfield and in schools. We brazenly started to wear struggle-branded clothing bearing Mandela's image and ANC slogans, even though the ANC was banned. We reproduced many of these images on T-shirts for the Hout Bay Youth Movement. The youth would bring their T-shirts and we printed them in members' backyards. They'd be worn everywhere, adding to the visibility of our movement.

My father had passed away in 1980, before the formalisation of HBAC. Our first rent-boycott march was on 13 May 1981, his birthday. There was a slight drizzle that day, and it felt like my father was giving his blessing and assurances to care for me. It made me feel stronger and more confident. My family was aware of my involvement in the community, or 'politics', as they referred to it. They were cautious at first, and gave their support passively. Later, this support became active when we openly challenged the authorities.

That first community march in 1981 was significant for several reasons, one being that government propaganda promoted the idea that people in coloured communities couldn't work together. The march proved the opposite. HBAC also encouraged workers living in our community to join progressive trade unions, including FAWU, the Commercial Catering and Allied Workers Union (CCAWU) and the National Union of Metalworkers of South Africa (NUMSA). They would even organise the community to collect and donate food for striking workers if the need arose. We were building unity in action, living out FAWU's slogan that an injury to one is an injury to all.

HBAC was eventually affiliated to the Cape Areas Housing Action Committee (CAHAC), a metro-wide federation of civic associations in Cape Town. This broke down the isolation the Hout Bay community felt, being geographically separated from the Cape Flats. We made our first leaflets by hand; even the illustrations were hand-drawn. We had no access to computers, so we photocopied them at night at the Divisional Council offices where I'd started working in 1982, and distributed them the next day. We were very busy.

This was a very difficult financial period for my family. After I left school, there was no money to support any further academic studies and I couldn't find work anywhere. If an employer looked at your senior certificate and saw that you left school in 1976, it was the end of the interview. There were no resources for the community activities I got involved in; resources had to come from the people running those organisations, which added to our personal financial struggles. In 1980, I worked at the Hout Bay Civic Centre for a short while, and then started working shifts at the Divisional Council Fire Station as a radio operator.

It was around this time that I decided to do a drafting course at the Bellville Technikon. In order to fit classes into my busy schedule, I would leave directly from work after a night shift, take public transport to Bellville, and then return from the technikon for work. There was barely time to touch base at home, except to get a change of clothes and grab the flask of black coffee and sandwiches that my mother prepared for me. Needless to say, it caught up with me physically. I had to drop something. I couldn't drop work, nor could I drop my community activities. So, despite my interest in the course at the technikon, I dropped out.

The launch of the UDF at the Rocklands Civic Centre on 20 August 1983 was a major event attended by 20 000 people. Hout Bay residents travelled in buses to the UDF launch as members of CAHAC, which was affiliated to the UDF. The Cape Youth Congress (CAYCO) had been formed a month earlier, in July 1983, and the Hout Bay Youth Movement was a member of CAYCO, so the youth went along to the UDF launch in their numbers too.

The formation of regional and national structures in various civic organisations linked communities sharing common struggles. People would often say, 'Ag, we can't do anything, we're only few', but this changed when residents began to see the power and strength of united action. Collective action motivated many people to become part of the struggle against apartheid. We learnt new methods of engaging the enemy state, and we drew strength from each other.

When CAHAC was formed in the early 1980s, only a few areas were focused on the issue of access to residential land. CAHAC mainly organised in areas with established council housing schemes and the issues they faced were rent-related. The major challenge facing us in Hout Bay was the shortage and lack of access to affordable housing, resulting in people building their own informal houses. These people were labelled 'illegal squatters', and the informal housing areas became a regular target for evictions and destruction by the authorities. HBAC would facilitate legal representation for arrested community members at the courts, and provided materials such as plastic sheets and wooden poles so that people could rebuild shelters that had been demolished by government officials.

I don't think CAHAC was ready for HBAC. Although Hout Bay also had housing, rent and maintenance-related issues, we insisted that we talk about the land question because people who occupied informal houses didn't share the kinds of housing issues that CAHAC was concerned with. There were a few CAHAC meetings where HBAC tried to put land struggles on the agenda, but these issues were never discussed. We then became aware that representatives from Bloekombos in Kraaifontein were also struggling to put their land struggle on the table in meetings with the UDF, and that the UDF wasn't ready to deal with this issue either. The collective support that we banked on was absent, although individuals like Angela Andrews and Henk Smith from the Legal Resources Centre assisted us, and Advocate Essa Moosa often went to the courts to defend local people who were arrested for illegal squatting.

On one such occasion, Essa met colleagues who remarked: 'It must be a big thing if you came personally to attend.'

'Yes,' he replied, 'it *is* a big thing.'

When Comrade Oscar Mpetha was arrested in 1985, and when Crossroads went up in flames in 1986 and the struggle for land and the challenges of informal settlements finally came into the spotlight, HBAC had already been involved in the land struggle for several years. During this time, we were called on to assist other informal settlements facing similar evictions in areas such as Noordhoek, Redhill in Simon's Town, Vrygrond, Elsies River and even Lawaaikamp in George.

Around this time, I married Shantaal Adams, who also became an activist. There was little choice if she was going to be with me – she realised that the struggle was my life. Our first child, Fidel Che, was born in 1984.

In 1985, two Hout Bay students, Rodney van Neel and Reagan Cloete, were detained. During December of that year, we organised a campaign for their release. There was a candlelight vigil in solidarity with all detainees, and we created pamphlets. While we were distributing the pamphlets in the community, the neighbourhood kids, who loved working with us, took handfuls of pamphlets and ran ahead. The police picked one of them up and asked where they'd got the pamphlets. The child must have innocently replied 'Dicki'.

A police van pulled up as I arrived at my mother's house. We had an outside toilet on the stoep, so I ran into the toilet and pulled my sister in with me. 'Sit on the toilet pot,' I told her, 'and if anyone knocks on the door, you must undress, open the door a little and then kick it closed. Say to them, "Can't you see I'm on the toilet?"'

When the police knocked on the door this is exactly what she did. They searched the rest of the house and left defeated. We phoned the local Catholic priest, who gave me a lift out of the area. I wore a black scarf like a nun. When we were stopped at a roadblock near Bakoven, the priest wound his window down a little way.

'Yes?' he said.

'Oh, sorry Father!' the police replied, and waved us on.

A few nights later, the police found me at my place in Lotus River. For three months, I was detained under the state of emergency regulations. Although I wasn't detained in terms of Section 29 of the Internal Security Act, I was kept in isolation in the Wynberg Police Station cells for a long time before I was transferred to Victor Verster Prison via Caledon Square Police Station. Patty Presence was also being detained at Victor Verster at the same time.

I was put in an empty section with three other detainees, and after a few weeks they transferred us to the bigger A-section. The cells on the first and second floors of the jail were all full. The third floor was only half full, and yet they kept the four of us together on the fifth floor on our own. Of the three other detainees, I only knew Comrade Mandla, a trade unionist. The other two, a gangster and a Rasta, were unknown to both of us, and we suspected that these guys were informants locked up with us to monitor our conversations.

The security police interrogated me regularly while in detention. There were two things I could do: lie down and cry or stand firm and fight. I was scared and unsure of what was going to happen to me, but posing that question to myself helped. Once I had decided to stand firm and fight, the next question was what action I could actually take. I told myself that there were again two options: I could be uncooperative and let them do whatever they wanted with me, or I could play a psychological game with them.

I ended up doing a bit of both. I acted disorientated and, in time, most of the uniformed policemen at Wynberg Police Station, both white and non-white, thought I was there for no reason. I managed to win their sympathy. All of them were prepared to do small things for me, such as bringing me newspapers or food. On the other hand, the security police thought I was very stupid. I pretended not to recognise them or know which day of the week it was. I would bungle their questioning by acting like I didn't know what was going on, but I'd be laughing in my heart as they fell for my strategy. They played good cop, bad cop, but that didn't work because I seemed to want nothing from the good cop and everything from the bad cop.

The security police showed me a lot of photographs of MK operatives, some of whom I knew but hadn't worked with closely. The security police were adamant I knew Ngconde Balfour, Tony Yengeni and his wife, Lumka. They regularly questioned me about Shirley Gunn, Johnny Issel, Wilfred Rhodes, Trevor Manuel, Joe Marks, Cecyl Esau, Neville van der Rheede and Leon Scott. It was tough, but I stood my ground. Then, out of the blue, Patty Presence and I were released.

Nobody was ever detained as a result of my detention and interrogation. As difficult as it was, the battle that I picked and the way that I chose to fight that battle was right for me, and ultimately for the people around me as well.

My detention in 1985 happened during the height of the land struggle in Hout Bay. Community members had become openly defiant and no longer erected shacks out of sight high up on the mountain, but in places visible from the main road. The courage they displayed when fighting back was amazing. Their motto was: 'You can break our shacks today and lock us up, but we'll come back and rebuild them.'

While I was in detention, the provincial administration requested a meeting with community leaders to discuss access to land. I think the timing was strategic: the administration had probably realised that they couldn't break the spirit of the people of Hout Bay, so they tried another tactic: having me detained to take me out of circulation. However, the communities refused to meet with the administration until I had been released. Two weeks after my release, I received a message that a meeting had been set up. White home-owners were putting pressure on the government to sort out the 'squatter issue', and by then the informal settlement community was openly defiant. Even the police and the officials whose job it was to break down shacks were scared to go into these communities. The white property owners and Hout Bay Ratepayers Association were very worried and thought they could regain control by putting pressure on the government to do something – the main reason the government agreed to negotiate with us. The eventual agreement was that a forestry site belonging to the municipality would be given over to the informal settlement community.

By then, the white people of Hout Bay regarded me as enemy number one. In a meeting with the chairperson of the ratepayers association, I had to make an effort to put the man at ease.

'Look, we don't want to burn down your houses,' I said at the start of the conversation. 'We just don't want you to burn down ours.'

About twenty minutes into the discussion, the chairman said: 'You know what, Dicki? I was so scared to come and see you because everyone painted you as a terrorist. I expected a *huge* guy, and here you are, small and gentle, and you don't spit fire.'

This brought me to a powerful realisation: our people were so under-resourced, and yet we instilled fear in those who wanted to cross swords with us in our struggles against apartheid.

I was recruited into the Ashley Kriel Detachment in 1988. For me, the appeal of MK wasn't only the military operation; the organisation had other objectives, such as making the country ungovernable, campaigning to support MK operatives, and building community organisations in order to strengthen centres of peoples' power, which I was already involved in. I obviously had a very public profile at the time, though, and I was under intense security police surveillance because of my human rights activism and land struggles in particular. My primary concern was therefore how strong I would be if the security police captured me. Not only would they want to detain me, but everyone connected to me too. Having considered the responsibilities and consequences, I joined MK to serve as commander of the Southern Suburbs unit. In time, I recruited others to work with me. My commander was Anton Fransch, who also trained me.

My MK training was very different to that of a conventional soldier fighting on the battlefield. I was to be an urban guerrilla, and my training centred on caching military hardware safely, finding targets, doing reconnaissance, working with MPM and SPM limpet mines and getting out of the way quickly after executing operations.

My second detention came after Mandela's release in 1990. I was busy planning a demonstration around access to land in the city. We were going to take to the streets near Parliament and present our memorandum there. The demonstration was planned for 6 April, Van Riebeeck's Day, the day the NP celebrated the anniversary of the arrival of the Dutch in the Cape. A few days before the march there was a terrible fire on Chapman's Peak. I had buried three large metal boxes of weapons on the mountain, and as the fire became more intense, I became increasingly worried: could the intensity of the heat trigger the explosives, potentially injuring or killing people nearby? I had worked at the fire station, so I knew the access route. I decided to retrieve the three boxes when the fire had subsided and put them in a safe place. However, I couldn't find Comrade Patty or Comrade James Madikiza to help me. Comrade Claude van Neel wasn't around either, and while Comrades Solomon 'Manni' Julies and Hilton Moses were on my list of potential recruits to call, I decided against them. In the absence of Patty and James, I considered another comrade, Cecil Nomqala, from the Eastern Cape. He and Comrade Kenny Tokwe had been introduced to me by his mother after they were shot by the police and badly injured, and I had taken them to a doctor in Grassy Park. I picked up Cecil at his workplace – the BP garage on Victoria Road in Hout Bay – and we drove to Chapman's Peak. I instructed him to stay in the car – a white Toyota Cressida with a large dent in the fender – to be on the lookout for strange movements and alert me if there were any. I retrieved one of the three very heavy metal boxes and carried it to the mouth of a tunnel that ran underneath the road, then went back for the second box. While I was busy taking out the second box, four firefighters came up the pathway towards me. I didn't know any of them and they didn't know me. I knew I was in trouble.

They demanded to see the contents of the box. I had to think fast. 'Ek kan vir julle help en julle kan vir my help,' I said. (I can help you and you can help me.) I took out my wallet. I had R150 on me and said they could have the R150 if they helped me carry the box. I told them that the box was full of papers and I had been asked to fetch it for the ANC. After a short discussion among themselves, they agreed to help me. They carried the box to the mouth of the tunnel and, because they had seen the first box there, I decided to ask them to get the third box out as well.

I let the firefighters carry the boxes to the car, indicating to Comrade Cecil to hide his face. The four men put the boxes in the car and Comrade Cecil and I drove off. I realised that I had to cover my tracks quickly because the firemen could start talking, so I dropped off Comrade Cecil, went home, took out the boxes and cleaned them, checked the contents and stored them in the broken-down car standing in my mother's driveway. I intended to cache them properly the next day, but before I had a chance to do so, the police came looking for me.

I was apprehended at the advice office in the Casa Del Mar building. When I saw the four firefighters with the police, I knew I was busted. The police said that when they heard the suspect had driven off in a badly dented car, they knew it was me. While the police searched the office, I gave loud, seemingly innocent instructions to the comrades about work they had to complete that morning. Those instructions were coded: I was really telling them to get word out to the AKD. I then got up to go to the toilet. Claude was streetwise and immediately followed me. I instructed him to get to my house and clean up, and then to connect with Patty and James to cache the boxes. Soon afterwards, the security police told me they were taking me home to search the house, and I cooperated. By the time we arrived, Claude had already removed anything incriminating. I was then taken to Wynberg Police Station and locked up in a cell. Meanwhile, Comrade Moeka Ismail helped Claude and Patty to move and cache the guns and explosives.

While I was in the Wynberg Police Station cells, I heard through the security police that Mark Henry was in custody. Just five months previously, Anton had taken me through final routine checks of the AK-47 and limpets, and informed me that someone had deserted the AKD safe house. On 17 November 1989, two weeks after I'd seen him, Anton was killed by the security forces. I assumed the security police were going to ask me about Mark, but they didn't. Instead, they asked me about Anton, whether or not I had known Ashley Kriel and whether I knew Shirley Gunn, Tony Yengeni and many other comrades. I told the cops I knew nothing.

I was held under Section 29 in the Wynberg Police Station cells for about three months. A series of security policemen interrogated me, among them Jeffrey Benzien, Ashley Kriel's killer. I played the same psychological game I'd used the first time I was detained, and they all thought I was the stupidest person they had ever picked up. Eventually, they seemed to believe my story and I was released.

When I decided to be a member of MK it was not because I liked war, but because I wanted peace. My intention was to contribute as much as possible to achieving liberation. Being part of MK was stressful and challenging, but looking back I can say that I'm glad I kept on and finished the race. People generally weren't surprised when they learnt that I was part of MK, given the intensity of my activism.

After the first national elections in 1994, a transition process for local government was negotiated. In the interim before the local government elections, the previous administration ran local government, but there was no guarantee that the apartheid-era municipalities would deliver services to all residents. Transitional political heads were appointed, consisting of 50 per cent apartheid-era politicians and 50 per cent struggle activists from civic organisations, trade unions, the ANC and other political organisations. In Hout Bay we had a very dynamic and transparent process to choose our local non-statutory representatives. The transition was discussed in a series of public meetings at the local civic centre, and all these meetings were packed to capacity. Even though they took place in Hangberg, members from all the informal settlements were present.

The agreed-upon process was that the public – specifically Hout Bay residents who could not vote before 1994 – could nominate candidates for the transition period. An open voting process would follow and seats would be allocated according to the outcome of the vote. The voting roll had to include candidates from the different geographic and demographic communities in Hout Bay. But then we heard that only one seat was allocated for the Hout Bay community in that Hout Bay Transitional Council, as the PAC and other organisations had taken up the rest of the 50 per cent of allocated seats. Neither the ANC nor the CAHAC representatives would grant us an audience, and we eventually had to threaten to disrupt the process should they continue to ignore us. We then persisted at the metro negotiations until they agreed to allocate three out of six seats to local organisations: one seat to Hangberg, a working-class area; one to Hout Bay Heights, a middle-class area; and one to the informal settlements. The remaining seats were allocated to the PAC, the Western Cape Civic Association (WCCA) and the Informal Settlement Movement. I received seven out of the twelve votes on the Transitional Council on my nomination as mayor and was elected as mayor of Hout Bay for the duration of the interim period.

At my inauguration, I announced the scrapping of all rental arrears and placed a moratorium on evictions. The officials, many of whom had worked for the old provincial administration, were fuming, claiming it to be illegal. But we were going to change those laws.

By the time the first local government elections came around in 1996, I was ready to step out of public life. I thought I had completed my task; we now had a democracy that needed to run its course. However, the community felt strongly that I should be a candidate in the local government elections, and there was a contingent of leaders in the Western Cape, including Dullah Omar, pressurising me to stand, as the ANC needed people to lead and train newly elected councillors. Eventually I conceded. Seven municipalities in the Cape Metro contested the elections. I was contesting in the South Peninsula Municipality. Out of twenty-nine wards contested in this municipality, the ANC only won one – mine.

It was a four-year term, from 1996 to 2000. I earned R2000 a month, which could not even cover my travelling costs to municipal meetings. The municipality did not make any resources available for constituency consultation, and we had to fight to get access to municipal halls for constituency meetings. Every Wednesday I had an open consultation evening where community members could register complaints. Line upon line of people came with their challenges and problems. I also had a report-back meeting every month, alternating between the harbour and Imizamo Yethu communities.

I was overwhelmed. I was not in charge of the council and I couldn't interfere in the administration. I served my term to the best of my ability, but I decided not to stand for public office elections again. Since then, the ANC has been unable to win the Hout Bay ward.

In 2010, there were violent clashes between evicted informal housing residents and the Cape Town Metro Police when the City of Cape Town evicted many families and obtained a court order to resettle them. My political consciousness did not allow me to do nothing and I once again got involved in the community's struggle for access to land in Hout Bay for working-class people. There's still unfinished business for me there: the unequal distribution of land has never been resolved. People of the harbour and Imizamo Yethu are living on land that is overcrowded, and there are no plans to de-densify these areas and develop new sites in Hout Bay for working-class people. I believe that the government needs to expropriate land to develop housing for working-class families. I became involved in the struggle to build a better life for all. We have a democracy now, but our people remain poor. The government can do a lot more. Nevertheless, we enjoy equal access to opportunities, so it's up to each individual to take advantage of this democracy we enjoy.

The struggle for equality in South Africa has consumed most of my life and, dare I say, at a price. There has been little compensation in return. I went through the demobilisation process, and I applied for a special pension but never received a response, not even an acknowledgement letter. However, I do at least receive medical support from 2 Military Hospital in Wynberg.

My decision to get involved in the struggle was never about personal gain. I wanted everyone to have a better life, where everyone is free. I've got four children: Fidel Che, who was born in 1984; Loriyaan, born in 1990; Ashanti, born in 1994; and Leejay, born in 1995. I now have two grandsons too – Raul and Rafael – and a granddaughter, Farrah. I want to spend the last years of my life watching them grow into young men and women, equipped to take advantage of the opportunities presented by this hard-fought battle for a society in which they can live their lives to the fullest.

14

Patrick Presence

Loyalty Deep as the Ocean

I SAW MY FIRST AK-47 at Dicki Meter's house. He approached me in 1989 and asked if I was ready to work for MK. I was more than ready. I had heard about people leaving South Africa to fight apartheid, and I told myself that I would fight too. I wanted to leave the country, and I would have if I'd had someone to go with me, but Dicki told me that there were MK comrades in town.

The first military training I received was also from Dicki: handling an AK-47, hand grenades and limpet mines. My combat name was Samuel; Dicki's was Reggie. My first and only operation took place in December 1989, when we blew up the railway line near Wittebome Station. I remained in the car and Dicki planted the limpet mine. I wasn't scared; I'm not a fearful person.

My father's name was Arthur, but some people called him Attie. I remember very little about him, or the harbour community, called Texas, where we lived then. He drowned when I was very young. I was born on 31 March 1958 and he died in 1962. I have memories of running to him when he came back from the sea. He'd pick me up and give me some fruit from his fishing basket. Many years after my father died, I'd walk down Karbonkel Road in Hout Bay Harbour and have visions of him drowning at sea. I was never able to make peace with his death. When I was in school, I couldn't concentrate on what the teachers were saying because my mind wasn't there; I was always thinking about my father drowning.

When my father passed away, my family split up. I was only four, and I was sent to live with one of my grandfathers. My paternal grandfather's name was Jan, but he was known as Johnny. He was from a farm in Ceres. My father's side of the family is of Khoisan descent. My maternal grandfather's name was Karl Adam Meisenheimer, and the community knew him as Charlie. His father was German and his mother was Indian. Both my grandfathers wanted me to live with them, and they ended up fighting over it. I can still remember them shouting at each other.

Eventually, I went to live with my grandfather Johnny and my grandmother Christine, while my mother and my little sisters stayed with her parents. We all lived in council cottages, just one street apart, so I spent time in both houses, although the two families didn't get along. When I came home from school, I would change, eat and then go over to visit my other grandmother.

My mother married another man when I was still young. As a child I thought he was unkind to her, but as I grew up I realised he was only teasing. He was a big man and my mother was a small woman, but she was quick to raise her fists. He would never have lifted a finger to hurt her, though.

Dicki Meter and I attended crèche together. I found Dicki crying on the first day and I said that I would take care of him, although he tells a different story. After a year at crèche I went to Hout Bay Primary. Mr Manuel was the principal of the school and he was also our scoutmaster. He was a good man, and it was he who brought the Sea Scouts to Hout Bay. As many of our fathers were often at sea, he taught us the kinds of life skills we would have got from them, such as how to build a fire. When I was about twelve years old, Mr Manuel took us to the Cosy Corner restaurant in Wynberg. It was my first time eating in a restaurant and I wondered, 'Is this how rich people live?'

I remember a particular bus journey with my grandmother, when I was in primary school. There were empty seats in the front of the bus but she insisted on standing. 'Grandma,' I said, 'there are seats in the front. You can sit there.'

'Be quiet,' she whispered. 'The seats are for white people.' I didn't understand, so I persisted. I wanted to know who the white people were. 'The women sitting there,' she said softly. 'The seats are for them. Now keep quiet. No more questions.'

This and an incident on the beach made me very scared of white people. I had gone to the beach by myself and crossed over the Disa River mouth. On the other side, a white man appeared from the bush with a whip in his hand. 'You damn *hotnot!*' he shouted at me. I panicked, jumped back over the river mouth and fled home. I could not understand why the man had threatened me like that – I didn't know how I could have done anything wrong. At home, I told my grandmother what had happened. She wanted to *moer* me because we weren't allowed on that side of the beach. We had to stay on the harbour side of the river mouth, but I was young and didn't understand; there weren't any signboards yet. From that day on, I didn't like white people and I was very angry with them. As a young teenager, I wanted to kill them all – not my grandfather, though; the *other* white people.

I had many friends at primary school. Dicki was – and still is – my best friend. We were in crèche together, in school together, in the struggle together and in jail together.

Sea Scouts was great. We especially enjoyed camping away from Hout Bay, which happened twice a year. The first time I went on a camp it was to Gilray Camp in Grassy Park, a residential area surrounded by bush. We pitched the heavy army-style canvas tent with its huge, heavy centre poles in the bush and camped there for about a week. Akela Tina was the Cub Scouts' leader and I was Tina's favourite cub.

I started playing sport in school, and this helped me take my mind off my father's death. I enjoyed playing rugby and soccer, and I played in three soccer teams. I would play in the third team game, then come off, play in the second team game, come off and then play in the first team game. Three games in a row, all in one day.

I was probably twelve years old when Dicki, Samuel and I started the Eagle Stars soccer club, which still exists. We also started the Bonny Boys. In one of our meetings, I told the players that Bonny Boys wasn't a good name, so we proposed that everyone think of a suitable name for our club and bring suggestions to the next meeting, where the new name would be chosen. After soccer practice that day, I walked past Bay View Road and it struck me that that was a great name for our club. The name I proposed was chosen and we became the Bayview Rovers. The club kept its name in later years and still plays in the Wynberg League. Soccer took up a big space in my life, and I became something of a local legend. I was a very enthusiastic player, and I have a scar from breaking my hand when I landed awkwardly after a bicycle kick.

Besides playing soccer, I was also a regular spectator. The first game I watched was at Hartleyvale Stadium, and I went with my grandfather Charlie and his friend Oupatjie. I was about nine. There were thousands of people watching – whites and blacks. There were no orderly queues when you entered Hartleyvale Stadium, and you could easily get crushed as people pushed and stampeded to get in through the narrow turnstile at the entrance. Inside, the white section took up three quarters of the stadium, while we sat in the smaller section apart from them and on top of each other. Some of us stood throughout the game while the whites had nice seats. On our side of the stadium, the guys smoked dagga pipes. There was so much smoke that it looked like fires were burning. The police were present, but our people were cautious and put out their pipes and joints when the police walked through the stands. None of this bothered me though – I was there to watch soccer.

White clubs like Hellenic and Cape Town City played at Hartleyvale. At the time, all the has-been English football players would come to Cape Town to play for these clubs. My favourite team was Cape Town City, but I couldn't play for them because I was black. There were black teams then, but they didn't have stadiums that I knew of. They also didn't have the same level leagues. When the coloured leagues started, they played at the William Herbert Sports Ground in Wynberg, but they were not like Hellenic, and they played against lower-level leagues.

My grandfather Charlie often came to watch our Bayview Rovers games. He would sit in his car and watch me play. I was eager to score goals and I scored a lot of them. My best goal was scored against a professional team at Hartleyvale. Although Hartleyvale was for white clubs, we got invited to a multiracial football social in the 1980s. We played Cape Town City's second team, at night under the floodlights. Scottish footballer Andy Donnelly was the goalkeeper. He'd come to play for Cape Town City when he was done with playing professional football in England.

When I walked onto the grass, I thought, 'What type of grass is this?' It was so soft and bouncy that my soccer boots kept sinking into it. When the ball was kicked, it went so far – *shooooop* and then *GOAL!* 'What's up with this ball?' we all wondered. We scored three goals against City, who scored eighteen. We had the talent, but on the grass we didn't have the technique. Nevertheless, I was glad I had scored a goal against a professional team, and against Andy Donnelly! I always say that if I had lived in England, I would have played for England; and if I was a 'born free', I would have played for Bafana Bafana.

As a teenager, I could not concentrate much in high school because every day I had visions of my father drowning in the bay. That's why I never swim, and I'm still scared of the sea. But I think school prepared me for life, particularly because my teachers started speaking about politics. I finished school in 1974, when I had completed Standard 8. I had passed every standard, but I couldn't continue with Standards 9 and 10 because there was no money for that, so I went to work. My first job was at the fish factory, in the cold-storage department. I didn't stay there long, though, because I couldn't stand it when the white bosses shouted at the workers. I got really angry with them, and they fired me. I was chased away from all my jobs.

I then worked for an engineering company in Stikland in Bellville with Dicki's brother Faldie. To get to work, we'd catch a bus to Wynberg, a train from there to Salt River, and then another to Bellville. By the time we got to work, I'd be exhausted. We were welding buses for the Golden Arrow bus company, and my job was to grind frames. It was a tough job because we worked with iron. I was eighteen at the time and I had just finished school, so I didn't really know what it was like to do hard manual labour. When teatime came, I'd nap during the ten-minute break, and during lunchtime I slept as well. On our way home I slept on the trains and buses, and when we got home I slept again. I was always exhausted.

I sustained an injury at the engineering company when a steel splinter got under my visor and flew into my right eye. The doctor removed it and the hole closed after a month. A few years later, when I worked for a boat-building company in Hout Bay, fiberglass fumes came into contact with that eye. I worked late that night and by the next morning my eye was red and inflamed. I think a combination of the two work injuries caused blindness in that eye.

After the job in Stikland, I worked at Atlantis Diesel Engines (ADE) for one year. ADE was a government job-creation project intended to employ residents in the newly established township of Atlantis on the West Coast, thereby halting the influx of coloured and black people to Cape Town. Businesses in Atlantis got tax and rates incentives, and labour was subsidised too, but once the subsidisation period ended, most of these businesses closed down. While working at ADE, we stayed in Atlantis during the week and only came home on weekends. The company was building engines for the SADF trucks. I was fired for handing out UDF pamphlets to the workers – management told me that I was a terrorist and that I couldn't work there any more. Two security workers escorted me out the gate. At that time, Shirley Gunn was in Hout Bay for the Hout Bay Action Committee meetings, and Dicki introduced me to her. We spoke about politics and our problems, and I got involved with the action committee. Dicki and I were very young, only around twenty years old.

I was twenty-three when I met Nicolene through Kalla, my aunt. The two of us became friends and then started to talk about marriage. Nicolene is from Okiep in the Northern Cape. When I told her mother that I was taking Nicolene as my wife, she said she could see I would take care of her daughter. Nicolene's father wasn't as accepting of me. I had visited Nicolene's family in Namaqualand, but when Nicolene fell pregnant her parents came to Cape Town, wanting to know what the hell was going on.

We got married in the Heathfield Trinity Methodist Church in 1983. Nicolene's father didn't come to the wedding. Nicolene was the apple of his eye and he'd had other plans for her that did not involve me. After we got married, though, he accepted both me and our child, and eventually we became very close. Of all the sons-in-law, I was the only one allowed in their house.

When he got sick, we cared for him in Kraaifontein. He lived with us there until the day he died.

Two weeks before Nicolene was due to give birth in 1983, we travelled to Namaqualand, where I was due to play a soccer match in Okiep. On the day of the game, a blisteringly hot Saturday, I drove to the venue by car, and the club players and supporters went by bus. The bus broke down, and the players were tired and a bit drunk by the time they arrived. It was so hot that the game was postponed. I was still at the field when I heard that Nicolene had gone into labour. We rushed to the hospital in Nababeep, which is twenty kilometres from Okiep. Our son Adrian was born on Sunday morning, and a few hours later the busload of soccer players turned up to see the baby.

I was not able to celebrate Adrian's third birthday with my family in 1986, because I was detained during the state of emergency. This was my first encounter with Jan Louw, a security policeman. They caught me at home and took me straight to Victor Verster Prison in Paarl. They told me I was a terrorist. Dicki had been detained before me, but was not yet at Victor Verster when I arrived. I was behind bars for about three months, and I wrote letters to Nicolene from prison. She was pregnant with our second child at the time.

Detention only made me stronger and more committed. I told myself that I would get out, that Mandela had been in prison for a long time and that these few weeks were nothing in comparison. Mandela inspired me, and I remained physically and mentally strong.

I met other comrades in Victor Verster: Trevor Manuel, Wilfred Rhodes, Joe Marks, Maxwell Moss and the lawyer Vincent Saldanha. I was in a single cell in Section D, but we discussed politics together in the library. We also went to church in the prison.

I was released in November 1986. The security police dropped Dicki and me off at the Parade in Cape Town and told us to get going. So we ran. We didn't have any money, but we took the train to Wynberg and a taxi home to Hout Bay. Nicolene was working as a receptionist at the Chapman's Peak Hotel, and after I arrived home, I went there straight away to see her. I had missed my family very much while I was in detention.

Carmy was born in 1987. Dicki drove Nicolene, Auntie Bettie – an experienced midwife – and me in Brother Vos's Mini station wagon to the Retreat maternity ward. Nicolene's contractions had started and there we were, crammed into the tiny Mini. We had taken Auntie Bettie just in case something happened on the way. Our daughter was born on 3 January.

*

In my MK underground cell, I worked with Dicki. He was the only person I knew until Leon Scott visited me in 1990, when Dicki was in detention, because an arms cache had to be removed from Hout Bay.

During this time, I ran into the security policeman Jan Louw again, in Hangberg. He drove up to me in a blue car and said, 'Patty, you will see what's going to happen.'

'Go to hell, man,' I replied. He said he was going to get me.

It was early morning when they handcuffed me and beat me up at Wynberg Police Station. I didn't shout at all as they hit me, and I didn't say anything. I just stood there. This made them angrier. They knew about the military hardware that we had moved and wanted to know where it was.

Soon after that, there was gang warfare in Hout Bay. The Rastafarian gang had been taxing the shebeen owners and drug dealers, and every shebeen owner had to pay the gang to trade. If they didn't pay, they would be hurt or killed. A rival gang started to retaliate and many people lost their lives. I had to do something. 'I'm going to kill the gangsters,' I thought to myself. 'Dicki and Shirley can get angry at me, but I'm going to put a stop to this. People can't die for no reason. I'm going to show them.' I took an AK-47 and walked up the street, holding the gun above my head. The gangsters could come; I was ready for them. When I reached the top of the street I fired on them. They shot at me, but missed. A few guys armed with handguns joined me. The gangsters came running towards us, about twenty of them, and I aimed the AK at the leader. Then I heard a voice telling me, 'Patty, what are you doing? Think this through. You are not a murderer.' So I shot past them, up in the air, and they ran away shouting, 'These bastards have AKs!' The other gang scattered too.

Dicki arrived soon after the incident. He'd just returned from a workshop in Wellington and the comrades had been waiting for him when he pulled up at his house. They told him what had happened and that he must go to my place. He came, took the firearm from me and told me to run because the police were already in the area.

A week after the shooting incident, Jan Louw and two others from the security police arrived at my place at about 11 p.m. We lived in the maisonettes at the harbour then. Nicolene had just returned from a wedding, and Adrian and Carmy were there too. Dicki had taken the AK, so I stood in the dark stairwell, hitting the metal railing with a long stick to make a sound like a gun. 'I'll kill you,' I shouted, 'Just come up the stairs!' It went on like this for what felt like hours. More vans pulled up outside. Eventually, the security policemen ran up the stairs. At this point, it was just Nicolene and me; my brother had taken Adrian and Carmy to their grandmother's place because they were screaming and crying. The security cops managed to get into the house, and then it was a fight. All I had was the stick, but I fought like hell. I beat them up, and Nicolene fought too. She took a policeman's pistol and I was shouting: 'Nicolene, leave the fucking gun!' Then they got me, handcuffed me and took me away. The furniture was upside down and the place was a complete mess.

They took me to Wynberg Police Station, to the cells at the back. It was late at night. I was questioned by a white security policewoman with long dark hair who operated with Jan Louw. She asked if I was a wrestler because she couldn't believe that a small man like me could beat up three large, highly trained policemen.

Dicki got hold of a lawyer after I was charged with assaulting police officers and attempted murder for shooting a Rasta in the leg. The police dropped the assault charges and tried to get my lawyer to do a deal with the Rastas to drop the attempted murder charges in exchange for the AK, but by then I didn't know where the AK was. Fortunately, I was released the next morning.

I was eventually acquitted on both charges, and I didn't have to appear in court. The Rasta who'd been shot in the leg said it was me who shot him, but the police didn't know what firearm had been used. I'd fired the AK several times, but without aiming to hit the gangsters, and I definitely wasn't the one who shot the Rasta in the leg because it was a tiny wound, perhaps from a handgun. If it had been a bullet from the AK, his leg would have been seriously injured.

I still vote for the ANC. My loyalty can be stretched forever. My son Adrian is like me; we don't talk much, but he has always been behind me. He believes that what I did was right. He was the first to throw stones at the police in 2010 when the Democratic Alliance (DA), with the support of the police, evicted people living in informal housing on the mountain. Nicolene was also one of the first out there during the evictions, and she was shot in the leg with a rubber bullet. She never could just stand by and do nothing. Meanwhile, Carmy, with her struggle background and knowledge of politics, persuaded her in-laws to become ANC supporters.

In 2002, I bought a kombi, got a taxi permit and started my own business. I drove up and down from Hout Bay to Wynberg for three years until we hired a driver. We eventually sold the taxi because it was too much trouble and generated little income. It was a good business idea, but the driver messed up the taxi and the profits went towards wages and maintenance, so we didn't make much and the business wasn't viable. That was my last job.

Fortunately, Nicolene has worked consistently over the years. One of her most recent jobs was a one-year contract monitoring fishing quotas at the harbour. The City's anti-poaching project employs former combatants. As the wife of a veteran, Nicolene qualified to be part of the project. She has been able to support the family as the breadwinner, and gave me the opportunity to be involved in the struggle.

Nicolene says that, in hindsight, she wouldn't choose to live her life in the same way, at the same intensity. Her primary consideration would be our kids. We were so close to the struggle and politics that we couldn't see the bigger picture. Now, when we look back, we can see a complete picture, and because we made sacrifices, we are aware of how everyone around us made sacrifices too.

Since 2015, Patrick suffered a series of seizures and strokes that left him bedridden and requiring intensive palliative care. Thanks to the efforts of AKD members, Patrick received access to medical care as a veteran. He underwent extensive assessment at 2 Military Hospital in Wynberg and was diagnosed with Alzheimer's. After being discharged, he stayed in Chatsworth, Malmesbury, with Nicolene. Unfortunately, his condition worsened over time, and he passed away on 25 September 2017. His spirit lives on in the hundreds of lives that he touched and the courage and commitment he displayed, which encouraged so many people who knew him. Hamba kahle, Comrade Patty. Rest in power.

15

Timothy Jacobs

Education for Liberation

I LEFT SOUTH AFRICA in 1989, aged seventeen, and returned after receiving military training at the ANC's Cassius Maake camp in Tanzania. In 1990 I returned the same way I had left – across the Zambezi River into Zimbabwe, thinking of all the stories I'd heard about comrades drowning. I could hear lions roaring and couldn't tell how close or far away they were. I travelled to Harare, then to Bulawayo and from Bulawayo by taxi to Plumtree. A group of us walked into Botswana and were picked up by a comrade, who drove us to Francistown. At a roadblock, those of us who could not speak Setswana were told to remain silent or pretend to be asleep. The comrade replied to the policemen in Setswana, and fortunately they didn't bother the rest of us.

We were picked up again at Francistown and made to stay in the back of a truck like labourers, all the way to Gaborone, where I met James Ngculu. I was put up in a house and I was alone most of the time. James visited me periodically and gave me instructions. One night, I was told that I was going to link up with an MK comrade named Thabo, who would help me cross the border into Bophuthatswana. Before I left, I was given about R400 and told to go straight home; I would be contacted there.

At about 6 a.m. the next morning I boarded a bus back to South Africa. I had to give my Makarov pistol to Thabo. He told me that when I reached the first town, I must catch the next bus to Mafikeng Station. He assured me that no one would think it strange I was there because there was a coloured area nearby, so people would think I was from that area.

From Mafikeng I took a train to Kimberley and then another to Cape Town. I was sharing the third-class compartment with guys who were drinking, and to avoid any questions they might have I bought them a bottle of brandy to keep them happy. During the journey, I prepared myself mentally for the questions I would get at home and came up with the legend that I had left school and ended up on the streets of Durban before deciding to return home.

In Cape Town, I took a bus to Hout Bay. One of the first things I learnt when I got back home was that Dicki Meter had been arrested and Patty Presence was not in Hout Bay. I told myself to keep calm. Soon after I returned, a comrade arrived in Hout Bay with my clothes, which I had not taken with me when I left Botswana. I was instructed to stay put until I received further orders. I became very frustrated. During training, I had imagined that the armed struggle would be like all the other revolutions that I had read about – the liberation of Cuba, Angola, Mozambique and Zimbabwe. It would surely be the same in South Africa: MK comrades would walk the streets with AK-47s. But that did not happen.

I don't know much about my family history. I have never attempted to speak to anyone about it. I don't have the passion to find out as other people do. Maybe it's because I choose not to hear about the past.

I know that John Jacobs, my dad, was originally from Cape Town. His parents passed away many years before I was born. His family was forced out of Hout Bay and Steurhof and moved to another area in the Hout Bay valley. Then the Group Areas Act was enforced there too, and they moved again, to the Texas area of Hangberg, which was the property of Oceana Group. My parents would later move to a two-bedroom council flat, Number 8, Block MM, where I was born.

My dad was a fisherman and worked for Cape Coast and Oceana. I had just started school when the boat he was working on capsized off the West Coast. He was badly injured and instructed to stop working. He received a disability grant, and died of cancer in 1988.

My mother was born Margaret Cloete and is originally from Port Nolloth in the Richtersveld in the Northern Cape. I don't know my grandparents on my mother's side either because they too passed away before I was born. They were a Catholic family and my mother was educated in a convent school. Like many people from rural areas, she migrated to the city to find work and a better life. She ended up in Hout Bay, processing fish for South African Sea Products, an Oceana Group company, until she retired. She died in 2005.

My parents had eight children: five boys and three girls. The eldest was Martin, who left home when he was young. He lived on the streets in Cape Town as a stroller, and has since passed away. Next came Carol, then Joseph, who became a maintenance worker for private gated communities in Hout Bay. Francisco was in and out of prison, having turned to crime to survive. Then there was Mario, better known as Howie. Joan and Dorothy followed, and I am the youngest, the *laatlammetjie*, born on 13 January 1972, about ten years after Dorothy. We are Catholic. Our names either come from the Bible or we were named after members of our family. I am named Timothy, after my uncle, and my second name is Emmanuel.

Growing up in Hout Bay was good. The harbour community was like a big family; everyone knew everyone else. Growing up, I experienced that cohesion, but I also realised that something was wrong. Our parents worked themselves to the bone, and most of the time children were left unsupervised, although there were always caring adults around. When we went to the beach on the Chapman's Peak side of Hout Bay, we were curious as to why we were not allowed to swim there. The coloured policemen would ask us what we were doing in the area, and confiscate any pine cones we had taken from the trees.

I grew up tough. My parents were not highly educated. When my dad was boarded and went on a disability grant, the large household had to survive on my mother's meagre wage. Nevertheless, there was something to eat every day, although it might only have been bread. We did not generally have luxuries except for once or twice a month and at the end of the year when our parents received work-related bonuses and did Christmas shopping.

All my siblings slept in the larger of the two rooms in our flat but, being the baby, I slept with my parents. In the 1970s, Joseph moved to a council flat to stay with the mother of his child. His son was two years younger than me. Carol moved out in the 1980s when she got a one-bedroom flat. She worked for Amalgamated Fisheries, which was bought out by I&J, and then she worked for Pick 'n Pay in Constantia. Carol's daughter is three years younger than me. The rest of us stayed in Block MM at the foot of the mountain. I was not particularly close to any of my siblings because of the age gap between us, but I was close to my nephew Benedict, my niece Auriol and my cousin Arthur.

None of my brothers and sisters were able to achieve much in life. None completed matric or received any sort of professional training. I am the only one among my siblings with a high-school and tertiary qualification. My immediate family may have had ambitions and life goals, but it did not seem like it. That was the norm. There were few role models around us. I could count the teachers in the community on one hand, and I didn't know of any other professionals. It was only in the 1980s, after the Tricameral Parliament was set up and Hout Bay Heights was developed, that a coloured middle class emerged and lawyers, social workers and other professionals moved in and I came to know about these professions.

My parents were not involved in politics, but my dad was politically aware and my mom learnt about defending her rights as a member of the Food and

Canning Workers Union, which became the Food and Allied Workers Union. My brother Mario was interested in politics to a degree. I started learning about politics through reading newspapers and discussing what was wrong in the country at home.

I went to Sentinel Junior Primary from 1978 until 1987, from Sub A to Standard 8. I recall the awakening of my political consciousness in Standard 3 when Mario wrote something about the 1976 student uprisings for me for a school oral. I participated in art classes and games afternoons at the Hangberg Civic Centre and it was there that I met Dicki Meter. Dicki and my older siblings regularly talked politics at home, and I remember a march against poor service delivery in which Mario and my sister Carol were involved. In 1983, my father attended the launch of the UDF in Mitchells Plain, and I started to become more politically aware.

When I was in Standard 5 in 1984, there were student uprisings, and the next year there was a schools boycott. I became actively involved in politics because of this. The whole school participated and we elected an SRC. I got to know about the Hout Bay Action Committee, the Hout Bay Youth Movement and about national politics. Someone would drop off banned political reading material and say: 'Read it, don't ask questions and pass it on.'

When Ashley Kriel was killed on 9 July 1987, I went to Dicki and told him that I wanted to do what Ashley did – fight against apartheid. Dicki told me not to come to him with mad ideas; I was fifteen years old and had to finish school. Dicki was being reasonable, but I was upset; 1987 was a year of mass student action and Ashley's death had ignited us – we really wanted to be part of what Ashley had been part of. Nevertheless, I completed Standard 8 at Sentinel and applied to St Owen's Boys High School in Retreat to complete Standard 9 and matric. I didn't know at the time that St Owen's was political – even more so than Sentinel.

St Owen's admitted coloured and black students, despite government regulations requiring that students be separated by race. There was a margin of integration in Catholic schools, and although black students were not in the majority, they were accepted. Politics was part of the school culture and there was open discussion with the teachers, many of whom were foreigners. During church services we prayed for Madiba and detainees, and there were *Release All Detainees* stickers in the classrooms. At noon, we would say the rosary and I always prayed for those who were politically persecuted. There was an opportunity at St Owen's to finish my Catholic confirmation classes, but I had other things on my mind. I remember thinking, 'Jesus will under-stand. We need to liberate South Africa.'

The schools in Retreat, Lavender Hill, Heathfield and Steenberg formed the Retreat Student Action Committee (RetSAC). The Congress of South African Students (COSAS) was banned, so we formed new structures aligned to COSAS and held meetings with students after school to decide what protest actions we would take.

I completed Standard 9, but one term into matric I decided to leave the country and join the ANC. Dicki arranged everything. My thinking at the time was that if Dicki did not send me across the border, I would walk. He said I was too militant, and that I would either end up dead or in prison, but I think he realised that the best option was to send me out of South Africa.

I left in 1989, when I was seventeen, leaving a note at home that said I had been accepted at another Catholic school in Natal and did not want to burden the family because I knew that they would not agree to my going to a school so far away when there were good Catholic schools in Cape Town. Mario helped; he advised me to throw my bag of clothes out of the bedroom window so no one would see I had packed when I walked out of the house. Dicki met us at the bus stop and took us to Cape Town. There, they put me on a Greyhound bus headed for Johannesburg. That was the last I saw of Dicki for some time.

In Johannesburg, I was met by Richard Ishmail. He left me in Hillbrow for a few hours, then came back and took me across the border to Botswana, where he deposited me with James Ngculu. I was booked into a hotel for about two days before my real journey began. I travelled from Gaborone to Francistown, and from there to the Botswana–Zimbabwe border. We walked from the Botswana border to Plumtree, then took a taxi to Bulawayo, where we stayed for a few days before travelling to Harare by train. The final leg of our journey was crossing the Zambezi River into Zambia.

We finally arrived at a big transit camp in Chelston, Lusaka, where I had disagreements with the camp command because the ANC refused to send me to a training camp. They wanted to send me to the Solomon Mahlangu Freedom College (SOMAFCO) instead. 'Do you tell every young person who comes here that they must go to school?' I asked them angrily. 'I don't want to go to SOMAFCO!' As a result, I was stuck at Chelston for a few months.

Intelligence within MK was rigorous and they caught quite a few people in the transit camp who were working for the apartheid regime. We had to write our biographies for the screening process; there were people arriving from all over South Africa, so someone would be able verify the details if necessary. Nevertheless, the camp had been attacked before I arrived, and the camp commander's house had taken the brunt of an explosion. Only the kitchen remained intact; the rest of the house was completely destroyed.

One day, I got the shock of my life when Chris Hani arrived at Chelston and I was called in to meet him. Chris told me that people in Cape Town were asking what had happened to me. 'Comrade Chief of Staff, you must ask the commander of the transit camp what will happen to me,' I replied. He must have, because the next day I was on a plane to Tanzania.

I was taken to the Cassius Maake ANC training base, a former PAC camp. We heard that the Tanzanian government considered the PAC's armed struggle in South Africa ineffective, and the PAC had subsequently vacated the camp, but we were never sure what really happened. Cadres at Cassius Maake were trained for a maximum of three months and then sent back to South Africa, so I was happy.

There were very few of us at Cassius Maake – about fifteen cadres in total, and only one female comrade, Lerato. Once, we visited the centre at the nearby Yusuf Dadoo training camp to watch movies because we had no electricity at Cassius Maake. The comrades at Yusuf Dadoo camp were not allowed to see us, so our faces were covered.

One thing I loved at the camp was the jazz hour on Monday evenings. Everybody would take to the floor, singing revolutionary songs and dancing, and we felt like warriors. Jazz hour built our morale. It gave us the feeling that we were going home to liberate our people, and we felt that if the enemy came we were prepared to take them down.

When I was on kitchen duty, comrades would often get angry with me because I made them sing. They had to stand in a queue for their breakfast or lunch, but before they got their food I made them sing four revolutionary songs. Normally we only sang one song. 'No, no, no,' I would say, 'the masses want to see you sing before you eat.'

We had to guard the camp day and night. The 'break-my-heart shift' was from 2 a.m. to 4 a.m., when we stood at our posts alone in the dark. There were big rats and lots of snakes in Tanzania and sometimes we would wake with a snake in the tent. The wind was always blowing and we would hear trees falling and wonder if – or when – one would fall on the tent while we were sleeping. The next day we would chop up the fallen trees for firewood. Each of us also had to carry fifty litres of water from the stream to the camp every day.

I don't know if we can call ourselves cadres of a special type, but I think that if you were trusted enough to be part of MK you were a special cadre of the ANC. We had a fierce love for the struggle and a strong commitment to it. We became part of a bigger family and we were prepared to do things for that family that we would not do for other people. To us, the cause was worth dying for. The love for the revolution bound us together and the bond between

MK comrades was powerful; it did not matter how old you were or where you came from.

For the first time, I encountered comrades who had been in Angola. Some of them desperately wanted to go home but could not; others were identified to go and fight the armed struggle in South Africa. I listened to their stories and heard about the mutiny at Pango camp and how comrades were killed there. They also showed us their wounds from the war with UNITA, which was supported by the apartheid government. South Africa spent millions on UNITA to fight the MPLA and MK. I understood this to mean that the apartheid government knew that the military wing of the ANC was a force to be reckoned with, and spent that money because they feared MK.

The political education I received in the camps and the non-racialism of the ANC was incredible. There was a strong focus on soldiers' intellectual development. We would read books, then discuss the content and how it related to the struggle and to building South Africa. I read about the revolution in Bulgaria and fell in love with that country. I was drawn to books about Che Guevara and stories about Fidel Castro and how he defended himself in court. I read a library book every third day and I made sure that I read every edition of the ANC's journal, Sechaba.

During my time with MK, I was repeatedly told to go back to school. The camp commander told me that the ANC could even facilitate studies at any university outside South Africa. But I felt differently. I was militant. I needed to go back home to fight with an AK in my hand.

Once I had completed my training at Cassius Maake, the ANC again wanted to send me to SOMAFCO to finish matric, but I was adamant: I needed to go home. They tried to coax me with pilot training at a military academy in a socialist country because, they argued, the new South Africa would need people with these skills, but I refused. I didn't want to be a pilot. I wanted to go home and be part of the revolution.

I was taken back to Chelston transit camp for a day, and then to the house where Pallo Jordan and a comrade named Don stayed. One day, they took me to Steve Tshwete's house nearby and I realised that I was staying in the area where the ANC leadership lived. I remained in Zambia with Comrade Don for a few days, and then was sent back to South Africa the way I'd come – across the Zambezi River into Zimbabwe, then via Plumtree to Botswana and the border.

Once back in South Africa, I discovered that the ANC was unbanned and had agreed to negotiate with the apartheid government. I was very frustrated because this meant I'd lost the chance to use my military training in the armed struggle. I became very upset, so Dicki arranged a meeting with the MK high command in the Western Cape, and that's when I met Shirley Gunn and Aneez Salie. Aneez explained what the ANC had decided about the armed struggle – that is, that MK would remain operational for the time being. As a soldier, I accepted the order I was given by my superiors, and returned to Hout Bay and waited. After some time, Dicki gave me a message from the high command: I must go back to school to finish matric. So I went back to school. Hout Bay had a brand new high school by then, and I completed matric there in 1991.

The following year, I decided to study a three-year diploma course in journalism at the Peninsula Technikon in Bellville. At the end of the course, they refused to give me my diploma because I hadn't completed my in-service training, which I eventually did at a community publication I helped start in Hout Bay.

In the mid-1990s I demobilised, and in 1996 I became involved in business. Over the years, those oppressed by apartheid had got to understand industries as labourers, not as owners. We started making money when the industries began to be transformed, but we did not know about proper financial management and tax implications because there were no government structures in place to guide emerging black entrepreneurs.

I decided that the only way to empower myself was to do business courses. I completed several introductory courses in the late 1990s and early 2000s and that is when I read about the University of Cape Town's Graduate School of Business. I applied for the Associate in Management course and started in 2008. That was the first step to an MBA.

Looking back, I believe that the ANC was correct in advising me to go back to school. I always remind people that although I was given the opportunity to join the ANC's armed struggle, education was seen as the best weapon to empower and build South Africa. I sometimes wonder how my life would have turned out if I had agreed to go to SOMAFCO or train as a pilot. Maybe I would be flying Boeings around the world, or have the skills needed to work in government.

Most people didn't know where I went when I left the country to join MK. At my fortieth birthday, Aneez, Melvin Bruintjies and Dicki were present. Aneez came in late and asked to say a few words after Melvin had made a speech. I didn't know that they were going to speak about my life in MK. My aunt turned to Dicki and said, 'All these years you did not tell us that you were the one who allowed this boy to leave the country.'

In 2010 I was appointed to the ANC Regional Task Team and later elected onto the Regional Executive Committee of the ANC, where I was responsible for the Economic Transformation and Rural Development portfolio.

I married Jastine on 13 January 2007, and we have three children: two boys, Carlito and Trey-José, and a girl, Tashlyn. I also have a child from another relationship, Griffin, who stays with his mother. Jastine is the pillar in my life. She was in the fishing industry for a number of years, learning all the ins and outs of the industry by working both day and night shifts for a major fishing company. She has an entrepreneurial spirit and sold biscuits and other products on the side, and we decided that that would be enough. Together, we took the first steps to her becoming an entrepreneur.

Jastine and I initially stayed in the informal settlement in Hangberg, and after that we rented a two-bedroom flat in a subdivided house in Hout Bay Heights belonging to former Rivonia trialist Denis Goldberg. We now have our own house. Although my father's family was forcibly removed from the Hout Bay valley and Steurhof, we did not bother with land claims. My aunt is currently staying in the council flat where my mother used to live. My three sisters and one of my brothers rent council flats in the harbour. Mario stays with Carol. My cousin Arthur died in 2005 after being stabbed, and my cousin Benedict died in hospital from injuries he sustained when he was hit by a car.

Things have changed dramatically in the Hout Bay community, maybe because the world is changing. Social cohesion in the community doesn't exist as it did before. There seems to be no future for the people of Hangberg. If you are born here, you will remain here. It is as if people accept their conditions because of how the community is structured. Most of the children end up in the same circumstances as their parents – without a future. Only a few people from Hangberg go on to university or other tertiary education and move out of the area.

As youngsters during apartheid, we could not walk freely on the white side of Hout Bay. We now live in a democracy, yet that side of Hout Bay is still a predominantly white area because of racial differences in social capital. I believe that service delivery needs to be fast-tracked so that the standard of living of historically disadvantaged citizens is raised to the same level as that of historically advantaged citizens.

16

Charles Martin

Till the Sun Sets

T HE MOST IMPORTANT reason for sharing my story is to acknowledge
the people who crossed my path and the experiences I shared with them.
I often ask whether it was chance that we met or if it was part of a greater
design. I grew up in the church, an institution I both love and loathe, and
have spent most of my life in the Christian ministry.

My involvement in MK began in 1988, when I was serving at a local parish
in Bonteheuwel. I was recruited by Melvin Bruintjies, in the midst of immense
political turmoil, personal suffering and the sacrifices of many brave men,
women and children in our country, and Bonteheuwel in particular. There was
a raging debate in church circles about the legitimacy of the armed struggle,
and I gave serious thought to the ethics of joining the struggle as a minister in
the church. The South African Council of Churches (SACC) was under attack
from conservative right-wing elements for its support of the struggle, particularly its support of the armed struggle. Frank Chikane, general secretary of the
SACC, responded to the debate in a way that articulated my own view. He wrote:
'There are people in South Africa who are not living in the townships who have
the space and the luxury to debate the matter, but people in the townships do
not have this space and luxury. For them it's a matter of life and death.' This
profound statement helped me make my decision: apartheid was a crime
against humanity and everything at our disposal should be used against it.

I was born on 15 June 1959 in rural Paarl, seventy kilometres north of Cape
Town. My working-class parents and extended family were pillars in the lives
of my siblings and me. As children we were able to play safely in the streets,
day and night. We were surrounded by vineyards, mountains and unspoilt
nature, where we would go hunting. Our childhood days were filled with
joy and happiness, without any awareness of our parents' daily struggle to
survive and the simmering struggle for democracy in South Africa.

Most people in the coloured community of Paarl were unconcerned about the struggle and lived their lives in isolation from the daily persecutions suffered by our fellow South Africans; the propaganda machine of the National Party government and its surrogate forces was hugely successful in winning the hearts and minds of our people.

Francis Martin, whom everybody called Siena, is my mother. Her parents died when she was very young, and she and her siblings were sent to stay with different family members, separated from each other and scattered. I can only imagine how that trauma must have impacted them. What I saw, though, is that it made my mother very compassionate and also very strong. She always stood up for herself and others, and she cared for the poorer members of the family. On weekends, I often accompanied her to visit her sickly brother in Simondium. We would come back to Paarl late on Saturday or Sunday evenings, often having to hitchhike all the way back, as no public transport was available. My mother always gave to those who had less than us, such as clothing to children whose garments were threadbare. She was also the person in the family who organised funerals.

My mother was a domestic worker most of her life. When I was a little boy, she cleaned for a white family in Goodwood. I remember going with her on the long train journey to her workplace, leaving Huguenot Station in Paarl early in the morning, getting off at Goodwood Station, walking to the house, and coming back home again in the late afternoon. I'd spend the day playing happily in the white people's house, but can't recall interacting with anyone there other than my mother.

On Fridays, we went shopping in the Paarl town centre, and I took comfort holding my mother's hand when we crossed the old, rusty iron bridge over the fast-flowing Berg River. When she saw someone being ill-treated by shop employees, she would always say something and involve herself. She was a caring, kind-hearted woman who did not tolerate the abuse of people.

Being a humble housewife with a sense of justice, my mother became involved in the local community and regularly took part in organising rent boycotts and occupying the rent office. She would later join the ANC and the ANC Women's League when her children got involved in the struggle. It was wonderful for me to see her transformation from housewife to struggle activist.

My father, known by all as Pa Willie, was a quiet, hard-working man. We were seven children in the family and he had to work extra hard to provide for us all. He worked at Royal Baking Powder for many years, and when it closed down he worked at KWV distilleries. During the harvest season, he worked in the vineyards, pruning and cutting grapes, and I went with him to do gardening work for a white family on Saturday mornings. He worked hard and never complained.

I fondly remember our Sunday trips to the cemetery in Paarl to clean the graves, which involved the whole family. After we'd cleaned the graves, my father, uncles and the boys would disappear into the open veld next to the cemetery and hunt rabbits. We also foraged for kukumakranka, a fragrant plant with a white flower that blooms at Christmastime. We'd pick the plant and put it inside the breast pockets of our jackets because of its beautiful fragrance. My father loved outdoor life and besides hunting he took us fishing. His mother died when he was very young, and he'd had to fend for himself and his younger siblings. He could cook and bake bread, and he contributed much to their household.

I'm the second eldest of my siblings; Rachel is two years older than me. William is a year younger than me; David is a year younger than William; then there's Melvin and my sisters Dalene and Zelna. My childhood was tough but very happy. My grandfather had a big house on a large plot in Paarl and my siblings and I grew up there with our cousins. My parents, aunties and uncles looked after all of us.

I started school at Amstelhof Primary School when I was five years old, and I failed Sub A dismally because I was so young. I spent the remainder of my primary school years at the Huguenot Congregational Church School, which was linked to the Bethel Congregational Church parish. Paarl was a very small town and my parents knew the teachers. In fact, my Sub A teacher, Juffrou Cupido, had taught my father in Sub A too. The teachers had everyone's respect in our close-knit community. Our principal, Meneer Kulsen, was strict but very kind. Meneer Sammy Kannemeyer showed great patience to those of us who struggled with *handwerk* (woodwork). We received love and compassion from Juffrou Mavis, Juffrou de Wee and Juffrou Adonis in Sub A and Sub B. Juffrou Rita Green *moered* the hell out of us in Standard 2, yet we all loved her. Meneer Arendse in Standard 3 was also very kind. When his beloved dog went missing, he rallied us to search for it one afternoon. Sadly, we didn't find his dog, but we ate up all the lovely food he provided for the search party.

In primary school, my three best friends were Ian Swarts, Solomon Davids, and Trevor Erentzen. Ian's mother taught at the school and his father was a shoemaker who worked from his garage. We spent a lot of time together in his workshop, trying our hand at repairing shoes. I still remember the smell of leather, glue and shoe polish.

My father used to take our family and others on annual outings and camps to the Breede River in Worcester. We camped under a big brown army tent, and we had so much fun together playing in the river. During one such outing, my mother called me over and told me that she had just heard on the radio that Ian had drowned on holiday in Namibia. I was devastated, and for a long time I avoided walking past Ian's house because of the memories it brought back. Not long before this tragedy, a girl in my class had also drowned in a farm dam. Our teacher said she got stuck in the mud.

Trevor, Solomon and I remained together from Sub A to matric. Our paths separated after that. I recently met up with Solomon, who is now a retired teacher, and I learnt from him that Trevor died a few years ago.

In 1963, when I was four years old, our community was affected by the Group Areas Act. The apartheid government threw the coloured people out of their houses, churches and mosques. Bethel Church, where we went, was in the part of town that was proclaimed white, and we had to build another church in Paarl East – the coloured part of town. While we built our new church, we continued going to Sunday school at Bethel in the white area. We went there by bus, which cost a few cents. We built the new Bethel Church on a big plot that had lots of small bluegum trees on it, and the pupils of our church school were paid two cents for every tree that was uprooted.

Our minister at Bethel was Reverend John Thorne. He was also the principal of our primary school at the newly built church. Later, he became my supervisor when I did my ministerial probation in Westbury, Johannesburg.

Reverend Thorne was politically conscious and would not let people forget that our Bethel Church congregation had been forcibly moved by the Group Areas Act. As a remembrance, he erected a memorial plaque on the church premises.

During Bethel's recent centenary celebration service, Reverend Thorne came to Paarl to attend the celebration with his former church congregants. We went to our old church in the white area to hold the service, but they refused to open the church doors for us. We held the service outside in the yard, and Reverend Thorne shed tears.

Reverend Thorne left our church in Paarl in 1975, and was succeeded by Reverend Abraham 'Abe' John Reginald Maart, who would become my mentor. In Paarl and in the broader ecumenical and progressive circles he was fondly known as 'Meneer'. When he arrived, the young people in the church were mesmerised by him. He had an afro and a master's degree from Cambridge University, and he preached about justice, the South African political situation and the need for the church to oppose apartheid. He encouraged us to raise our heads high, stand up for our rights and face the world proudly. He brought life into the church by involving people in its activities, starting group discussions in church services and prayer meetings, allowing the youth to preach from the pulpit, and sending us on youth-work training courses.

Something in me woke up. I'd always wanted to be a minister, but I was unable to see myself as part of the conservative church. With Reverend Maart, however, I saw an alternative. He regularly invited preachers and speakers from the Western Cape to preach in our church on Sundays, such as Professor Daan Cloete from the University of the Western Cape, and from all over the world too. In this way Bethel Church was transformed and the congregants were educated. This exposed us to the broader progressive theological thinking in the ecumenical church and the world, as well as activism and activists. Through Reverend Maart's influence, the Bethel Church youth became involved in the Catholic Church's Young Christian Students (YCS) movement in 1976. YCS was a very progressive youth movement. It was part of the broader Mass Democratic Movement and operated on university campuses all over South Africa. By nature of its constituencies, it crossed racial, cultural and class barriers. I joined the YCS and this had a strong influence on my theological and political thinking.

Between 1976 and 1979, Reverend Maart arranged for many of us to attend training programmes on leadership and theology presented by progressive para-church organisations in the broader ecumenical movement, which prepared me for my life ahead as a pastor and church activist.

However, Bethel Church was also thrown into turmoil during these years, as a part of the congregation thought Reverend Maart was *too* political, and he was under constant attack. The white right-wing religious movement was very active in South Africa then, particularly in the Western Cape, and orchestrated a campaign to infiltrate Bethel Church. Members of the Gospel Defence League used some of the conservative members of Bethel Church to launch a dirty-tricks campaign against him, claiming he was a communist, overly political and had stolen the church's money. In response, the broader Congregational Church in the Western Cape sent a delegation to Bethel to investigate the allegations against Reverend Maart. When the church delegation arrived for the meeting with Bethel's parishioners, about fifteen of our youth members, myself included (sporting an afro), awaited them with placards.

The progressive members of Bethel Church won this battle, and the right-wing members broke away and formed their own church. Meanwhile, the security police were getting worried about Bethel Church, and Reverend Maart in particular. They started a long campaign of harassment that culminated in them setting the reverend's car alight in the churchyard and flooding Paarl with pamphlets claiming he was a thief who was misleading congregants. A counter-campaign was launched and we won that battle too.

I was in matric in 1976, and was marginally involved in protest action and throwing stones, but I was not part of any organised political formation outside of church structures. In mid-1977, I got my first job as a reception clerk at the new Paarl East hospital, which had been built for the coloured community. The hospital's white management was extremely racist and disrespectful towards all black workers. One day we stood up against them, and called a meeting with management in which I was very vocal. All of us were fired. Thereafter, the big boss at the hospital's human resources department met with each of us individually, and told us that if we apologised we would get our jobs back. It was one of the biggest choices I ever had to make. My income contributed to the household and as the eldest son, I felt obligated to support my family. On the other hand, my conscience would not allow me to apologise to management. I was permanently fired. Thankfully, my parents never held it against me. They were proud of the stand I had taken.

My destiny was decided when Reverend Maart registered me for the National Youth Leadership Training Programme (NYLTP) in Hillcrest, Durban. NYLTP was initiated by the mainstream churches as a programme to train church youth workers. It brought together young people across the barriers of class, colour, culture and geographical location. Next to Reverend Maart, NYLTP was the most powerful influence in my early adult life. Amazing educators crossed our paths at NYLTP. Among the prominent South Africans who taught there was Professor Khoza Mgojo, who later became a TRC commissioner and my New Testament professor at theology school. Others were Dr Stanley Magoba, who became a PAC leader, and Desmond Tutu.

At NYLTP we spoke freely about the pain apartheid caused us, and our dreams for South Africa. We confronted our prejudices and how we had been shaped by our education and experiences. Deep friendships developed among the people in our group. For the first time in my life I experienced what it was like to put my life in the hands of others. Years later I would again experience this deep sense of trust and belonging in the AKD.

NYLTP was part of an overall church youth programme known as 'Give one year of your life'. It meant doing the four-month course in Hillcrest and spending the rest of the year as a youth worker in a local parish. This was the second big decision I had to make: even though I was convinced it was the right one, it once again had a financial effect on my family. However, my parents stood behind me and so did my brothers and sisters.

I returned to Paarl at the end of 1979 and worked as a voluntary youth worker for Bethel Church. David Esau, one of the wealthy congregants, gave me R50 a month. I was staying with my family, earning nothing from the church, and living with the guilt of being unable to contribute anything to the household. While I was volunteering, my siblings Rachel, William and David worked to support the family.

My political involvement deepened with my youth work in the church. I felt ready to work with young people and present to them the alternative theology of liberation. That, I decided, was going to be my ministry. During this time, however, the security police regularly harassed me and the church youth. They waited outside the church gates while we held our meetings on Friday evenings and sometimes they beat us up. One of the security policemen, Mr Daniels, known to activists as 'Oom Daan', later found out who my mother was and constantly followed and harassed me. It was a sign of things to come.

From 1980 to 1982 I studied theology at the Federal Theological Seminary of Southern Africa (Fedsem) in the township of Imbali outside Pietermaritzburg. I was politically conscious and a fervent adherent of liberation theology by then. Fedsem has a proud history of political consciousness and our lecturers were mostly black. Among them were eminent theologians, such as Dr Khoza Mgojo, Dr Sigqibo Dwane, Dr Alpheus Ngobese, Dr Ian Darby, Bennie Witbooi, Dr Bonganjalo Goba, Dr Andre Kaltenrieder and Dr Brian Banwell. Fedsem was federal and ecumenical. It consisted of three colleges: Albert Luthuli College, which catered for the Congregational, Presbyterian and Volkskerk churches; John Wesley College, which catered for Methodists; and St Peter's College, which catered for Anglicans. I was a student at Albert Luthuli College.

Fedsem was constantly harassed by the apartheid government and other political factions. The area in which the institution was based was an Inkatha stronghold, and Fedsem was regarded as a breeding ground for communists and ANC-aligned priests. Students in later years reported having to flee for their lives when Inkatha impis descended on the campus to attack them.

My years at Fedsem were very happy. I enjoyed the ecumenical, multiracial and multicultural community of staff and students and was thrilled by its theological orientation, which focused on African, contextual and liberation theology. As students we supported the local struggles and actions of the broader democratic movement in the Pietermaritzburg townships and suburbs. Theological students of all races lived and studied together under the noses of the apartheid rulers who disallowed racial and cultural integration.

On one occasion, the security police raided our campus, pulled us out of our classes and arrested us, bundling us en masse into their yellow vans and holding us in detention for a day.

In my final year, I received the Albert Luthuli College best-student award but I told our principal that while I appreciated the acknowledgement, my philosophy on education did not allow me to accept the award. Education, I explained, should be non-competitive and promote growth and sharing. I was shocked when some students accused me of racism, alleging that I'd refused the award because it carried the name of an African intellectual leader.

I completed my theology degree at Fedsem in 1982 and graduated in 1983. My parents and members of Bethel Church travelled by kombi all the way from Paarl to Pietermaritzburg to attend my graduation ceremony. They were brimming with pride the day Bishop Dwane capped me.

Having graduated, I was now ready to start my career as a trained minister. The church assigned me to Westbury in Johannesburg, formerly a black township that had since been declared a coloured area by the Group Areas Act. Black people who had lived there were moved to Soweto and coloured people were placed in their old, dilapidated houses.

I arrived in Westbury as a young priest in 1983 and crossed paths with Reverend John Thorne again. He was the minister of the local Congregational parish in nearby Bosmont, and was appointed my supervisor for my two-year probation period. I met YCS members who attended a community meeting at my house and I became the YCS chaplain for high school students living in Bosmont and Westbury. I also met Father Albert Nolan, one of South Africa's leading contextual and liberation theologians and a patron of YCS. He'd authored *Jesus before Christianity*, which was our bible in the progressive church youth movement. The book articulated what many of us believed about religion, faith and ministry in a context of oppression and exploitation.

During my time as a parish priest in Westbury, there was a man who befriended the local comrades. He tried to forge a close relationship with me too, but I kept my distance. We became suspicious of him when we found out he was allocated a council flat in Newclare. He was from Cape Town and a student at the Rand teachers' college, so it was odd that he had been able to jump the long housing queue and receive a council flat. We later discovered that he was a police informer. This was not my last encounter with him.

My two years in Westbury deepened my theological curiosity and thinking. I assisted parishioners in the task of reflecting on and understanding our role as believers ruled by a government that defended a crime against humanity in the name of the God we served. Despite my previous theological training, I now think of this as the true beginning of my education.

Our parishioners were slowly exposed to the Westbury Residents Action Committee (WRAC) and community issues, and our church became a place for community meetings. Once, over a weekend, WRAC turned the church into a clinic and offered health screenings for the Westbury community.

I worked closely with two prominent members of WRAC who had a big influence in my life: Auntie Florrie Daniels, who was in her sixties, and her son Elvis, a medical student at the University of the Witwatersrand. After I preached my last sermon in the Westbury parish on Christmas day in 1984, it was Auntie Florrie and Elvis and his two nieces, Venisha and Samantha, who bid me goodbye on the N1 as I left for Cape Town. I carried that act of kindness with me.

Some church members had regarded me as overly political and I was reminded of what Reverend Maart endured in Paarl. Dealing with conservative congregants was tough, but I persisted, and won over a few people through projects demonstrating that part of our pastoral responsibility involved addressing social and political issues in the community. I knew I wouldn't convert the whole parish; instead, I handpicked a few people to mentor so that they could continue the work when I left.

I was ordained in 1985 in the Bonteheuwel Congregational parish in Cape Town, working full-time and doing my honours degree in religious studies at the University of Cape Town on a part-time basis. When I arrived in Bonteheuwel that year, some community activists approached me to serve on the local UDF Area Committee, but I made it clear that I was not a politician. I worked in the church and my role in the community was supportive: I provided sanctuary to people on the run from the security forces, arranged funding for them when they were in hiding, and organised prayer meetings for parents whose children had been detained and imprisoned, building their morale and helping them understand and support their children. Many parents were thrown into the struggle by their children's actions, and they didn't know what to do because they didn't understand the situation.

It was around this time that Melvin Bruintjies came into my life. He was immersed in the church and was politically active in Bonteheuwel. We knew him as 'Jesus', because he always attended community and political meetings with his Bible.

Melvin took me to the Churches Urban Planning Commission (CUPC) office in Lower Main Road, Observatory and introduced me to Johnny Issel.

Johnny explained the Western Cape political situation to me, and we reflected on the role of the church and that of ministers in the struggle for democracy. One of the weaknesses in theology was the lack of continuous social analysis: many of us who were trained as ministers had no clue what was happening in society. Johnny encouraged me to join CUPC as a board member. Coincidentally, the regional Congregational Church appointed me as their representative on the CUPC board too.

In Bonteheuwel I worked closely with the youth formations in the MDM. I became good friends with Evelyn Holtzman, a trade unionist. At that stage, Bonteheuwel was one of the most militant townships in the Western Cape and activists were targeted, harassed and detained without trial by the government and its security police. The streets saw constant battle scenes between the angry youth and police, the billowing black smoke of burning-tyre barricades a symbol of their rage. I conscientised some of my parishioners, and a few, young and old, joined the MDM. During this time I ran into the police informer again. There was a protest at the Bonteheuwel town centre and I witnessed the police violently beating up students. Afterwards, I overheard him bragging about how many students he'd beaten.

The government feared that Bonteheuwel was ripe for insurrection and as a result they targeted the community. The repression was extreme.

On 7 March 1986 Pastor Gottfried Kraatz was deported from South Africa and fifty-six of us were arrested while saying our farewells to him and his wife at D.F. Malan Airport in Cape Town. We were beaten, briefly detained and put on trial for disorderly conduct. Siraj Desai was our lawyer and succeeded in getting the charges dropped against all of us. A year later, during the second state of emergency, a brave Lutheran couple from America, Brian and Susan Burchfield, both pastors, were also deported because of their support for our struggle. As the repression intensified, young activists were sent to me for sanctuary. June Esau and I once transported a number of them to their families in Piketberg and Citrusdal, and we were caught in a road block in Malmesbury on our way home. June evaded arrest, but she was subsequently served with a banning order. I was arrested and spent about a year in Victor Verster Prison. Prior to this detention, I'd had a taste of apartheid prisons during a few short stints in police cells. Be that as it may, not knowing the exact reason for my detention and being aware of the brutality of the security police caused some initial anxiety. However, my time at Victor Verster turned out to be a very valuable experience. There were many other comrades at the prison and we held political discussions. Listening to the stories of comrades from various communities strengthened my resolve to not be intimidated by the apartheid state. The most disheartening moment was leaving comrades behind when I was released.

I had seen and lived the cruel repression of apartheid, so when Melvin approached me to join MK, I no longer felt any moral, ethical or theological conflict about joining the armed struggle.

I played a largely supportive role in the AKD. This was logistically difficult as I also had a parish to run and broader political work to do, such as coordinating political campaigns and support for MDM activities in Bonteheuwel. I was very politically active, but I had a low profile and my role as a priest offered convenient cover. People knew me as a minister who arranged prayer meetings, went with mothers of Section 29 detainees to protest at the security police headquarters in Cape Town, spoke at meetings here and there, and worked with the youth. My biggest fear was that if I was exposed, the government would use the opportunity to accuse me and the ANC of misusing the pulpit and the church. However, the way the AKD operated with regard to discipline and organisation appeased my qualms. The commitment and maturity of fellow cadres I was connected to was inspiring. There was no bravado, just determination to do what the ANC and the country demanded of us. In addition, I was amazed to discover that most AKD members I worked with were deeply committed people of faith or, if not believers, deeply spiritual. At a time when the apartheid government was launching a concerted campaign to discredit progressive formations in various faiths, it was a blessing to pray and reflect together.

All the AKD's military operations were linked to clear political objectives, and supported MDM campaigns and activities. I had contact with three members: my commander Melvin Bruintjies, Heinrich Magerman and Seiraaj Salie. I had no knowledge of the others. My first mission was to deliver materials to Seiraaj at Buttrim, a button factory in Epping Industria, where he worked. After that, I arranged safe houses and finances, and later I was asked to identify suitable recruits for the Paarl unit. I identified Charles Chordnum, my second cousin. Years later, I heard that Charles was involved in one of the AKD's last operations, blowing up the Paarl Magistrate's Court with a limpet mine. I also recruited Pete Arendse, who became a general in the post-apartheid SAPS.

There were two tragic incidents that were particularly difficult to handle as a member of the AKD. One was the loss of twenty-two-year-old Coline Williams and twenty-year-old Robbie Waterwitch on 23 July 1989. They were both good friends of mine. I had moved to the corner of Thornton and Boeschoten Roads in Gleemoor, Athlone, soon after marrying Helena in

1989. I heard the explosion that killed them from our home. I went out to see what had happened, and the owner of a nearby hardware store said that a gas bottle had exploded, but I suspected it was an MK-related blast. I walked home, not knowing Robbie and Coline were lying dead and mutilated not far away.

We soon found out what had happened on the SABC news, which referred to the two as 'terrorists'. I will never forget the response of my wife's apolitical cousin: 'If Robbie is a terrorist, then I am one too.'

The AKD asked me to go to the Williams family and tell them about Coline's death before they were approached by the police or media. They wanted me to speak to the Waterwitch family as well, but I said I didn't think it was appropriate because I didn't know Auntie Hettie, Robbie's mother, and believed that somebody who knew her well should go.

The memory of that evening in the lounge with Mrs Williams and Coline's sister, Selina, will be etched in my mind forever. Before I went, I realised that I did not have the courage to speak to them alone – how do you tell a mother that her daughter has been blown up? So I deviated from my commander's instructions and went to the Williams' pastor, Father Frank de Gouveia of the Bonteheuwel Catholic Church, to ask if he would accompany me. He did not hesitate, and we went to the Williams' home together.

When we broke the news, Mrs Williams froze and fell silent. Selina started to cry. Father Frank and I spent a while there, comforting them. I asked Mrs Williams and Selina to keep quiet about my visit, as I feared that it might expose me as a member of MK. It might have been safer for a non-member to break the news to the family, but we wanted to do it as soon as possible and I was the obvious choice.

I was unsettled for a few days after that, overcome with sadness at the loss of these two committed young activists. Coline's death affected me deeply. She was serious about the struggle, and involved in many political, youth and community structures. She'd often popped in at my place and we'd talk about life and theology. Robbie lived down the road from me in Gleemoor, and he had come to chat to me every Sunday afternoon – I'd actually seen him the Sunday preceding the blast.

Coline and Robbie's deaths united Cape Town activists in their resolve to continue the struggle. Multitudes from many different political and religious orientations, including Qibla, a radical Islamic group, gathered at their funeral service at St Mark's Catholic Church in Athlone. Father Peter-John Pearson spoke about the struggle with bold conviction, impressing on everyone that Coline and Robbie's deaths would not deter us. I marched in the procession with their coffins, from the church as far as Athlone Police Station, where I was overwhelmed by anger when I recognised the police informer from Westbury standing there with a smile on his face.

The second tragic incident happened not long afterwards, in November 1989, when I was working at the Western Province Council of Churches at Community House in Salt River. Melvin came to me and said there had been a shoot-out between an MK soldier and the security forces in Athlone, so we went together to Kromboom Road and waited helplessly for more news. Later that day it was confirmed that the slain comrade was Anton Fransch.

I knew Anton from Bonteheuwel, and it was I who had taken him to a farm in Elgin and handed him over to Shirley Gunn on his way into exile three years earlier, in 1986. The night before he left, we spent time together at the Moravian Church house in Lansdowne Road. The last memory I have of Anton was him atop a horse on the farm in Elgin.

The security police were obsessed with assassinating Shirley Gunn, Aneez Salie and Johnny Issel. All three comrades were set up for being killed when their faces were shown on national TV as wanted persons. In Shirley's case, the security police accused her of bombing Khotso House – part of a plan to discredit MK and the AKD. In 1990, Shirley was captured. Her baby, Haroon, was taken from her and placed in a children's home, with the cooperation and support of social workers who violated the rights of a little boy and inflicted the most horrendous type of trauma on him, his mother and his father.

I was tasked with going to the SACC National Conference at Pentech in Bellville to enlist a delegation of SACC members to accompany us to the security police headquarters in Loop Street to demand the return of Haroon to Shirley and their immediate release. When I arrived at the conference, I met Professor Khoza Mgojo, my former theology professor, who served on the SACC's structures. I asked him to intercede on my behalf with Reverend Frank Chikane, the general secretary of the SACC, to table the issue of Shirley and Haroon at the conference. Professor Mgojo returned disappointed and told me that Reverend Chikane was not at all keen on tabling the matter. Reverend Chikane's stance angered me, and I saw it as the antithesis of what it means to be Christian – not to mention the fact that the reverend had himself been targeted by the security police. I had thought that the conference would understand that Shirley had been set up, and that the SACC would stand up for Haroon and use the opportunity to stand in solidarity with us. But the matter did not even get on the SACC's conference agenda.

The AKD was incensed by this inadequate response. I don't think that the

ANC responded in the way it should have either, as I gather there was little support given at the time.

The bombing of Khotso House finally became a national issue at the TRC. Adriaan Vlok, the apartheid minister of law and order who had masterminded the Khotso House bombing and the planned assassination of Shirley, washed the feet of Frank Chikane, who'd survived an attempted assassination by poisoning. However, Vlok never apologised sincerely to Shirley and Haroon. He used the Bible and a newfound religious conversion to support and justify the nondisclosure of crimes against humanity perpetrated by the state.

I supported the TRC wholeheartedly nevertheless, and I knew that we had limited capacity to address the country's complicated past. At the same time, I did not support some of the actions and conclusions of the TRC. It is not possible to forgive a person if that person does not ask for forgiveness or tell you what you must forgive them for. We know that some people told lies and hid many things. Some only came forward to tell their story because others had spoken, and they had no intention to reveal the truth. A lot of people got away with a lot of things and, in a way, we were forced to move on for the sake of national reconciliation. In some cases, we ended up giving credence to a type of cheap grace. Vlok, who proclaimed that he was a transformed 'church man', should have come to Shirley, Aneez and Haroon with his social workers and security policemen and said, 'I was the one who instructed these people to do what they did to you, and I am sorry.' Those are the things that make for real forgiveness, and real peace.

I demobilised in 1992. Non-statutory force members were called to Faure and I took the R22 000 package. I didn't want to join the SANDF because I am a community person at heart, but after some time I decided to enlist – chaplaincy seemed like a role I could play, providing support and boosting peoples' morale. I joined the navy as a chaplain in the Reserve Force.

Being a chaplain in the navy was extremely challenging. The navy personnel belonged to diverse religious faiths and they did not understand that a chaplain's role was to provide support to all members of the navy, regardless of their beliefs. Much of my time was spent reorientating the theological outlook of some of my colleagues.

I was later called to help effect a parliamentary imperative that required the Department of Defence to ensure that all force members acquire a Grade 9 qualification by 2011 and matric by 2020. Hundreds of general workers in the navy did not have a Grade 9 qualification; in fact, many were illiterate. In order to remedy this, I started the South African Navy ABET project, although it went beyond my remit as a chaplain. In order to continue the project in the proper capacity, I applied to the navy to remuster, and I was made a full commander. I subsequently started a navy matric school, and over fifty members of the South African Navy have since completed matric.

Throughout the early 1990s, I worked at the Theology Exchange Programme (TEP), which later became the Centre for South–South Relations (CSSR). We arranged international exchange programmes for church and community activists between countries in the Global South, including Nicaragua, the Philippines, Brazil, Bolivia, Uganda, Tanzania and Palestine. We identified challenges faced by these countries and compatible contexts with the idea of learning from each other. Issues we focused on were HIV and AIDS, gender, democracy, development, transitional politics, South–South solidarity, the role of civil society in struggles and transition, and liberation theology.

In 1994, I was involved with church organisations setting up a national elections-monitoring network for South Africa's first democratic elections, and TEP brought activists from Nicaragua and the Philippines to share their expertise with us. In hindsight, I believe that our network and the monitoring we did during the elections made a significant contribution to the work and task of the Independent Electoral Commission.

For the next ten years I did administrative and project work in Catholic schools in the Western Cape for the Catholic Institute of Education (CIE), and afterwards I worked as a consultant on the Elandskloof restitution farm near Citrusdal. Elandskloof was returned to a few families under the land restitution programme, which was implemented shortly after democracy. The farm was managed by a committee of beneficiaries and the Department of Land Affairs was appointed by the court as the administrator. I was part of a two-person team that took over the administration on behalf of the department. Bethel Church also put in a claim to the Land Claims Commission, but it has not yet been settled.

On Sunday 7 May 2006, Reverend Abe Maart fell ill during a Holy Communion service at Bethel Church and was admitted to hospital. A few days later, he died of an aortic aneurysm. His death was an enormous blow to the parish and the Paarl community, especially the poor and downtrodden from his ministry. Reverend Maart's funeral attracted thousands of people from the community, and Parliament and the Western Cape government issued a statement about his role in the community. It was a fitting send-off for a man so dedicated to Paarl and to our struggle, and who suffered immensely for his beliefs. He was laid to rest in Paarl's Heroes' Acre.

When I go to the cemetery to bury people, I think of the cost of our struggle. I remember brave women such as Ivy Kriel, Mrs Bruintjies and Ma Scott, Leon Scott's mother. These women were harassed by the security police due to their own involvement in the struggle and that of their sons and daughters. I also remember how Ghadija Vallie and I led mothers to the security police headquarters in Loop Street in 1985 to demand the release of Section 29 detainees. I remember Auntie Florrie and Elvis, Pastor Gottfried Kraatz, June Esau, and Brian and Susan Burchfield. These people, among others, built my understanding of what it means to serve God. Their heroism and selfless dedication always came to mind when I offered Holy Communion with the call to offer our body and blood as a living sacrifice. Their resilience in the face of hardship and repression recalls the words of Christ, who said, 'No greater love can any person have than to lay down one's life for one's friends.'

When I reflect on the AKD, I'm filled with pride. I was part of a group of people with integrity, commitment and dedication. Some of our members lost their lives and we will carry that pain until we die. We joined MK as part of our commitment to the struggle. Scared as we may have been at times, we were prepared to lay down our lives for freedom, right until the end. In this respect, one memory stands out for me: when Madiba was released from prison, while others were celebrating, the AKD was tasked to carry out operations that same night, as the sun was setting. Such was our struggle – continuing until the sun set. And the sun has not yet set; there is work to do for the poor and the exploited. That struggle continues, a struggle in which the AKD played a part.

I don't think I will ever go back into full-time parish life. I have discovered the joys of working with people in a way that does not impose restrictions on me. I have found great happiness in determining my destiny, which has been informed by so many people who have crossed my path. I look at some of my dear friends who are church ministers and I can see how limited their perspective and understanding of life is. The struggle opened my eyes to so many people, issues, skills and opportunities, and as a result I have outgrown parish life. Once you have experienced the world, it is difficult to go back and live within narrow parameters.

Helena and I have three beautiful sons. Anton is the eldest and is named after Anton Fransch. Kent was named by Helena, and Charles is named after me. Helena and I separated in August 2012. Initially, I felt guilty for denying my sons the benefit of a full family life. It took a while for me to realise that we inflicted more pain on our children by being together and we had to free our sons from the pressure of siding with either parent. Today, I believe that our separation is in everyone's best interests and I feel less guilt. My sons and I have a good relationship and that is the most important thing to me now.

I have tried to tell my story in a respectful way. That is a requirement from the Bible – if you speak about something that has the potential to harm, do it gently, kindly and with respect. You must be mindful of why are you telling your story, why are you keeping a certain memory alive. In my case, it's not to inflict any injury or pain, but to leave a message. The history and operations of the AKD alone speak volumes. My plea is that the members move on with gentleness and kindness, which has always been one of the hallmarks of our detachment.

17

Heinrich Magerman

The Truth Will Set Us Free

W AR ISN'T EASY, but ours was a just war: as people of conscience, we had to take sides. People were forced to take to the streets and others were forced to go underground. I began actively opposing the apartheid system in high school and my participation deepened at the University of the Western Cape through my involvement in progressive Christian organisations. I joined MK because I believed in truth. Truth is like oil in water – it always surfaces. When judged for our response to the demon of racism and apartheid, we can look people in the eye because we were on the right side. God forbid the day any future generation is confronted with the choices that we had to make.

I alone bear the responsibility of sharing the story of the Macassar Unit. Andrew Adams and Paul Endley have passed away, and the other surviving member, Desmond Stevens, has elected not to share his story. I hope my story does justice to our unit's contribution.

Heinrich Magerman is an odd name for a South African classified as coloured. My parents' peers have children named Ulrich and Elrich, though, so maybe it has something to do with their generation's choice of names. At times, especially when I was involved in the struggle, people were confused by my German name, as I was very far from being German. At one stage I even considered changing my name.

My father, Johannes Magerman, was born in 1945 into the old NG Sendingkerk founded by the Dutch Reformed Mission Church. In 1950, Reverend Isaac David Morkel, a progressive thinker, founded the Calvyn Protestant Church, a breakaway from the old NG Sendingkerk, because he could find no scriptural justification for racial segregation. Many people from Namaqualand embraced this new church. My father and his mother, Rosina, were first-generation Calvyn Protestant Church members. My life has been shaped by their beliefs.

My father, usually known as John or Johnnie, grew up in Komaggas, a small town west of Springbok in the Northern Cape, and he attended primary school there. The nearest high school was in Springbok and the travel costs and boarding fees prohibited him from continuing his education. Later, my grandmother Ouma Rosina moved the family to Nababeep, where copper mining was an economic drawcard. She didn't marry my paternal grandfather, Sam Damon; she married Tol Adams, a miner who worked for the O'Okiep Copper Company. Papa Tol did not accept my father as a member of the family. His half brothers and sisters loved him dearly, but the tensions at home eventually drove him away. When my father completed primary school, he left Komaggas in search of his biological father in Cape Town.

My grandfather, Papa Sam, was married and living in Ravensmead, and his family welcomed my father. I have a big family as a result, which had its advantages as my brothers and I were showered with love. Papa Sam was a loving old man with whom we developed a close relationship.

Time gradually softened Papa Tol's heart. When we visited him and Ouma Rosina in Nababeep, we were warmly embraced. Papa Tol was older, and I think we got the benefit of the love that he had denied my father. Ouma Rosina wrote to my father every month. After he'd read the letters, he'd give them to us to read as well. Her letters would update him on all the people in Namaqualand he'd known as a child, and we would get our kisses and short messages at the end of the page.

My father's first job was at Conradie Hospital in Cape Town, where he befriended my mother's sister. When he visited her home, he met my mother and they fell in love. His next job was as a messenger at the old Cape Provincial Administration offices in Wale Street, where the Western Cape Provincial Administration offices are currently housed. For the rest of his life, my father worked as a messenger and driver at the Trust Bank, now the ABSA building, in the centre of Cape Town.

I have fond memories of going to work with my father in the early 1970s – going up and down in the lift was the highlight. When I got my driver's licence, I stood in for him when he went on leave. Whenever I see the ABSA building I am reminded of him. Another fond memory I have of my father is that he had a gramophone and we'd listen to gospel records, such as the Kings Messengers Quartet.

My mother's name is Hannah – spelt with an 'h' as in the Bible, as she would always say. My second name is Samuel from the biblical story of Hannah, who desperately wanted a child. After praying to God to give her a son, she conceived and gave birth to a boy whom she named Samuel. My mother's nickname was Titte and her maiden name was Priga. There is still debate in the family about the origin of her surname; according to stories I've been told, Priga was derived from *piriga*, the Khoi word for horse.

My mother was the youngest of her nine siblings. She was born in 1944 in Vanwyksvlei, a beautiful, tranquil settlement in the Northern Cape. In the Great Depression of the early 1930s, her father, a farm labourer, uprooted the family: everything they owned was put on the back of a big lorry, and they drove off to eventually settle in Cape Town. There were a few stops in between: Calvinia, De Doorns, Worcester and finally Goodwood. When Goodwood was declared a white area under the Group Areas Act, they were forced to move to Bishop Lavis.

My grandparents on both sides of my family were poor but dignified, hard-working people. My maternal grandfather worked for South African Railways for many years. Later in life, he became the janitor at the Dutch Reformed Mission Church in Bishop Lavis, which he cleaned and opened for services for many years. My early childhood years were spent in Bishop Lavis in my grandparents' house. There was a large guava tree in the garden, and we looked forward to eating guavas in winter. There were other fruit trees too – a mulberry tree, fig trees and even a grapevine.

My grandparents had an old wood stove, which was the heart of the house, and while cooking my grandmother would whistle Dutch Reformed Mission Church hymns. Sunday lunches were grand three-course meals with a formal set-up: everyone sat at the table and Ma prepared a huge spread – roast chicken, potatoes and salads, and stews in winter. Our grandfather was a big presence in our lives, stern and serious, and there were clear rules and discipline in the home.

I have three brothers. I am the eldest, born on 2 October 1968. Johann is two years younger than me, Michael was born in 1976 and Calvin in 1979.

I went to Elnor Primary School in Sub A, and at the end of the year I was top in my class. Because I have very small eyes, Principal Cloete joked that *die ogies is nie daar nie, maar die breins is daar* (the eyes aren't there, but the brains are there).

After living with my maternal grandparents in Bishop Lavis, we lived in Mountain View Road in Matroosfontein. When small sub-economic houses were developed in Elsies River, we moved to Clarke Estate. The houses looked like a train, attached like carriages, and unlike our previous house, it was cramped, with little space for us to play. The distance to our new school, Range Primary, was also greater. When Principal Klein, who lived in Bellville South, saw us walking along the road to school, he'd often offer us a lift. Our teachers were like mothers, fathers or guardians to us, as our own parents had to work long hours.

I was about six when I joined the church brigade. My involvement as a schoolboy, both in the church brigade and the church youth, was my first encounter with organisations, and these experiences shaped my understanding and my character. In the brigade, we wore uniforms and belts denoting our rank. Our instructors were members of the Cape Corps, a military organisation for coloured men, so the brigade had military-style discipline. The brigade also had a band, and once a month on a Sunday we paraded in uniform accompanied by brass instruments and booming drums. This positive experience inspired me musically, and I later played the flute in the band.

Uncle Charles, who lived in the house opposite ours, owned a fruit, vegetable and fish business, and I helped him deliver fresh produce to his customers' front doors in Elsies River and Bishop Lavis. Every Friday, we made deliveries to the old-age home in Matroosfontein. Sitting on the back of his delivery bakkie was very exciting and felt like freedom to me.

My mother worked as a machinist at Gossard clothing factory, and later at Pep clothing factory in Epping. My father worked in town, so we often stayed with neighbours, and they were like our second parents. Our family became good friends with the Leeuw family. On Friday nights, the adults danced to music on the gramophone, kicking up the dust. Mr Leeuw was from the Eastern Cape and isiXhosa-speaking. Auntie Nontjie sold marshmallows from home, which she bought in bulk in Epping Industria. They were a mixed couple. What I better understood later in life was that some people, like the Leeuws, were already in interracial relationships, and they chose to 'become' coloured, despite apartheid's racial classification laws. Their surname, Leeuw, was originally Ngonyama, the isiXhosa word for 'lion'. They belonged to the Bantu Presbyterian Church and their son Cliffy became a priest and went to minister in the Eastern Cape. Many isiXhosa-speaking families lived in Matroosfontein. In general, the greater Elsies River area had a non-racial character.

In the early 1970s, my father was part of the first intake of men handpicked to be trained as evangelists by Reverend Morkel at the theological seminary of the Calvyn Protestant Church in Athlone. He'd had a turbulent youth and was once part of a street gang. One night, the gang decided to get up to trouble, but when push came to shove, the guys were cowardly and ran away. My father realised they weren't trustworthy and left the gang. He'd heard a sermon on the radio and, because he was sick of the life he led, he decided to convert. After he'd confessed and joined the church, he was eager to become an active member.

Thanks to his primary-school education, my father could already read and write, and at the seminary he was taught how to speak to an audience. He practised by standing in front of a mirror, which he did diligently. His life was radically changed, and so were ours.

He eventually became an evangelist, serving in the Matroosfontein and Macassar congregations. The Calvyn Protestant Church in Matroosfontein, operating from the Rhenish Church, soon became too small for the growing number of congregants. Next to the old church building was a large plot on which Reverend Daniel van den Heever, who had a good understanding of construction, built a massive new church and rectory. The reverend played an influential role in our church, and we were drawn in to assist him in many areas of his work. I learnt a lot about organisation, fundraising and entrepreneurship from him, and also important life skills and values, such as the value of hard work.

The reverend also got sausage and mince at a wholesale price, and a group of church sisters packaged the meat to sell to the community. They would then give me the list of orders to deliver on Wednesdays, and on payday on Fridays I had to collect the money from our customers. The bulk of the profits went to building the church, but I earned a little on each package sold. This incentive motivated me to sell more packages, and eventually I earned enough money to buy my first bicycle and tape recorder. My parents could not afford to give my brothers and me these things, because both of them had low-paying jobs: my father was working at the Trust Bank and my mother was a tea lady at the Volkskas Bank.

In the mid-1970s, Reverend van den Heever visited Macassar, a small working-class community with a few dust roads near the coast, close to Somerset West and Strand. He asked my father to minister to the people there, and my father agreed, so we moved from Clarke Estate to Macassar in December 1978.

Macassar had two sections: 'the scheme', which had been built by the apartheid government under the Group Areas Act in the early 1970s; and the historic Macassar area, which dated back to the late 1600s. New houses had been built in the scheme, and we got one of them. It was slightly bigger than our Clarke Estate house, and it was next to the Eerste River, near the highest sand dune on the Cape Flats. This new home gave us the opportunity to appreciate the natural environment – the trees, dunes, rivers, mountains and the ocean. There was a rabbit in our yard, springbok in the dunes, and *turksvye*, or prickly-pear trees. There was space to play, and we swam in the river and enjoyed the nature surrounding us. Elsies River had seemed like a concrete jungle in comparison.

I attended Macassar Primary School, which was initially housed in a prefab structure. At the end of my first year, the school moved to a beautiful new building. My father integrated quickly into the community and became chairperson of the school committee, which meant I had to be a well-behaved boy. I performed well academically and received many academic prizes.

To earn pocket money, I delivered newspapers in the early morning before school. Sunshine or rain, I rode my bike over the N2 to collect the newspapers in Firgrove – about five kilometres away – and then back to the N2 and over the bridge to deliver the newspapers to my customers, before returning in time for school. Later, I got a Saturday job through a congregant who had a mobile grocery-hamper business, and we delivered the hampers to customers in Macassar and to farms in Stellenbosch. In time, we made up the hampers ourselves and I continued distributing them, with the bonus of a free hamper for our household. I also worked as a general assistant to a painter, and I tended people's gardens in the white, middle-class area of Somerset West. I had a wide variety of jobs at primary school and high school, and if I wanted to go somewhere, like on a camp, I funded it myself.

I took my schoolwork extremely seriously, but it was difficult to study at home, where I shared a bedroom with my three brothers. Fortunately, a couple in our church, Sammy and Sophia Louw, took me under their wing. They lived in one of the houses in Marvin Park that the AECI Dynamite Company had built for its staff, and from Standard 8 to Standard 10, I studied in their home during exams. In matric, my schoolteachers Philda and Harold Hickley also made their house available for me to prepare for my final exams.

I won many book prizes for my hard work at school and I was very active culturally. I was involved in the school choir and sang soprano, and I was in the youth brigade. The brigade was not the same as Boy Scouts, but we learnt similar things, such as different methods of preparing fish, including baking it in clay on a fire. We went on several camps, where we met children from other brigades. Those camps were later taken over by the apartheid government's 'winning hearts and minds' propaganda programme, which targeted young people.

Things started to change during this time. At high school, I belonged to a Christian student organisation called the Vereniging van Christelike Studente (VCS), and every June holiday we travelled to different parts of the country, such as Kimberley, Port Elizabeth and Namaqualand. My father did not have a car then and we could not travel anywhere, so these trips were wonderful experiences that opened my eyes to what was happening elsewhere in the country.

I later became a VCS leader. This was in the heat of the struggle in the mid-1980s, and through VCS I met people like Charlie Martin and Allan Boesak, both of whom were reverends presenting political topics for discussion and debate. The character of VCS was dramatically changed and shaped by those debates, and we as young people developed a deep awareness that our spirituality could not be divorced from our social realities. It became clear to me that if we called ourselves Christians and true believers, there was no way we could accept the apartheid system. We believed we were duty-bound to actively oppose apartheid, even violently if need be.

Resistance was on the rise and the youth became actively involved in the struggle. We resisted the Tricameral Parliament in 1984, and the Management Committee (MANCOM), the undemocratic local authority structure that the apartheid regime had imposed on coloured communities. Newly qualified teachers, mainly from the University of the Western Cape, came to teach at our school. They were young and radical and we formed strong connections with them.

I was part of a group of students leading protests at my school. Principal Solly April, a lay preacher, once forcibly took me out of my class and insulted and assaulted me because of my views. I did not change my stance, though, and told him I would continue standing for what I believed to be right. He could not fault me – our protests were disruptive, but I was a good scholar. In my view, he dehumanised himself through his actions, advocating a type of Christianity devoid of truth and blind to the criminality of apartheid.

I turned eighteen in 1987, my matric year, and in October I went for my driver's licence test. One of my teachers loaned me his car to practise driving, and kind Reverend van den Heever asked his son Russel to take me to do the test. The Somerset West Traffic Department was extremely racist and punitive and I had to repeat the test seven times. But I was determined in everything I did, and persisted until I eventually got my licence.

After matriculating, I started a BA degree at UWC. It was 1988 and the many political campaigns at the university made me aware of the different approaches to the struggle. Melvin Bruintjies recruited me into the AKD that year. I had met Melvin a year earlier through his work at the Churches Urban Planning Commission and through the Inter-Church Youth, which was affiliated to the Western Province Council of Churches. Our involvement in the church contributed to our success in the underground since no one believed people like us would be involved in MK.

Desmond Stevens, Paul Endley and Andrew Adams were trained and deployed before me, but when they underwent more advanced training I joined them so that I could also carry out operations, if necessary. Melvin trained us in reconnaissance and in the handling of firearms and explosives, specifically limpet mines and hand grenades. By then, my father owned an old car and because I had a driver's licence, I was tasked with transporting arms for our unit and for storage, as well as assisting with operations.

My primary role was to drop off Paul and Andrew at the targets. They carried out the operations, and I picked them up at prearranged locations and took them home safely. Together, we set off explosions at the Stellenbosch Magistrate's Court, the Paarl Magistrate's Court and the Somerset West Municipal Offices. Our last mission was the railway line in Eerste River. Our operations always got excellent media coverage, which included information about the estimated damage we had caused to the buildings that had been targeted. We knew that we were part of a bigger detachment because our operations were sometimes synchronised with others, but we had no knowledge of the AKD beyond our Macassar unit.

Because I had a relatively high political profile in Macassar as a result of my student and community activism, the security police often turned up at my parents' house. My poor mother always had to deal with them, chasing them away from the house when they came looking for me.

While my father may not have understood my involvement in politics, he showed support in his own way. On a number of occasions I travelled with him to Namaqualand and we began to connect more deeply. I walked with him during his pilgrimage to the hills and rocks near Ouma Rosina's house and accompanied him when he visited his cousins and friends. I even went to church services that he led there, and he'd ask me to pray or to read a passage from the Bible. In hindsight, I realise that he was passing something on to me, creating a space for me to develop.

Towards the end of the 1980s, I became deputy chair of ICY and things changed fundamentally for me. The churches launched the national Standing for the Truth Campaign in May 1989. It resolved to develop non-violent actions against apartheid and called for peoples' organisations to be unbanned, exiles to be allowed to return, political prisoners to be released, and, ultimately, the abolition of apartheid. The WPCC took the lead in the province and Allan Boesak led a big march in Cape Town. On 19 August 1989, thousands of protestors arrived in buses to reclaim the whites-only Strand beach and Bloubergstrand on the West Coast as part of the Mass Democratic Movement's Defiance Campaign. The atmosphere was jovial and we had a wonderful time in the sun, even as heavily armed policemen took up positions along the road. Protestors were picnicking, swimming, singing or praying. Archbishop Desmond Tutu was with us, wearing a yellow sunhat with the slogan 'Free The Beaches' and a T-shirt that read 'Just Call Me Arch'. We'd ignored police orders to disperse, so he held a prayer service to persuade the police not to use force against us, but protestors were nevertheless shot with birdshot and others were *sjambokked*. The actions of the police, as well as our successful occupation of the beaches, sparked more defiant protest actions in the weeks to come.

In a Helderberg protest held on a Sunday, police shot a protester named Xavier. We realised we needed to respond to the incident, particularly when we learnt that Xavier would be paralysed for life. We wrote letters to the editor of *Die Burger*, and there was coverage in a local Helderberg newspaper and the *District Mail*. I was asked to speak with Lionel Abrahams, chief warden at the parish of St Joseph the Worker, about using the church to hold a prayer service for Xavier. It was agreed that we could, and we informed the whole community about the service. It was encouraging and inspirational to find that there were people in the community prepared to mobilise against injustices and lend their support. Dullah Omar acted as Xavier's attorney and won the case and fair compensation for him. We were very pleased with the outcome.

I was in my third year at UWC in 1990, four years before our democratic breakthrough, when Melvin narrowly escaped arrest. The security police, armed to the teeth, had surrounded the home he shared with his wife Ruth in Wynberg, prepared to kill him. Melvin went underground and our contact with him became limited. Then Desmond was arrested and detained for thirty days. I realised I had to keep away from the police and I went into hiding.

Three weeks after Desmond was arrested, however, I was detained. I was dating Spesilene, the woman I would later marry, and I made the mistake of trying to visit her one Saturday night, even though I knew the police were looking for me. Police reservists were monitoring the area and I must have been spotted on my way to her place. I realised I was being followed when I saw a police van behind me, not far from Spesilene's house. I ran to the house and started knocking on her door. The police arrived as the door opened and I was arrested.

Reverend van den Heever came to the Macassar Police Station where I was being held. He was unaware of the depth of my involvement in politics, and had turned up simply because he knew I was a God-fearing person. From my holding cell alongside the reception area I heard him saying, 'It's a terrible mistake, it can't be him, not Heinrich!' The policeman on duty said they had been looking for me and the reverend asked what I had done.

'Sir,' replied the policeman, 'he did not steal anything, but he is undermining the state.' I don't know whether the reverend was relieved or not. My father also didn't really understand what I was involved in, or, if he did, he didn't let on. He didn't engage in political discussions at home as my mom did, but before he went to sleep he would pray aloud and the refrain was always, 'If my children struggle in life give them the grace and wisdom to get up.'

I was transferred to the Strand Police Station and held in solitary confinement. The security police then interrogated me at their offices in Alexander Street in Stellenbosch, not far from the Regional Services Council. I had visited the council building as an eight-year-old boy with Reverend van den Heever when he delivered the building plans for our new church. It was also where we held protests around our community struggles.

Words cannot express the terror I felt in the hands of the security police. When I was detained, Desmond was in the last week of his thirty-day stint in detention. The security police used the detention-without-trial legislation to interrogate me about organising the community, intimidating members of MANCOM and generally causing havoc. During interrogation, however, I was relieved to realise that the security police didn't have a clue about my MK involvement.

I spent two weeks in solitary confinement at the Strand Police Station. The loneliness was excruciating, but I at least had access to a Bible. I drew strength from the Book of Amos, and my resolve to oppose the brutal and oppressive apartheid government was strengthened.

From Strand I was transferred to Victor Verster Prison in Paarl and held there for a further two weeks. Victor Verster was a marginally better place to be because I had contact with other comrades when we were let out of our single cells during the day. This gave me strength. I never saw my parents and my siblings, as they were denied access to me. My mother travelled all the way to Victor Verster Prison once, but the prison authorities were very unkind to her. She had been under the impression that she would see me, but they told her to hand over the clothes she had brought me and leave. Michael, my youngest brother, managed to smuggle in a note to say that he loved me and was thinking about me. It meant a lot.

The whole experience was extremely traumatic and very tough. Professor Brian O'Connell, the rector of UWC, was our pillar of strength throughout it all. He lived in Strand and was the chairperson of the Detainees' Parents Support Committee (DPSC), which arranged legal representation for detainees. The DPSC sent a lawyer to see me at Victor Verster and when she told me that she was my legal representative, I burst into tears; she was the first person to enquire about me.

Soon after my release, I went to stay with Reverend Pierre van den Heever, the secretary of the WPCC. I turned twenty-one and held a church service on my birthday. Charlie Martin spoke, and I used the R500 the DPSC had given me on my release to buy refreshments. It felt important to be surrounded by people whom I loved and who cared for me.

As the country transitioned into democracy in the early 1990s, it became clear that we needed an association that would focus on housing and civic matters in the community. We started the Macassar District Civic and Resident Association (MACDRA) with a group of older residents in the community, and then we formed the Macassar Advice Office. We convinced the St Stephen's Catholic Church to provide space for the advice office, and the Social Change Assistance Trust (SCAT) funded it so that it could be open from Monday to Friday, as well as in the evenings.

MACDRA became a very influential organisation. I was part of the collective leadership that led marches to the MANCOM committee members' houses, along with Desmond Stevens, David Kennel, Ron Halford, Samuel Kleyn, Vincent Shabangu and Desmond's father-in-law, Pieter Jacobs. Things heated up. Through our mobilisation, we forced MANCOM chairperson Sydney Kuhn and other committee members to voluntarily resign. Unfortunately, a member of the Tricameral Parliament coerced them into withdrawing their resignations, and our efforts were reversed. We nevertheless refused to give up.

I completed my studies at UWC in 1991, but the only available teaching post was in Postmasburg in the Northern Cape. I was not prepared to take it because I was too involved in the Macassar community. My parents agreed that I should continue working as a volunteer at the Macassar Advice Office, despite the financial impact this had on the family. I volunteered full-time and Antony Cupido, a member of the advice office committee, occasionally gave me R100 from his salary. I was also briefly appointed by the South African Democratic Teachers Union (SADTU) in Helderberg as an organiser for the region.

During this time Mr Africa, the principal of the primary school I'd attended in Macassar, informed me about a temporary teaching post that had become available at the school. Later that year, I got the temporary job. I continued to be active in the community and participated in a COSATU-led march. When a permanent position became available the following year, I applied for it. Mr Africa called me in and said that he would never appoint me, because he assumed that when there was a march I would be there and not in the classroom. I felt that I was being denied the permanent post because of my political stance and activism, despite what I had achieved. This happened after Mandela's release and the unbanning of political organisations, but it was clear to me that in many ways we were not yet free.

In the period between 1990 and 1993, various criminal charges were laid against me and other community activists for our attempts to render MANCOM ineffective. Taswell Papier, who had defended members of the AKD, was our attorney on some of these cases. In one case, five of us were arrested and charged with intimidation – I was cited as first defendant. Eventually the charges against the other four were dropped, but I was found guilty. The verdict of the Pretoria judge who presided over the case in the Strand Regional Court stated that there was a spirit of intimidation in our actions and that I represented that spirit. Two young attorneys, Terrie Morkel and Jaco Olivier, took up the matter on appeal. I was in Namaqualand when the matter was heard at the Cape Town High Court. That weekend, I read the verdict in *Rapport* newspaper: '*Onderwyser onskuldig oor intimidasie*' (Teacher not guilty of intimidation). I was immensely relieved; my ordeal was over.

Contrary to popular belief, we were still involved in MK after the signing of the Groote Schuur Minute in May 1990 – the resolution between the ANC and the apartheid government to end the climate of violence and intimidation in the country. During the demobilisation process a few years later, the SADF came to retrieve limpet mines that I had stored without detonators in my parents' backyard. Arms were also retrieved from the AKD's long-term storage places, such as the Helderberg Nature Reserve.

I am saddened by the entire demobilising process. In hindsight, I feel that we were robbed and misinformed. I understand that ignorance of the process does not exonerate one, but the fact is that the demobilisation process was fundamentally flawed. The interview and ranking process was rushed, and I got the distinct impression that we – members of the non-statutory forces – were discouraged from integrating into the new South African National Defence Force. With my university degree, I was ranked as a lance corporal, but there was no broader orientation given about other possibilities I could have pursued, such as in the South African Police Service. I demobilised and received R22 000, but those who didn't demobilise got a far better deal in term of pension buy-back because their years of service in the non-statutory armed forces were taken into account when they integrated. I felt discriminated against because I had chosen to become a teacher in the public service rather than integrate into the military.

*

After our democratic elections in 1994, I continued to be actively engaged in community issues, taking up the struggles of the people. I was elected by the ANC to serve as deputy secretary of the South-East Metro Region, the biggest region in the Western Cape at the time, which included Khayelitsha, Mitchells Plain and Stellenbosch. I coordinated the Helderberg elections during this period, and served as the political education officer for the region, becoming involved in the first ANC national political education school.

With the democratisation of local government and because of my community involvement, the ANC chose me to serve on the Cape Metropolitan Transitional Council as well as on the Helderberg Municipal Council. This was when my local government career started. There was a certain irony in this: unbeknownst to the councils, our Macassar Unit had set off explosions in the buildings where we met, including the Strand municipal building, the Somerset West municipal offices, and the magistrate's court.

By 1995, I had to decide where to take my career: work in local government or remain a schoolteacher. Teaching was the logical choice, as I would be contributing in my field of expertise – education. However, I was fascinated by the transition period, so I became an ANC councillor in the Helderberg municipality, serving as deputy chairperson of the executive committee and chief whip. I was also one of six ANC representatives to serve on the Unicity Commission, a unique statutory body responsible for overseeing the transition of six different sub-structures into the City of Cape Town as we know it now.

I also worked in Blue Downs and Eerste River, and continued to be involved in MACDRA, the homegrown organisation that represented the working-class struggles of the Macassar community. In December 1996, disaster struck when a sulphur stockpile on the AECI Dynamite Company's premises ignited. The wind came up and blew toxic sulphur dioxide in the direction of Macassar. On the night of the disaster, I was in my mother's kitchen and we could smell pungent fumes. MACDRA took the lead in the response to the disaster, and cooperated with the fire brigade and the police.

The people living closest to the fire were immediately evacuated. However, the physical effects of sulphur dioxide poisoning had life-threatening effects on people with respiratory problems. One asthmatic resident died that night as a result of inhaling the fumes. To take up a class action lawsuit we would have to build plaintiff cases within the entire community, and I became the community's public representative. Taswell Papier and Vincent Saldanha, who worked for the Legal Resources Centre, advised us. Through them we negotiated with AECI.

Ultimately, on the advice of our lawyers, we agreed that we would not take the class action litigation route. However, we successfully lobbied various parliamentary standing committees and President Mbeki appointed a commission of inquiry to investigate the incident.

In 1996, I applied for a special pension, as did many others who served in the struggle. However, both Desmond and I were born on the wrong side of the 1967 cut-off date and we were disqualified because we were too young, a decision that I found unfair as we had not been asked our ages when we joined MK. For me, the struggle was always about putting other people first. My youth was consumed by it, and this affected my relationships. The emotional toll requires psychological healing. I never put myself or my wife Spesilene first, which resulted in my first marriage breaking up. Drinking and over-eating became my coping mechanisms. The stress of life in the underground, and an unhealthy lifestyle of always being on the go and not eating properly, caused me to become overweight. By 1997 I was diagnosed with diabetes and became insulin-dependent.

When I met Janine Kock she was active in the ANC, and she later became the chairperson of the ANC Youth League in the Strand. We had so much in common, and we debated political issues late into the night. Janine and I got married and we have two children: Jaihne Limpho, our daughter, is named after Chris Hani's wife and Anne Limpho Falatsa, a close comrade and fellow councillor who died. Our son Heine's second name is Sipho, which means 'gift' in isiXhosa. It's a supreme honour to be a parent, and I am very happy.

In the first democratic local government election in 2000, I was nominated to serve as a candidate for the ANC in the Macassar ward. The ANC and the New National Party (NNP) were the main contenders in the local elections. The ANC's overall provincial performance was poor at the time, receiving only 39.7 per cent of the votes, whereas the NNP got 49.9 per cent. The Macassar and Rylands wards were the only wards in the City of Cape Town where the ANC won majority votes in those elections.

When the results were announced, the ANC was taken aback by their poor performance. However, the result in our working-class Macassar ward and in the middle-class Rylands ward affirmed all our hard work and the confidence of the community. We had learnt from the elections since 1994, so in the 2000 elections we knew exactly what our approach should be. We had the trust of the people, which had been earned over time. Even my father, who had voted for the NNP during the 1994 elections, voted ANC when I became councillor, which made me proud.

When I was nominated as a councillor, there were two factions in the ANC in the Western Cape: the Mcebisi Skwatsha faction and the Ebrahim Rasool faction. I tried to remain neutral. My deployment as sub-council chairperson was delayed, but I took it with grace. It was a full-time position and the pay was better. I am glad my mother was alive to see me appointed. She was the one who'd had to deal with the security police coming to the house, and who always supported us throughout the struggle. I also suffered at the hands of elements within the ANC who staged a sit-in at the sub-council offices in Blue Downs, accompanied by a journalist from the *Daily Voice* – without first raising their concerns with the ANC structures. This was deeply disconcerting but did not deter me.

By the mid-2000s, internal political battles and factional infighting within the ANC in the Western Cape informed my decision to quit serving as a public representative. When the post for provincial manager for Project Consolidate was advertised, I applied for it because I could see that the ANC in the Western Cape was losing focus on being people-centred, but interested only in building their various power bases. To me it was never about having to choose between ANC leaders; leaders are elected and the electorate should direct the leaders' conduct. The leadership battle took on a life of its own, and that was the year I decided I'd had enough.

This was the best move I could have made at the time. My life thus far had always put other people first, but this position provided me with the space to focus on my children and myself. I'm no longer prepared to compromise my time with my children or cause further disruption in their lives. I now lead the Community Development Workers Programme in the Western Cape – a partnership programme working across the three spheres of government, which is designed to improve community access to government services. We have the ability to effect change, helping people to help themselves through the work we are doing.

I think many are in denial about what it took to participate in the struggle. To some people it might sound heroic, as if it was an adventure, but the choice to be an MK soldier was never an easy one. Our patriotism and our desire to stand for the truth drove us to the point where we were prepared to make the ultimate sacrifice. We stood in the shadow of death all the time. It was not about being heroic but about serving and being responsive to the demands made on our generation.

18

Charles Chordnum

No Greater Life

O N THE DAY that Nelson Mandela was released from prison, I participated in one of the Ashley Kriel Detachment's final operations. Like
many others, I was driven by the inhumanity of apartheid to become actively
involved in anti-apartheid struggles, beginning with youth activism when I was
fourteen years old. Eight years later, I was recruited into Umkhonto we Sizwe
under the command of the AKD.

I was born into a Christian family and raised with Christian values. Respect
and discipline were paramount. My parents, Doreen and Chris Chordnum,
provided my siblings and me with an education and the skills to fend for
ourselves. They instilled in us a culture of sharing too: in our one-bedroom
house we shared a bed, clothes and food.

I am the second eldest of four children: Russell is the eldest and Phillidah
and Christo are younger than me. I was born on 24 March 1967 and named
after my paternal grandfather, Charles Jimmy Chordnum, and my late maternal grandfather, Alphonso John Andrews. My maternal grandfather trained
and practised as a nurse at Paarl Hospital. During his leisure time, he practised
boxing, which he learnt as a youngster during World War II. He was a proud
and disciplined individual, always meticulously dressed when engaging with
the public – a characteristic that distinguished him among his peers. He was
also an avid reader and a devoted family man, who nurtured strong family
values in his children. These values held firm over time, despite the harsh
reality we faced.

My mother is one of ten children, the eldest of the girls and respected
among her siblings. I was fortunate to have met all her brothers and sisters,
and I had a special relationship with Auntie Rachel, or Auntie Ray, as she was
called. She was a remarkable person who battled the odds to raise two sons
single-handedly and educate them through to tertiary level. She understood

the struggle and supported those who were involved. Later on, when I was on the run, she did not hesitate to provide me with a safe house.

My father is one of seven children and the only son. His father died when he was very young, and his mother, my grandma Sophie, was responsible for raising her children on her own. My father left school at a young age to work and help his mother fend for the family financially.

Grandma Sophie stepped in to help look after my siblings, our cousins and me while our parents were at work. We accepted our family dynamics and its challenges, which were similar to those of other working-class families around us.

As youngsters, we played games in the streets, including *drie blikkies* and *kennetjie*, where a short stick is flipped into the air by a longer stick. We also played street rugby and street cricket, which were played everywhere in rural coloured communities of the Boland. My uncle Gerald showed great skill and promise as a rugby player, and he had fans on and off the field. He played a very influential role in my upbringing, and introduced me to outdoor adventures such as mountain climbing, swimming in rivers and exploring neighbouring farms. My siblings and I loved exploring our surroundings. On Saturday mornings we'd meet the elders at a local barber, where we were introduced as '*Boeta se klong*' (Chris's boy) or '*Alphonso se kleinseun*' (Alphonso's grandchild). This contributed to a strong sense of belonging.

The Group Areas Act affected my family like it did all other non-white families in the early 1960s. I was born after the forced removals and raised in the newly established coloured area in Paarl East, or Onder-Paarl. Stories about Bo- (upper-class) and Onder- (working-class) Paarl shaped our social consciousness from an early age. My siblings and I were often told stories about the house in Bo-Paarl in Eiland Street, Bella Vista, on the other side of the Berg River, where our family had lived and where our community had once been. It was rezoned as industrial property and many Jewish shop owners and retailers moved into the area. The Rembrandt Tobacco Corporation's factory was built there, which became a massive economic driver in Paarl.

My grandparents also owned property in Bo-Paarl. The family house was next to the old Bethel Congregational Church, which was relocated to Evans Street in Onder-Paarl, where it still stands today. The church, led by Reverend John Thorne and Reverend Abe Maart, played an instrumental and unifying role in Paarl, fighting against the forced removals and driving Christians to fulfil their social responsibility to oppose injustice.

Our family did not immediately relocate to the newly established Amstelhof area. I have memories of us living with my grandmother for a period before we moved to 327-A Bokmakierie Street. Government housing for non-whites was less than decent. The two-room units resembled a hostel, or compartments on a train, and we could hear the neighbours' conversations deep into the night. We suffered the indignity of sharing an outside toilet and bathroom, which had an overhanging showerhead and a loose standing tap below. Every house was equipped with a Dover coal stove in the kitchen, where our food was cooked and water was warmed for washing and bathing. The eight-square-metre kitchen doubled as a dining room and lounge, and we did our homework around the kitchen table. This room led into the bedroom, which we all shared, with a curtain partitioning the space. On one side was my parents' bed, and on the other was the bed that my siblings and I shared.

I spent most of my childhood at 327-A Bokmakierie Street; it is where my memories as a barefoot boy reside. Four of my cousins lived in a house opposite ours with their parents, Uncle Floors and Auntie Joanie Willemse. We were together most of the time and an older cousin, Jacque Philander, or 'Boetatjie', acted like an older brother to us younger kids.

Our backyard had a few fruit trees, a flowerbed, a patch of lawn and a protea tree. My mother enjoyed gardening and each year she would plant different types of seasonal flowers. During springtime, the colourful display of flowers would brighten the garden and the annual flowering of the protea lured beautiful woodpeckers. My siblings and I collected wood for the stove, and on weekends we woke up early to start the fire to boil water for coffee and bathing. Fetching water outside was the boys' responsibility with our father, while my sister helped my mother wash the dishes and clean the house. The family had a dog named Snipsy, which we all had to take care of.

My mother trained at the Athlone Teachers' Training College, but fell pregnant while studying and couldn't complete her training. After she married my father, the rest of her adult life was dedicated to helping support the family. She worked as a retail assistant and deli attendant at OK Bazaars in Lady Grey Street, our local retail area, and she'd often come home with leftover cold meats and salads. She spent a large part of her working life at OK Bazaars, but also worked for Wellington Dried Fruits in the same street. Her survival skills and management of our family's meagre income rubbed off on me, although her wisdom is one of her finer skills that I am still unable to master.

My father was the family's main provider. He worked as a bricklayer in the construction industry. When contract work was scarce in the Western Cape, he found work as a builder in other towns and provinces and would sometimes be away for a month or two at a time. Though physically taxing, bricklaying was a rewarding career then. His work took him all over the country for more than fifty years, working for different companies. He also had a passion for music, something he shared with his brother-in-law. They formed a brass band with a few friends from the neighbourhood and entertained the local community on special occasions, free of charge.

My parents worked tirelessly from Monday to Friday. On weekends, and after payday, family and friends would gather for braais and drinks, and the neighbourhood children would all play together. This was at a time when each child was everyone's child; when discipline and respect were the order of the day; when husbands would surprise their wives and children with chocolates and packets of chips as tokens of their love and appreciation. It was a time of Chappies bubblegum, Wilson's sweets and gumdrops; when women dressed stylishly and men wore three-piece camel suits and pointed shoes at Christmas and on the long road to church.

Because we came from a staunch Christian background, we had to pray and read the Bible when we woke up in the morning, when we came home from school, when we had dinner and when we went to bed at night. Before we went to bed we had to be clean, with our teeth brushed, our shoes polished, and our pants and shirts cleaned and ironed, ready for the next day. On Sundays and mid-week, we went to church and attended prayer sessions. Respect for elders was enforced. When passing an elder, the correct thing to do was to greet them properly, looking them in the eye. When somebody was begging next to the road or knocking at our door for help, we had to try to assist them. My mother never indulged in alcohol or cigarettes and was a member of the church's Susters-Vereniging (Sisters Union). On Sundays, she would wear her black-and-white church outfit, with a little clutch bag in which she carried her Bible and hymn book. Before going to church, each child would get two cents for the collection box and we would be watched to ensure we did not pocket it.

I remember the day my father stopped smoking. It was a Saturday when I was about ten, and we were riding on his bicycle to watch rugby at the local sportsground, me on the handlebars and Russell on the back seat. My father pulled over at the local shop to buy a packet of Rothmans. When he came out, he stopped, said 'no' and went back into the shop to exchange his cigarettes for suckers and Wilson's blocks, which he gave to us. I never saw him smoking again. When I was about thirteen or fourteen, he stopped drinking too, became a born-again Christian and really turned his life around.

My family relocated to Lantana, which was next to a vineyard and apricot farm. Although it was still a working-class community, the move offered our family the opportunity to get a bigger council house: a three-room semi-detached house, with an inside bathroom with a bath and toilet. Most houses in the community had outside toilets, and my friends would jokingly say to me, '*Jinne* Charles, are you guys really shitting in your house?'

I frequently visited friends and schoolmates who lived on farms, and experienced first-hand the difference between the lifestyles in our semi-urban community and farming communities. We didn't have much in the way of resources, but they had absolutely nothing: no electricity and barely any living space: two or three families would share a two-room house. The farmer's house was always some distance from where the farmworkers stayed, and they were not allowed to come within a 100-metre radius of it. At one of my friends' places, a river formed the boundary between the white farmer's house and the farmworkers' homes. When we crossed the little bridge and heard the dogs barking, we knew we had to retreat.

I have vivid memories of the bread boycott and the 1976 student uprising, which took place when I was nine years old. I remember coming home from school when the police shot teargas at student protestors, which I inhaled. I remember the bus boycott as well. Buses were the main mode of transport for working people travelling to and from town. During the boycott there was a stream of people, defiant and strong, walking to and from work instead of going by bus.

Moving from Amstelhof to Lantana meant my siblings and I had to attend a new school, the Afrikaans-medium William Lloyd Primary. My mother would take us to school in the mornings on her way to work in town, and in the afternoons after school we stayed with Grandma Sophie until she fetched us again. We did that every day until we were old enough to walk home on our own. In theory, this gave us more time to do our homework – something we rarely did.

Charles Harris, my English teacher, introduced me to politics. He'd give us his opinions on the 1976 student uprising and his thoughts on the African struggle for independence from colonial masters. He saw Zimbabwean independence in 1980 as a massive victory and admired Robert Mugabe, whose question 'Why do we have to subject ourselves to being ruled when we can rule ourselves?' was very influential at the time. Like all institutions, William Lloyd had its own class dynamics. There was a clear divide between middle-class and working-class learners, preferentially skewed towards middle-class learners. This never deterred us working-class children from socialising across class boundaries and achieving academically and on the sports field, though. We were tough and determined to succeed despite the odds, and we praised one another when we excelled.

Sport was an important part of my life. Our principal at William Lloyd Primary, David Samaai, had played tennis at Wimbledon in the 1950s and trained tennis players both at school and the local tennis clubs. My uncle Sinclair Andrews introduced me and the other boys to rugby, which was played under the banner of the South African Rugby Union (SARU), part of the South African Council on Sport. SACOS supported non-racial principles by encouraging interaction between coloured, African and Indian communities, rejecting outright the apartheid government's racist programme. Sport was another site of struggle, and the SACOS slogan was 'No normal sports in an abnormal society'. Our club, Young Standards Rugby Football Club, was the oldest rugby club in Paarl and one of the oldest clubs in the Western Province. It formed part of the Paarl Rugby Union, an affiliate of SARU. SACOS-affiliated sporting bodies mostly trained at the historic *kraal* next to the Huguenot Station, where our grandfathers and grandmothers had played sport in their youth.

Not all coloured communities united under the SACOS banner, though. Some played sport under the apartheid government's sports federations, which caused major tensions among us. The system of divide and rule was greatly at play here. Those who played under the federations were generally either members of the SAP or the Coloured Corps in the SADF. They lived in our communities and spied on our resistance.

I learnt so much from team sport and the network of players and administrators. My mother's youngest brother, Gerald, who was like an older brother to me, was an excellent rugby player and represented his high school at regional and national levels. He was famous for his long runs off the scrum, wearing the Number 8 jersey. His involvement in sports and outdoor activities encouraged me in the same direction and I eventually ended up playing for the Under-19 Young Standards Rugby first team, which went on to claim the league title. Gerald was politically active at school, and in 1980 he was detained for fourteen days. My mother had always looked out for him, so in return Gerald often babysat my siblings and me, and he actively developed our political awareness.

I attended Paulus Joubert Secondary School in the 1980s. The school mainly accommodated children from the neighbouring areas: Amstelhof, Lantana, Magnolia Flats and the surrounding farms. Most of our parents who made it to secondary school had also attended Paulus Joubert.

My first two years at high school were traumatic. I found myself in an environment where I had to fend for myself, with little guidance from my older brother and cousins. Luckily, my strong religious background drove me to join the Vereniging van Christelike Studente (VCS), of which Reverend

Allan Boesak was a patron. Priesthood appealed strongly to me then, but my involvement in student politics soon took centre stage.

My beliefs were challenged, and two biblical scenes resonated with me at the time: the reaction of Jesus when he found the Holy Temple being used for gambling and personal gain, which angered him so much that he chased everyone out of the temple; and Moses leading the enslaved Israelites out of bondage in Egypt to the Promised Land. These stories inspired me to fight the evil apartheid system to obtain justice and freedom.

The VCS exposed me to issues beyond the school environment, especially the state's repressive handling of the unrest in the Vaal Triangle. This coincided with the UDF's 1983 'Don't Vote' campaign. I started listening to the voices of resistance and became part of a group that got together during break time for discussions about apartheid's gutter education and the Tricameral parliamentary system.

At the same time, playing sport allowed me to meet comrades like Johan van Zitters, a former activist from the Congress of South African Students (COSAS), and the brilliant Daniel Pietersen. Daniel had shared a platform with Allan Boesak at a meeting we organised under the banner of the Boland Students Action Committee (BOSAC) in the early 1980s. During this mass meeting, which took place at the Roman Catholic church in Paarl, Daniel told the crowd, 'Hoe meer jy kry, hoe stiller bly jy.' (The more you get, the quieter you become.) He directed this statement at teachers and other professionals who remained silent to protect their own interests as the struggle intensified.

My activism evolved during these years, and I was radicalised by my peers and teachers. Zaid Shaik in particular took me under his wing. He guided my thinking and gently instilled confidence in me over time. I also met teachers from the University of the Western Cape and teachers' training colleges, who shared their ideas. I had started high school as a devoted conservative Christian, elected as chairperson of VCS, but as the years progressed, my consciousness transformed into that of a social activist, and this prepared me for militant action.

My first actions in the liberation struggle were during the run-up to the Tricameral Parliament elections in 1984. COSAS led the fight at school level by rallying against the institutionalised prefect system, and campaigning for the recognition of a democratically elected Student Representative Council at our school. I was privileged to be elected as a representative on the first democratically elected SRC at Paulus Joubert.

COSAS's student leadership in Paarl organised across the length and breadth of the district, not only in schools in coloured communities, but also in black communities such as Mbekweni. I was in and out of the African townships, even though it was prohibited. State propaganda mainly focused on creating divisions between coloured and black communities across the country. This was to deepen the racial divide and keep us apart.

Under the banner of COSAS, we waged many battles against unjust laws, which sometimes led to direct confrontation with the security forces and the riot police and caused general unrest across town. Confrontations with the police during August 1985 led to the SAP's brutal killing of Adri Faas, a student activist from UWC. Although the government restricted attendance at his funeral, thousands of mourners turned up. The crowds multiplied as his coffin was carried down Drakenstein Road, and that led to further violent confrontations with the police. Our town became ungovernable.

At this point, Zaid Shaik's organisational skills made it possible for us to present our fight in a structured manner. With his mentorship, we organised a number of well-supported activities, including a mass rally at New Orleans Secondary School, which was interrupted by the security police and the Paarl riot squad. Students were led off the school premises and some of us were detained in terms of Section 50 of the Internal Security Act. The apartheid police hoped that by detaining the student leadership and isolating the 'troublemakers' from the community, all activities would die down and the situation would normalise.

I was detained at Allandale Prison in Paarl, together with Japie Cornelissen, Philemon Davids, Tommie Matthee, Mario Julies, Muawia Moerat, a comrade by the name of 'Lompie' and another innocent youth. We were all very young (I was eighteen) and being held together helped. Most of the warders were from our local community and some knew us because they lived in Paarl, and they took messages to our families and friends on the outside. After fourteen days we were released. Soon afterwards, on 20 July 1985, a state of emergency was declared.

The state of emergency banned many organisations, including COSAS, so we had to become creative. We regrouped after our release and continued our BOSAC work. With the Paarl Students Association (PASA), we continued to mobilise high-school and university students. Many individuals in leadership positions were banned or restricted under the state of emergency regulations, and many activists were randomly detained across the country. The state's actions showed that it was facing a serious crisis nationwide.

Reverend Abe Maart roped me in to serve on the coordinating committee of the consumer boycott to support its activities and increase pressure on the apartheid state. We gave communities much-needed information about the rent and consumer boycotts, and also information about those incarcerated on Robben Island. My participation in UDF structures, including SACOS, intensified. By this point, the divide between racist sports bodies and the anti-apartheid formations supporting non-racial sport under SACOS and the UDF was clear. In 1986, my matric year, the *Rapport* Cycle Tour brought this division to a head. SACOS viewed the hosting of the rebel cycle tour in Paarl as an insult and an assault on the non-racial peoples' movement, and started mobilising to disrupt it. The tour wasn't cancelled, but it was redirected away from Paarl East. Then, a few days before the event, the house of Mr Kulsen, the co-organiser of the tour and chairman of the local cycling club, was petrol-bombed.

There was a warrant out for my arrest due to my alleged involvement in the bombing, and a few other suspects were arrested, including Adwell West, Mario Julies and John Steenkamp, who was later exposed as a police informant. Two others, John Kearns and Titus Hendricks, tried to skip the country, but they too were arrested. Charges were later dropped against Mario and Adwell. John and Titus were held under Section 29 and charged with terrorism and furthering the aims of a banned organisation – the ANC. Titus was convicted and imprisoned on Robben Island.

During the second state of emergency in 1986, I was detained, along with a number of comrades, for around six months. For the first three months, we were held at different police stations and moved every other week – from Klapmuts to Paarl, Malmesbury and Worcester. The security police were trying to disorientate us, and make it difficult for our parents to visit us. For the last three months, we were held at Victor Verster Prison. By then, the Detainees' Parents Support Committee had started organising and supporting parents, while the Paarl Advice Office coordinated parent visits to detained family members in different police stations and prisons. My family suffered, especially with the subsequent detention of my sister Phillidah, who was held under the state of emergency regulations at the Worcester female prison for six months that year.

After we were released, Phillidah told me there was someone she wanted me to meet. 'I'm bringing the person tonight; make sure you're here,' she said. That evening, she introduced me to a man I had not met before. 'This is Charles Martin,' Phillidah said. 'Your cousin.' In the course of the evening, I learnt that Charlie and I had both grown up in Paarl, but we had not met because Charlie and his family lived in Magnolia Flats, which we knew as 'the

Flats'. Our impression of people who lived there was that they were tough guys; they did not stand back for anyone. After completing matric in the 1970s, Charlie had left Paarl to pursue his career as a priest and participate in the liberation struggle. This meeting foreshadowed our involvement in MK.

I matriculated at the end of that year. There was an agreement in our community that when we finished school we would dedicate one year to the Paarl community, so in 1987 and 1988 I volunteered at the Paarl Advice Office, based in the 1-Up Centre in Newton, opposite Mbekweni. My main responsibilities were organising the unemployed youth as members of the Paarl Youth Congress (PAYCO), building BOSAC and PASA, and general administrative work. I loved the work of helping others, particularly arranging and preparing visits to political prisoners on Robben Island, and it felt good to serve my community, especially after the advice office had supported my parents through my detentions.

The advice office received financial support from the Social Change Assistance Trust, a Norwegian funding agency, and we worked as volunteers, receiving a nominal fee of R600 per month, which we shared between unemployed comrades and worthy causes. The advice office also provided paralegal advice and galvanised legal support from the Legal Resources Centre and other advice offices. This was during the time when the apartheid state-owned and white-owned businesses were unfairly dismissing black workers and abusing workers' human rights. We mediated on behalf of workers between employees, employers and the Department of Labour, and during this period the ranks of the youth movement swelled.

Over time, I built up a network of people that reached into even the most conservative parts of Wellington. Japie Cornelissen and I recruited young activists to build the youth and student movement and we connected with veteran trade unionists who linked us to younger workers in the clothing, textile and paper industries in the surrounding areas of Pniel and Kylemore.

The security police were serious about isolating us from our communities and in 1987 I was once again detained under the state of emergency regulations, and held at Victor Verster Prison. It was hell. Detention took its toll on me and I started fantasising about escaping and going into exile. While at Victor Verster, I met more senior Western Cape activists, including Johnny de Lange, Ngconde Balfour, Bulelani Ngcuka, Maxwell Moss, Neville van der Rheede, Zoli Malindi and Willy Simmers. Trevor Manuel was also there for a period of time. My political education continued: when they spoke, I listened.

When I was released later that year, I went straight back into the thick of things. I suppose the threat of imprisonment always felt more real to me than the threat of losing my life. But when comrades like Ashley Kriel and Anton Fransch were killed, the cruelty and severity of the apartheid system became apparent. It was a hectic period in my life and my relationship with my family became strained. My great-uncle Barend Andrews had been elected as a member of the apartheid government's Tricameral Parliament in 1984, and throughout the 1980s he shared a political platform with Adriaan Vlok, the notorious minister of law and order. I did not hide the disgust and hatred I felt towards Uncle Barend. Another point of contention was that my mother's brother served on the Paarl Management Committee, which was responsible for the municipal administration of the Paarl East area. I had a number of explosive confrontations with him, which affected my relationship with my family. As the 1980s drew to a close, my parents left Paarl and relocated to Eerste River, hoping that my active involvement in politics would subside.

In 1989, after volunteering at the advice office for two years, I enrolled for a Bachelor of Administration at UWC. It was during this period that my cousin Charlie Martin recruited me into the AKD. I was trained by my commander, Andrew Adams, to handle weaponry, including an AK-47 and Makarov pistol, and explosives such as limpet mines and grenades, and instructed in how to prepare and execute operations. After years of suffering under apartheid and experiencing violence first-hand, the ability to fight back was empowering.

Being an MK cadre required the utmost discipline and meticulous execution of operations. Self-glorification had no place in it. Andrew and I conducted reconnaissance for the execution of the Paarl operation. Our mission was linked to Nelson Mandela's release from prison and his first public address at the Grand Parade in Cape Town on 11 February 1990. Andrew and I wanted to watch him walking free from prison, but our operation required us to be in the field at the time, awaiting a signal from our command centre that would either give us the go-ahead or tell us to stand down.

Our initial target was the Conservative Party offices, due to the CP's refusal to participate in the negotiation process between the apartheid government and the liberation movement. When Mandela addressed the crowds from the balcony of City Hall, he said, 'The factors which necessitated the armed struggle still exist today. We have no option but to continue.' This was considered an endorsement of the continued existence of MK and the AKD, and we were given the go-ahead for the operation. Andrew and I headed for the CP offices, but when we arrived there was a lot of activity around the place, so we resorted to plan B: either the local police station or the municipal office. The local police station was also ruled out due to possible casualties given the packed holding cells at the back. The municipal offices therefore became the target.

The operation went smoothly and our careful planning meant that no one was killed or injured. Nevertheless, I breathed a sigh of relief when it was over. Andrew and I spent the night at my aunt Eleanor's house in Lantana, and he left the following day.

I didn't demobilise in 1992 with the bulk of the non-statutory force members. I was unemployed at the time and so I decided to explore my career options with the SANDF.

Prior to my first deployment in 1997 at the Youngsfield Military base in Ottery, Cape Town, I reported to the Wallmansthal Military Base in Pretoria, along with other combatants from MK and APLA. The integration programme presented there allowed us to share our respective experiences in the underground and in exile, the operations we'd participated in and our expectations for the new South Africa. The conclusion of the ranking and integration process demanded that we undergo conventional basic statutory training, which was conducted under the watch of representatives from an integration committee to prevent incidents that could derail the process or cause any further strain between the different armed forces. However, senior white SADF soldiers provided the training and this caused tempers to flare because of bullying and their abuse of rank and authority. This was a challenging period for me because the demanding environment caused a lot of stress that I had to learn to manage. I was miserable, surrounded by former SADF members as well as former non-statutory force guys who I believed started to conform to the more conservative culture.

I have since learnt that politics is not absolute and changes with time. One day, out of the blue, my great-uncle Barend Andrews asked to speak to me at my house in Paarl. This would be our first conversation and I struggled to accept his invitation to meet. I consulted Reverend Abe Maart to ask his opinion about it. He said that if we were willing to embrace and reconcile with whites in post-apartheid South Africa, what stopped us from embracing family members whom we regarded as sell-outs? He pointed out that I was working alongside members of the former SADF, who had murdered so many of our people, including members of the AKD, so what reason did I have for not extending the same reconciliatory hand to my uncle? He advised that I approach the meeting with Barend with an open mind. This, for me, was the start of crossing the divide.

I maintained contact with a few people who'd been politically active, but it wasn't until 2007 that I saw Andrew Adams again – at AKD member Richard Ishmail's funeral in Cape Town. I took him back to the house where he and I had stayed that night in February 1990 when we'd executed an operation, and I re-introduced him to my aunt. I later discovered that he had been involved in multiple AKD operations, which did not surprise me given his skill in the field.

My employment with the SANDF in Cape Town gave me the opportunity to focus on family. I was married to Shireen, with whom I'd had a relationship since our school days, and my permanent appointment at the SANDF granted us a three-bedroom flat at the military flats at Castle Court in Zonnebloem. I didn't stay with the SANDF for long, though. Eventually I opted to complete my tertiary education instead, and I enrolled at Cape Technikon to pursue a national diploma in public management. After graduation, I applied for a master's degree in public administration at the University of Stellenbosch and received a scholarship.

Once I'd completed my postgraduate degree, Bruce Kannemeyer, the municipal manager of Stellenbosch municipality, recruited me to work with him. I assumed duty in the mid-2000s as a policy researcher and remained at the municipality until 2009, after which I took up employment with the Breede Valley municipality. In 2010, the municipality changed from an ANC majority council to a DA majority council. All the resultant restructuring, sidelining and politicking got the better of me, and in February 2014 I threw in the towel.

Around this time, my family life suffered tremendous blows, including the break-up of my marriage. I moved out of our family home in Paarl and settled in the small town of Wolseley, about thirty-five kilometres outside Worcester. I never imagined it would be so difficult; loneliness was the worst part. Adjusting to a life on my own and staying afloat affected me deeply.

My first Christmas and New Year away from my three children was terrible. The following year I decided to invite my parents and siblings to my place, as well as Charlie Martin. In the spirit of reconciliation, I invited my great-uncle Barend Andrews too, along with his daughter Gertrude, her husband and their daughter, Abigail. It would be our last social gathering with all of us together, committed to becoming closer as a family. Our path to healing ended abruptly with Uncle Barend's death, and then Gertrude's murder on 7 June 2013. Our contact with Abigail, his only granddaughter, was severed when she resettled outside the Western Cape with her father.

I relocated to the Free State a year later, working in service of local government. I currently live in the small rural town of Vrede, a previously white-dominated suburb with an agricultural economy. When the different municipalities were re-categorised in 2001, most of the areas were demarcated afresh and some municipalities were lumped together to make them more economically viable. The result was that little attention was paid towards the provision of services for remote towns like Vrede. The roads are littered with potholes and economic activity has completely declined. The municipal work-force has limited capacity, whilst whites still predominantly own the means of production. My childhood home and struggle life feels far away from here.

I've found it difficult to find myself in this new democracy and to reconcile with my family and move on. But my parents have helped me in this regard. While they did not support what we were prepared to do for the struggle, they have played a very supportive role in helping me adjust to my circum-stances and embrace our new democracy. My children are the centre of my life. Shastelle's second name is Ruth, after Ruth First. She is a town planner for the Western Cape government. Sammy's second name is Colene, after Coline Williams, and is studying international relations at the University of Stellenbosch. My son, Charles Junior, my youngest, is named after me. He is now in high school and we have a very close relationship. I am very proud of all of my children and owe a lot of gratitude to my ex-wife Shireen, who keeps the family together and has instilled strong family values in our children.

In February 2016, after a longstanding relationship, I married Shandre in her hometown of Worcester. She is the light in my life, providing great sup-port to me, my children and the rest of my family. At the beginning of May 2017, Shandre resigned from her work in Worcester and joined me in Vrede. Her family and I connect easily and I foresee a great family relationship unfold-ing over the next few decades.

My life has been strengthened by the sacrifices of others who served before me and with me to achieve our freedom and a humane society, including heroes like Nana Abrahams, Norman Pietersen, Anton Fransch, Ashley Kriel, Coline Williams, Robbie Waterwitch, Adri Faas, Neil Moses, Oliver Tambo, Chris Hani, Lilian Ngoyi, Oscar Mpetha and Zoli Malindi.

During the struggle, we held a shared belief in a just society. Our beliefs are now enshrined in our Constitution and in the Bill of Rights that our elected government is entrusted to realise. The rest – ensuring our aspirations and dreams are reached and that our democratic government is held account-able – is up to each one of us.

Abbreviations

ADE: Atlantis Diesel Engines
AKD: Ashley Kriel Detachment
ANC: African National Congress
APLA: Azanian People's Liberation Army
AWB: Afrikaner Weerstandsbeweging
BA: Bachelor of Arts
BAAB: Bantu Affairs Administration Board
bergies: homeless people
BBC: British Broadcasting Corporation
BISCO: Bonteheuwel Inter-schools Congress
BOSAC: Boland Students Action Committee
BP: British Petroleum
BSc: Bachelor of Science
CAHAC: Cape Areas Housing Action Committee
CAP: Community Arts Project
CARA: Coline, Ashley, Robbie and Anton Memorial
CAYCO: Cape Youth Congress
CBD: central business district
CEO: chief executive officer
CIA: Central Intelligence Agency
CLOWU: Clothing Workers Union
COSAS: Congress of South African Students
COSATU: Congress of South African Trade Unions
CP: Conservative Party
CUPC: Churches Urban Planning Commission
DA: Democratic Alliance
DG: disability grant
DPSC: Detainees Parents Support Committee
EOH: Ernest Oppenheimer Hall
FAWU: Food and Allied Workers Union
Fedsem: Federal Theological Seminary of Southern Africa

FRELIMO: Mozambique Liberation Front

FRU: Film Resource Unit

HBAC: Hout Bay Action Committee

ICY: Inter-Church Youth

IFP: Inkatha Freedom Party

JC: Junior Certificate

LLB: Bachelor of Laws

MACDRA: Macassar District Civic and Resident Association

MANCOM: Management Committee

MDM: Mass Democratic Movement

MK: Umkhonto we Sizwe

MPLA: People's Movement for the Liberation of Angola

MWASA: Media Workers' Association of South Africa

MYM: Muslim Youth Movement

NGO: non-governmental organisation

NIC: Natal Indian Congress

NICRO: National Institute for Crime Prevention and Rehabilitation of the
    Offender

NIS: National Intelligence Service

NNP: New National Party

NP: National Party

NUSAS: National Union of South African Students

NYLTP: National Youth Leadership Training Programme

PAC: Pan Africanist Congress

PASA: Paarl Students Association

PE: Port Elizabeth

Pentech: Peninsula Technicon

REC: Regional Executive Committee

RPMC: Regional Political Military Committee

SAAF: South African Air Force

SABC: South African Broadcasting Corporation

SACC: South African Council of Churches

SACOS: South African Council on Sport

SACP: South African Communist Party

SADF: South African Defence Force

SAIRR: South African Institute for Race Relations

SAMVA: South African Military Veterans Association

SANDF: South African National Defence Force

SAP: South African Police

SAPS: South African Police Service
SARHWU: South African Railway and Harbour Workers Union
SARU: South African Rugby Union
SATOUR: South African Tourism
SATS: South African Transport Services
SOMAFCO: Solomon Mahlangu Freedom College
SRC: Student Representative Council
TAU: Technical Assistance Unit
TEP: Theology Exchange Programme
TRC: Truth and Reconciliation Commission
UCT: University of Cape Town
UDF: United Democratic Front
UDW: University of Durban-Westville
UIP: United International Pictures
UNISA: University of South Africa
UNITA: National Union for the Total Independence of Angola
UWC: University of the Western Cape
VC: vice chancellor
VCS: Vereniging van Christelike Studente
VP: vice-president
WCRF: Western Cape Relief Forum
Wits: University of the Witwatersrand
WPCC: Western Province Council of Churches
WRAC: Westbury Residents Action Committee
YCS: Young Christian Students

Glossary

bakkie: pickup truck
boere: members of the apartheid police, prison service or security forces
boeta: boy; brother
Casspir: armoured personnel carrier
coolie: derogatory term for person of Indian descent
dagga: marijuana
dhal: a dish made with lentils or other split pulses
dompas: passbook, compulsory for black men to carry in white urban areas under apartheid law
dorpie: small town
fokken: fucking
fokkol: fuck all
gram dhal: type of dhal made with chickpeas and flour
gumbas: dances
hotnot: derogatory term for people of Khoisan descent
jinne: an exclamation of surprise
juffrou: miss
Kan 'n man dan nie?: Can a man not…?
koeksister: traditional Cape Malay plaited doughnut dipped in syrup
kiewiet: plover
keffiyeh: scarf worn around the head
kombi: minibus
kraal: traditional African village of huts; an enclosure for livestock
laatlammetjie: a child born many years after their siblings
Labarang: Eid
meneer: mister
moer: beat up
nikah: Muslim matrimonial vows
padkos: food to eat on a journey

pap: maize-meal porridge
rondawel: hut
rooiaas: red bait
Sammy: dergoatory term for Indian man
skrik: fright
sev: crunchy chickpea noodles
sjambok: a long, stiff whip, originally made of hide
stoep: veranda
swart gevaar: black peril
takkies: sports shoes
ubuntu: philosophy of compassion and humanity towards others
zol: marijuana

Index

Williams, Mrs 346
Williams, Selina 85
Wilson College 95
Wits 95–100, 168, 169–170, 189–190
Wittebome High School 300–301
Wittebome Station railway line, operation at 297, 315
women's role in struggle 49, 67, 68, 200, 350
Woodstock Police Station, operation at 142, 257–258
World War II 3, 246
WPCC 15, 123–124, 132–133, 154, 359, 360
WRAC 343

Xavier (protester) 361

YCS 339, 342
Yengeni, Tony 55, 71–72
Young Africa Group 234
Young Christian Students 339, 342
Young Standards Rugby Football Club 374
Yusuf Dadoo training camp 330

Zambia 17, 20–21, 161, 172–173, 329–331
Zemaar, Zayne 147
Zimbabwe 97, 148–149
Zuma, Jacob 243